Tomorrow's Geography
for Edexcel GCSE Specification A

Mike Harcourt • Steph Warren

Hodder Murray
A MEMBER OF THE HODDER HEADLINE GROUP

The publishers would like to thank the following individuals, institutions and companies for permission to reproduce photographs and illustrations in this book:
Airfotos: 2.24 p36; Grahame Austin: 1.1 p2; Axiom Photo Agency: 8.27 p179; Corbis: 1.13 p9; Ros Cowdery: 6.3 p113; Paul Creighton: 8.19 a–b p173; Sue Cunningham Picture Library: 8.5 & 8.6 p167, 8.8 p168, 8.10, 8.11 & 8.12 p170, 8.13 p171; Ecoscene: 5.1 p89, 5.14 & 5.15 p96; Environment Agency: 5.16 p97; John-Paul Fanning: 7.25 p149; Kate Findlay: 7.29 p152, 7.30, 7.32 & 7.34 p153; Oliver Fitzsimons: 7.23 a–b p148; Geoinformation Group: 4.7 p72, 8.16 p172, 8.20 p174; Geoscience: 1.32t & b p16, 1.38 p19; Mike Harcourt: 2.15 p33, 2.18 p35, 2.23 p36, 4.8 p72, 4.12 p73, 4.23 p80, 5.2 c–d p90, 5.7 p92, 5.8, 5.9 & 5.10 p93, 7.1 p137; Robert Harding Picture Library: 2.19 p35, 3.2t, b, l & r p48, 3.20 p58, 3.30 p64, 5.14 p96, 5.15 p96t, 5.21tr & bl p100, 7.20 p146, 7.41 & 7.42 p159, 7.45 & 7.46 p160, 8.28 & 8.29 p180; Sian Holtom: 1.32 p16; Kingfisher Photography: 1.10 p7; Life File Photo Library: 5.24 p102, 6.36 p132; the Oracle Shopping Centre, Reading: 8.18 p173; Ordnance Survey: 1.24 p13, 1.26 p14, 1.40 p21, 2.40 p47, 3.32 p67; Panos Pictures: 2.16 p33, 2.37, 2.38 & 2.39, p45, 3.29 p64, 4.25 p82, 4.30 p84, 5.12 p95, 5.21 p100tl & br, 5.26 p105, 5.28 p107, 5.29 p108, 6.12 & 6.13 p118, 6.14 p118, 6.15 p119, 6.29 p129, 6.37 p134; Lucy Phipps: 1.2 a–b p4, 1.20, 1.21 & 1.23 p12, 3.8a p52, 4.24 p81, 7.16 & 7.17 p144, 7.19 p145; Popperfoto: 5.20 p113, 6.7 & 6.8 p115, 6.29 & 6.30 p129, 6.31, 6.33 & 6.34 p130, 6.39 p135; Ewan Reid: 7.24 p149; Science Photo Library: 1.31 p15, 4.13 p73, 5.19l & r p99; Skyscan: 1.28 p14, 2.24 p36, 5.15 p100; Skyscan / © Air Images: 1.35 p18; Dominic Tester: 1.16 p11; Topham Picturepoint: 5.11 p94, 7.11 & 7.12 p141; Steph Warren: 1.3 & 1.4 p4, 1.17 p11, 1.25 p13, 1.27 & 1.28 p14, 2.33 a–d p43, 3.8b p52, 3.17 & 3.18 p57, 3.19 p58, 3.28 & 3.29 p63, 5.2 a–b p90, 5.4 & 5.5 p91, 7.1 p137, 7.40 a–b p158, 8.22 & 8.23 p175, 8.24 p176; Fiona Woolf-Brears: 3.13 p54, 3.14 p55, and the A level geographers of Blessed Hugh Faringdon Catholic School, Reading.

Maps on pages 13, 14, 21, 47 and 67 reproduced from Ordnance Survey mapping with the permission of the Controller of Her Majesty's Stationery Office, © Crown copyright.

Every effort has been made to trace and acknowledge copyright. The publishers will be happy to make suitable arrangements with any copyright holder whom it has not been possible to contact.

Orders: please contact Bookpoint Ltd, 130 Milton Park, Abingdon, Oxon OX14 4SB. Telephone: (44) 01235 827720, Fax: (44) 01235 400454. Lines are open from 9.00–6.00, Monday to Saturday, with a 24 hour message answering service. You can order through our website at www.hoddereducation.co.uk.

British Library Cataloguing in Publication Data
A catalogue record for this title is available from The British Library

ISBN -10: 0 340 79965 X
ISBN -13: 978 0 340 79965 5

First published 2001
Impression number   10 9 8 7 6
Year   2005

© Copyright Steph Warren and Mike Harcourt 2001

All rights reserved. No part of this publication may be reproduced or transmitted in any form or by any means, electronic or mechanical, including photocopy, recording, or any information storage and retrieval system, without permission in writing from the publisher or under licence from the Copyright Licensing Agency Limited. Further details of such licences (for reprographic reproduction) may be obtained from the Copyright Licensing Agency Limited, of 90 Tottenham Court Road, London W1T 4LP.

Cover photos from Photodisk, photograph of Machu Picchu is taken by Tim Smith.
Project management and typesetting by Cambridge Publishing Management.
Illustrations by Oxford Designers & Illustrators Ltd.
Printed in Italy for Hodder Murray, an imprint of Hodder Education, a member of the Hodder Headline Group, 338 Euston Road, London NW1 3BH.

Contents

Chapter 1	The physical world	2
Chapter 2	The human world	22
	Case Study: Land use in an urban area in an MEDC: Reading, UK	40
	Case Study: Land use in an urban area in an LEDC: Bangalore, India	44
Chapter 3	The economic world	48
	Case Study: Intensive wet rice farming in an LEDC	54
	Case Study: Changes affecting farming systems in the EU	56
	Case Study: Computer development in Bracknell	62
	Case Study: Fiat, a TNC, in Brazil	65
Chapter 4	The natural world	68
	Case Study: Papua New Guinea	82
Chapter 5	Managing the environment	89
	Case Study: Recession at Walton-on-the-Naze	92
	Case Study: The Mississippi River flood, 1993	98
	Case Study: The Broads	102
	Case Study: Desertification in the Sahel	104
	Case Study: Doñana National Park	106
	Case Study: Oil extraction in the Amazonian rainforest	108
Chapter 6	Managing hazards	111
	Case Study: MEDC Hurricane Floyd in the USA, Sept 1999	113
	Case Study: LEDC Cyclone One Bravo, Bangladesh, May 1997	117
	Case Study: LEDC Earthquake in Turkey, 1999	128
	Case Study: MEDC Tottori Earthquake, Japan, Oct 2000	131
	Case Study: Mount Pinatubo, Philippines, June 1991	132
Chapter 7	Managing Tourism	137
	Case Study: The impact of tourism on Ayia Napa, Cyprus	141
	Case Study: The impact of tourism on Zanzibar, East Africa	144
	Case Study: The impact of tourism on the Pennine Way and Malham, UK	148
	Case Study: The impact of tourism on the Inca trail to Machu Picchu	152
	Case Study: The impacts of tourism have led to the need for management of the Maldives	157
	Case Study: Yosemite National Park, USA	160
Chapter 8	Managing urban areas	164
	Case Study: São Paulo, Brazil	166
	Case Study: Urban areas in MEDCs are subject to constant change in their land use: Reading, Berkshire, UK	172
	Case Study: There are many challenges facing managers of all large urban areas: environmental problems in Cairo, Egypt	178
Appendix A:	Sample Examination Answers	182
Index		189

1 The physical world

Figure 1.1 Aerial photo of Swanage facing north

Coastal processes produce distinctive landforms that are subject to change

How are coasts eroded?

The coast is a narrow strip between land and sea. It is under continual attack from waves at the base of the cliff and other processes on the cliff face. (You should always refer to these processes when answering a question on landform formation.) Many of the same processes are used by both the sea and rivers to erode land. The theory box below should be referred to throughout this chapter to understand the processes of erosion.

> **The processes of coastal erosion:**
>
> **Hydraulic action** – this is the pressure of the water being thrown against the cliffs by the wave. It also includes the compression of air in cracks: as the water gets into cracks in the rock face, it compresses the air in the cracks; this puts even more pressure on the cracks and pieces of rock may break off.
>
> **Corrasion** – sand and pebbles carried within waves are thrown against the cliff face with considerable force. These particles break off more rocks which, in turn, are thrown against the cliff by the breaking wave.
>
> **Corrosion (solution)** – this is a chemical reaction between certain rock types and the salt and other acids in seawater. This is particularly evident on limestone and chalk cliffs where the water is a milky blue at the bottom of the cliffs due to the dissolved lime (see Figure 1.1).
>
> **Attrition** – this is a slightly different process that involves the wearing away of the rocks which are in the sea. As the boulders in the sea continually roll around, they chip away at each other until smooth pebbles or sand is formed.

These processes are the main ways in which the sea erodes the base of a cliff. However, coasts are under attack from other processes on the cliff face such as weathering and mass movement.

What are the main types of weathering?

There are three main forms of weathering: physical, chemical and biological. Not all of them occur on every coastline, but combinations of them are usually evident.

Physical weathering – Freeze-thaw weathering or frost action is when water makes its way into cracks in rocks. If the temperature falls below freezing, the water will expand as it turns into ice. This expansion puts pressure on the rock around it and fragments of rock may break off. This type of weathering is common in highland areas where the temperature is above freezing during the day and below freezing during the night.

Chemical weathering – Rainwater contains weak acids that can react with certain rock types. The carbonates in limestone are dissolved by these weak acids and this causes the rock to break up or disintegrate. This can be seen on limestone statues or limestone pavements, for example at Malham (see Chapter 7).

The physical world

Biological weathering – This is the action of plants and animals on the land. Seeds that fall into cracks in rocks will start to grow when moisture is present. The roots the young plant puts out, force their way into cracks and, in time, can break up rocks. Burrowing animals, such as rabbits, can also be responsible for the further break-up of rocks.

Figure 1.3 Soil creep in the Cuckmere Valley, East Sussex

Figure 1.2 Biological weathering in (a) Zanzibar, and (b) South Africa

What is mass movement?

Mass movement is when material moves down a slope due to the pull of gravity. There are a number of different types of mass movement, but for the purposes of this chapter, only soil creep and slumping will be discussed.

Soil creep is the slowest downhill movement of soil. Gravity will pull the water that is contained in the soil down a slope. The soil will move downhill with the water. As this happens very slowly, it's not possible to see it happening, although it does move more quickly after heavy rainfall. The slope may appear rippled (like sheep paths around the hill). These ripples are known as terracettes. Figure 1.3 shows evidence of soil creep on a slope.

Slumping is common on the coast. Also known as rotational slipping, it involves a large area of land moving down a slope. Due to the nature of the slip, it leaves behind a curved surface. This is very common on clay cliffs. During dry weather the clay contracts and cracks; when it rains, the water runs into the cracks and is absorbed until the rock becomes saturated. This weakens the rock and, due to the pull of gravity, it slips down the slope on its slip plane.

Figure 1.4 Slumping east of Bowleaze Cove, Weymouth

What affects the rate of coastal erosion?

Waves are the main agents of erosion on coasts. Their power is determined by a number of factors. The two main factors are the wind speed and the distance over which the wind blows over open water; known as the fetch. The longer the fetch, therefore, the stronger the wind and the more powerful the wave. The south-west coast of England experiences south-west winds that may have blown for several thousand kilometres.

Waves are created by a transfer of energy from the wind to the sea. As the wave approaches the coast, it begins to lose energy due to friction with the beach. The more gentle the beach's incline, the more energy the sea will lose. On steep beaches, however, the wave retains much of its energy until it reaches the beach and consequently forms a destructive wave.

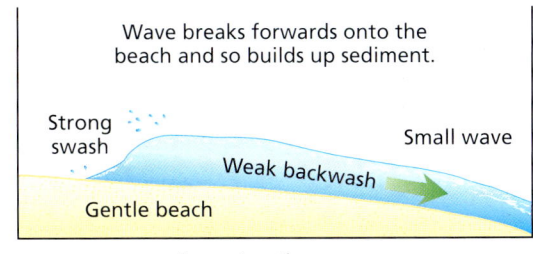

Waves can be either destructive or constructive. In this part of the chapter we will discuss destructive waves as they are mainly responsible for coastal erosion and for taking sediment away from coastlines. They have a number of characteristics:

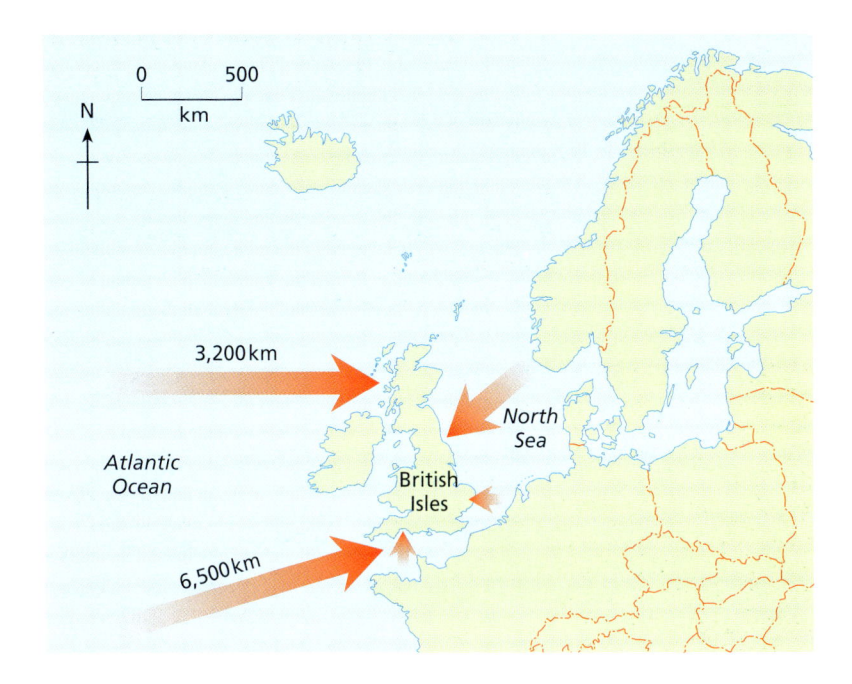

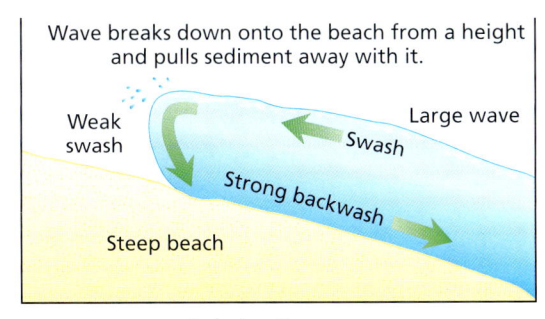

Figure 1.5 Diagram showing the fetch of waves around the British coast

- The backwash is much stronger than the swash and is therefore able to carry sand and pebbles away from the shore.
- They break frequently; there are between 10 and 15 every minute.
- They are high in proportion to their length.
- They are generally found on steep beaches.

The type of rock on a coastline also affects the rate of erosion. If the cliffs are made from resistant rock, like granite, they will erode more slowly than cliffs made from less resistant rock, such as clay. The rock's structure can also have an effect on the rate of erosion. Rocks that are well jointed or with many faults, such as limestone, will erode more quickly as the waves exploit these lines of weakness. Cliffs that are gentle and well vegetated will be more resistant to mass movement and weathering than cliffs of bare rock. This will also affect the rate at which they can be eroded by the sea.

What landforms are created by coastal erosion?

A number of distinctive and dynamic landforms are formed by destructive waves. These include headlands and bays; cliffs and wave-cut platforms; caves, arches, stacks and stumps.

Figure 1.6 Destructive and constructive waves

Headlands and bays

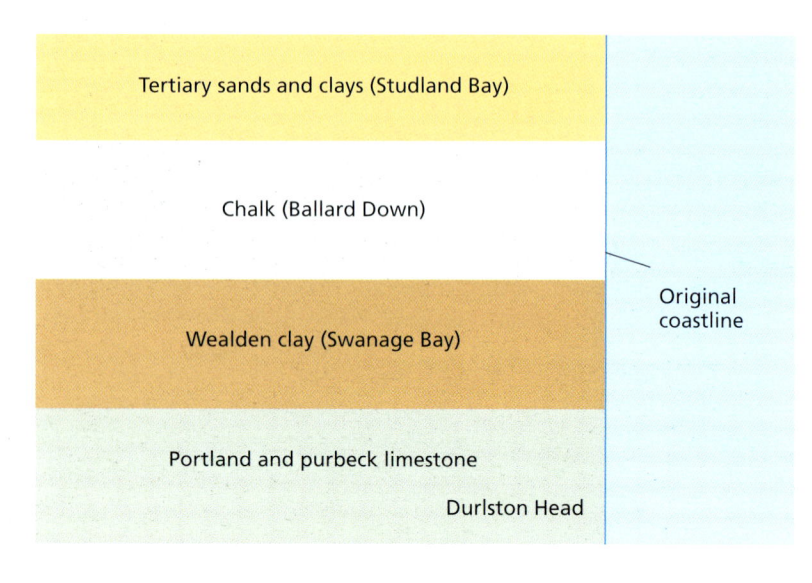

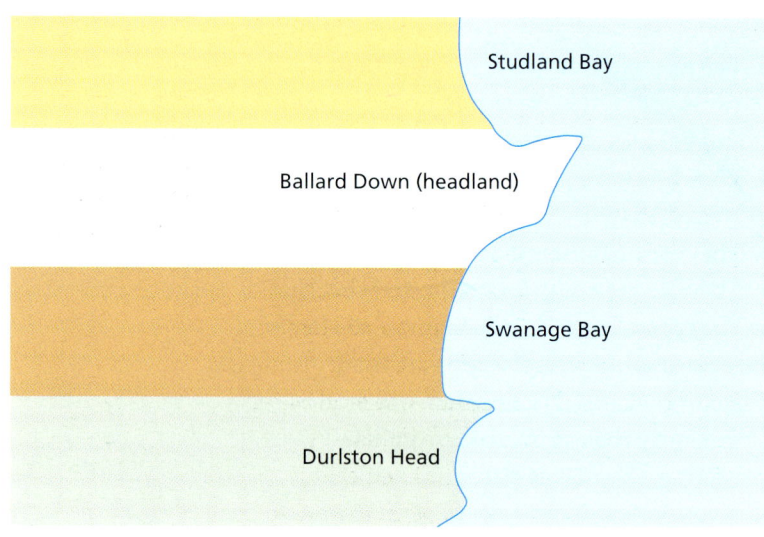

Figure 1.7 The formation of headlands and bays

On coastlines where rocks of varying resistance lie at right angles to the sea, the bays are the softer rock and are indentations in the land. The headlands are the more resistant rock and protrude into the sea (see Figure 1.7). As the bays are made from a less-resistant rock type, the erosion rates are greatest at first. In time, as the sea cuts the bays back, the waves reaching the coast are less powerful because they have to travel over a longer expanse of beach. At this point the headlands, which are further out to sea, start to experience the more powerful waves and are eroded at a faster rate than before.

Headlands and bays are clearly shown on the aerial photograph of Swanage (Figure 1.1).

Cliffs and wave-cut platforms

Headlands are usually formed from cliffs. When the sea moves against the base of the cliff using corrasion and hydraulic action (and if the rock type is limestone or chalk, corrosion (see page 3)), it undercuts the cliff and forms a wave-cut notch. Above this notch, an overhang will form; in time, it will fall into the sea as a result of the pressure of its own weight and the pull of gravity.

The sea will then continue to attack the cliff and form another notch. In this way, the cliff will retreat, becoming higher and steeper (see Figure 1.8). The remains of the cliff rock, now below the sea at high tide, form a rocky, wave-cut platform. As a result of erosion and weathering, some boulders will have fallen from the cliff onto the platform. As the width of the platform increases, so the power of the waves decreases, as they have further to travel to reach the cliff.

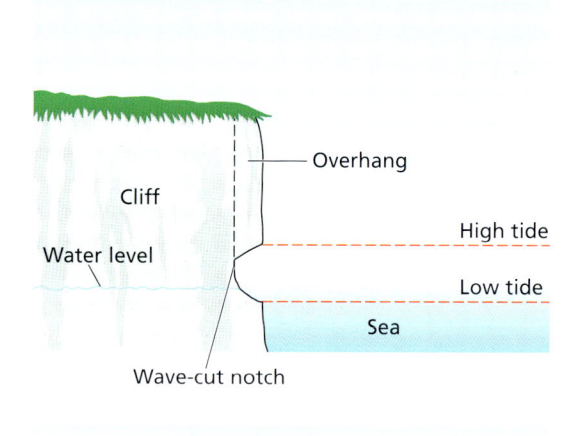

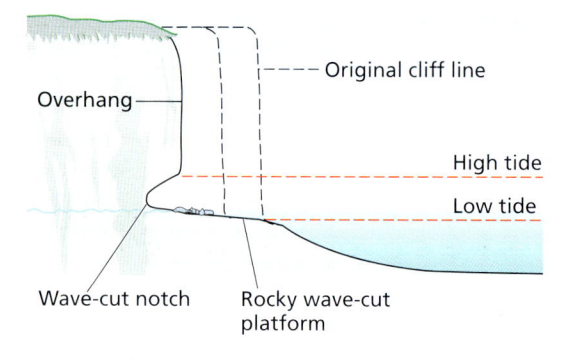

Figure 1.8 The formation of cliffs and wave-cut platforms

The physical world

Caves, arches, stacks and stumps

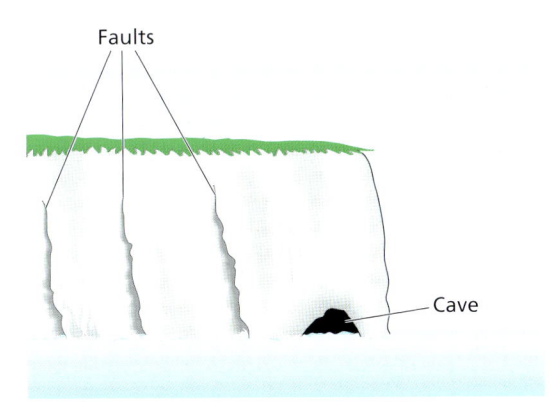

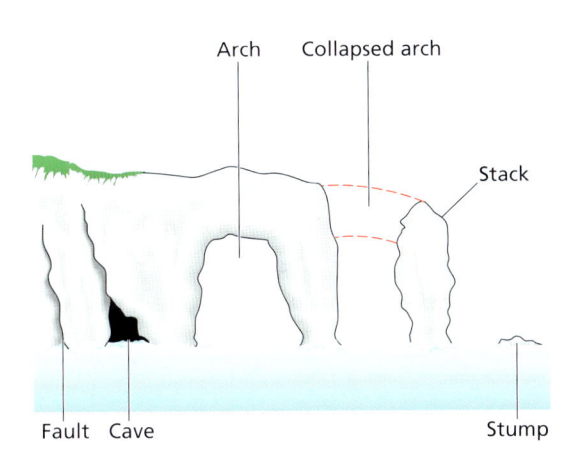

Figure 1.9 The formation of caves, arches, stacks and stumps

These are formed in rocks that have a fault or line of weakness. The action of the sea will exploit the fault, through erosional processes such as hydraulic action. In time the fault will widen to form a cave. If the fault is in a headland, caves are likely to form on both sides. When the backs of the caves meet, an arch is formed. The sea will continue to erode the bottom of the arch. Weathering will also take place on the bare rock faces. As the sea undercuts the bottom of the arch, a wave-cut notch will form. It will collapse in time, as it is pulled down by the pressure of its own weight and gravity. This leaves behind a column of rock not attached to the cliff, known as a stack. Continued erosion and weathering will lead to the formation of a stump that is only visible at low tide (see Figures 1.9 and 1.10).

Figure 1.10 Photo of the coast east of Durdle Door in Dorset to show erosional features

How does the sea transport material around the coast?

The sea transports material in much the same way rivers do. Sediment is transported by the sea in the following ways:
- Large stones are rolled along the sea bed in a process known as traction.
- Small sand-sized particles are bounced along in a leap-frog movement called saltation.
- The process of carrying sand and clay-sized particles within the water is known as suspension.
- The process of carrying minerals dissolved in the water is known as solution.

As we explained earlier, the direction of the waves hitting a beach is determined by the prevailing wind which also influences the power of the waves. If the wind is blowing at an angle to the beach, the waves (swash) will approach the beach at this angle, transporting the sand and pebbles with them. The wave always returns to the sea in a straight line at 90° to the coast (backwash). As the water is being pulled by gravity, it will take the shortest route back down the beach. In this way, material is moved along the beach until it meets an obstruction. This is known as longshore drift (see Figure 1.11).

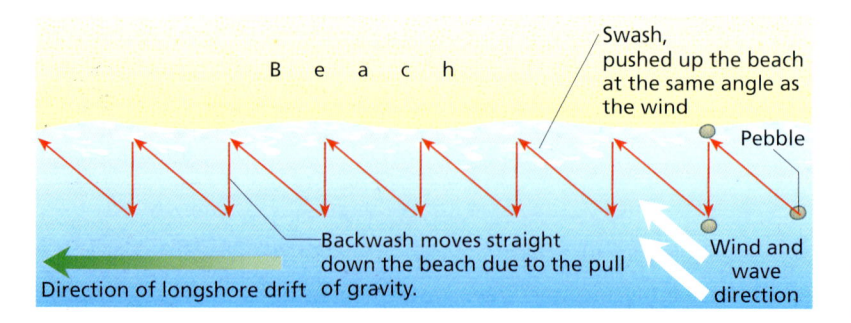

Figure 1.11 Diagram of longshore drift

What landforms are created by coastal deposition?

The other type of wave which operates in coastal areas is a constructive wave (see Figure 1.6). As its name suggests, this wave builds rather than destroys the coastal environment. It deposits sand and pebbles that form beaches. Constructive waves have a number of characteristics:
- The swash is more powerful than the backwash and therefore deposits sediment on beaches.
- They break infrequently at a rate of 10 or less per minute
- They are long in relation to their height
- They are usually found on gently sloping beaches.

Constructive waves form a number of landforms in coastal areas. These include beaches, spits and bars.

Beaches – Beaches are perhaps the most easily recognised and named coastal feature around the British coast. A beach is an area of land between the low tide and storm tide marks and is made up of sand, pebbles and, in some places, mud and silt. They are formed by constructive waves, often in bays where the waves have less energy due to the gently sloping land and as a result deposit material. They can also be found along straight stretches of coastline where longshore drift occurs. Seaside resorts often build groynes to keep beaches in place and to reduce the effects of longshore drift (see Chapter 5).

Spits – A spit is a long, narrow stretch of pebbles and sand which is attached to the land at one end, with the other end tapering into the sea. It forms when longshore drift (see explanation on page 7) occurs on a coastline. When the coastline ends, the sea deposits the material it is transporting because the change in depth affects its ability to transport the material further.

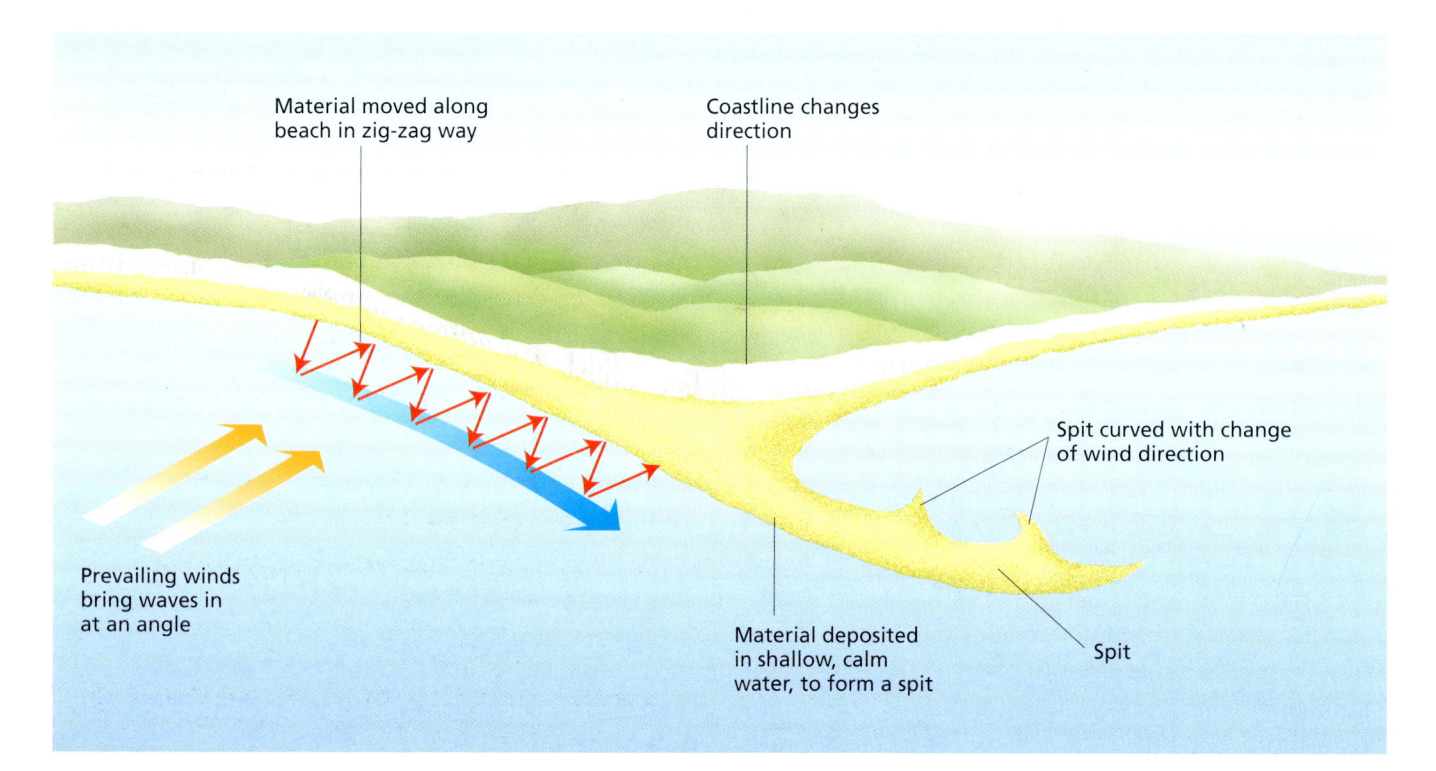

Figure 1.12 The formation of a spit

If there is a river estuary, then the meeting of the waves and the river causes a change in speed which results in both the waves and the river dropping their sediment. In time, the material builds up to form a ridge of shingle and sand known as a spit. On the land side, silt and alluvium are deposited and salt marshes form. The wind and sea currents may curve the end of the spit around. Spits are very dynamic, which means that their shape and form continually change. If spits are present on a coastline, it should be possible to determine the direction of longshore drift (see Figure 1.13).

Bars – If a spit develops in a bay, it may build across it, linking two headlands to form a bar. This is only possible if there is a gently sloping beach and no river entering the sea. In this way, bars can straighten coastlines.

An example is Slapton Ley in Devon which also has the characteristic lagoon formed behind the bar where any run-off water is trapped and slowly seeps through the bar to the sea.

Figure 1.13 Hurst castle spit, Hampshire

ACTIVITIES

Higher

1 Draw a field sketch of Figure 1.1. Include the following on the sketch:
   a 4 landforms created by erosion,
   b 2 landforms created by deposition,
   c 2 forms of coastal protection (see Chapter 5),
   d 2 processes which occur on this coast.
   e Name the rock types (see Figure 1.7).
2 What is the difference between corrasion and corrosion?
3 What is meant by the term 'fetch'?
4 List three differences between constructive and destructive waves.
5 Using only an annotated diagram, explain how wave-cut platforms are formed.
6 Explain the process of longshore drift.

Foundation

1 Match the term with its correct definition.

Term	Definition
Corrasion	The wearing away of rocks which are in the sea.
Corrosion	The wearing away of cliff by the rocks in the sea.
Attrition	A chemical reaction between certain rock types on seawater.

2 Longshore drift is the process used to transport material along the coast. How does it work?
3 What is meant by the term 'fetch'?
4 List 3 differences between constructive and destructive waves.
5 Draw a field sketch of Figure 1.1. Include the following on the sketch:
   a Landforms: headlands, bays, stack, wave-cut platform, spit.
   b Processes: slumping, longshore drift.
   c Coastal Protection: rip rap, groynes (see Chapter 5).

River processes produce distinctive landforms in their valleys

How do the characteristics of a river and its valley change?

Rivers begin in upland areas and make their way downhill to the sea. A river starts at its source and meets the sea at its mouth. As it makes its way to the sea, the river channel (the area in which a river flows) and its valley experience a number of changes. The river becomes wider and deeper as it is joined by other, smaller rivers (called tributaries); the point at which rivers meet is known as a confluence. The river valley also changes: the sides become less steep, the gradient decreases and the shape of the valley changes from a V to a broader shape, almost like a flat-bottomed U.

The land that is drained by a river system is called a drainage basin; the boundary of the drainage basin, usually made up of highland, is called the watershed.

As a river moves downstream, the changes that occur mostly relate to differences in the river's energy. When it is in an upland area, a river has the power to erode downwards, as it is way above sea level, and it forms a V-shaped valley. As the gradient (slope) of the valley decreases, the river uses its energy to transport the material it has eroded. Due to the lack of gradient, it begins to erode sideways (laterally). As the river moves closer to sea level, the gradient decreases further. Although the river is still eroding sideways at this point, deposition is the most important process and the valley becomes wider and flatter. This change from erosion to deposition helps to explain the change in landforms and the shape of the river valley as the river moves towards the sea (see Figure 1.14).

The long profile of a river shows the steep gradient at the source gradually becoming more gentle until the river reaches sea level. These changes usually show a river to be split into three sections, known as the upper, middle and lower courses (see Figure 1.14).

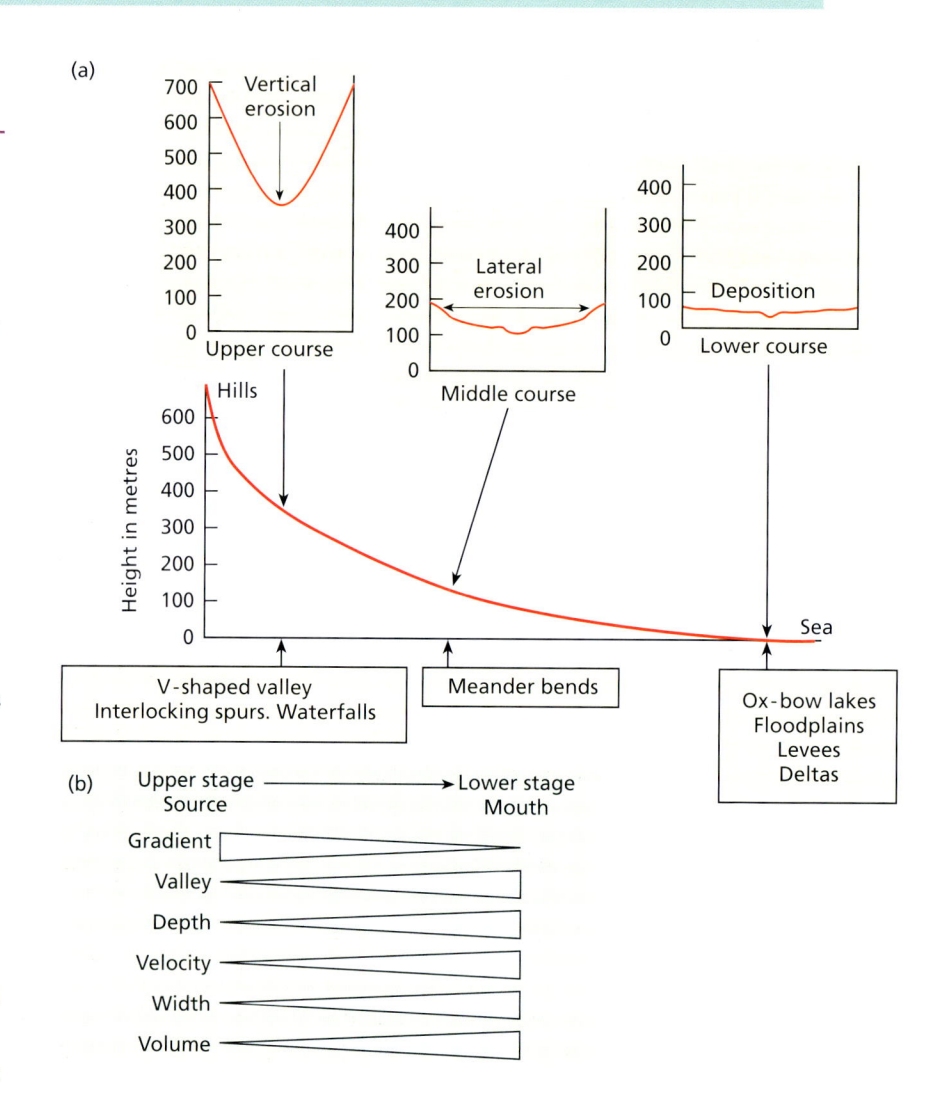

Figure 1.14 The features of a river's course

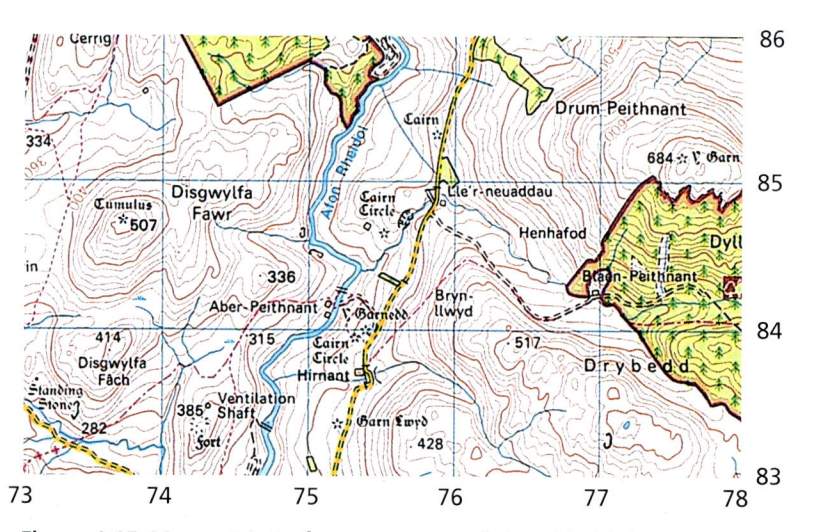

Figure 1.15 Map extract of upper course of river Rheidol

Figure 1.16 River Rheidol's upper course

ACTIVITIES

Activities for Figures 1.15 and 1.16

1. Draw a cross section of the valley between grid reference 737 848 (spot height 507 m) and 776 852 (spot height 684 m).
2. Mark the following on your cross section: the River Rheidol, minor road.
3. Using Figure 1.16 to help you, describe the course of the river's channel and its valley shown on the map extract.
4. The photograph was taken at grid reference 752 843; in which direction was the camera pointing?

As a river moves downstream, its discharge also changes. Discharge is the amount of water passing a specific point at a given time and is measured in cubic metres per second. The discharge depends on the river's velocity and volume. The volume is the amount of water in the river and the velocity is the speed of the river. The velocity times the volume is the river's discharge.

As a river moves towards the sea, its discharge will increase because of the increased volume as more tributaries join the river. The velocity of the river is determined by the amount of water which is touching the river's bed and banks. If the river is deeper, there will be less contact between the river and its banks and bed, therefore less friction will occur and the river velocity will be greater.

What landforms can be found in river valleys?

A river's course can be split into three sections. In the upland area at the start of the river, there is the upper course. Features of the upper course include V-shaped valleys, interlocking spurs and waterfalls.

Figure 1.17 Interlocking spurs

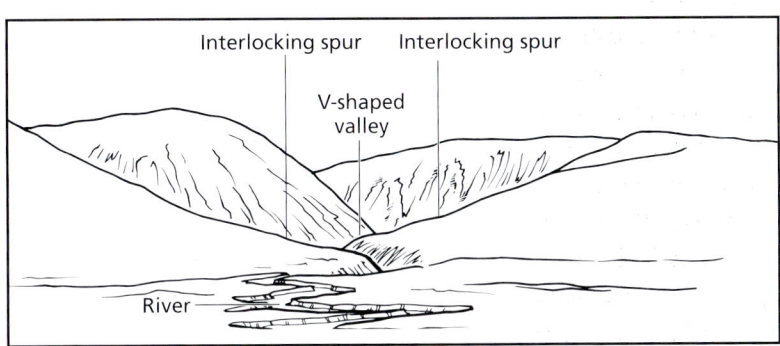

V-shaped valleys and interlocking spurs

In the upper course, the river is small and because most of its water is in contact with its bed and the banks, there is a lot of friction. Ninety five per cent of the river's energy is used to overcome this friction. A result of this is that the river flows more slowly here than in the lowlands. The rest of the river's energy is used to erode downwards, hence the characteristic V-shape of the valley. As the river winds its way down between barriers of more resistant rock, spurs which interlock down the valley are formed (see Figure 1.18).

Figure 1.18 Field sketch of Figure 1.17

Waterfalls

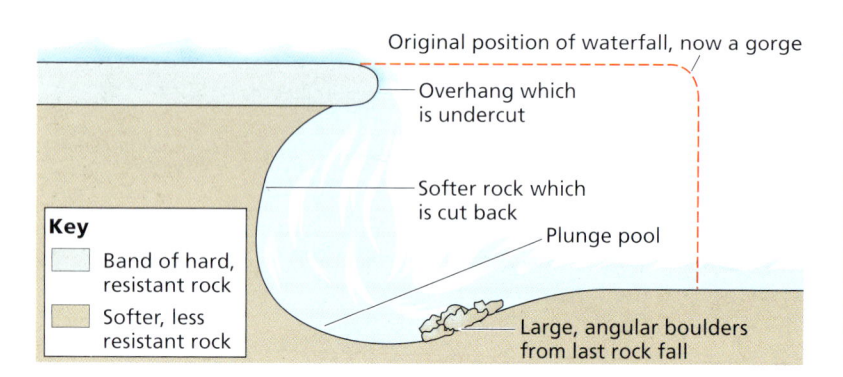

Figure 1.19 Waterfall formation

Key: Band of hard, resistant rock / Softer, less resistant rock

Labels: Original position of waterfall, now a gorge; Overhang which is undercut; Softer rock which is cut back; Plunge pool; Large, angular boulders from last rock fall

A waterfall forms when a river crosses a band of less resistant rock, after flowing over relatively hard, resistant rock (see Figure 1.19). The sudden drop in the river's course that results is known as a waterfall. The softer rock is cut back more quickly, leaving an overhang of harder rock. In time, due to the pull of gravity, the harder rock becomes too heavy and falls into the river below. As the water splashes back from the plunge pool, hydraulic action against the back wall of the waterfall (see theory box, page 3), also erodes the softer rock. Over time the waterfall moves back or retreats up the valley, often forming a gorge.

The deep pool below the waterfall is known as a plunge pool. It is deeper than the rest of the river because of the power of the water falling into it (the Meiringspoort waterfall has a drop of 60 m and a 9 m plunge pool). It contains large boulders that have fallen from the overhang and smaller rocks that have been eroded off the back wall of the waterfall. The river erodes these rocks by the process of corrasion (see theory box, page 3).

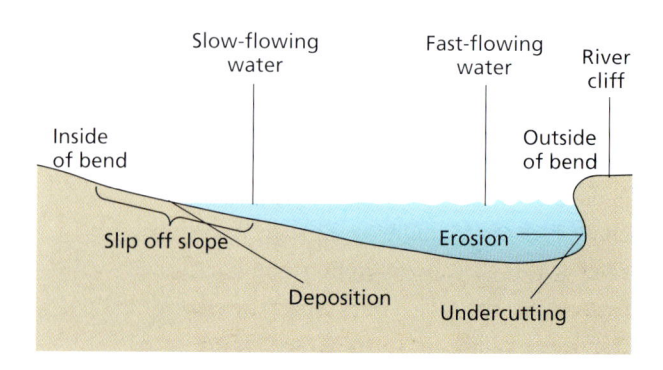

Figure 1.21 Meiringspoort waterfall, South Africa

In the middle course, the river is deeper as a result of being joined by a number of tributaries. Less water is in contact with the channel which means that there is less friction and the river has more power to erode. The river erodes laterally (sideways), rather than vertically (downwards), as there is less of a gradient in this part of a river's course because the valley is flatter with more gentle slopes. A meander bend is one feature of the middle course which is caused by this increase in lateral erosion.

Figure 1.20 Meander bend, Ardèche River, France

Figure 1.22 A cross-section of a meander bend

Labels: Slow-flowing water; Fast-flowing water; River cliff; Inside of bend; Outside of bend; Slip off slope; Erosion; Deposition; Undercutting

Figure 1.23 Zambezi gorge formed by the retreat of the Victoria Falls

The physical world

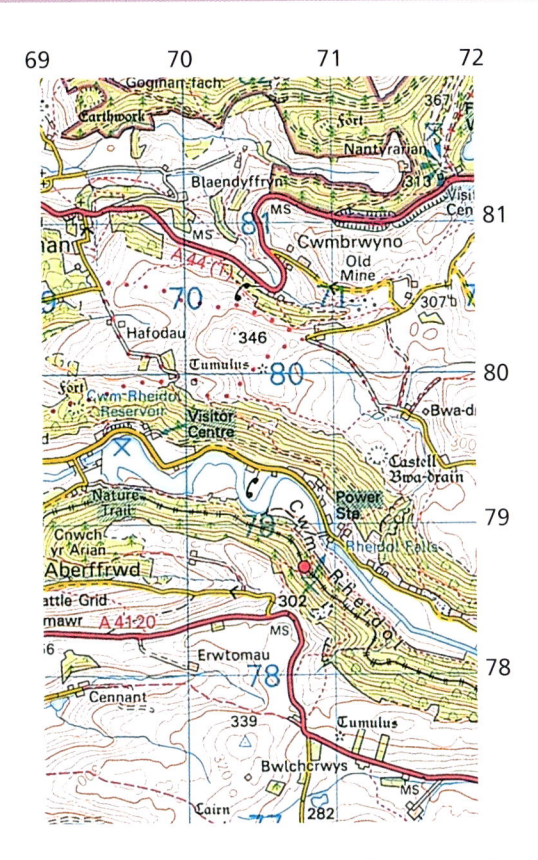

Figure 1.24 Map extract of middle course of river Rheidol

Figure 1.25 River Rheidol in middle stage

ACTIVITIES

1. Draw a cross section of the valley between grid reference 703 803 (spot height 343 m) and 704 776 (triangulation pillar 339 m).
2. Mark on your cross section: nature trail, woodland, track, A4120, River Rheidol.
3. Describe the course of the river shown on the map extract.
4. The river becomes much wider at this point. Why?
5. Draw a field sketch of the photograph in Figure 1.25 to show the main features of a river in its middle course.
6. Primary activities have declined in this area:
    a. Support this statement using map evidence.
    b. How has the area been developed to provide jobs for local people? Use map evidence in your answer.

The outside of a meander bend has the deepest water because this is where the greatest erosion takes place and forms a river cliff. The water is moving fastest at this point and therefore erodes the bank using corrasion. The water moves more quickly on the outside due to the lack of friction because of the river's depth and consequent lack of contact with the bed and banks. A slip-off slope forms on the inside of the meander bend because of deposition. Deposition occurs on the inside because the water is moving more slowly and is shallower. As a result, there is more friction here and the river is less powerful. The river is therefore unable to carry its load and deposition takes place. An underwater current takes some of the eroded material from the river cliff across the river and deposits it on the slip off slope (see Figure 1.22).

In the lower course of the river, the channel is wide and deep and is surrounded by a wide valley floor. The velocity of the river is greater as there is less friction with the channel. The slopes of the valley and the gradient of the river channel are very gentle. The river's main process has now become deposition as a result of the large load of eroded material (such as sand and silt) that it is carrying. However, there is still some lateral erosion taking place. A number of features, such as ox-bow lakes, flood plains, levees and deltas, can be found in the lower course.

The physical world

Figure 1.26 Map extract of lower course of river Rheidol

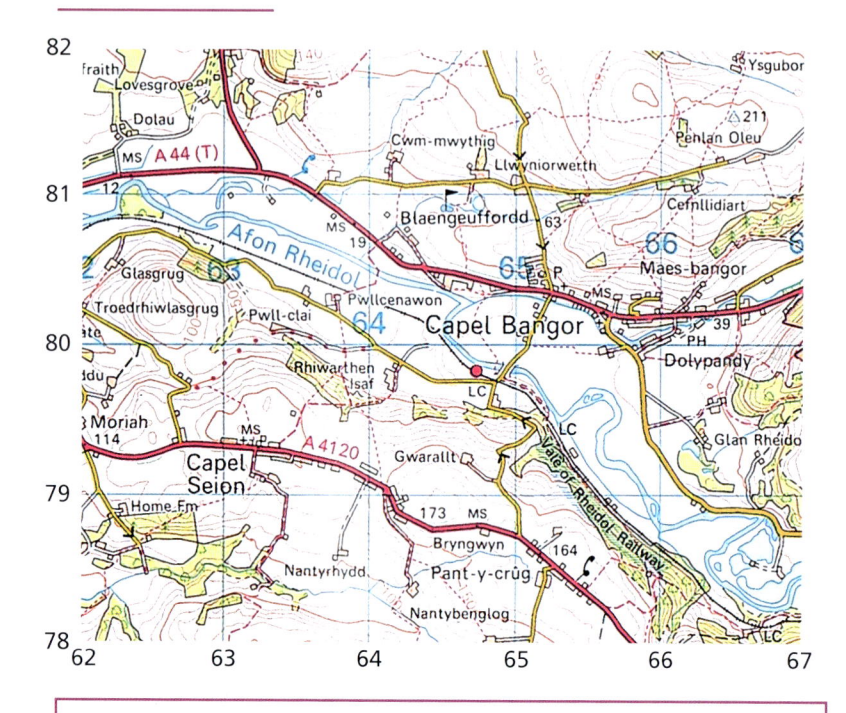

Figure 1.27 Lower course of river Rheidol

Figure 1.28 Meander bend almost an ox-bow lake

ACTIVITIES

1. Draw a cross-section of the valley between grid reference 665 815 (triangulation pillar 211 m) and 645 789 (spot height 173m).
2. Mark the following on your cross-section: A44, River Rheidol, Gwarallt farm, Cefnllidiart farm, railway line.
3. Measure the width of the flood plain.
4. What evidence is there to show that the river channel has changed course? Use diagrams to help your answer.
5. Describe and explain the route of the A road.

Ox-bow lakes – In the lower course of the river, meander bends become very large. With continual erosion on the outside of the banks and deposition on the inside, the ends of the meander bend become closer (see Figure 1.29). When flooding occurs, the river is able to cut through the gap and, in time, forms a new straight channel. Continued deposition of alluvium at times of low flow, results in the old bend of the river becoming cut off. This is called an ox-bow lake.

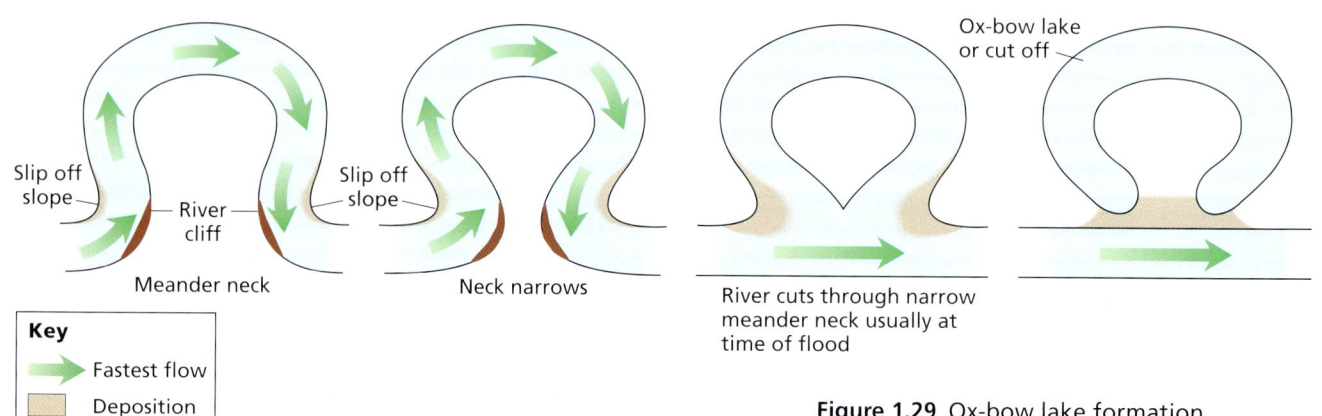

Key
- Fastest flow
- Deposition
- Erosion

Figure 1.29 Ox-bow lake formation

Flood plains and levees – A flood plain is the low flat area of land on either side of a river. It can be found in the middle course of a river, but is more usually found in the lower course. When the river contains too much water to stay within its channel, it floods the surrounding land. As it moves away from its channel, it becomes shallower and friction increases. The river has less energy and, therefore, must drop some of the load it is carrying. It drops the largest amount of material close to the river channel. After a number of floods, this builds up to form levees (see Figure 1.30). The river water drops the heaviest material first.

Another contributing factor to the formation of the flood plain is the migration of meanders downstream. Meanders are formed by lateral erosion which causes the bend to move across and down the valley in the direction of the river's flow. The outside of the bend, where erosion is greatest, moves the bend in that direction and the inside bend fills in the flood plain with the deposition that occurs there.

Deltas – When rivers meet the sea, they do so in a variety of ways, one of which is a delta. This is a low, flat area of land that is formed through river deposition. There are two types of delta: bird's foot and arcuate.

A bird's foot delta is composed of fine sediments called silt. As the river meets the sea, it loses velocity causing it to drop some of the load that it is carrying. In time, this deposited material blocks the river channel and the river has to split to go around it, forming new channels called distributaries. An example is the Mississippi delta which flows into the Gulf of Mexico.

An arcuate delta is more common. It is formed from coarse sediments such as gravel or sand and is triangular in shape. Because the sediments are coarse, the river deposits its load easily and forms many new channels to get to the sea; therefore it has many distributaries. An example is the Nile delta. Calm seas with few currents aid the development of deltas.

Figure 1.31 Satellite photo of the Mississippi delta

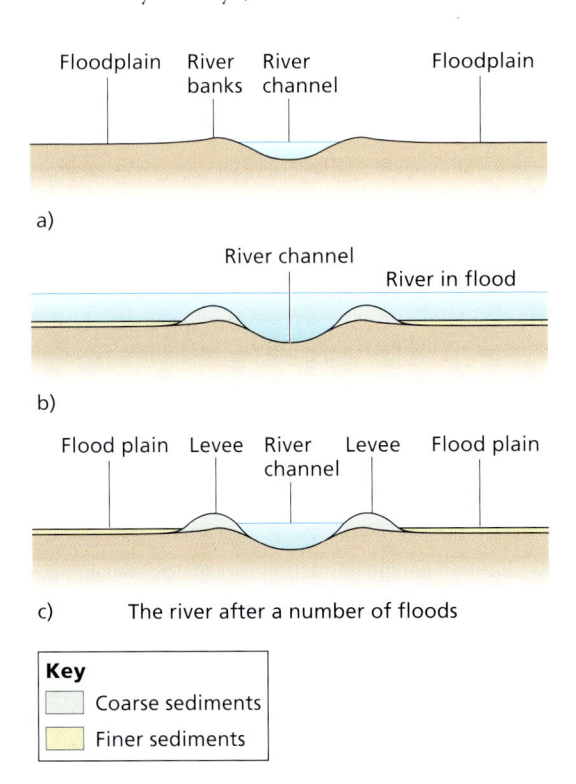

Figure 1.30 Levee and flood plain formation

ACTIVITIES

1. Look at the diagram showing the formation of a waterfall (Figure 1.19). Draw your own series of annotated diagrams to show how a waterfall is formed.
2. Look at Figure 1.20 which shows a meander bend on the Ardèche River in France. Draw a labelled field sketch of the photograph and explain how this bend has formed.
3. The photograph in Figure 1.28 shows a meander bend. What is likely to happen to this bend in the future?
4. Draw a sketch of the delta shown in Figure 1.31. Mark the features of a delta on your sketch.

The characteristics of valleys can be changed by glaciation

Figure 1.32a Corrie, arête and pyramidal peak during glaciation

Figure 1.32b Corrie, arête and pyramidal peak after glaciation

How are glaciers formed?

When snow collects on the ground, it has many air spaces. As it becomes deeper, air is squeezed out as a result of the weight of the snow above, which compacts the snow or ice. (This is what happens when you make a snowball; if you press it hard enough, it becomes a ball of ice as all the air is removed.) With time and repeated snowfalls, the ice becomes thicker and then, due to the pull of gravity, gradually starts to move down the slope. When ice moves, it is known as a glacier.

How do glaciers erode?

Glaciers erode by two main processes:
   As a glacier moves down a valley, it puts pressure on the valley sides and bottom. This pressure creates heat. (If you push your hands together, they will become warm because of the pressure you are using.) The heat causes a small amount of ice to melt, the water runs into cracks in the valley sides or bottom and almost immediately refreezes because of the cold temperatures. As the glacier moves, it then pulls away some of the rock face. This process is known as plucking.
   The rocks that have been removed from the hillsides by plucking (and freeze-thaw weathering) are carried in the ice of the glacier. As they move down the valley, they wear away (erode) the valley sides and bottom causing more rock to be broken off. This process is known as abrasion.

What landforms can be found in glaciated valleys?

As a glacier moves down a valley, it carves out a number of distinctive landforms: corries, pyramidal peaks, arêtes, truncated spurs, hanging valleys, ribbon lakes and U-shaped valleys. Eroded material, known as moraine, is also deposited on the valley sides and bottom.

Figure 1.33 The formation of a corrie

Corries – Corries or cirques are armchair-shaped hollows. They have a steep, rocky back wall, often up to 200 metres high in the UK but much higher in the Alps. The corrie is fringed by sharp ridges, known as arêtes. They begin to form when the snow that accumulates on high mountain slopes is compacted into ice. After a time, the ice starts to move due to the pull of gravity and as it moves, it carves out a corrie, usually in an area that already has a small depression (see Figure 1.33). The ice erodes by plucking and forms the steep back wall; the hollow is formed by abrasion. After glaciation, the corrie can be filled by a small lake known as a corrie lake or tarn.

The rotational movement of the ice causes greater pressure at the bottom of the steep back wall and in the base of the hollow than it does at the front where the ice leaves the corrie. Because there is less pressure, erosion rates at the front of the hollow are slower. A rock lip forms here which can be increased in size by deposition of moraine. This works as a dam after glaciation, and a corrie lake or tarn forms behind it. Freeze-thaw weathering (see page 3) occurs at the top of the steep back wall and adds rocks to the ice. These become embedded and are used in the process of abrasion.

Arêtes and pyramidal peaks – If two corries form next to each other on a mountainside, their sides will be both steep and rocky. The piece of land between them will be a sharp ridge of rock (arête) that is continually attacked by freeze-thaw weathering and plucking. If corries form on at least three sides of the mountain, the top of the mountain will become a sharp peak of jagged rock known as a pyramidal peak (see Figure 1.34). This is continually sharpened by frost action and plucking.

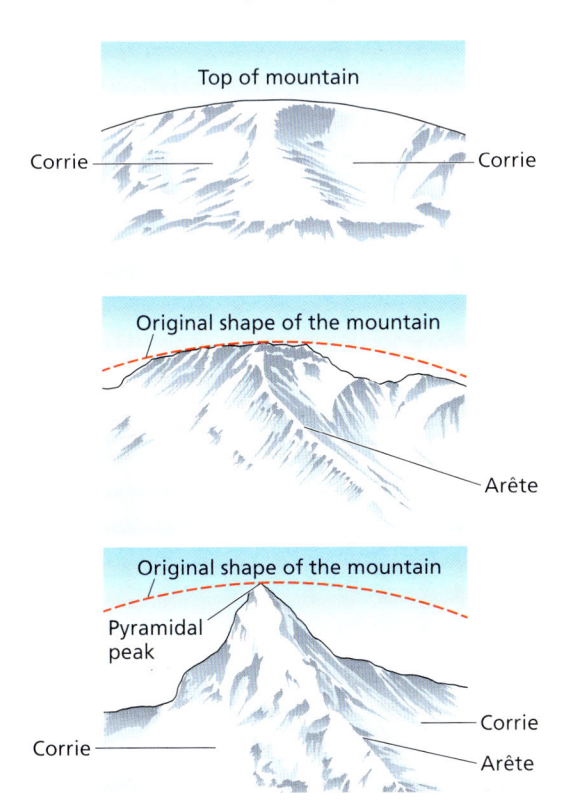

Figure 1.34 Arête and pyramidal peak formation

The physical world

ACTIVITIES

Use Figures 1.35 and 1.36 to help you to answer the following questions.

1. Name two corrie lakes.
2. Name a ribbon lake.
3. Name one arête.
4. Work out the difference in height between:
a. the spot height at Blea Water and the pyramidal peak,
b. the spot height at Haweswater reservoir and Blea Water,
c. What is the total difference in height?
5a. Study the aerial photograph of the Blea Water area.
b. Find Blea Water and draw a sketch of this area of the photograph. In your sketch, include two arêtes, a pyramidal peak, the steep back wall of the corrie, the corrie lip and Blea Water.

Figure 1.35 An aerial photo of Blea Water and Small Water

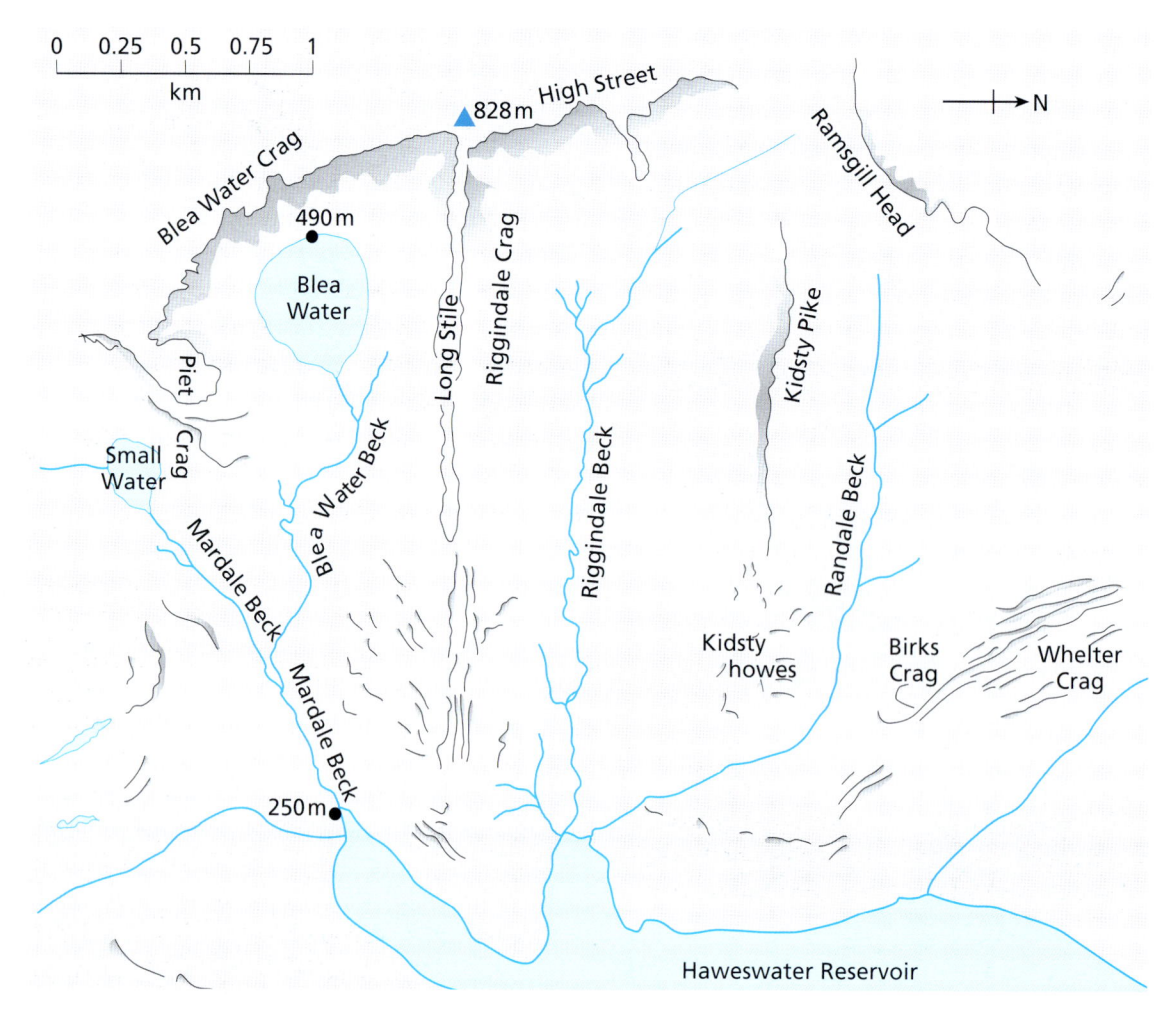

Figure 1.36 Blea Water map

U-shaped valleys and truncated spurs

A U-shaped valley is formed by a valley glacier. A valley glacier will completely fill a valley in an upland area. By doing this, it has far more power to erode the whole valley than the original river which only flowed across the valley floor, winding its way around crops of more resistant rocks to form interlocking spurs (see page 11).

As a glacier moves down a valley, its immense power erodes any rock in its path. It does not need to go around crops of harder rock but simply removes them. In this way, interlocking spurs are cut back to produce truncated spurs (see Figure 1.37). The valley, which used to be V-shaped with a river in the bottom, now has steep walls of bare rock for its sides and a flat bottom and it is also straighter than it was before glaciation. These are the characteristics of a U-shaped glaciated valley.

Figure 1.38 U-shaped valley

Hanging valleys – The main valley glacier is very powerful due to the amount of ice that is being moved and the pressure that it exerts on the sides and bottom of the valley. Other valleys, which contain tributary streams, are smaller and therefore do not contain as much ice. For this reason, they are not cut down as much as the main valley. After the ice has melted, these tributary valleys remain high on the sides of the main valley. The streams that flow in them now reach the main river by a waterfall down the steep sides of the main valley (see Figure 1.37).

Ribbon lakes – These are long, narrow lakes that can be left in a valley after glaciation. They are formed when the glacier meets a band of softer rock that it can erode more quickly. This leaves a groove in the valley bottom which, after glaciation, becomes filled with water. An example of a ribbon lake is Wastwater in the Lake District.

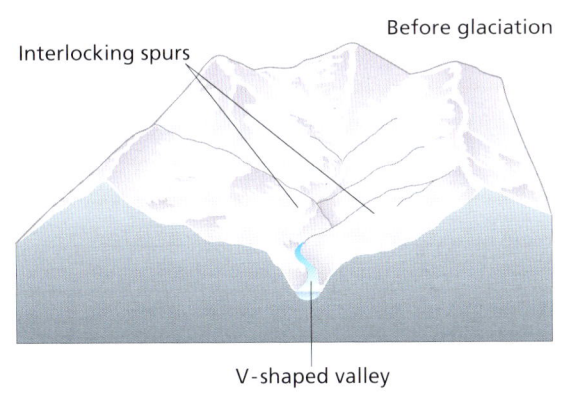

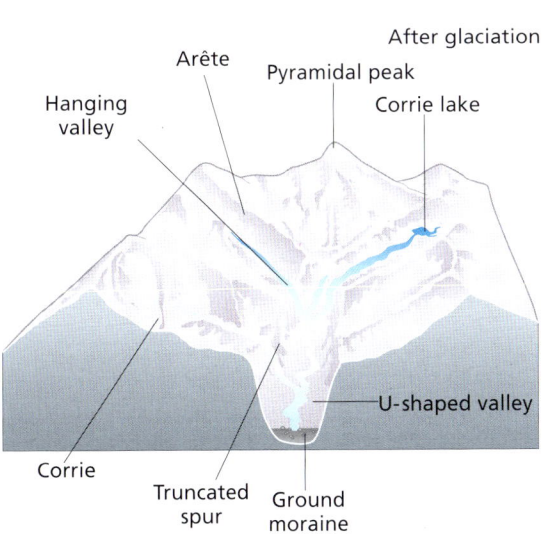

Figure 1.37 U-shaped valley formation

Figure 1.39 Types of moraine

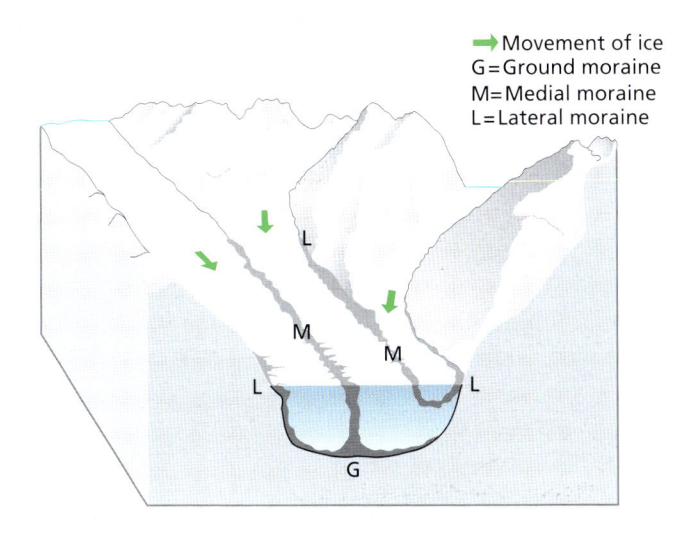

Moraine – Moraine is the material that is transported and deposited by a glacier. Four types of moraine can be found in glaciated valleys. The glacier collects moraine through the processes of freeze-thaw action, abrasion and plucking. Moraine deposited on the valley sides is known as lateral moraine. Ground moraine is deposited beneath the glacier and forms the flat valley floor. If two glaciers meet, their lateral moraines join to form medial moraine. The fourth type of moraine forms when the glacier reaches warmer temperatures and can no longer move down the valley; at this point, it can no longer carry its load.

The moraine deposited here is called terminal moraine. Terminal moraines may also block valleys so that ribbon lakes form behind them. An example is Buttermere in the Lake District.

ACTIVITIES

1   Using the map extract in Figure 1.40:
a   Draw a cross section of the valley between grid reference 455 138 (spot height 754 m) and 503 134 (spot height 474 m).
b   Mark on your cross section: the Haweswater reservoir, woodland, minor road, path, crags.
c   Compare the shape of the cross section you drew for Figure 1.15 with the one you have drawn for Figure 1.37.
d   Explain the differences in shape.

Sample Examination Questions

Higher tier

1   Study the photograph in Figure 1.10:
  a   Draw a sketch of the photograph. Include on it: a stack, arch, cave, stump. (4 marks)
  b   Was this photograph taken at high or low tide? (1 mark)
  c   Give one reason for your answer. (2 marks)
  d   There is a white area shown on the beach. What is it made of and how did it get there? (3 marks)

2   Study Figures 1.15, 1.24, and 1.26. How does human use of the valleys in the map extracts change as you move from the upper to the lower stage of the Rheidol River? (2 marks)

3   Study the map extract of the Lake District in Figure 1.40
  a   Compare the shape of Haweswater reservoir and Blea Water. (2 marks)
  b   Which side of the mountains are the corrie lakes on? (1 mark)
  c   Why is the valley floor so wide in grid square 43 17? (2 marks)
  d   Describe the route of the A592 shown on the map extract. Use map evidence in your answer. (3 marks)

Total 20 marks

Foundation tier

1   Look at the photograph in Figure 1.10.
  a   Complete the table below to show if the features are present on the photograph. (4 marks)

Feature	True	False
Arch		
Spit		
Cave		
Stump		

  b   Was this taken at high or low tide? (1 mark)
  c   Give one reason for your answer. (2 marks)
  d   There is a white area shown on the beach. What is it made of and how did it get there? (3 marks)

2   Study Figure 1.24. Name two ways that people use the valley. (2 marks)

3   Study Figure 1.40, a map extract of the Lake District.
  a   Compare the shape of Haweswater reservoir and Blea water. (2 marks)
  b   Which side of the mountains are the corries on? north / north east   south / south west   (1 mark)
  c   Why is the valley floor so wide in grid square 43 17? (2 marks)
  d   Describe the route of the A592 shown on the map extract. Use map evidence in your answer. (3 marks)

Total 20 marks

Figure 1.40 Map extract of a glaciated upland area

2 The human world

Rates of population change vary from place to place and over time

Global population change

On 12 October 1999, the world's population reached 6 billion. Rapid population growth is a recent phenomenon in the history of the world. It is estimated that 2,000 years ago the world's population was about 300 million. For a very long time the world's population did not grow significantly and periods of growth were followed by periods of decline. It took 1,600 years for the world's population to double to 600 million.

In 1750 the world's population was estimated at 791 million, with 64 per cent of people living in Asia, 21 per cent in Europe and 13 per cent in Africa. In 1900, the world's population had increased to 1.7 billion. The main growth areas at this time were in Europe, North America and Latin America. The percentage of people living in Asia had dropped to 57 per cent and in Africa to 8 per cent. The growth in the world's population accelerated after 1900, increasing to 2.5 billion by 1950, an increase of more than 50 per cent increase in just 50 years. The really rapid growth in the world's population, however, took place between 1950 and 2000. In this period, the world's population increased to 6.2 billion, a 250 per cent increase. Figure 2.2 shows the year when the world's population reached each billion and the number of years it took between each billion.

The main reason for this rapid growth in population is the reduction in the death rate in less economically developed countries (LEDCs). The United Nations estimates that the world's population will reach 9 billion by 2050. Of this increase, Asia will account for 60 per cent, Africa for 20 per cent and Latin America for 9 per cent. The number of people in Europe will decline to 7 per cent, less than a third of its peak at the beginning of the twentieth century. While the population of Europe was three times that of Africa in 1900, by 2050 the population of Africa will be three times that in Europe.

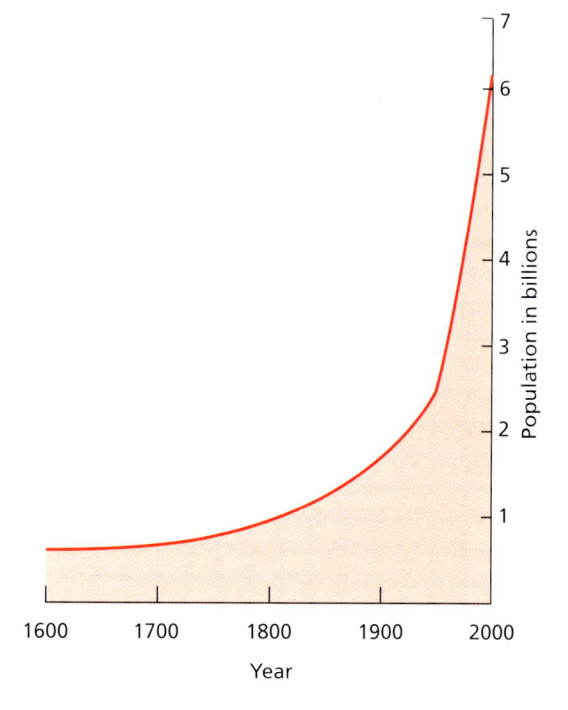

Figure 2.1 Graph of world population

Date	Billions	Years taken to add 1 billion
1804	1	
1927	2	123
1960	3	33
1974	4	14
1987	5	13
1999	6	12

Figure 2.2 World population growth, 1804–1999

In 1900, 70 per cent of the world's population lived in LEDCs. This rose to 80 per cent by 2000 and is expected to rise to 90 per cent by the year 2050.

The world's population will continue to grow after 2050. The United Nations' long-range population projections indicate that the population will reach 9.7 billion by 2150 and stabilise at 10.5 billion after 2200. Some sources theorise that the world's population will reach a peak of 12 billion before it starts to decline.

Predicting future population growth is a very uncertain process. Some demographers suggest that the population will start to decline rapidly in 50 years' time due to falling birth rates. In the last 20 years, birth rates have been dropping in all countries. In western Europe and Japan, the average birth rate is 11 per thousand. If this continues over a number of years, then the total population of the world will begin to fall, as it has done in Sweden and Italy.

ACTIVITIES

1. Draw a line graph to show the projected world population growth from 2000 to 2200. In which areas of the world do you think most of the growth will occur?

2. Draw a pictogram to show the percentage of people living in LEDCs and more economically developed countries (MEDCs) in 1900, 2000 and 2050.

Figure 2.3 Pie charts showing the proportion of the world's population in LEDCs and MEDCs

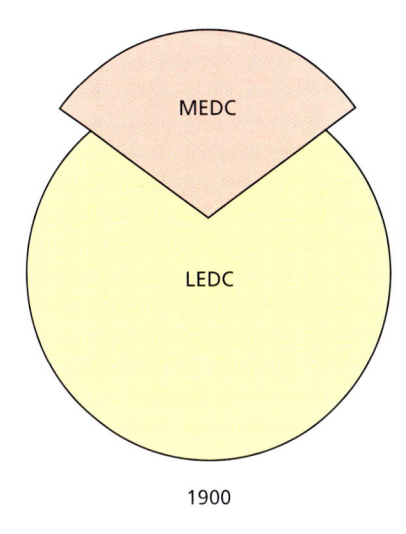

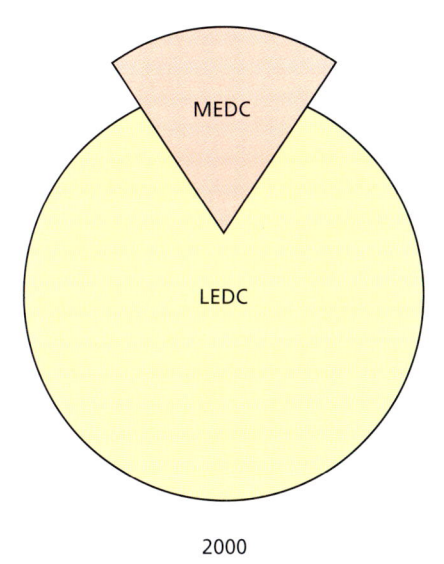

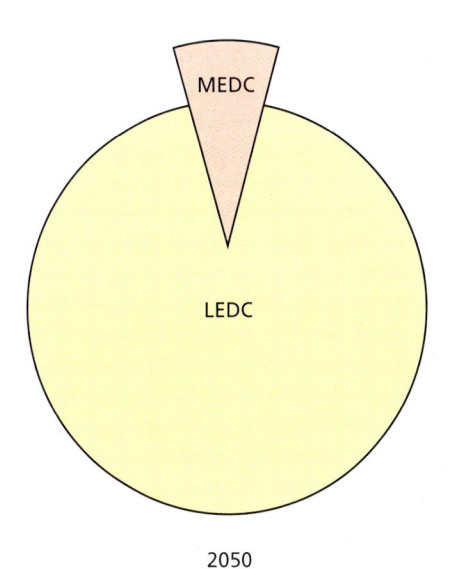

1900

2000

2050

The human world

What causes population to change?

The population in an area can change for two reasons:

1 Increases or decreases in birth and death rates.

2 The number of people moving into or leaving the area. People who move into an area are called immigrants and those who move away are called emigrants.

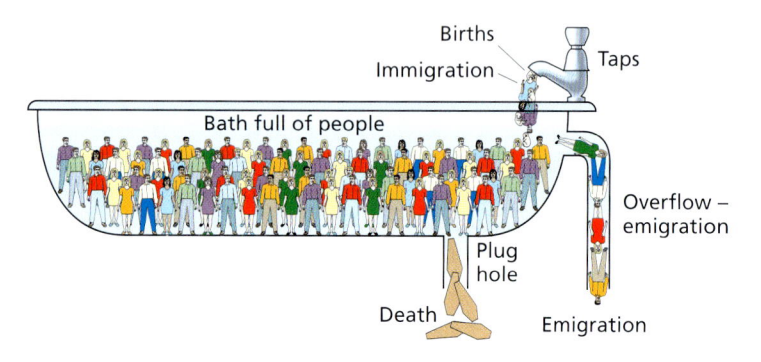

Figure 2.4 What causes population to change

What are birth and death rates?

The major reason for population changes, whether in a particular country or the world as a whole, is a change in birth rates and death rates. The **birth rate** is the number of live babies born in a year for every 1,000 people in the total population. The **death rate** is the number of people in every 1,000 who die each year. The **natural increase** is the difference between the birth rate and death

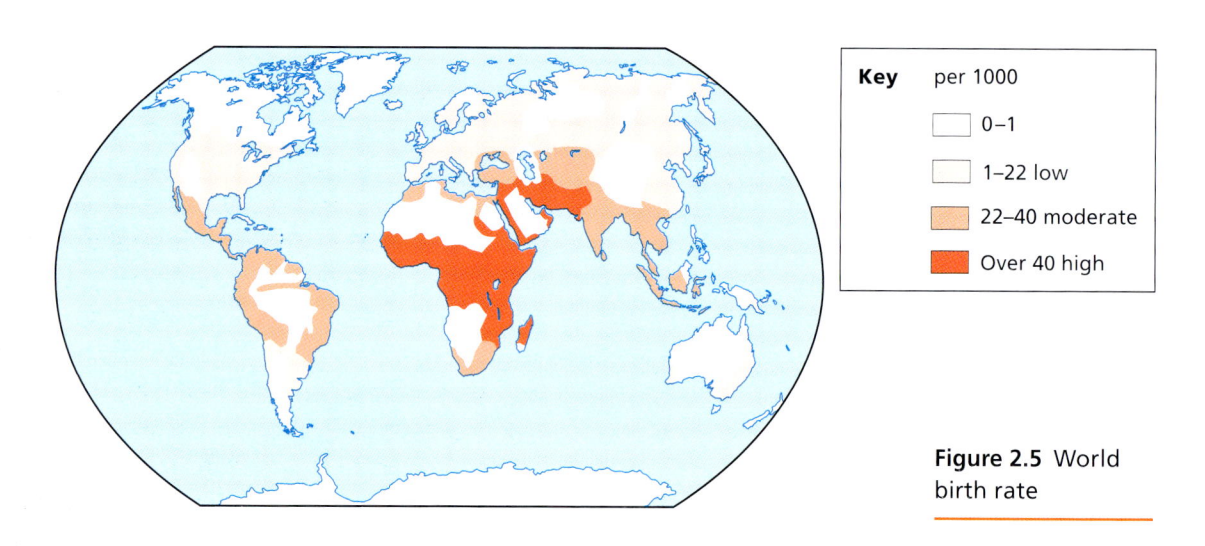

Figure 2.5 World birth rate

Key per 1000
- 0–1
- 1–22 low
- 22–40 moderate
- Over 40 high

ACTIVITIES

1 Look at the table below. According to this table what will the population of the world be in 2050?
2 What factors might cause this estimation to be wrong?
3 Study Figures 2.5 and 2.6. Describe the distribution of areas with high birth and death rates.

	Population 2000 (millions)	Births per 1,000	Deaths per 1,000	Natural increase	Doubling time in years	Projected population 2025 (m)	Projected population 2050 (m)
World	6 067	22	9	1.4	52	7 810	9 000
More developed	1 184	11	10	0.1	809	1 236	1 200
Less developed	4 883	25	9	1.6	42	6 575	7 800

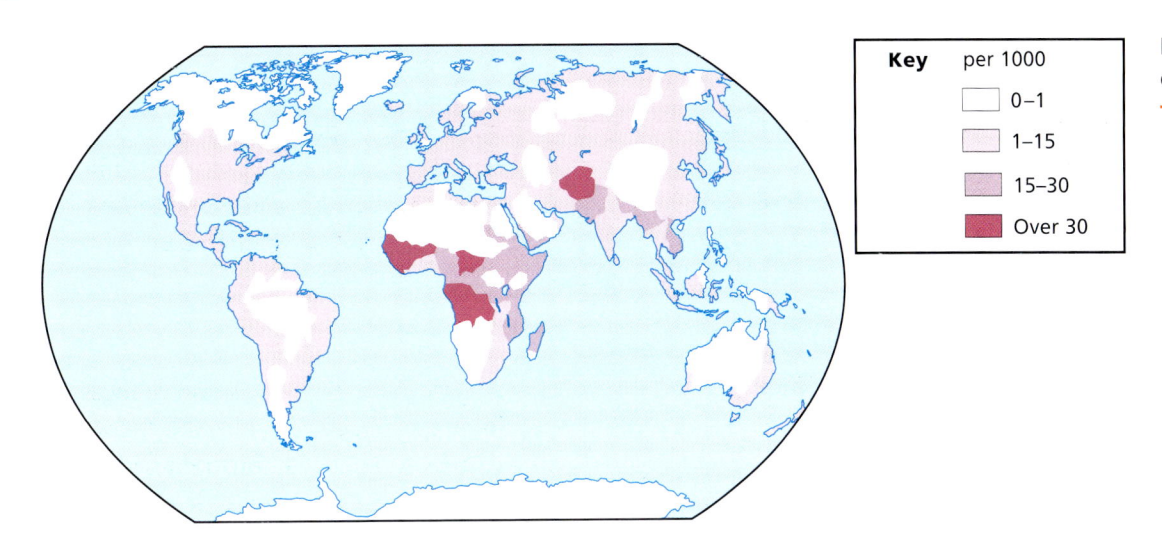

Figure 2.6 World death rate

rate. If the birth rate is higher than the death rate, then the total population will increase. If the death rate is higher than the birth rate, then the total population will decrease.

Natural increase is usually expressed as a percentage per year:

$$\text{Natural increase (per cent)} = \frac{\text{birth rate} - \text{death rate}}{10}$$

Why are birth rates decreasing?

Many countries such as China, India, Indonesia and Singapore have attempted to decrease birth rates through the introduction of family planning programmes. These programmes are not usually effective unless they are combined with greater wealth and progress in education. Educating women provides them with information on ways to control fertility, lengthens the time girls spend in school, raises the age of marriage and delays their child-bearing age.

Birth rates in India

India has had a family planning programme since 1930 but has struggled to reduce its birth rate. Its birth rate is currently 27 per thousand, which is almost twice that of China and above the average rate for LEDCs. Because so many Indians live in rural areas it has been difficult to monitor family planning campaigns. In the 1970s, India tried to introduce compulsory sterilisation for men with more than three children, but it was largely unsuccessful. India is not a wealthy country and has poor communications and education. The population is also made up of people with a variety of cultures, languages and religions. All of these factors make it very difficult for the government to enforce a family planning programme. It is likely that by the year 2035, India's population will be the largest of any country in the world.

Falling birth rates in Spain

In 1970, the birth rate in Spain was 2.86. In 1980 it was 2.21 and in 1999 it was 1.27. This is the second lowest birth rate in the world (Italy has the lowest). The reasons for this rapid decrease in Spain's birth rate are the improved quality of life and education, an increase in contraceptive use and the speed with which the country has undergone social changes. The percentage of students in further education has risen, particularly among the women. This has led to a massive increase in women in the workforce. The most important reasons for the decrease in birth rate are the increased number of single people in the population and the increase in the mean age of women when they have their first child. This mean age started to shoot up in 1988. Now most Spanish women have their first child between the ages of 30 and 39. The mean age in 1975 was 26, in 1995 it was 30.

Figure 2.7 The demographic transition model

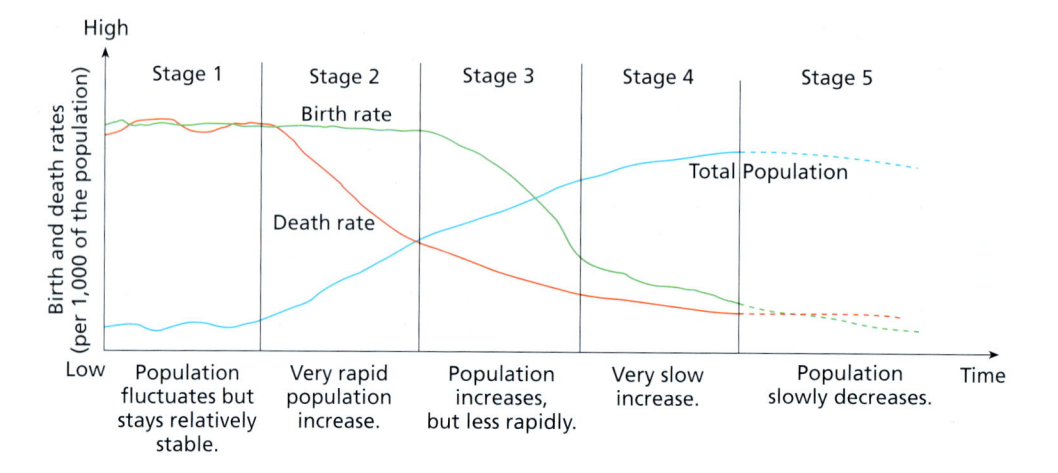

What is the demographic transition model?

The demographic transition model literally means 'population change model'. This very useful model shows how dynamic (subject to change) population is. The demographic transition model shows population change in two ways:

1. change over space: a number of countries at the same time can show the population characteristics of a different stage.
2. change over time: a country will theoretically progress through the stages.
The model is based on what happened to the birth and death rates in western European countries.

Each of the stages of the demographic transition model has specific characteristics. These are the characteristics you can expect for each stage and possible reasons for the changes between stages:

Stage 1 – Only a few of the poorest countries of the world are still at this stage when birth and death rates are high. They also fluctuate, leading to a small growth or decline in the population. There are many reasons for this:

- little access to birth control,
- because many children die in infancy (high infant mortality), parents tend to have more children to compensate in the hope that some will survive,
- children are needed to work on the land to grow food for the family,
- children are regarded as a sign of virility in some cultures,
- religious beliefs (e.g. Roman Catholics and Hindus) that encourage large families,
- death rates, especially among children, are high because of disease, famine, poor diet, poor hygiene, little medical science.

Stage 2 – This is the stage of most rapid population growth; birth rates remain high, but death rates fall rapidly causing a high population growth. Many less economically developed countries are in this stage. The reasons for this could be:

- improvements in medical care,
- improvements in sanitation and water supply,
- the quality and quantity of food produced improves,
- transport and communications improve the movements of food and medical supplies,
- decrease in infant mortality.

Stage 3 – Birth rates now fall rapidly while death rates continue to fall. The total population increase slows. Many of the newly industrialised countries are at this stage. The reasons for this could be:

- increased access to contraception,
- lower infant mortality rates means there is less need to have a bigger family,
- industrialisation and mechanisation means fewer labourers are required,
- as wealth increases, the desire for material possessions takes over the desire for large families,

- equality for women means that they are able to follow a career rather than being pressurised into having a family.

Stage 4 – Both birth rates and death rates remain low, fluctuating with 'baby booms' and epidemics of illnesses and disease. This stage is characteristic of many of the more economically developed countries and results in a steady population.

The table below shows examples of populations changes over time and space:

Is there a fifth stage? A Stage 5 was not originally thought of as part of the demographic transition model, but some countries are now reaching the stage where their total population is declining because birth rates have dropped below death rates. One example is Germany, but many other western European countries such as Italy, Spain and the UK may well be entering Stage 5.

	STAGE 1	STAGE 2	STAGE 3	STAGE 4
Changes over space	Ethiopia / Niger	Sri Lanka / Bolivia	Uruguay / China	Canada / USA
Change over time	UK: pre-1780	UK: 1780–1880	UK: 1880–1940	UK: post-1940

ACTIVITIES

Higher

1 Every 10 seconds 45 people are born and 16 die somewhere in the world.
a How many more people are there in the world:
   i   every minute?
   ii every hour?
   iii every day?
   iv every year?
b What will the long-term effects be on a country with a very low birth rate?

2 Study the following figures for birth and death rates per thousand for England and Wales between 1701 and 2001.

	1701	1721	1741	1761	1781	1801
b.r	36	35	37	36	36	37
d.r	34	36	36	32	29	22

	1821	1841	1861	1881	1901	1921
b.r	34	31	32	33	30	21
d.r.	21	20	21	20	17	13

	1941	1961	1981	2001
b.r.	15	17	14	12
d.r.	13	11	12	11

a Use the figures above to draw a graph for birth and death rates. Use the same axes.
b Draw vertical lines on the graph to divide it into the four stages of the demographic transition model.
c Which year shows the greatest natural increase in population?
d Which is the only year to show a natural decrease in population?

3 Draw a sketch of the demographic transition model. On your sketch extend the lines for the birth rate, death rate and total population to show what a fifth stage might look like.

Foundation

1 Every 10 seconds 45 babies are born and 16 people die somewhere in the world.
a How many extra people are there in the world (the difference between those being born and those that die):
   i   every 10 seconds?
   ii every minute?

2 Use the figures in the table to draw a graph of birth and death rates for England and Wales between 1701 and 2001.

3 Indonesia has a slogan of '2 is enough' to promote their family planning policy. Invent your own slogan and incorporate it on a poster for family planning.

Population structure and characteristics vary from place to place

Population structure

The structure of the population can be classified according to a number of different factors including age, sex, ethnicity, religious beliefs and occupational groups. Knowing about the structure of the population helps us, for example, to predict changes in the working population, the demand for housing and the provision of services for the young and elderly. It also allows us to make comparisons between areas in the same settlement, different settlements and LEDCs and MEDCs.

Who lives where in the USA?

Figure 2.8 shows the percentages of ethnic groupings for three states in the USA. (Ethnic means a group of people who have similar cultural characteristics, such as language, colour, religion and nationality). Ethnic groups usually migrate to a place where they may form a minority within the total population. Nearly all the world's countries and cities have several ethnic groups and minorities. These groups are rarely spread out evenly, but tend to concentrate in areas of a country or parts of a city. The three states clearly show differences in ethnic composition and reflect the main areas of migration.

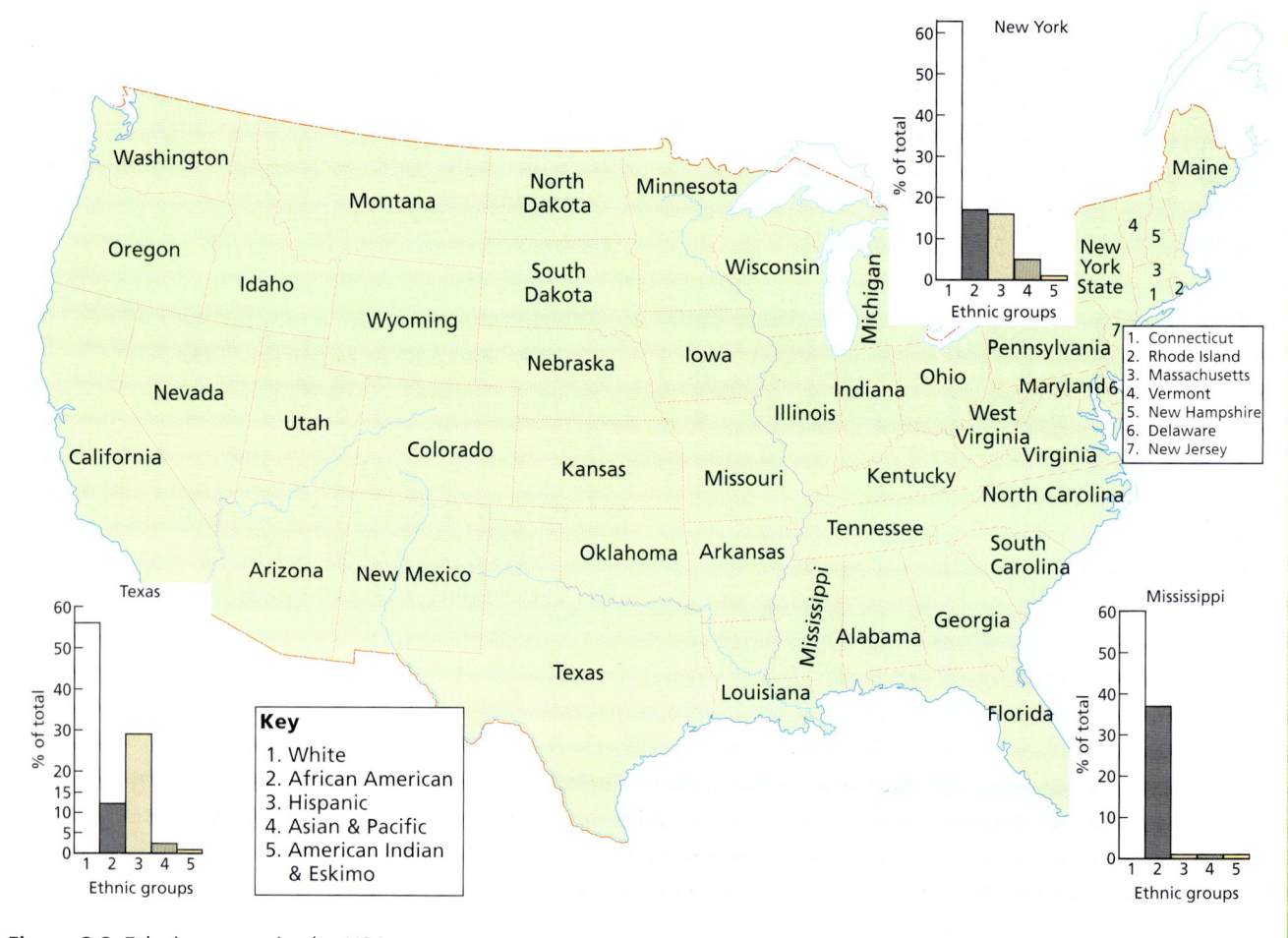

Key
1. White
2. African American
3. Hispanic
4. Asian & Pacific
5. American Indian & Eskimo

1. Connecticut
2. Rhode Island
3. Massachusetts
4. Vermont
5. New Hampshire
6. Delaware
7. New Jersey

Figure 2.8 Ethnic groups in the USA

The human world

In the UK information about the population is collected in a census which is a questionnaire that is delivered to all households once every ten years. The first census was administered in 1801 and, apart from an interruption for the Second World War, there are accurate figures up to 2001. Most nations in the world now conduct regular censuses. This can be very difficult in a country as large as India, which conducted the world's largest census in February 2001. About 2 million enumerators (census collectors), drawn from the ranks of schoolteachers and government employees, interviewed 200 million households on economic, educational, demographic and social details. One of the main problems to be overcome in India is obtaining proper data, especially in rural areas. The census commissioner has stated that, 'This time the questionnaire is being redesigned and maximum publicity will be given before the census so that people come forward with more information. Our past experience shows that there has been a poor response from women, especially in some parts of Punjab, Haryana and Uttar Pradesh. This time our efforts will be to improve on that count.'

What are population pyramids?

The most important demographic characteristic of a population is its age-sex structure. Population pyramids (also known as age-sex pyramids) graphically display this information.

Population pyramids display the percentage or actual amount of a population broken down by sex and age. The five-year age groups on the Y-axis show the long-term trends in the birth and death rates but also reflect shorter-term baby booms, wars and epidemics.

There are three key types of population pyramids: rapid growth, slow growth and negative growth.

Rapid growth

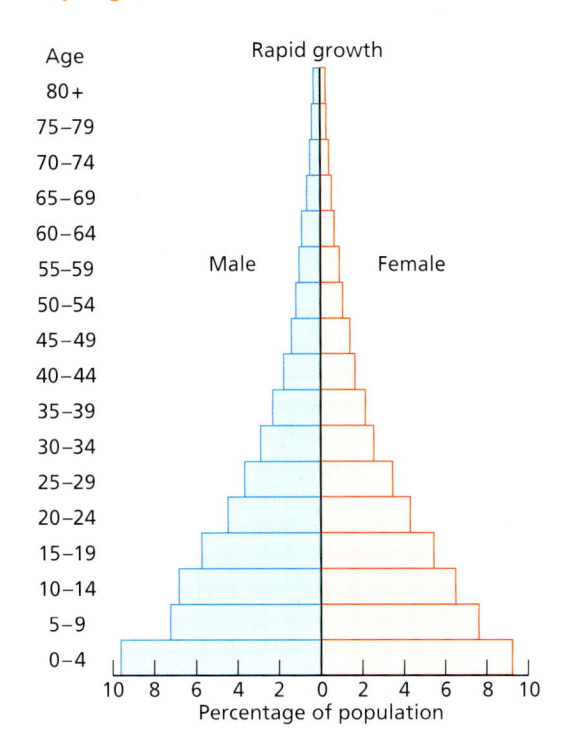

Figure 2.9 Population pyramid for Kenya

This pyramid of Kenya shows a triangle-shaped pyramid and reflects a high growth rate of about 2.1 per cent annually. The age-sex pyramid for Kenya is typical of a country in the less economically developed world that is experiencing rapid population growth. The wide base indicates that there are large numbers of dependent children aged 0–14 in the total population, the result of high levels of fertility. The top of the pyramid is narrow and indicates that only a small proportion of the population lives to old age. This type of population structure is likely to have a number of important implications:

- Limited resources will be stretched to meet the needs of the large number of dependent children for schooling, nutrition and health care.
- As this group reaches working age, a large number of jobs will need to be created to enable them to support themselves and their families.
- As this group reaches child-bearing age, it is likely that fertility rates will remain high, with continued high rates of natural population increase.

The human world

Slow growth

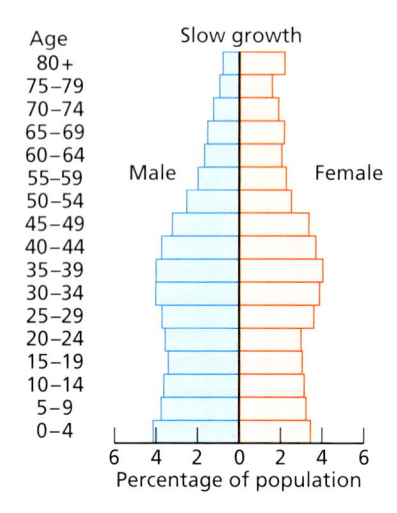

Figure 2.10 Population pyramid for USA

In the USA, the population is growing at a rate of about 1.5 per cent annually. This growth rate is reflected in the more oblong-like structure of the pyramid. Note the bulge in the pyramid between the ages of about 30 to 50. This large segment of the population is the result of the economic expansion in the late 1950s and 1960s. As this population group moves up the pyramid, there will be a much greater demand for medical care, pensions and other services for the elderly. This shape of pyramid is typical for a country in the more economically developed world.

Negative growth

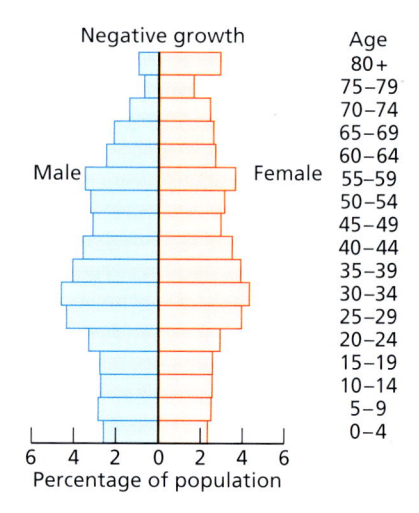

Figure 2.11 Population pyramid for Germany

Germany is experiencing a period of negative growth (−0.1 per cent). As negative growth in a country continues, the population is reduced. A population can shrink due to a declining birth rate and a stable death rate. Increased emigration may also be a contributor to a declining population. After the Second World War, workers from several southern European countries, especially Turkey, were encouraged to emigrate to Germany. The bulges in the 25–45 age groups in the 2000 pyramid show the children of these emigrants.

Several European countries have begun to take on this shape and can be compared to the possible fifth stage of the demographic transition model.

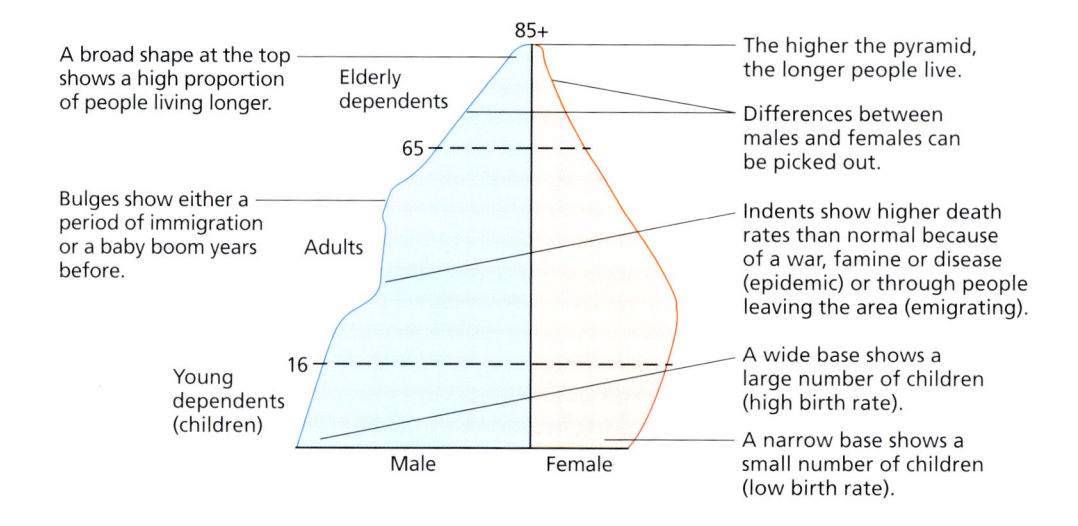

Figure 2.12 Examiner's tip interpreting a population pyramid

- A broad shape at the top shows a high proportion of people living longer.
- Bulges show either a period of immigration or a baby boom years before.
- The higher the pyramid, the longer people live.
- Differences between males and females can be picked out.
- Indents show higher death rates than normal because of a war, famine or disease (epidemic) or through people leaving the area (emigrating).
- A wide base shows a large number of children (high birth rate).
- A narrow base shows a small number of children (low birth rate).

The human world

ACTIVITIES

Higher

1. What does the term 'ethnic group' mean?
2. Look at the table below showing the ethnic composition of three states in the USA.
   a. Draw a pie graph for each state to show the different ethnic groups.
   b. Suggest reasons why the structures differ for the three states.

   Race percentage of population

State	White	African American	Hispanic	Asian Indian	American
California	51	7	30.5	11	0.5
Idaho	90.5	0.5	7	1	1
Arizona	68	3	22	2	5

3. Study the population pyramids for Kenya, the USA and Germany.
   a. Describe the population structure of Kenya.
   b. What are the differences between the three pyramids? Use data in your answer.

4. a. Use the data in the table below to draw modified population pyramids. (Draw only four bars.)
   b. State whether each country is experiencing rapid growth, slow growth or negative growth.

   Percentage of people in selected age groups for UK, Ethiopia and Ireland

Age	0–19		20–39		40–59		60+	
	M	F	M	F	M	F	M	F
UK	13	12	15	15	12	12	9	12
Ethiopia	28	28	13	13	6	6	3	3
Ireland	18	14	11	7	17	14	10	9

Foundation

1. Name the different ethnic groups in the USA.
2. Look at the table showing different ethnic groups in three US states.
   a. Draw a pie chart for each state.
   b. Which state has:
      i. the highest percentage of whites?
      ii. the lowest percentage of Hispanics?
      iii. the most even distribution of ethnic groups?

3. Below are two population pyramids. One is for Sweden and the other is for Mexico.
   a. Which pyramid is for Mexico and which one is for Sweden?
   b. Give reasons for your answer.
4. Look at the population pyramid for the USA (Figure 2.10). Information from this pyramid was used to complete the following table.

Country	Ages	Male %	Female %
USA	0–19	15	14
	20–39	16	16
	40–59	11	12
	60+	7	9
	TOTAL	49	51

   a. Draw similar tables for Germany and Kenya.
   b. Which country has the greatest percentage of its population in the age range:
      i. 0–19
      ii. 60 +
      iii. 20–59
   c. Describe three differences between the population pyramids for Kenya and Germany.

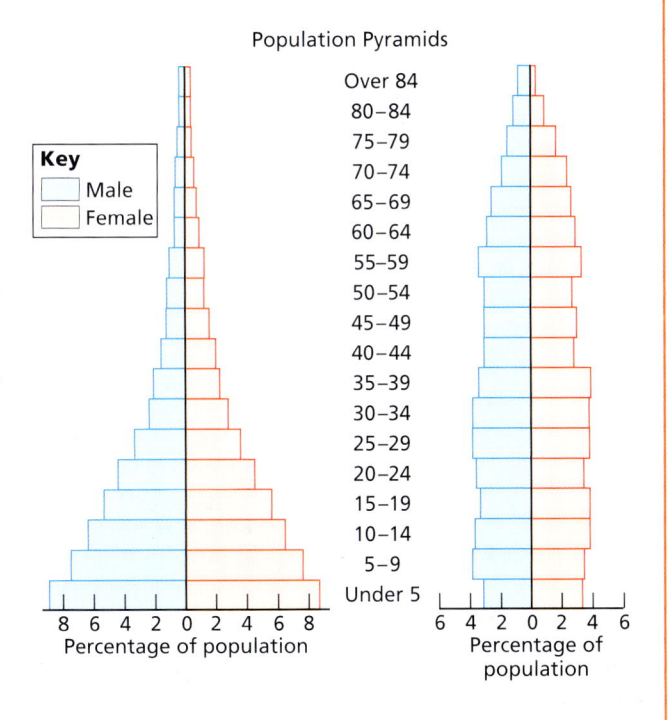

Figure 2.13 Population pyramids for Mexico and Sweden

How does the structure of rural and urban populations differ?

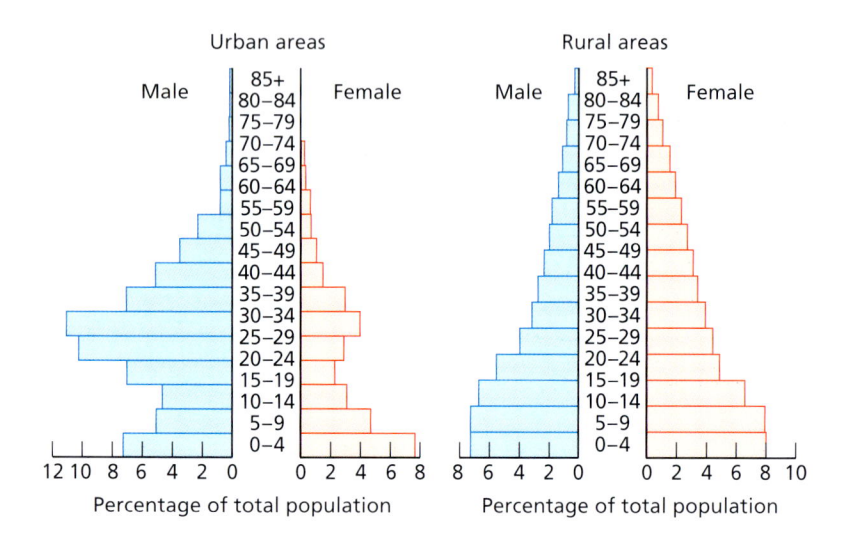

Figure 2.14 Contrasts in urban and rural population structures in an LEDC

In LEDCs there is often a marked difference in the population structure of rural and urban areas. In rural areas, there is often a shortage of young adults, particularly males, as a result of migration to the cities. This may cause rural birth rates to fall, although this is not always the case as many migrants to the city are only temporary.

Migrants often return to their villages when they have earned sufficient money to survive for another year. The urban population structure is likely to show a bulge in the 20–35 age range as well as an increase in the youngest age groups, reflecting the children of the young adults. Figure 2.14 shows a characteristic population pyramid for a rural and an urban area in Peru, an LEDC.

In MEDCs young adults also move to the cities in search of job opportunities and the 'bright lights'. In contrast, there is a movement away from the urban areas to the rural areas:

1 by people nearing retirement age who are looking for an improved quality of life,
2 by couples with high incomes looking for larger homes and a better environment in which to raise their families.

What are youthful and ageing populations?

When a country has a high number of children, it is said to have a youthful population, but when a country has a high number of elderly people, it is said to have an ageing population. Both of these situations can give rise to a variety of problems for a country. Children and old people depend on the economic support of the adult working population. If the percentage of either children or the aged is high, then more money and resources have to be made available for resources like schools, hospitals and nursing homes. These resources have to be provided by the economically active population.

What is the dependency ratio?

The dependency ratio is the relationship between the working population and the non-working population. For ease of calculation, the active population is taken as all those people aged 15 to 65, whether they are employed or not, and the non-active as those under 15 and over 65.

The dependency ratio is calculated using the following formula:

$$\text{Dependency ratio} = \frac{\%\text{ pop aged 0–14} + \%\text{ pop aged 65+}}{\%\text{ of population aged 15–65}}$$

In Sweden 18 per cent of the population are under 15, 20 per cent are over 65 and 62 per cent are aged 15–65. Therefore the dependency ratio for Sweden is:

$$\text{D.R.} = \frac{18 \text{ per cent} + 20 \text{ per cent}}{62 \text{ per cent}} = 61$$

The ratio for MEDCs usually lies between 50 and 75. In LEDCs, the ratio is typically higher, often over 100; the dependency ratio for Mexico (using figures from the population pyramid in Figure 2.14) is 104.

What are the problems of an ageing population?

In countries like the UK, the ageing of the population is an increasingly worrying problem. In 1950 there was only 1 pensioner for every 5 economically active people. Today this has increased to 3:5, which is causing a strain on the provision of state pensions as they are funded by the taxes of those people in work. It is obviously going to become increasingly difficult for the government to provide adequate pensions for the over-65s.

Do the over-65s have a right to a state-funded pension? What can be done to ease the situation? These are possible solutions:
- Increase the taxes paid by the working population.
- Raise the age of retirement.
- Abolish state pensions and make people pay for their own private pension plans.

With an increasing number of over 65s and life expectancy increasing all the time, there will be a much greater demand for health care and support services. At present hospitals are already short of bed space and specialist nursing for the elderly. The number of residential and care homes is likely to increase dramatically, but they are very expensive (they can cost up to £2,000 a month and many people have to sell their homes to finance their own care). At the moment, the government guarantees to pay the cost of care for those who cannot afford it, but as numbers are set to rise, can this be guaranteed in the future?

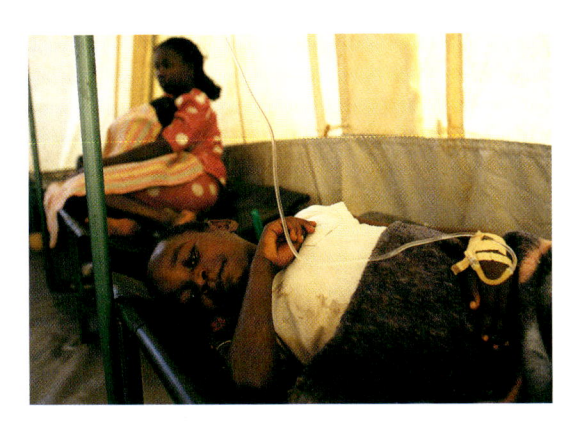

Figure 2.16 Sick children in an LEDC

What are the problems of a youthful population?

The large numbers of children is one of the main problems facing governments of LEDCs. Over 40 per cent of the population of Africa is under 15. This puts an enormous strain on the economies of these countries as they try to provide this huge number of children with education, health care and food. Attendance at secondary schools, especially in rural areas, is very low which results in large numbers of unqualified workers. Disease among children is prevalent, with common (yet curable) complaints like measles and diarrhoea sometimes leading to death because of the lack of trained medical practitioners and of necessary medical resources such as vaccines. It is impossible for governments in LEDCs to finance the ever-growing number of children.

Original house converted to residential care home.

Modern extension built due to increasing demands of an ageing population

Figure 2.15 A residential care home in Hertfordshire

ACTIVITIES

1. Draw typical population pyramids for the following areas:
   a. rural area in an MEDC,
   b. urban area in an LEDC.
2. Define the terms 'youthful population' and 'ageing population'.
3. Explain the problems caused by an ageing population.

> People live in a variety of settlements of different sizes.
> These settlements are often made up of distinct zones.

Physical and economic factors affect the location, shape and growth of settlements. Settlements do not happen accidentally or grow by chance. There is always a good reason why a settlement is where it is.

The land on which a settlement is built is called the site. The original decision to locate a settlement in a particular place would have been influenced by many factors. Most settlements were built by farming communities who would have needed a site that met all or as many as possible of their needs. The following factors were all important:

- access to a permanent supply of water,
- well-drained land that was free from flooding,
- land that was sheltered from strong winds and storms,
- land that faced south to gain maximum warmth from the sun,
- fertile land for arable crops and pasture for livestock,
- timber for fuel and building.

If a settlement grew, it was probably because it had many of the above factors as well as a good situation. (A settlement's situation is its location relative to its surroundings.) A good situation allows a settlement to grow and develop into a central settlement surrounded by other settlements. This central settlement is likely to grow into a market town as it is easily accessible from all the other settlements. Routes would focus on the central town and trade would develop, leading in turn to a growth in service industries.

Physical factors affecting the site of a settlement

Water supply – Settlements that are located close to rivers, lakes or springs are called **wet-point sites**. Figure 2.17 shows how a line of villages has developed alongside springs at the base of the hill. These settlements are called **spring-line settlements** and are one type of wet-point site. As water infiltrates into the hillside, it percolates through the porous rock. When the water reaches impermeable rocks into which it cannot soak, it issues forth as a spring.

Those who live in settlements located close to rivers have to be careful to build their houses above the flood plain. If houses are built too close to the river, there is a chance that if the river floods, serious damage to property can occur. This was shown in many areas of England during the autumn of 2000. Settlements were flooded from York in the north to Uckfield in the south.

Settlements that are sited above the flood plain are called **dry-point sites**. The city of Ely in Cambridgeshire was originally built on a slightly higher area of land surrounded by marshland. The photograph of Ely (Figure 2.18) shows the original site standing out above the flat fenland.

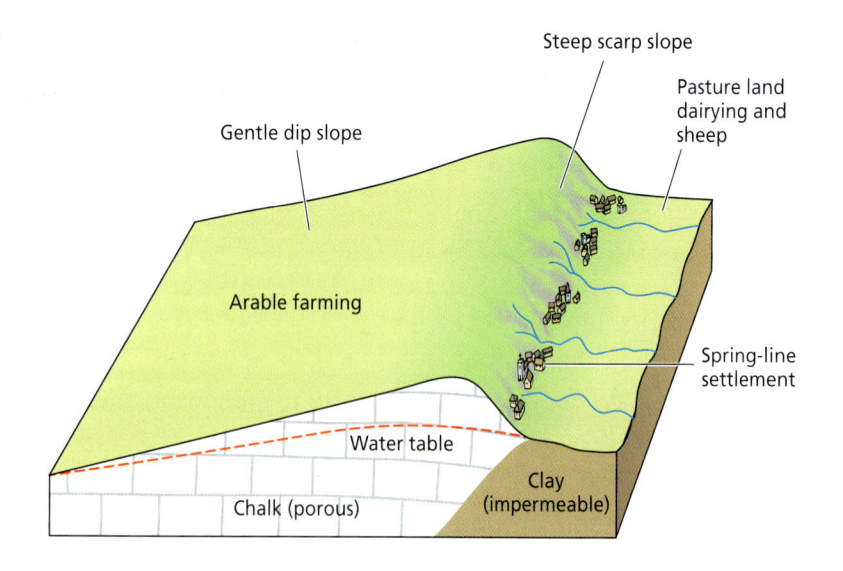

Figure 2.17 Diagram of spring-line settlements

Figure 2.18 Ely

Aspect and shelter – In the northern hemisphere, south-facing slopes receive more sun than the north-facing slopes and are therefore warmer. The south-facing slopes are also sheltered from the cold northerly winds. More settlements and agricultural land are therefore sited on the south-facing slopes (see Figure 2.20).

Figure 2.19 An alpine valley in France

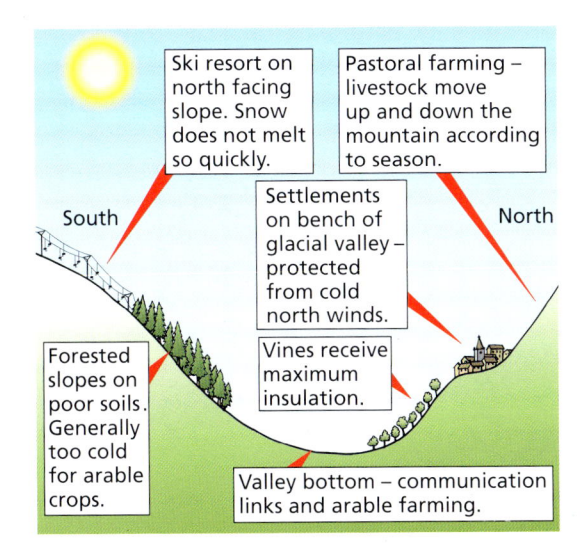

Figure 2.20 Land use in the Alps

Defence – Centuries ago, selecting a site for defence purposes was very important. A castle was often built on high ground overlooking the surrounding countryside. This is the case in Edinburgh and Lincoln. The town of Savignano in southern Italy was sited in a commanding position above a gap in the Apennine Mountains (see Figure 2.21).

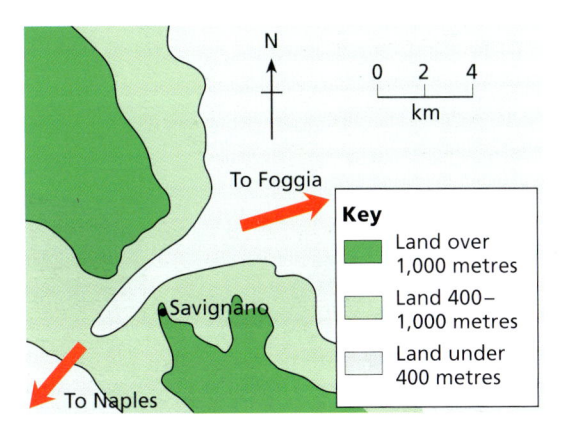

Figure 2.21 Map of Savignano

The original site of Paris was on the Ile de La Cité, an island in the middle of the river Seine. This protected the inhabitants from attack, as they were surrounded by water. Paris subsequently grew as it became a focus of routeways.

Venice is on the coast of north-east Italy, at the northern end of the Adriatic Sea. It is located at the mouth of the River Po which is a delta. The city is built on over 100 islands, split up by canals.

Figure 2.22 Map showing the site and situation of Venice

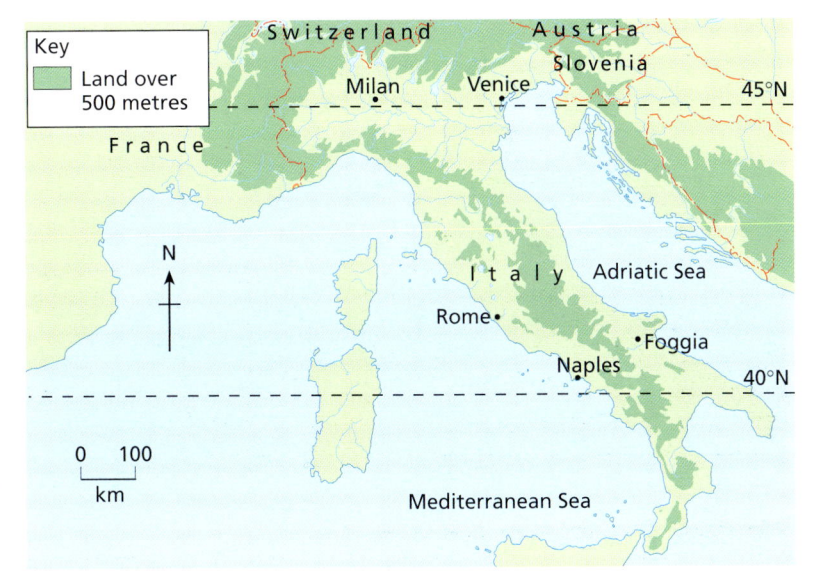

Figure 2.23 The Canale Grande in Venice

The canals act as 'roads' and are the only way, other than by foot, to travel around the city. The largest canal is the Canale Grande (see Figure 2.23). Venice's site was chosen because it provided a good defensive position. It later became a rich port, trading with cities all around the Mediterranean and western Europe. It is still an important city today, but much of its wealth is now based on tourism.

Many settlements are located on the inside of river meanders because they would only need to be protected in one direction. Examples include Yarm, Durham, Shrewsbury and Warkworth (see Figure 2.24 and the OS map on page 47).

Economic factors affecting the site of a settlement

Communications – Settlements often grew where rivers could be easily crossed. This might be at fords (Oxford and Hertford) or at bridging points. The lowest bridging point (the nearest point to the sea that could be bridged) was a particularly favourable site. Many large cities were originally sited at the lowest bridging point; examples include London, Hamburg, Paris and Exeter.

Other favourable communication sites were at the junction of valleys or in gaps through hills. Montgenevre and Briançon are in *cols* (gaps) in the Alps and straddle the French–Italian border (see Figure 2.25). Good communications often gave the settlement an advantage over others so it grew as a route centre. Traders would bring their goods to these accessible settlements and, in time, markets grew up there. Settlements also developed at favourable coastal locations. Ports such as Poole in Dorset and Sydney in Australia grew up around large natural harbours.

Figure 2.24 Photograph of Warkworth

Figure 2.25 Alpine routeway

Resources – Early settlers relied upon timber for both fuel and building material. A site close to woodland was therefore an advantage. Stone was also used for building, so proximity to a quarry was also useful. During the Industrial Revolution, coal was in great demand as a power source for factories. Many mining towns sprang up on the coalfields of northern England. The existence of oil reserves in various parts of the world, such as the Middle East and Russia, has been the reason for mining settlements to grow in these areas. Aberdeen in Scotland saw considerable growth with the development of the North Sea oil industry.

Settlement shapes

Settlements can be classified according to the arrangement of houses within them.

1 Nucleated or clustered settlements have the individual buildings grouped closely together. They often form at crossroads or route centres. They may have originally clustered close together for defensive purposes or because communal farming took place in the area.
2 Dispersed or fragmented settlements have individual buildings spread out. There is usually no obvious centre. They are often rural farming villages, where areas of woodland were gradually cleared.
3 Linear settlements have buildings on either side of a road, valley or the coast. Ribbon development is when housing grows out from a town along a main road.

ACTIVITIES

Use the OS map extract on page 47 to answer the following questions:

1 Give the name and a four figure grid reference for an example of each of the following. Do not use an example that has already been used in the text:
 a a dispersed settlement,
 b a nucleated settlement,
 c a linear settlement.
2 Find Alnwick on the map. Give six figure grid references for the following features found in, or close to Alnwick:
 a Alnwick information centre,
 b St. Leonard's hospital,
 c Alnwick museum,
 d the roundabout where the A1(T) meets the A1086.
3 Name the features found at the following grid references:
 a 208144
 b 192145
 c 253071
 d 237117
4 Describe the physical factors that affect the site of settlements.
5 How can good communication links affect the growth of settlements?
6 Compare the settlement shapes shown in Figure 2.26.

Extension

Choose a town in your local area.
 a Describe its site.
 b Why did your town grow while other settlements remained as villages?

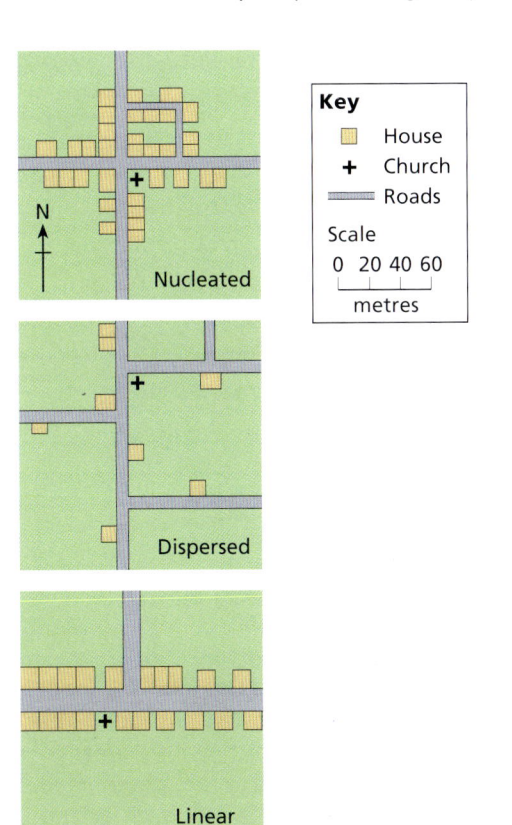

Figure 2.26 Diagram of settlement shapes

Urban Structure Models

By the year 2000 almost 60 per cent of the world's population and 90 per cent of the UK's population lived in urban areas. But what is an urban area? Are they all the same shape and structure? What determines their growth? Urban areas can be defined as areas of continuous development. Most urban areas in MEDCs have grown as employment and the need for housing has risen. Their initial growth was unplanned, but by the twentieth century most MEDCs urban development was being strictly controlled. This has had an effect on their shape and structure. During the twentieth century geographers tried to make sense of the patterns made by urban areas and devised a number of models which urban areas in MEDCs could be compared to. These definitions apply to all the models.

Zone 1: Central Business District; contains the major shops, offices and entertainment facilities.

Zone 2: Inner city area (twilight zone). This is an area of old housing and light manufacturing industry.

Zone 3: Low class residential. This is an area of poor quality housing, although the conditions are better than in Zone 2.

Zone 4: Medium class residential. This is an area of housing which was built between the wars. It is mainly semi-detached housing and council estates.

Zone 5: High class residential (commuter zone). This is an area of expensive housing on the outskirts of the city. It also stretches in to the countryside beyond the city.

Figure 2.27 Urban structure models

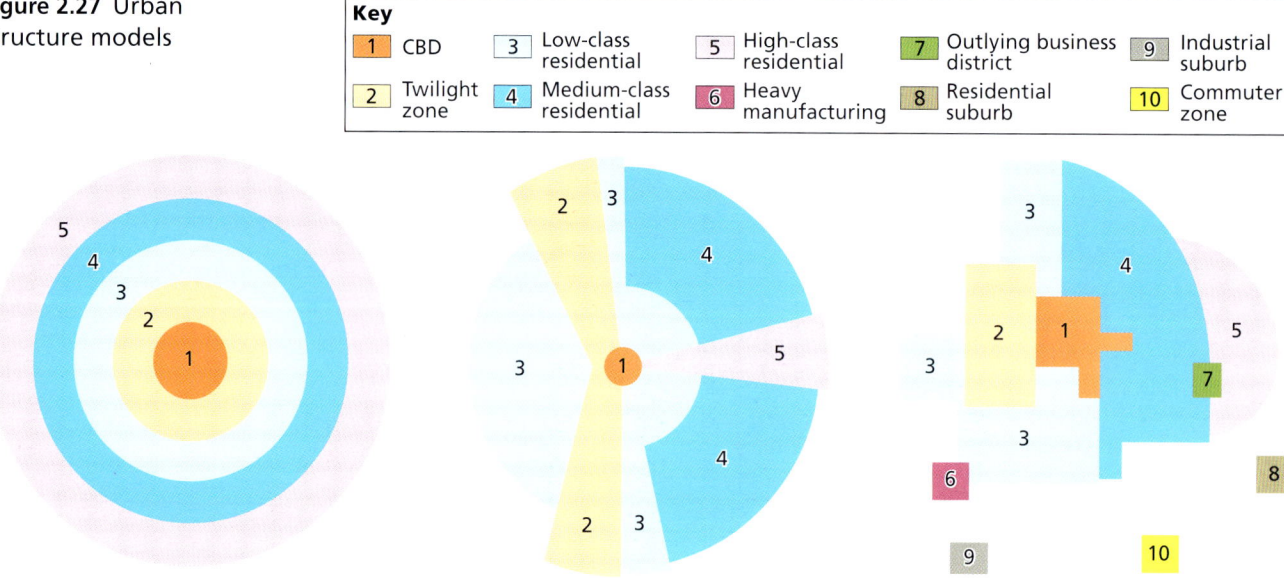

Key
1. CBD
2. Twilight zone
3. Low-class residential
4. Medium-class residential
5. High-class residential
6. Heavy manufacturing
7. Outlying business district
8. Residential suburb
9. Industrial suburb
10. Commuter zone

Concentric ring model
This model was devised by Burgess in 1924. It split the land use of the city into rings, starting from the centre. The idea was that urban areas grow equally in all directions.

Sector model
In the sector model, land use is arranged in wedges or sectors which radiate out from the city centre. It was devised by Hoyt in 1939. Its basis was that land uses are determined by the land accessibility.

Multiple nuclei model
Harris and Ullman devised this model in 1945. In this model the idea is that land uses only occupy small areas of the city. These areas are determined by a number of factors, such as land values or accessibility.

Tremendous growth has occurred in the number of people living in urban areas in LEDCs during the last half of the twentieth century. Geographers have tried to make sense of the patterns that have developed in these areas, but this has been made difficult by the speed of their growth. The result is that very little urban planning has taken place and there is consequently very little pattern to the cities.

The model which has evolved is true mainly for Brazilian cities, although it can be applied to other cities in the world. The main characteristics of the model are set out in Figure 2.28.

Zone A: Central Business District; contains the main businesses, shopping centres and entertainment of the urban area.

Zone B: Slums and tenements consisting of run-down housing, often overcrowded and sub-divided between a number of families (see Chapter 8). The tenements have very few amenities.

Zone C: High status housing. High-rise expensive modern apartment blocks, many have their own security guards.

Zone D: Poor to medium quality housing which probably started out as a shanty town. It has now been provided with some basic amenities (the periferia).

Zone E: Suburban high status, low density housing for executive and professional classes.

Zone F: Shanty towns (favellas in Brazil and bustees in India). Spontaneous squatter settlements.

Zone G: Low cost housing funded by the government which has basic amenities.

Zone H: Industry. Modern factories along main roads, sometimes with favellas in between.

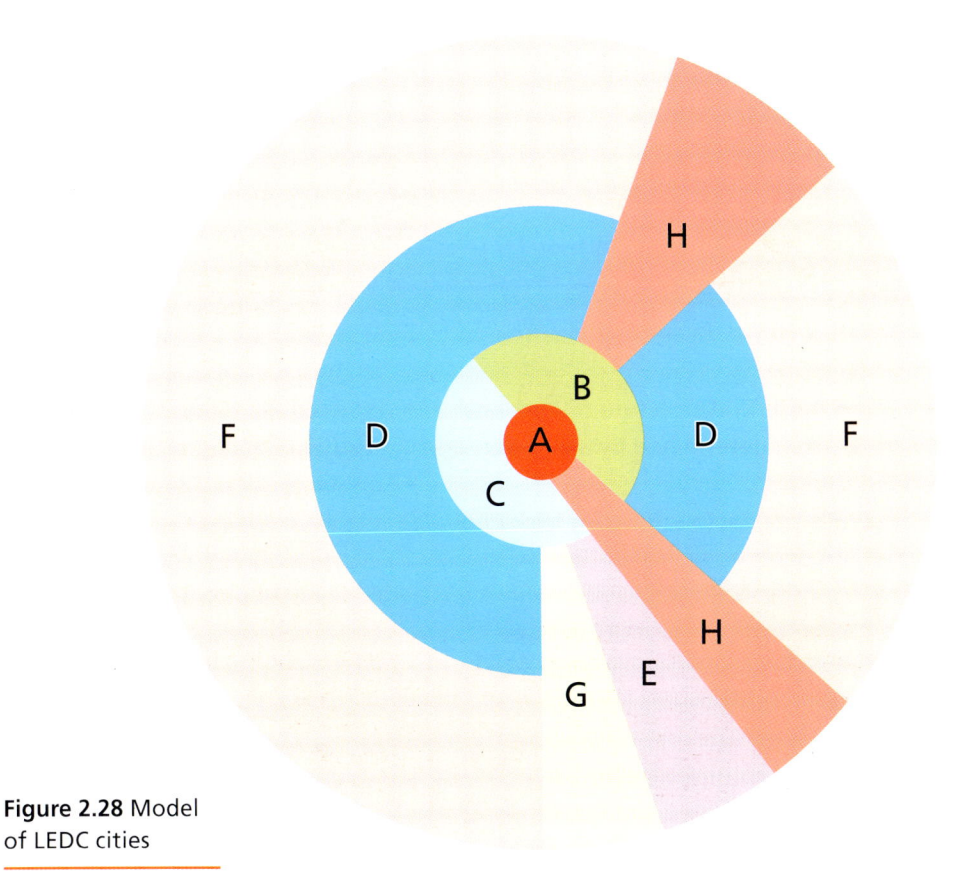

Figure 2.28 Model of LEDC cities

40 The human world

Case Study | **LAND USE IN AN URBAN AREA IN AN MEDC: READING, UK**

Where is Reading situated?

Reading is one of the largest urban areas in Berkshire. It is approximately 65 km from London, Oxford, and Swindon, and 110 km from Bristol. Reading is located in the Thames valley with the Chiltern Hills close to the north of the town. It is sited at the confluence of the Thames and the Kennet.

Why has Reading grown?

Reading first started to grow because of its accessibility. It is the meeting place of three important railway lines: from London Paddington to South Wales and the West Country, from London Waterloo to terminate in Reading, and the cross country line from the south coast of England to Scotland through major Midland cities such as Birmingham. There are also very good major road links, for example the A4 and then the M4 motorway linking London and Bristol. Reading's location in the M4 corridor, increasing its accessibility and closeness to London, means that it has grown considerably in the last 50 years. The original industrial base of the town were the 'three Bs':

- Bulbs: Suttons Seeds were based in the town.
- Brewing: there has always been a brewery in Reading. At present it is the large Courage brewery near Junction 11 of the M4.
- Biscuits: Huntley and Palmers were based in the centre of Reading.

In the late twentieth century, Reading has become known for its involvement with hi-tech Industries such as Digital, Motorola and NEC.

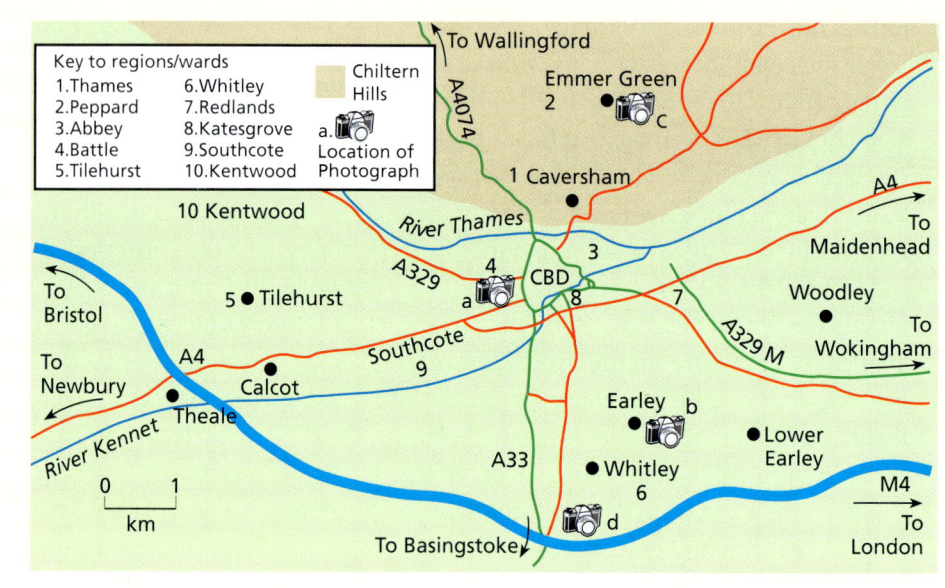

Figure 2.29 The site of Reading

1991 Census

	Ethnicity			Tenure and amenities				Skills		
	% white	% black	% Asian	% h'holds owner occupied	% h'holds no car	% lacking sharing bathroom/WC	% lone parent h'holds	% professional/ managerial h'holds	% skilled (manual & non-manual h'holds)	% partly skilled/ unskilled h'holds
3. Abbey	84.2%	6.2%	7.2%	48.9%	47.1%	7.1%	4.1%	41.9%	35.8%	17.2%
4. Battle	82.4%	8.9%	6.7%	73.2%	38.8%	3.7%	3.7%	34.9%	43.9%	18.4%
8. Katesgrove	86.1%	4.7%	6.6%	61.6%	41.0%	5.5%	4.4%	40.4%	33.3%	22.7%
10. Kentwood	93.9%	3.3%	1.6%	80.9%	21.9%	0.6%	3.3%	36.5%	42.7%	19.2%
2. Peppard	94.8%	1.0%	2.7%	87.5%	16.9%	0.3%	2.1%	52.6%	35.5%	11.1%
7. Redlands	82.7%	5.7%	6.0%	56.8%	38.0%	6.3%	3.7%	52.3%	29.1%	13.6%
9. Southcote	95.2%	2.5%	1.1%	58.6%	37.5%	1.0%	5.0%	30.6%	50.0%	17.0%
1. Thames	97.5%	0.4%	1.0%	92.7%	15.3%	0.6%	1.4%	70.3%	24.9%	3.3%
5. Tilehurst	97.1%	1.5%	0.9%	79.6%	24.4%	0.2%	1.8%	36.0%	51.3%	11.2%
6. Whitley	93.7%	4.0%	1.4%	49.5%	40.6%	0.4%	6.8%	24.0%	45.0%	20.0%

Figure 2.30 Census information for selected Reading wards

What has affected the shape of Reading?

The shape and structure of Reading has been determined by a number of factors:

- Physical factors: Reading is located in the Thames Valley. The confluence of the Kennet with the Thames is just east of the town centre. The courses of these two rivers have affected the shape of Reading (see Figure 2.29). The Chiltern Hills are to the north of Reading and have restricted growth in that direction.

- Human factors: the M4 motorway to the south of the town has stopped the town growing any further in that direction. It originally spread east–west along the A4, avoiding the river valleys but gaining shelter from the Chiltern Hills to the north. The most recent growth has been infilling which has mostly taken place to the south of the town. As can be seen in Figure 2.29, these roads affect the shape of the town as there is very little development to the south of the motorway.

The human world

What are the land use patterns in Reading?

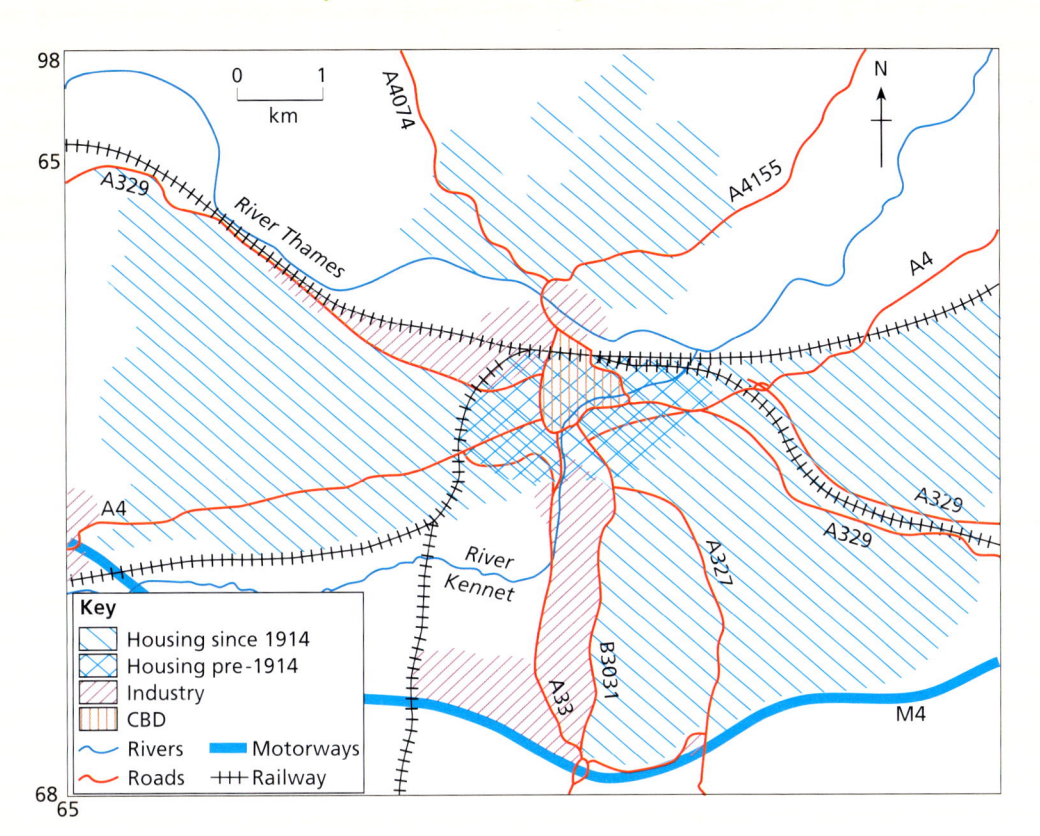

Figure 2.31 Reading's urban land use

Figure 2.32 Transect along the A4, Bath road

CBD – The CBD is a zone of renewal and redevelopment (see Chapter 8) which contains the most important shops, offices and entertainment facilities (Warner Village cinema). There are also important public buildings which include the library and town hall. Land in the CBD is in short supply and is, therefore, the most expensive land in the urban area. As a result of this buildings tend to be tall so that they take up the minimum amount of space, for example Queen's House, headquarters of Metal Box and the Prudential building. Another consequence of this is that the shops and other businesses in the centre of the town, for example Marks and Spencers and Heelas, must have a high turnover. The reason for this high demand for land is because it is the most accessible part of the town. Roads and public transport all converge on the centre of the urban area which makes it far easier to get into the centre of town.

Inner city area – This is the area just outside the CBD. Much of the high density housing was built between 1850 and 1914 (see Figure 2.31). The housing tends to be either two-bedroomed terraces in a grid iron pattern or larger semi-detached housing of the same age built along the main artery roads into the town. The industry is mainly light industry and small workshops. In many British cities the larger houses have been split into offices and bedsits or used for doctors' surgeries. In some cities the smaller terraced housing was replaced in the 1960s by high-rise flats.

42 The human world

Case Study — **LAND USE IN AN URBAN AREA IN AN MEDC: READING, UK** – continued

The suburbs – In Figure 2.27 the suburbs are zones 3 and 4 and consists of housing that was built after 1914. It consists of lower density housing, mainly semi-detached or detached. The houses tend to be bigger because the price of land is lower there. The majority of the housing is owner occupied, although there are some large out-of-town social priority estates, for example Whitley Wood (see Figure 2.33). Most of the houses have a garage and all have front and back gardens. There are also industrial estates which provide work for the residents; in many towns these are situated along the main roads.

ACTIVITIES

Higher

1 Describe the site of Reading.
2 Suggest reasons for Reading's growth.
3 Why are buildings in Reading's CBD tall?
4 Four different housing areas are shown in Figure 2.33.
a For each housing area justify the date when the houses were built.
b Using only photographic evidence, compare the housing types in housing areas A and B.
c Study housing area C. Describe the characteristics of this type of housing estate.
d Study housing area D. Why was this type of housing provided in the 1950s?
5 Study the census data for Reading in Figure 2.30. Choose 5 wards in different areas of the town.
a Compare and contrast the residents of these areas.
b Is there any relationship between the characteristics of the population and distance from the CBD? Use Figure 2.31 to help you.
c Does Reading have rich and poor areas?

Foundation

1 Describe the site of Reading.
2 Describe three human factors which encouraged the growth of Reading.
3 Why are buildings in Reading's CBD tall?
4 Four different housing areas are shown in Figure 2.33.
a Complete Table 1 below using the information in Figure 2.33 to help you.
b Look at housing area C. Describe the characteristics of this type of housing estate.
c Look at all the evidence provided. Give reasons to justify the age of housing estate A.
5 Look at the census information given in Figure 2.30. Choose 5 of the areas listed.
a What is the ethnic origin of the residents?
b Describe the tenure and amenities of the housing in your chosen areas.
c Which area has the most professional households?
d Where is it located in the town?
e Which area has the most manual and non-manual workers?
f Where is it located in the town?
g Is there a relationship between the employment of the residents and the distance of the housing area from the CBD?

Table 1

Photograph	No. of bedrooms	Garage	Garden	Area of city
a				
b				
c				
d				

Other land uses in this area are open spaces for playing fields and parks, schools and hospitals.

Commuter area – This consists of the expensive housing estates which have sprung up on the edge of the suburbs. Most of the housing is detached with 3–4 bedrooms and at least one garage (see Figure 2.33). During the last decade out-of-town shopping centres and entertainment facilities (see Chapter 8) have been developed in this area. This is because of the low land prices on green field sites and the greater accessibility they offer because the shopping centres usually cluster around ring road junctions. Many people have moved out of the town completely and live in the small villages in the rural area surrounding the town. This has become possible as a result of the wider ownership of cars in the last 30 years.

a. Inner city area – Pre-1914 housing close to Oxford Road

b. Suburbs – 1960s housing development in Earley

c. Suburbs – 1980s housing at Emmer Green

d. Suburbs – 1950s housing at Whitley Wood

Figure 2.33 Housing areas in Reading

Case Study: LAND USE IN AN URBAN AREA IN AN LEDC: BANGALORE, INDIA

Where is Bangalore situated?

Bangalore is in central southern India. It is situated on a plateau at a height of 920 m. It is the capital of the Karnataka state. It was founded in 1537 by Kempe Gowda and remained a small village for many years. In 1949, when the Bangalore Municipal Corporation was formed, it was still a small town. Since then Bangalore has experienced rapid growth.

Why has Bangalore grown?

Bangalore is known as the Garden City because there are many gardens within the city and many of the old roads are tree lined. Bangalore's reputation for being a beautiful city with a pleasant climate is one of the reasons for its growth.

When India gained independence from the UK in 1947, the Indian government decided to concentrate certain industries, educational and research centres at Bangalore. This was another major impetus for the city's growth, but the real growth of the city started when it became the capital of Karnataka in 1956.

The many new industries that were established in Bangalore in the late 1950s and 1960s led to a rapid increase in the size of the city. Many people came to Bangalore in search of employment which put a great strain on the city's infrastructure. The government and non-governmental organisations continue still to try to sort out this problem.

In the 1980s Bangalore became the location for the first major foreign investment in high technology in India (Texas Instruments). The growing reputation of the city, the pleasant climate and the cheapness of the labour (a computer analyst earns four times less than in the USA) has meant that many TNCs have been drawn to the city. During the 1990s Bangalore became India's most important centre for a number of industries, including the biotechnology, aerospace and Information Technology industries. Its population is growing by about 150,000 a year.

Year	Population (000s)
c. 1991	2660
c. 1981	916
c. 1971	1042
c. 1961	905
c. 1951	779
c. 1941	248
c. 1931	307
c. 1921	238
c. 1911	190
c. 1901	159

Figure 2.34 Changes in the population of Bangalore

What are the land use patterns of Bangalore?

As it is so difficult to discuss the land use of cities in LEDCs in a logical way, we will refer to the map in Figure 2.35 throughout this section. This will make it possible to locate the areas being discussed on a map of the city. A number of Bangalore's zones are described below:

Indiranagar – Zone E – This area of the city is located on the map to the east of the CBD. As can be seen on the map, it is 4–5 km from the city centre and very close to the airport. It is seen as one of the best residential areas in Bangalore. The area was developed in the 1970s and, from the start, was laid out for large, individually designed houses. The roads are tree lined which fits in well with the image of the city. Unlike other areas, the open public spaces are not filled with slum accommodation. However, within this wealthy suburb there are areas where the servants live. In these areas, you will still find chickens in the road and young children collecting water from a local well. Indiranagar has one industrial development, the Singapore Technology Park which brings no environmental problems to the area. The area has its own schools (Indiranagar High School) and hospital (HAL), which is one of the best medical institutions in the city.

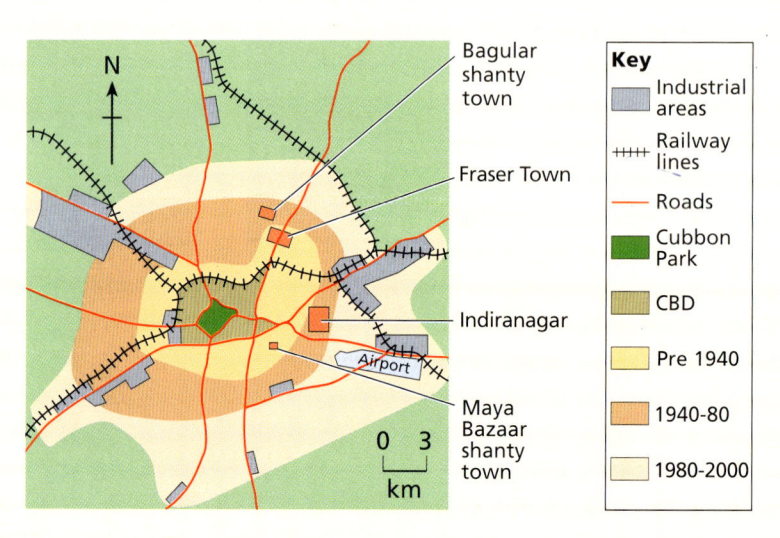

Figure 2.35 Map of Bangalore

Figure 2.36 Apartments in Indiranagar

Fraser town – Zone C – This is located approximately 3 km north-east of the city centre. It is one of the older parts of Bangalore, first settled during the British occupancy. At this time, the area comprised spacious bungalows with large gardens. The demand for land in Bangalore has led to the building of apartment blocks on the gardens of the bungalows. The apartments are expensive and are aimed at the middle to upper classes. However, the services in the area were built for lower density housing and the extra housing is putting a serious strain on the infrastructure.

Water in the area is rationed and there is a lot of pollution in local streams. Shanty towns have developed in the area to house the construction workers who are building the apartments. They need to be close to their work because of the lack of transportation and their inability to pay for it.

Maya Bazaar shanty town (Bustee) – Zone D – This is located approximately 3 km south east of the city centre on land that was originally owned by the army. It was first settled in the 1950s by migrant workers who built houses out of whatever they could find on vacant land. They had no basic facilities and a shanty town developed. Many of the buildings are now made from breeze blocks and therefore more substantial. The infrastructure in the area has improved as street taps and communal toilet blocks have been installed.

Figure 2.37 Houses in Bangalore

Bagular shanty town (Bustee) – Zone F – This is located approximately 5 km from the city centre and when it first grew up in the early 1960s it was on the outskirts of the city. The growth of the city means that it is now well within the city boundaries and other shanty towns have developed beyond it. It has a population of 6,000 living in approximately 900 houses on a piece of land that is bordered by a cemetery, two main roads and a railway line. The infrastructure is very poor, although it is better than it was. There is now a communal toilet block and washing facilities, some of the homes have electricity and water is provided by communal taps. However, there are still open sewers in the streets where children play.

Figure 2.38 Open sewer in Bangalore

Central Business District – Zone A – The centre of Bangalore is split into two parts by Cubbon Park. This came about because there was the original city with its fortifications to the west of the area and the British garrison to the east of it. When the British left, it was decided to keep the original trading area between the two parts of the city as a park. The large park still remains but it is surrounded by

ACTIVITIES

1 Draw a line graph to show Bangalore's population growth between 1901 and 2011.
2 Give two physical and two human reasons for the growth of Bangalore.
3 Describe the characteristic features of four of Bangalore's zones.
4 Explain the location of industry in Bangalore.

Extension

Compare the model of land use in LEDCs in Figure 2.28 with Bangalore's land use map in Figure 2.35.

The human world

LAND USE IN AN URBAN AREA IN AN LEDC: BANGALORE, INDIA – continued

high-rise buildings, commercial premises and busy roads characteristic of CBDs in MEDCs and LEDCs.

Industrial areas – Zone H – These are mainly found along the main roads leading out of the city and along the railway lines (as can be seen on the map in Figure 2.35). Much of the recent industrial growth in Bangalore has been in hi-tech industries that require fast transport links. For this reason the science parks have developed along the main roads on the edge of the city. There is also a large industrial area close to the airport.

Sample Examination Questions

Higher tier

1. Study the photograph of Warkworth (Figure 2.24) and the Ordnance Survey map extract. Find Warkworth on the OS map.
   a. What is the name of the farm marked A on the photograph? *(1 mark)*
   b. What land use is marked B on the photograph? *(1 mark)*
   c. What is the name of the river shown on the photograph? *(1 mark)*
   d. What is the number of the A road shown on the photograph? *(1 mark)*
   e. Which way was the camera pointing when the photograph was taken? *(1 mark)*

2. State the ways in which the houses in area C are different to the houses in area D. *(4 marks)*

3. There are some areas of Warkworth where houses have not been built. Where are these areas? give reasons why they are undeveloped. *(3 marks)*

4. Suggest why Warkworth grew up where it did. *(5 marks)*

5. What evidence is there that the land around Warkworth is good for farming? Use map and photograph evidence in your answer. *(3 marks)*

Total 20 marks

Foundation tier

1. Look at the photograph of Warkworth (Figure 2.24) and the Ordnance Survey map extract. Find Warkworth on the OS map.
   a. What is the name of the farm marked A on the photograph? *(1 mark)*
   b. What land use is marked B on the photograph? *(1 mark)*
   c. What is the name of the river shown on the photograph? *(1 mark)*
   d. What is the number of the A road shown on the photograph? *(1 mark)*
   e. Which way was the camera pointing when the photograph was taken? *(1 mark)*

2. Look again at the photograph. The houses at C are different to the houses at D. Describe their differences using these headings: size, gardens, location, one other difference. *(4 marks)*

3. Why have houses not been built on:
   a. area E,
   b. area F. *(2 marks)*

4. a. Describe the site of Warkworth. *(2 marks)*
   b. Give two reasons why Warkworth was built here. *(4 marks)*

5. What evidence is there on the photograph that the land is good for farming? *(3 marks)*

Total 20 marks

The human world 47

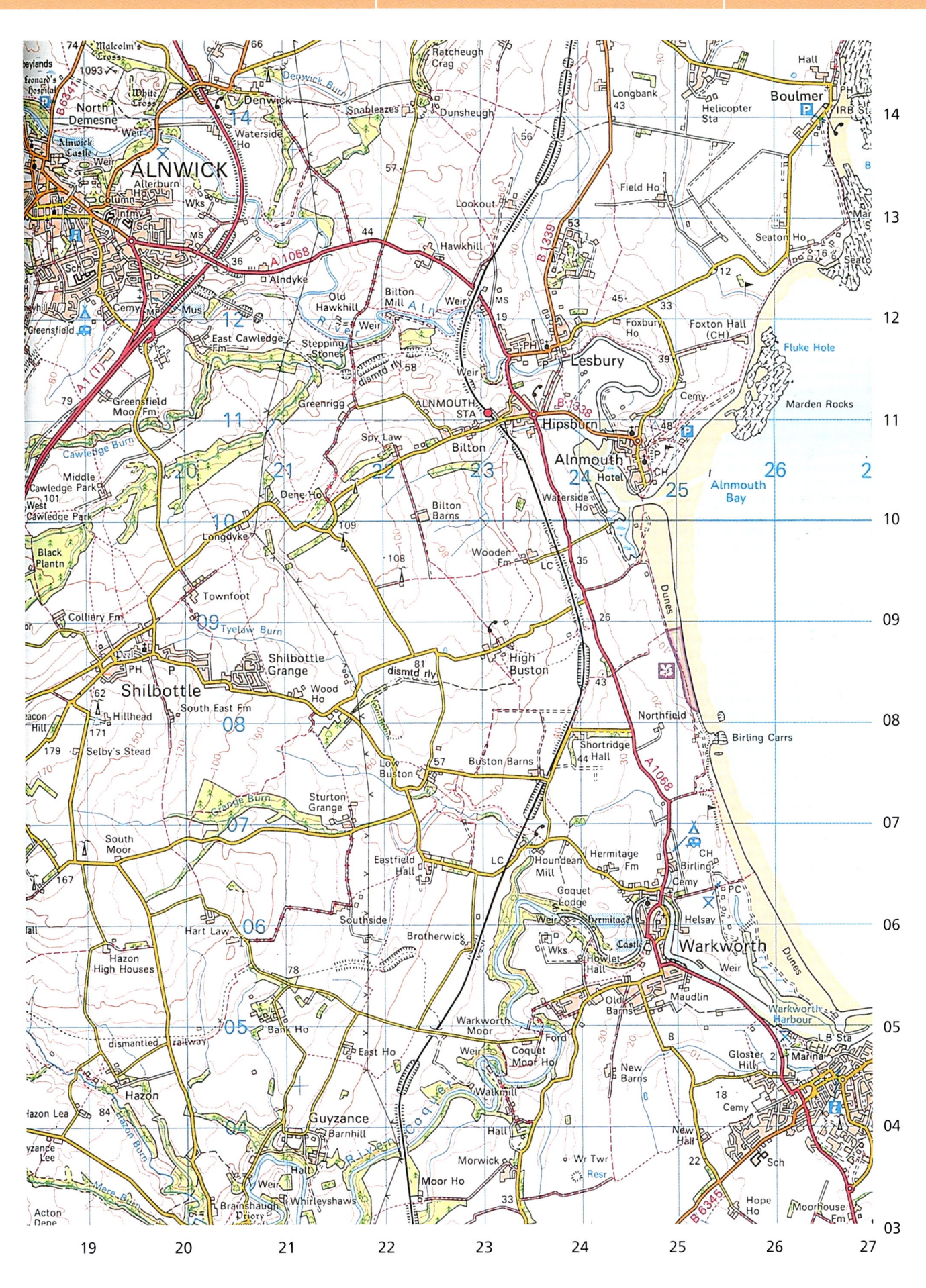

3 The economic world

People work in different economic systems

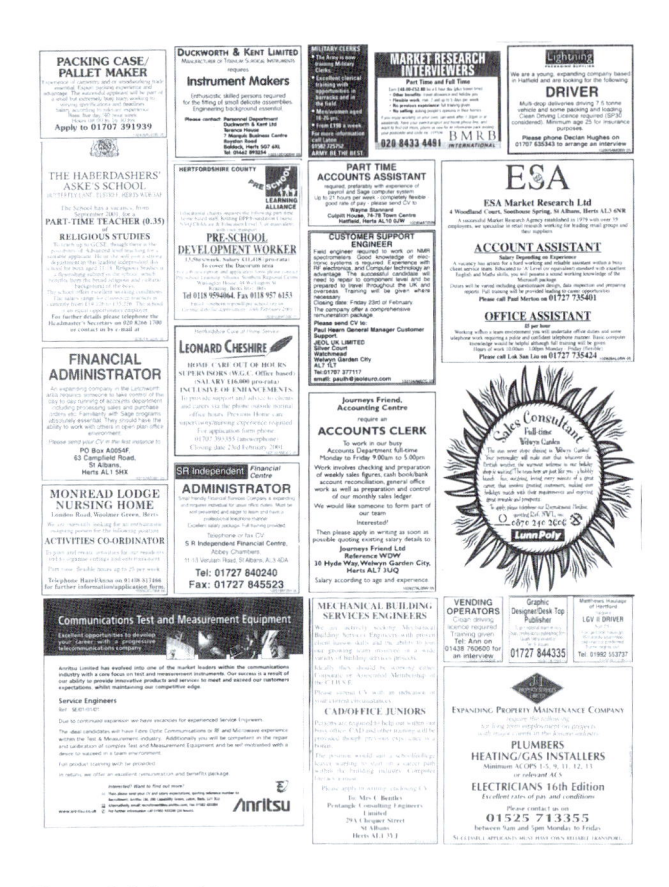

Figure 3.1 Local newspaper jobs

Figure 3.2 Different jobs

What are the sectors of industry?

Look at Figure 3.1 which shows advertisements for jobs offered in a local newspaper.

If you looked in your local newspaper, many of the jobs shown would be similar. In another country, the jobs on offer might be very different. Although there are hundreds of different jobs or occupations, they can all be classified into three categories.

- Primary industry is the extraction of raw materials from the ground or the sea. It includes farming, fishing, forestry and mining.
- Secondary industry is the manufacturing of goods using the raw materials from primary industry.
- Tertiary industry does not produce anything, but often involves the provision of different services. Teachers, solicitors, sales assistants and cleaners are all tertiary occupations.

It is usual to divide industry into these three sectors, but they are often linked together as one job relies on another. Figure 3.3 shows the stages in the production of a book. The raw material for the book comes from coniferous forests. The growing and cutting down of the trees is a primary industry. The wood is formed into pulp and turned into paper in a paper mill, which is a secondary industry. The paper is then used by an author to write the book, a tertiary industry. The book is then printed, another secondary industry. Finally the book will be transported to shops where it will be sold, both processes being tertiary industries.

The economic world   49

Felling trees

Paper mill

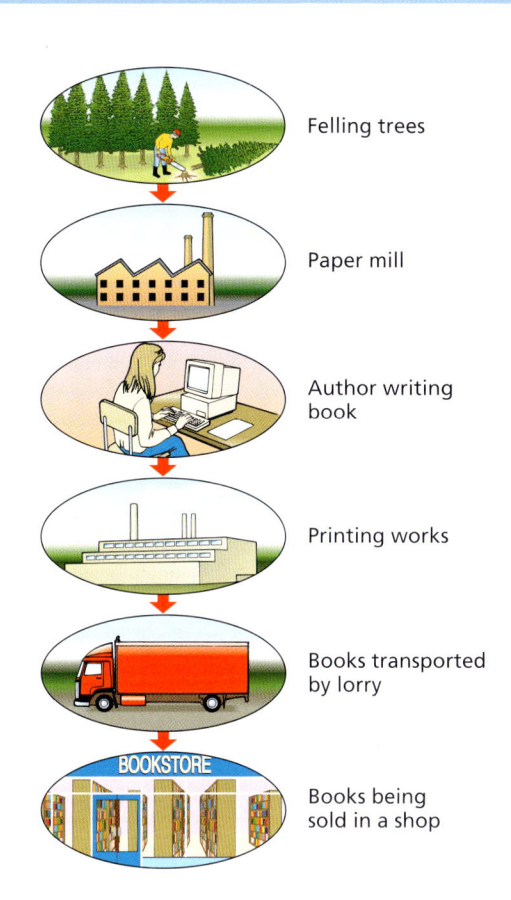

Author writing book

Printing works

Books transported by lorry

Books being sold in a shop

Figure 3.3 Stages in the production of a book

How do employment patterns differ between countries?

The relative importance of primary, secondary and tertiary industries can be used to compare the levels of development between countries.

Figure 3.4 shows divided bar charts for Mali, Taiwan and Germany. The bar chart for Mali shows that a high proportion of the population works in primary industries. This is a very common situation in an LEDC. The poorest LEDCs are in a similar position to that of the UK 150 years ago. They are in the early stages of economic development with most of their population still working on the land as farmers. In contrast, a high proportion of the workforce of an MEDC like Germany is involved in the tertiary sector. Up to 70 per cent of the workforce in some MEDCs with mature economies are in tertiary occupations.

Taiwan is a newly industrialised country (NIC) and has a strong manufacturing sector. Many transnational companies have factories in countries like Taiwan so that they can take advantage of cheaper labour and land. Up to 40 per cent of the workforce in NICs are involved in manufacturing.

Figure 3.5 shows the employment patterns for selected countries. This information has been plotted onto a triangular graph in Figure 3.6. You will see that LEDCs and MEDCs form separate clusters. Construction lines have been drawn on Figure 3.6 to show how Mali and Germany have been plotted.

Key
- Primary industry
- Secondary industry
- Tertiary industry

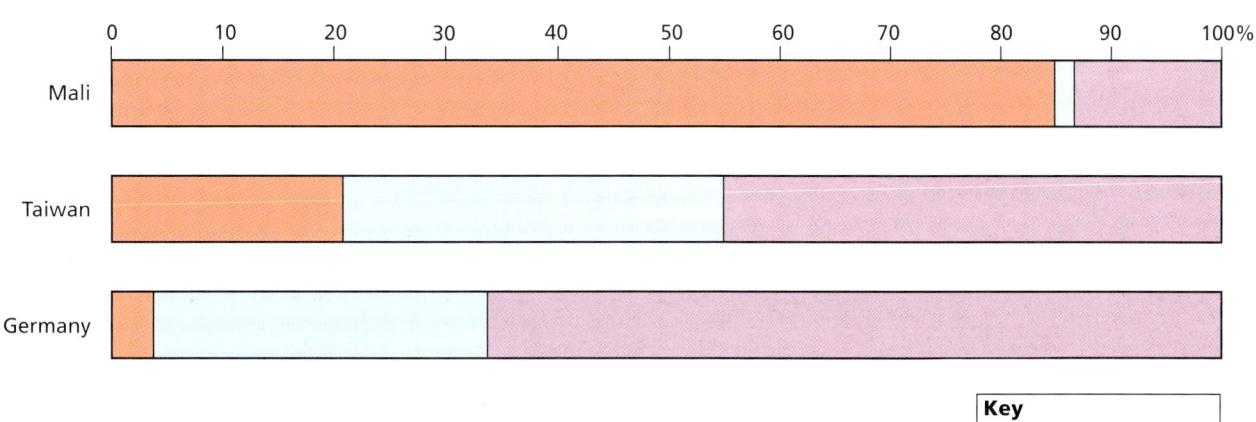

Figure 3.4 Divided bar charts for Mali, Taiwan and Germany

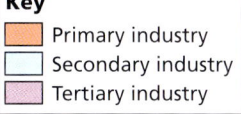

The economic world

Country	Number on graph	Primary	Secondary	Tertiary
Brazil	1	25	35	40
Bangladesh	2	57	10	33
Germany	3	4	30	66
Mali	4	85	2	13
Nepal	5	93	1	7
North Korea	6	18	32	50
Romania	7	31	44	25
Taiwan	8	21	34	45
UK	9	3	24	73
USA	10	3	21	76
India	11	62	11	27
Mexico	12	23	29	48
China	13	73	14	13

Figure 3.5 Table of employment patterns for selected countries

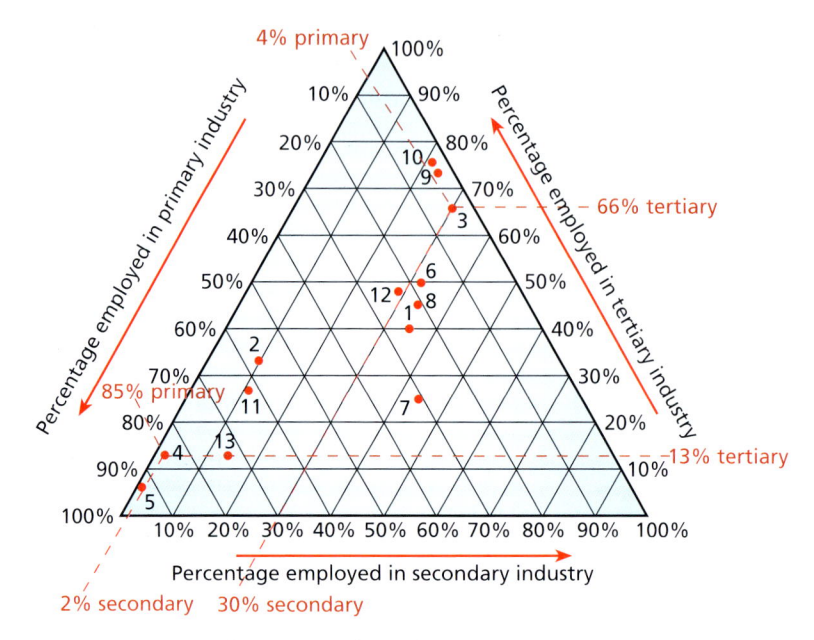

Figure 3.6 Triangular graph of employment patterns

How do employment patterns change over time?

All countries undergo changes in their economic systems. The graph in Figure 3.7a shows how the relative importance of the different economic activities in the UK has changed over the last 150 years. Three trends are apparent:

1 A steady decrease in the primary sector has been caused by:

a Improvements in technology led to increased mechanisation which has reduced the need for agricultural workers in particular.
b Many raw materials, for example iron ore and coal, have been used up or are cheaper to import from abroad.
c Jobs in primary industries are often seen to be 'dirty' and to have few career prospects. Workers prefer the better paid and less physically demanding jobs in the tertiary sector.

2 An increase in tertiary employment. This was gradual but steady until the Second World War, then this was slightly reversed due to increased manufacturing as part of the war effort. The growth in the tertiary sector increased rapidly in the last decades of the twentieth century. Most of this was in the new hi-tech industries such as micro electronics and in associated fields like research and development.

3 The manufacturing industries were steady until a decline in 1990s which mirrored the growth of the tertiary sector. The decline was due to the cheaper labour in LEDCs which encouraged manufacturing industries to locate there.

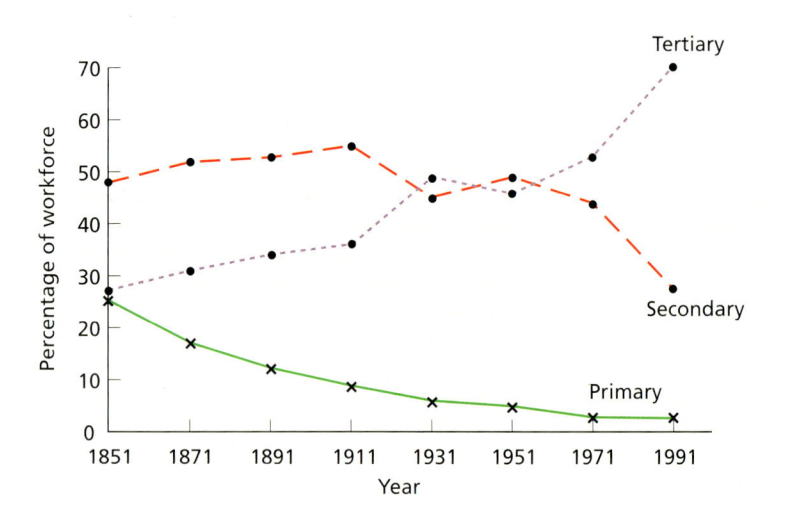

Figure 3.7a Graph showing changes in UK employment sectors

Employment patterns have also changed in LEDCs. The pie graphs in Figure 3.7b show how the three sectors of industry have changed in China between 1960 and 2000. The changes that can be seen on the graphs are typical of an LEDC:

- Primary industry decreases as the country becomes increasingly urban. The number of farmers decrease as rural workers migrate to the urban areas.
- Secondary industry increases as the country gradually becomes more industrialised.
- Tertiary industries increase to service the needs of the growing cities.

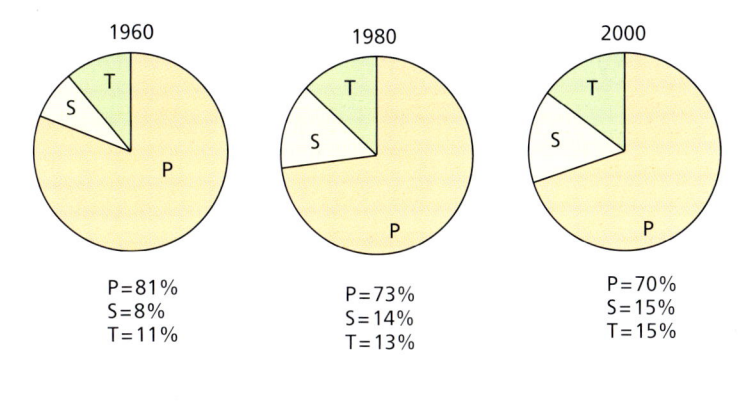

1960
P=81%
S=8%
T=11%

1980
P=73%
S=14%
T=13%

2000
P=70%
S=15%
T=15%

Key
P=primary S=secondary T=tertiary

Figure 3.7b Graph showing changes in China's employment structure

ACTIVITIES

Higher

1. Study Figure 3.1. Decide which sector of industry is represented by each advertisement. Tabulate your results and say why Figure 3.1 comes from a newspaper in an MEDC.

2. Use the figures in the Table 1 to construct divided bar graphs for the three countries. Describe and explain the differences between the graphs.

   Table 1

Country	Primary	Secondary	Tertiary
UK	3	24	73
Nepal	92	1	7
Mexico	23	29	48

3. Look at Figure 3.7a.
   a. When did the percentage of people working in secondary industries become greater than those in tertiary industries?
   b. For how many years did the percentage of people employed in secondary industry remain higher than the percentage employed in tertiary industries?
   c. Why was the percentage employed in secondary industries high during this period?
   d. Draw pie graphs for 1851, 1931 and 1991.
   e. Briefly describe what your graphs show.

Foundation

1. Look at the photographs in Figure 3.2 Decide whether each of them is a primary, secondary or tertiary job.

2a. Look at Figure 3.1. Decide whether each job is primary, secondary or tertiary. Add up how many are in each sector. Construct a table of your results and draw a bar graph to show your results.

b. Explain what your graph shows.

3. The following is a list of jobs involved in the manufacture of a motor car:
   - mining iron-ore,
   - turning iron-ore into steel at an integrated steel works,
   - transporting the steel sheets to a car assembly plant,
   - manufacturing a car at the factory,
   - selling the car.

   Draw a series of diagrams to illustrate these jobs and say which sector of industry each diagram represents.

Farming systems show different characteristics. All farming systems have been experiencing change

The characteristics of farming systems

There are many different types of farms around the world. The different farming systems can be split into distinct categories. Farming systems can be: intensive or extensive, commercial or subsistence, and arable or pastoral. There has also been a move in MEDCs towards organic farming.

- An intensive farm is one that has high levels of labour and/or capital input for a relatively small area of land. The output per hectare is high.
- An extensive farm is one that has low levels of labour and/or capital input for a relatively large area of land. The output per hectare is low.
- Commercial farming is when farmers grow crops or rear animals to sell at market to make a profit.
- Subsistence farming is when farmers grow enough food to feed themselves and their families. There may be a little left over for sale at market.
- Arable farms only grow crops.
- Pastoral farms rear animals. The only crops grown are fodder crops.
- Organic farming is farming that is environmentally friendly. Farmers do not use any chemicals and don't feed their animals with anything that has been grown using chemicals.

Figure 3.8 Different farming types

Extensive pastoral farming in Cape McClear, Lake Malawi

Intensive arable farming in Turkey

Markets: Lowestoft Birdseye peas, British Sugar Corp. Ipswich, Hovis flour mill, Norwich

Machinery: 7 tractors, 2 combines 2 seed drills, 3 ploughs

Flat land: 270 hectares

Soil: Fertile, deep boulder clay

Place: Farm in Suffolk

Climate: Rainfall 505mm Temps: Jan 3°C, July 17°C

Labour: 2 workers and Farmer

Figure 3.9 An East Anglian farmer's dilemma

The economic world

Physical factors

Soils
Fertility will effect the type of farming fertiliser loams: any type of farming usually arable.

Relief
Flat land is ideal for arable farming because large machinery can be used. Once the slope is more than 20° it is difficult to use machinery.

Aspect
This is the direction a slope is facing. South facing slopes are warmer in the northern hemisphere.

Climate
Temperature is very important for arable crops. Wheat needs over 15°C for 3 months during ripening and harvesting. Oats can grow at temps below 15°C. Rainfall is very important, not enough and crops will die, too much and they will be flooded. Wheat requires less than 750mm, whereas oats require over 1,000mm. Dairy cattle need over 800mm.

Human factors

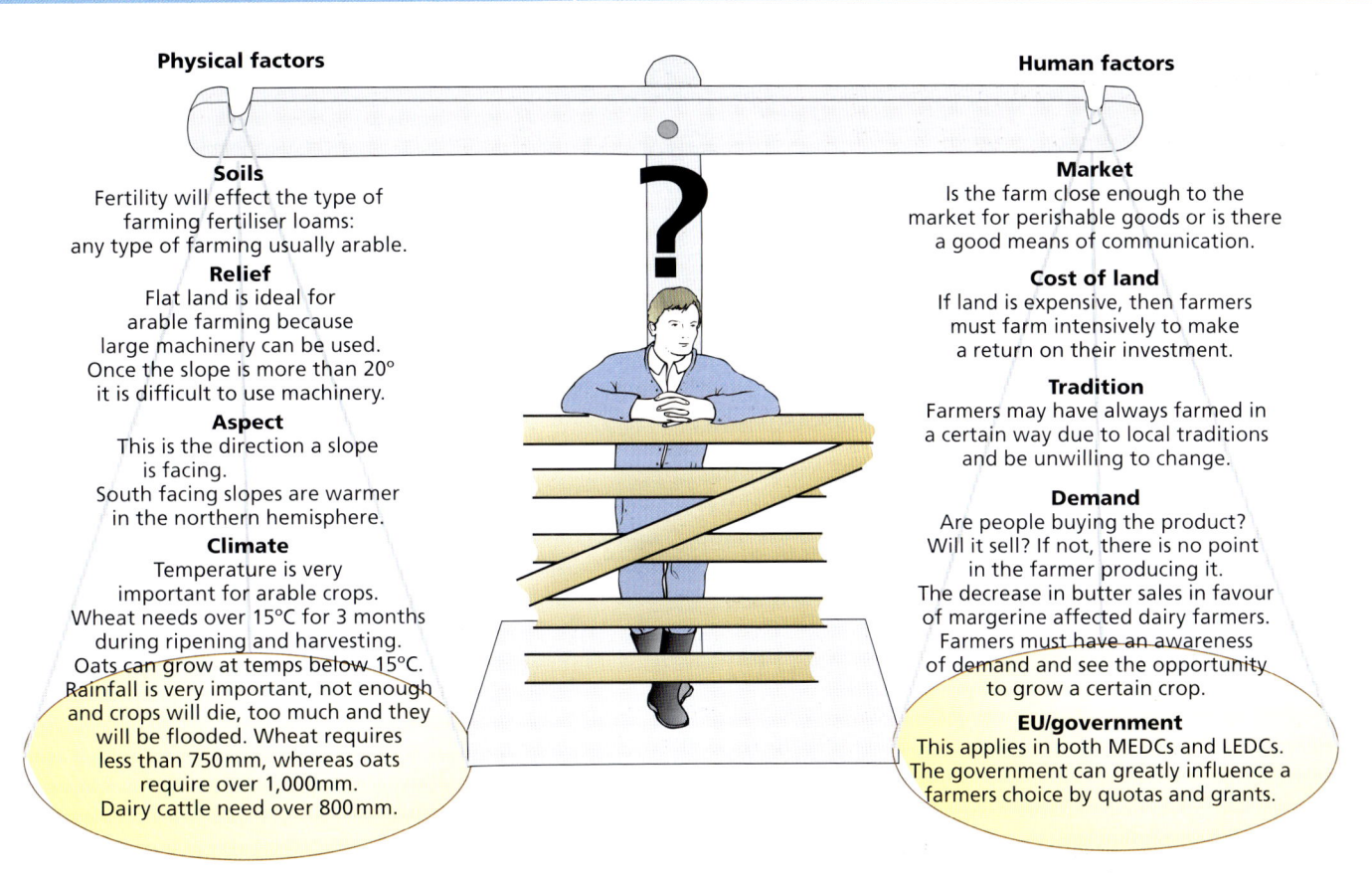

Market
Is the farm close enough to the market for perishable goods or is there a good means of communication.

Cost of land
If land is expensive, then farmers must farm intensively to make a return on their investment.

Tradition
Farmers may have always farmed in a certain way due to local traditions and be unwilling to change.

Demand
Are people buying the product? Will it sell? If not, there is no point in the farmer producing it. The decrease in butter sales in favour of margerine affected dairy farmers. Farmers must have an awareness of demand and see the opportunity to grow a certain crop.

EU/government
This applies in both MEDCs and LEDCs. The government can greatly influence a farmers choice by quotas and grants.

Figure 3.10 A farmer's decision

The factors that affect farming systems

There are many factors that affect the decisions that a farmer has to make. These factors can be classified into the following categories: physical, economic, political and human.

A farmer in the Lake District will be faced with many decisions about what to grow on his land. His first constraints will be the physical factors that he cannot change without great expense. He must then take account of the human factors, which can be just as important. Figure 3.11 shows a plan of a farm in the Lake District and the farmer's options. What would you do? Give reasons why?

Farmers in other parts of the country do not face the same physical restrictions. Their decisions are more affected by human factors. Read what the farmer has to say in Figure 3.9. What would you do? Give reasons why.

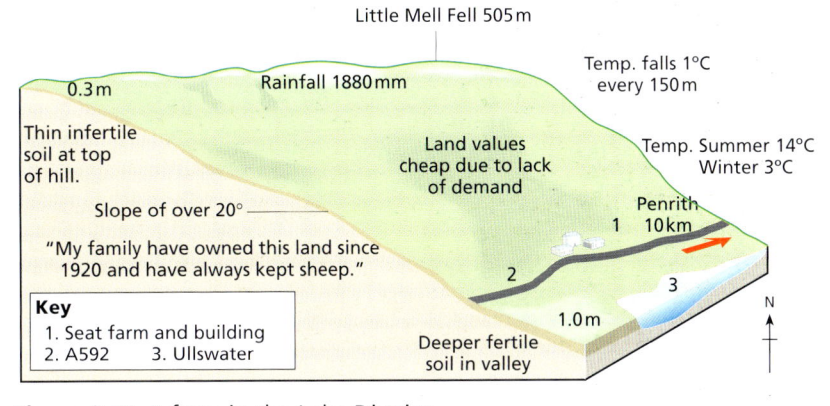

Little Mell Fell 505m
Rainfall 1880mm
0.3m
Thin infertile soil at top of hill.
Slope of over 20°
Land values cheap due to lack of demand
Temp. falls 1°C every 150m
Temp. Summer 14°C Winter 3°C
Penrith 10km
"My family have owned this land since 1920 and have always kept sheep."
Deeper fertile soil in valley
1.0m

Key
1. Seat farm and building
2. A592
3. Ullswater

Figure 3.11 A farm in the Lake District

ACTIVITIES

1. Choose one from each pair of characteristics to describe the farming system shown in the photographs.
   - arable / pastoral,
   - commercial / subsistence,
   - extensive / intensive.
2. Imagine that you are a farmer in the west of England. Research the physical and human characteristics of this area.
   a. Are human or physical factors more important?
   b. What type of farming would you choose?

Case Study: INTENSIVE WET RICE FARMING IN AN LEDC

The Philippines is a group of over 7,000 islands located north of Indonesia and south east of China. They have a population of 70 million, 70 per cent of which are farmers or farm labourers. The average farm size is between 1.5 and 2 hectares. Many farmers do not own the land they farm but rent it. They pay for their rent by giving a proportion of their crop to the landowner. Most of them are subsistence farmers producing just enough to feed themselves and their families. The ever-increasing urban population has to be fed with imported rice. The introduction of the Land Reform Act has attempted to redistribute the land to peasant farmers, but progress has been slow.

Since the 1970s the Filipino government has been trying to persuade farmers to grow more high yielding varieties of rice in a strategy known as the 'Green Revolution'. These varieties require fertilisers and pesticides which many of the poor farmers cannot afford and, as a result, raised yields were generally those of the richer farmers not the peasants. More recent research has focused on crossing traditional varieties, which have been grown successfully in the Philippines for years, with newer varieties.

Negros Occidental, Philippines

The case study concentrates on two different types of farms which have developed since land reform split up some of the large haciendas (plantations) that used to dominate farming on Negros, an island south east of Manila.

Maximo Casiendo's farm at Barangay Busay

This used to be part of a sugar plantation. In 1996 ownership was transferred to Maximo Casiendo under the Land Reform Act. The farm is in a flat fertile area about 70 m above sea level with rich clay/loam soils. The climate has an average temperature of 25 °C and 1,800 mm of rainfall, of which 80 per cent falls between June and December often during tropical storms (or typhoons – see Chapter 6). The farm is 2.6 hectares, which is fairly large for the Philippines. Most of the land is used to grow rice as well as maize with some vegetables and cassava. There are usually 2 crops a year and sometimes 3. The labour on the farm consists of Mr Casiendo and his 7 children; the two eldest (at 23 and 24 years of age) work full time on the farm and the others help out when needed. The farm owns a rice thresher which cost 22,000 pesos (£350). The rest of the village pay him 1 *cavan* of rice (50 kg) for every 10 *cavans* that they thresh using his thresher. Mr Casiendo does not own his own *carabao* (water buffalo) which are used to plough the land but hires one for 1,800 pesos (£28) per hectare when it is needed. All other jobs are done by hand.

Figure 3.13 A typical farm on the Philippines

Other inputs of the farm are:
- Fertilisers: 7–8 bags of nitrogen per year, 3 bags of complete NPK (nitrogen, phosphorus, potassium) and 2 bags of PK (phosphorus, potassium) per hectare.
- Pesticides: 2 litres per hectare of insecticide is put on the land to control leaf hopper insects and a herbicide is used to control weeds 3 days after the broadcasting (sowing) of the rice.
- Diesel: 30 litres per hectare is used for the rice thresher.

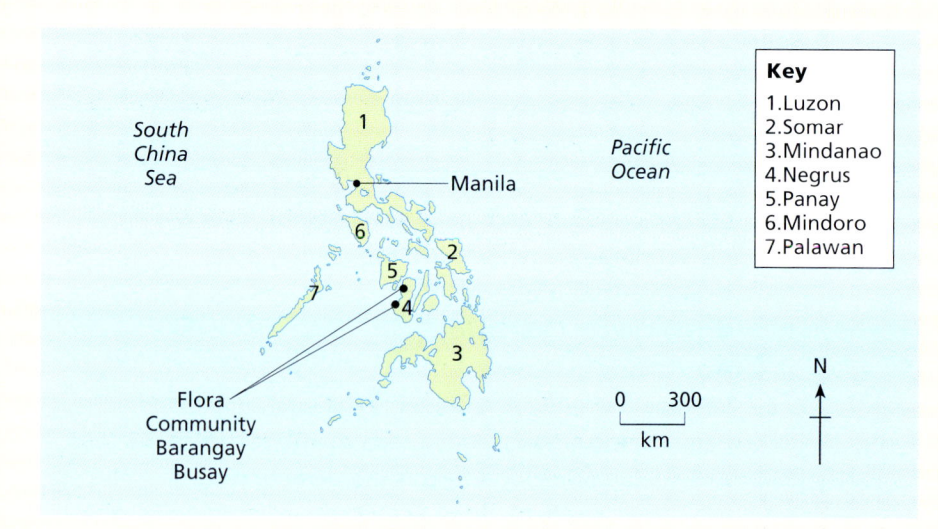

Key
1. Luzon
2. Somar
3. Mindanao
4. Negrus
5. Panay
6. Mindoro
7. Palawan

Figure 3.12 Map of the Philippines

The outputs of the farm are: 520 *cavans* of rice over two crops (100 *cavans* per hectare) and some maize. Most of the crop is for the family's consumption, although in a good year some can be sold.

The Flora community

In 1995 the Philippine government gave 76 hacienda workers an 86 hectare estate through the Comprehensive Agrarian Reform Programme. The estate is approximately 3 km south east of Kabankalan. It is in a lowland area with rich sandy loam soils laid down by the Hilabangan river. The Flora community received support through loans and technical help. The farm is worked on organic farming practices. Sugar cane and high value vegetables are grown for sale but rice is the main crop as it is the community's staple food. It is grown according to the MASIPAG rice farming system which uses no chemical fertilisers. Nitrogen is supplied from straw decomposition and the use of azolla, a nitrogen-fixing aquatic plant. The residue from sugar cane processing, known as 'mudpress', and rice hull ash are also used as nutrient sources. The community only uses its own seeds thus ensuring that they are organic. Weeds are controlled by crop rotation, good soil fertility and mulching. Insects are controlled by biological strategies such as the introduction of a predator. If it is needed, the crops are dried by solar or biomass energy.

The Hilabangan river provides a constant supply of water which is used to irrigate the crop in the drier season. They average 2.5 crops a year and their yield is 100 *cavans* per hectare.

The farmers are achieving the same yields per hectare as other farmers in the area who have to spend money on expensive fertilisers and other chemicals.

Figure 3.14 Organic rice farming

ACTIVITIES

Higher

1. Classify Mr Casiendo's farm. Use one of each pair of the following terms:
   - intensive / extensive,
   - subsistence / commercial,
   - pastoral / arable.
2. The floral community farms organically. Quote evidence to support this.
3. Describe the physical geography of the area in which the Flora community is located.
4. Two case studies are given on wet rice farming in the Philippines. Compare the two farms. Use the following headings: chemicals, intensity, farm organisation, outputs.

   Table 1

Mr Casiendo's farm	Flora community

Foundation

1. Classify Mr Casiendo's farm. Use one of each pair of the following terms:
   - intensive / extensive,
   - subsistence / commercial,
   - pastoral / arable.
2. Mr Casiendo's farm is not an organic farm. Use evidence to support this.
3. Describe the location of the Flora community.
4. Copy Table 1. Put the descriptions below into the correct column:
   - organic farming is practised,
   - 7–8 bags of nitrogen fertiliser is used,
   - owns a rice thresher,
   - 100 *cavans* of rice,
   - clay loam soils,
   - sandy loam soils,
   - farmer and his 7 children,
   - nitrogen from azolla, a nitrogen-fixing aquatic plant,
   - the farm is run as a community.

Case Study: CHANGES AFFECTING FARMING SYSTEMS IN THE EU

British farming seems to be continually in the news, generally with bad news. Why is this and what is happening to British farmers? For many years British farmers have had their incomes subsidised, first by the British government and then by the EU, in order to keep the price of food down. This support has recently started to be withdrawn, causing much heartache and protest. There seems to be no answer to the question as to why British farmers are being asked to farm less intensively and even to set aside land while thousands of people in the world are starving. British farmers are having to turn to other ways of making money due to the poor prices they are getting for their crops and animals (see Figure 3.15).

A study of Home Farm in the West Midlands

One farmer who has been faced with these problems is Nigel Redfern of Home Farm in Hampton in Arden close to the Birmingham conurbation. Mr Redfern farms approximately 200 hectares. The land is gently undulating, with fertile sandy soils and a climate which has summer temperatures of 16 °C and winter temperatures of 3 °C. The total annual rainfall is 700 mm. Due to the favourable climate, relief and soils, Mr Redfern is not restricted by physical factors as to what he can grow. He is far more influenced by human factors. His farm is a mixed farm on which livestock are reared and a variety of crops are grown. Markets for his livestock are close by: Banbury is 60 km and Uttoxeter 50 km away. He sells most of his arable crops to merchants who come to the farm.

How 183 ewes earned 18p

Income		Expenditure	
3 sheep @ £8.50	£25.50	Auction house commission at	£210.45
3 @ £4.00	£12.00		
38 @ £3.60	£136.80	VAT at	£36.83
9 @ £2.80	£25.50	Market insurance at	£5.49
28 @ £0.90	£25.20	CAP levy at	£0.50
43 @ £0.60	£25.80		
59 @ £0.05	£2.95		
Total	£253.45	Total	£253.27

Sheep worth less than crisps!

Sheep are being sold for less than the cost of a single crisp as livestock prices continue to fall. Calum Sinclair, a Scottish hill farmer, received a cheque for 18p yesterday after selling 183 ewes at market (see breakdown below). His profits are thought to be the lowest return ever on sheep that have been reared for five years. Last year it was headline news that unwanted ewes were selling at 25p, the price of a packet of crisps, but Mr Sinclair calculated that his profit on each sheep failed to reach a tenth of a penny, less than the cost of a single crisp. Mr Sinclair, who has farmed in the Scottish uplands for 49 years, said that he has never known prospects so bleak. Last year his sheep fetched £6 each while in 1996 they had received £26. He added that life was difficult but he kept hoping for better times.

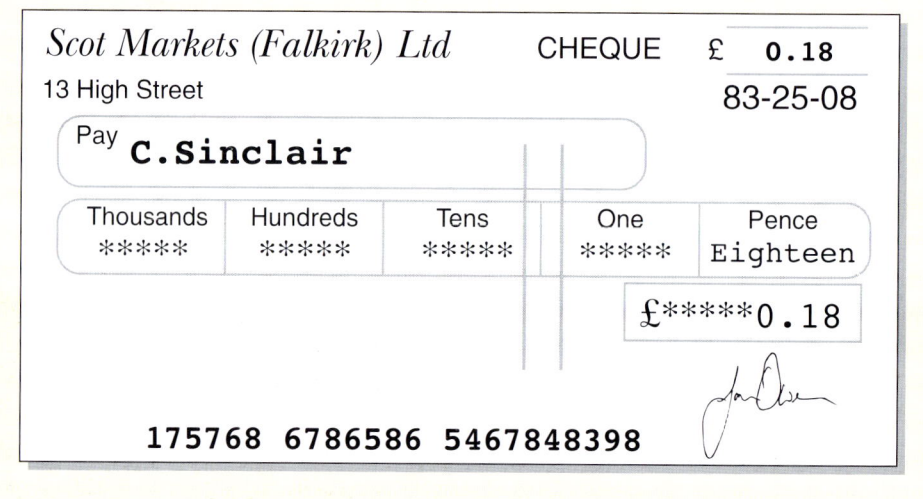

Figure 3.15 Newspaper report about Scottish farmer

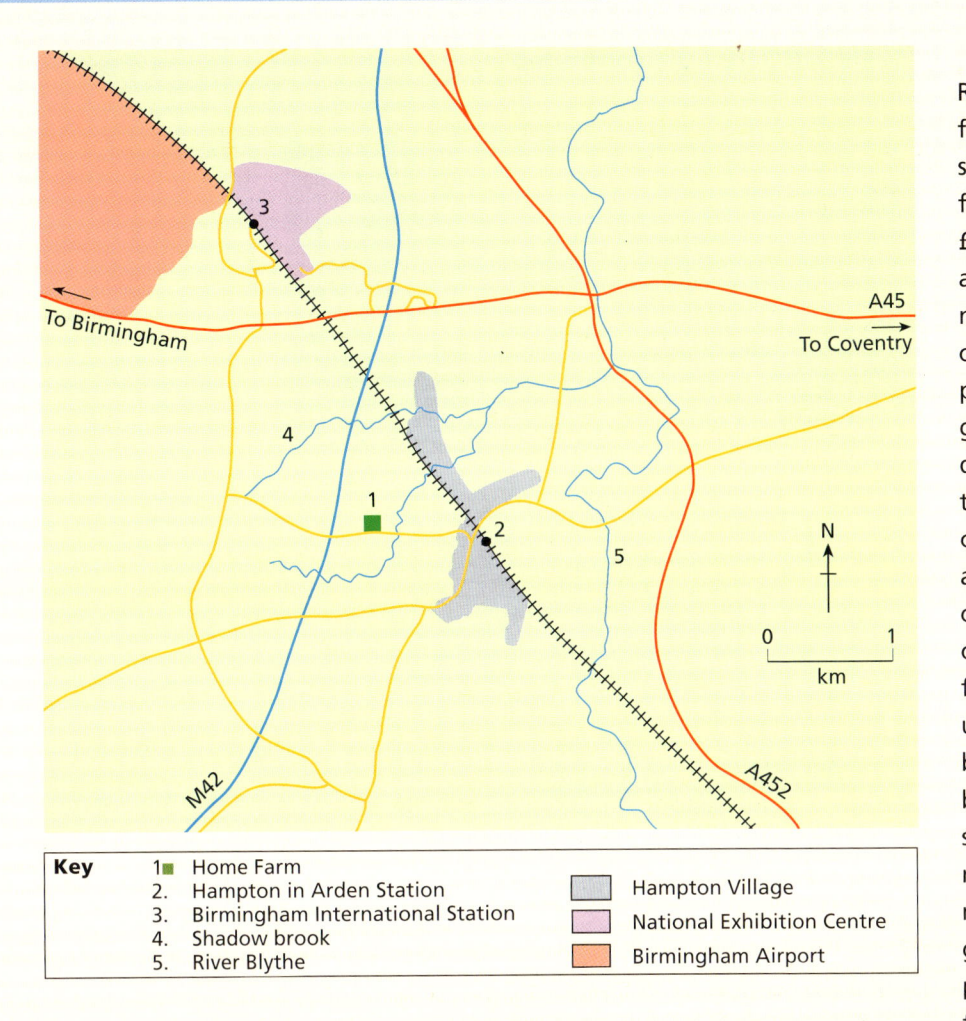

The economic world

57

Key
1. ■ Home Farm
2. Hampton in Arden Station
3. Birmingham International Station
4. Shadow brook
5. River Blythe
- Hampton Village
- National Exhibition Centre
- Birmingham Airport

Figure 3.16 Map showing location of Home Farm

During the last five years, Mr Redfern has begun to diversify his farm. This is due to the decrease in subsidies which meant that his income from the cereal crops decreased by £40,000 between 1998 and 1999, with a further decrease in 2000. There is now an area on the farm on which caravans are stored. For this to occur, planning permission had to be granted by the local council. It was delayed because of opposition from the Hampton Society, a local voluntary organisation which tries to oppose any changes to the area. Up to 20 caravans can be stored at an income of £250 per caravan per year (other farmers charge up to £500 depending upon the facilities offered). This has brought its own problems, however, because even though the caravans are screened, they can be seen from the road and two attempts have been made to steal them. Most of the gateways on the farm are now padlocked and are blocked by large farm machinery.

The farm has seen many changes over the years, with the building of new sheds for machinery and corn storage, and a dairy. The old cow sheds are not being used because of their restricted space and poor condition. However, the dairy also stands disused as Mr Redfern has decided that there is no point in putting in the hours looking after cows for the very poor return that he gets for their milk (milk costs approximately 45p a litre in shops of which farmers receive approximately 8p a litre). The farm's milk quota has been sold as has the herd of cows. The only animals left on the farm are the young bulls, which are being raised for meat, and a flock of 300 sheep.

Figure 3.17 Farming practices on Home Farm

Figure 3.18 Stored caravans at Home Farm

CHANGES AFFECTING FARMING SYSTEMS IN THE EU – continued

The latest diversification scheme is to convert the old cow sheds and outbuildings into accommodation for bed-and-breakfast visitors. These are either people who wish to holiday on a farm or are businessmen who are attending conferences at the NEC (National Exhibition Centre) which is only 2 miles away (see Figure 3.16). There is also the possibility of making the most of the fact that Birmingham airport is close by. This would involve people leaving their cars at the farm and, after an overnight stay, being taken to the airport for their flight. Mr Redfern would store the cars for £3 a day until their return. The cost of overnight accommodation is £30 for a single and £45 for a double room.

Another way in which Mr Redfern has diversified is to rent out certain fields for pony grazing; if a shed is also rented, this increases the price. Rent for part of a field is £30, but for use of a shed as well the price goes up to £100 a month.

In these ways Mr Redfern has tried to adapt to the changing circumstances of British farming and he hopes to be able to continue without getting into debt. One of his main problems at the moment is obtaining labour. Due to the poor pay and lack of promotion opportunities, very few people want to work on the land. This has caused a great shortage of labour. At present Mr Redfern runs the farm on his own, with the help of casual labourers and other farmers who are more fortunate with labour as they have older sons who want to work on the land. However, it is often his wife and four children (ranging in age from 7 to 14) who help out.

Figure 3.19 Farm buildings being renovated

Figure 3.20 Diversification

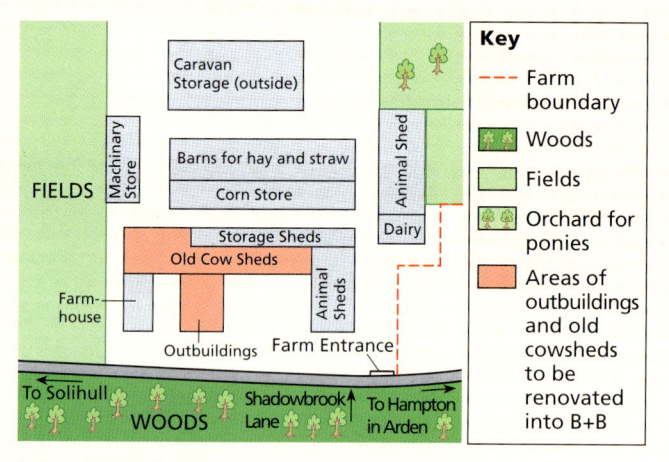

"Alf says he's had to diversify too – and selling beer's no longer on the management plan."

Figure 3.21 Plan of Home Farm

ACTIVITIES

1. Name the ways in which Mr Redfern has diversified his farm.

2. Home Farm is on the edge of the Birmingham conurbation. Draw up a list of the advantages and disadvantages of this position. Clues: communication links, urban fringe problems including crime.

3. What other diversification schemes might Mr Redfern introduce? The following websites may help you in your answer: http://www.nfu.org.uk or http://www.maff.gov.uk

The Common Agricultural Policy (CAP)

The way ahead – In the past, CAP used approximately 70 per cent of the EU's total budget but provided only 5 per cent of its income. There were many problems with this system (see Figure 3.22). This could not be allowed to continue as the EU needed to help other sectors of industry. New policies had to be developed which still support farmers but are less costly to the EU's budget.

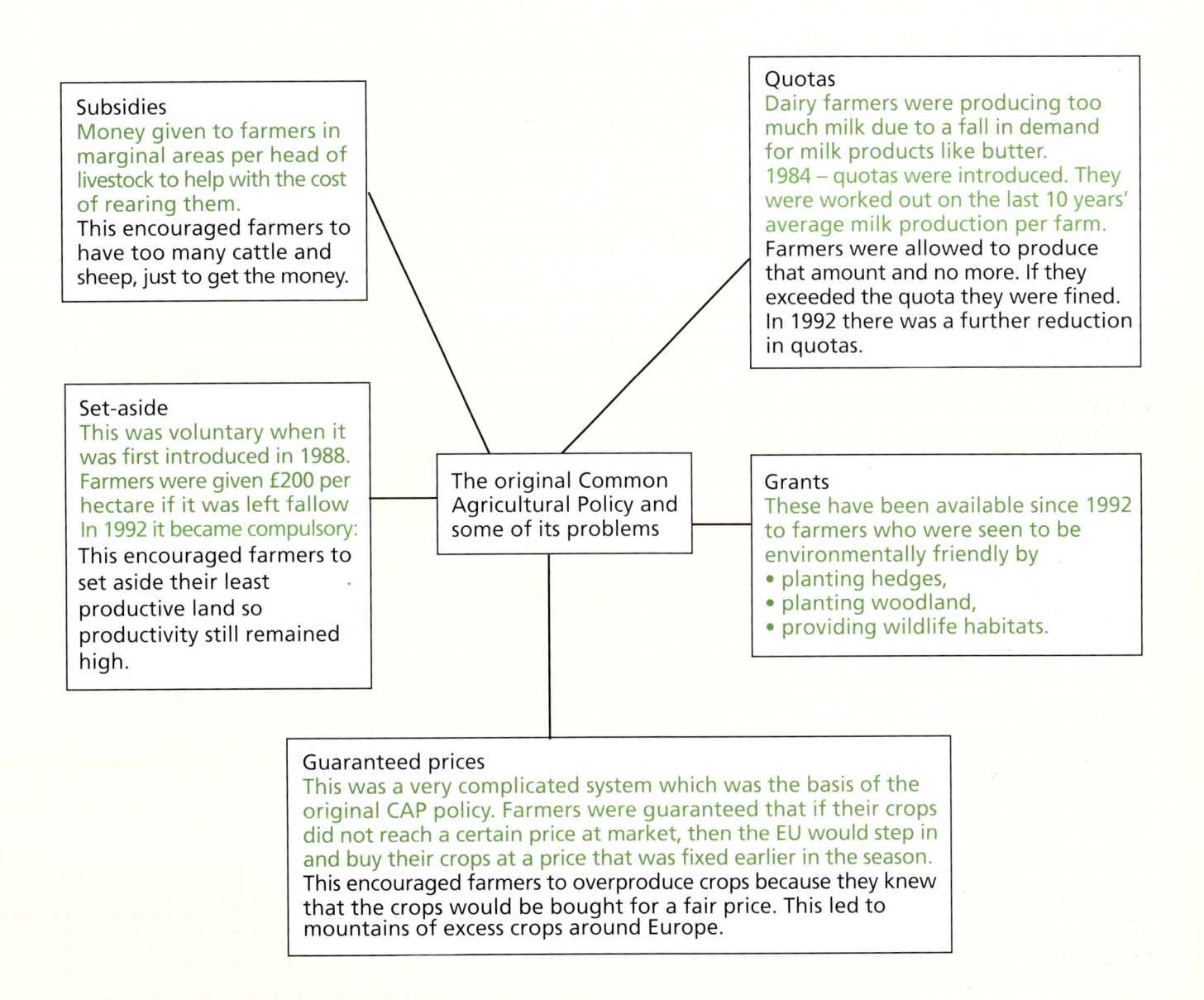

Subsidies
Money given to farmers in marginal areas per head of livestock to help with the cost of rearing them.
This encouraged farmers to have too many cattle and sheep, just to get the money.

Set-aside
This was voluntary when it was first introduced in 1988. Farmers were given £200 per hectare if it was left fallow In 1992 it became compulsory:
This encouraged farmers to set aside their least productive land so productivity still remained high.

The original Common Agricultural Policy and some of its problems

Quotas
Dairy farmers were producing too much milk due to a fall in demand for milk products like butter.
1984 – quotas were introduced. They were worked out on the last 10 years' average milk production per farm. Farmers were allowed to produce that amount and no more. If they exceeded the quota they were fined. In 1992 there was a further reduction in quotas.

Grants
These have been available since 1992 to farmers who were seen to be environmentally friendly by
• planting hedges,
• planting woodland,
• providing wildlife habitats.

Guaranteed prices
This was a very complicated system which was the basis of the original CAP policy. Farmers were guaranteed that if their crops did not reach a certain price at market, then the EU would step in and buy their crops at a price that was fixed earlier in the season.
This encouraged farmers to overproduce crops because they knew that the crops would be bought for a fair price. This led to mountains of excess crops around Europe.

Figure 3.22 Original EU policies (green type represents EU policy; black type represents the problem)

CHANGES AFFECTING FARMING SYSTEMS IN THE EU – continued

These are some of the policies which are now in existence:

- **Set-aside:** In 2000 farmers had to set aside 10 per cent of their farm if they were to receive the arable area payments which have replaced guaranteed prices for arable crops. To be eligible for arable area payments, the minimum plot size is 0.3 hectares. Farmers are now allowed to cut hay or silage from their set-aside land or let other farmers' livestock graze on it as long as there is no payment in cash or kind, but they are not allowed to grow food crops on it.
- **Arable area payments:** these are made per hectare to growers of cereal crops, oil seed rape, sunflower seed, soya beans, peas, beans and linseed. The farmer must re-apply every year, stating the areas of different crop growth. The eligible land had to have arable crops on it in 1991. Farmers can also claim for woodland and set-aside if the land was arable in 1991. The payments in 2000 were as follows:

Year 2000	Approx. payments
Cereals	£550
Oil seeds	£784
Peas, beans, lupins	£683
Linseed	£830
Set-aside	£550

- **Milk quota:** this is a restriction on the amount of milk a farmer may produce. The quota for individual farms remains the same as 1992. Farmers may buy and sell all or part of their quotas through 'bucket' shops. These are agencies that deal in quotas. They generally buy quotas cheaply in May at the beginning of the quota year and then sell them for a large profit in March when farmers are desperate to increase their quota so that they are not fined for producing too much milk.
- Quotas have also been introduced on sheep and beef cattle.
- **Woodland grant scheme:** grants are available to farmers who wish to plant woods on their land. The woods must be at least a quarter of a hectare in area and at least 15 metres wide.
- **Environmentally sensitive areas scheme:** farmers in 22 areas of the country, including the Broads and Pennine Dales, can sign a management agreement of up to 10 years with the Ministry of Agriculture, Fisheries and Food (MAFF). They may agree to plant hedges and maintain dry stone walls or protect wetland habitats. They are paid for their protection of the environment.
- **Hill farm allowance scheme:** this is paid to farmers in marginal areas who farm more than 10 hectares of land. It is a payment on the area of land they farm which is within the moorland boundary. In 2001 they will be paid £13.02 per hectare for their land up to the first 350 hectares and £6.51 for the next 350–700 hectares. Other land will be paid for at different rates.

ACTIVITIES

1. Explain the problems caused by the old policies of CAP.
2. Describe the new initiatives that have been implemented.
3. In your opinion, will the new policies be successful?

The factors affecting the location of secondary industries

Industrialists are faced with many decisions when trying to decide where to locate their businesses. The factors that affect the location of an industry can be split into physical, economic, political and human. Figure 3.23 shows the main factors affecting an industrialist's decisions, but it is easier to split them into:

- Physical factors: those which are related to the natural environment such as land, raw materials and energy.
- Human factors: these are about the influence of people such as labour, environment, government policy, transport, markets and capital.

Land
The factory needs sufficient flat land to build on. The price of the land is important.

Raw Materials
If raw materials are bulky or heavy, the industry will locate close to them to save on transport costs.

Environment
Industries nowadays are far less restricted in their location requirements. Many now look to what the area can provide for its workers before deciding to locate there.

Labour
The availability of a labour force is more important to some industries than others. Labour intensive industries such as car assembly need a readily available supply of labour.

Transport / Communication
The availability of a good transport network, roads, railways and airports is very important to modern industries. They wish to receive their components quickly and despatch the finished goods to market with the greatest speed.

Energy
This was a more important factor in the past; factories needed to locate close to a source of power, originally water, then coal. This is not so important now because many industries use electricity.

Markets
The importance of nearness to markets is dependent on the goods being produced. For example:
Fragile goods – need to be produced close to their markets so that they do not get damaged on route.
Bulky goods – need to be made close to the market because of high transport cost.
Service industries must locate at their market.
Market is not so important to other industries.

Capital
This is the money that is invested to start a business. The amount of capital will determine the size and location of the factory.

Government Policy
The British government has withdrawn many of its incentives which it used to encourage industries to locate in depressed areas. The EU now provides grants to these areas. Industries that locate there will receive assistance in the form of low rent and rates.

The factors that affect the location of industry

Figure 3.23
Diagram of factors influencing industrial location

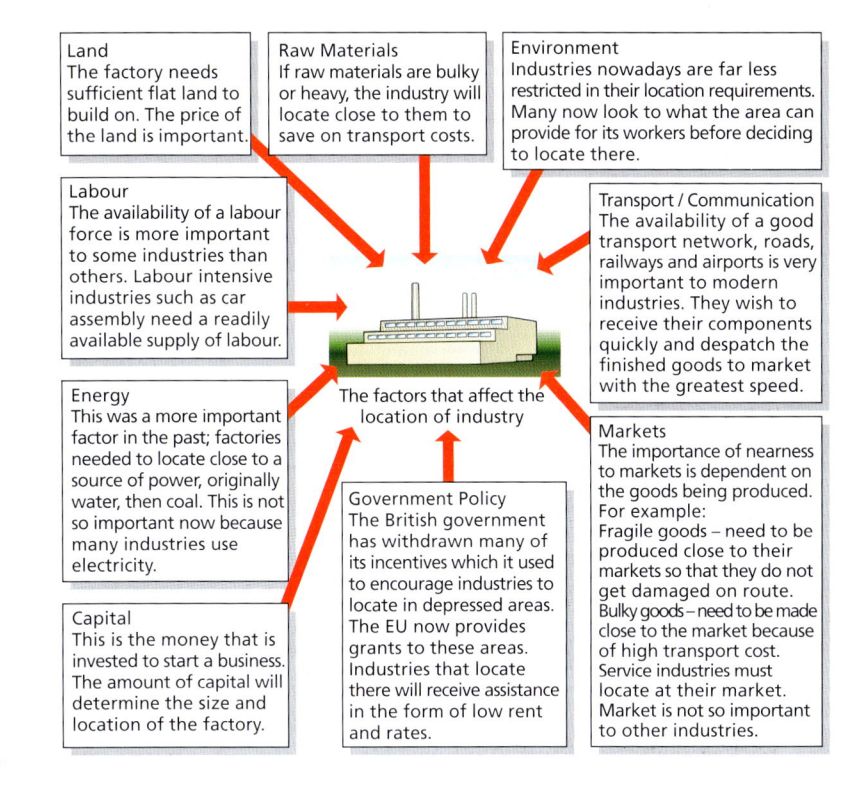

ACTIVITIES

1a In pairs, read the description of the four industries below.
   i   Iron and steel: this requires large amounts of iron ore, coal and water.
       It produces a bulky, heavy product. The factory requires a large site.
       Most of the processes are controlled by computers.
   ii Hi tech: this requires components which are small, light and expensive.
       It needs a large, skilled workforce. Very expensive equipment is required.
       Markets tend to be global. Workers demand high wages and an excellent quality of life.
   iii Brewery: this requires a large site and workforce. The main raw material is water.
       The product is bulky and requires large lorries to transport it.
   iv Textile manufacture: this is very labour intensive and uses a large factory.
       The main raw material is cloth. Depending on the clothes being made, markets tend to be global.
 b Complete the table below for each of the industries mentioned. Rank the factors for each industry from 1 to 7. The most important factor should be ranked number 1 and the least important number 7.
 c Analyse your results.

Industry	Transport	Land	Labour	Raw material	Environment	Capital	Market
Iron and steel							
Hi-tech							
Brewery							
Textile							

Case Study: COMPUTER DEVELOPMENT IN BRACKNELL

Modern hi-tech industries are those that involve the use of research and development to create high value, technology based products and processes. These industries are thought by many to be footloose. There are, however, a number of specific factors that affect their location.

There are a number of large concentrations of hi-tech firms in the UK. These include Cambridge (Silicon Fen), Silicon Glen to the north of Glasgow and the Thames Valley as well as a large concentration in Bracknell, Berkshire.

Why have hi-tech industries located in Bracknell?

There are a number of specific factors that have affected the location of the hi-tech industry in Bracknell:

1. Hi-tech industries require an excellent communication networks. Bracknell is located close to the M4 and M3 motorways (see Figure 3.24) which gives it access to the motorway system of the whole of Great Britain. The M4 is linked to Bracknell by the A329M and the M3 is linked to Bracknell by the A322 which is a dual carriageway. Bracknell is 20 miles from Heathrow airport and 50 miles from Gatwick airport. Both of the airports are accessible by motorway from Bracknell. It is also on the Reading to Waterloo train line which gives it access to Britain's rail network.
2. Hi-tech industries require a highly skilled workforce. The population of Bracknell and the surrounding area has grown considerably in the last 50 years. What is more significant is the growth in the 25–44 age range in the population. This shows an increase in the working population and, in the case of Bracknell, the population of skilled workers (see Figure 3.25).

There are a number of universities in the area with a good reputation for degree courses in computer technology. These include Royal Holloway, Brunel, Surrey and Reading, all of which are within a 20-mile radius of Bracknell.

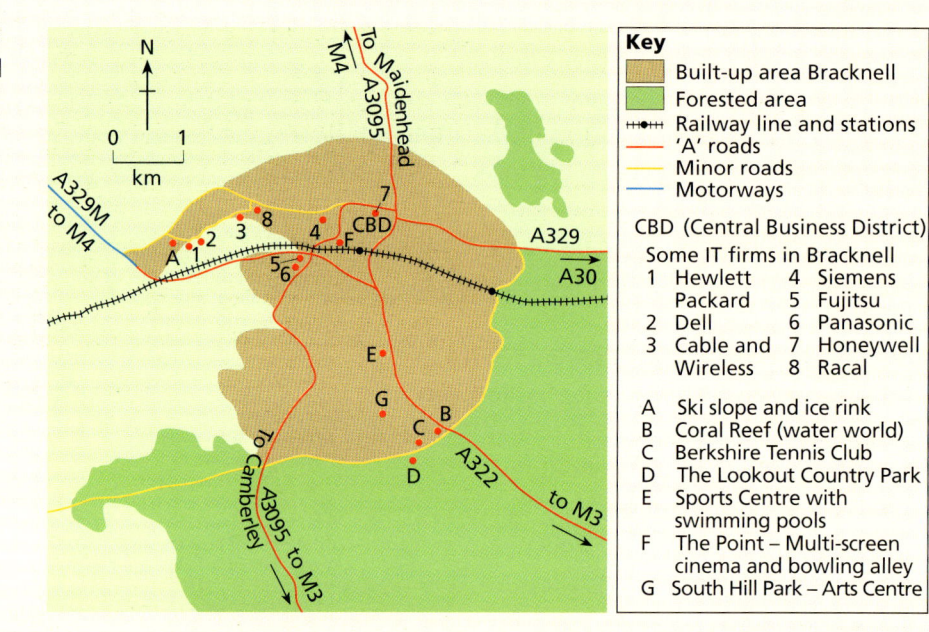

Figure 3.24 Map of Bracknell area

Key
- Built-up area Bracknell
- Forested area
- Railway line and stations
- 'A' roads
- Minor roads
- Motorways

CBD (Central Business District)

Some IT firms in Bracknell
1 Hewlett Packard
2 Dell
3 Cable and Wireless
4 Siemens
5 Fujitsu
6 Panasonic
7 Honeywell
8 Racal

A Ski slope and ice rink
B Coral Reef (water world)
C Berkshire Tennis Club
D The Lookout Country Park
E Sports Centre with swimming pools
F The Point – Multi-screen cinema and bowling alley
G South Hill Park – Arts Centre

Year	Population numbers
1951	23 408
1961	43 192
1971	64 135
1981	81 225
1981	95 949
1991	109 648
2001 estimate	112 319

Figure 3.26 Population numbers 1951–2001

Age	1951	1961	1971	1981	1991	2001
0–4	8	11	10	8	8	8
5–9	7	9	10	7	7	7
10–14	6	8	9	8	6	6
15–24	16	12	16	17	14	12
25–44	29	33	29	31	35	36
45–64	20	18	17	18	17	18
Over 65	14	9	9	11	13	13

Figure 3.25 Population percentage in age groups

3 Hi-tech industries require an area that can offer excellent leisure facilities. Bracknell has many leisure facilities of both a sporting and entertainment nature. There is a dry ski slope, ice rink, bowling, athletics, football and rugby clubs, leisure pool and swimming pool. The area around Bracknell has much to offer for people who prefer countryside leisure activities. There is a large area of coniferous forest to the south with open public access through the Look Out Country Park. Windsor Great Park is to the east of Bracknell which has unrestricted public access to people on foot or bikes. Further to the north are the Chilterns while to the south-west are Salisbury Plain and the Wiltshire Downs.

The artistic are also catered for with the South Hill Park Arts Centre which regularly puts on theatrical performances.

The list of hi-tech firms that have located in Bracknell include Hewlett Packard, ICL, Novell, Honeywell, Siemens, Dell and Panasonic. Their office complexes are very impressive with landscaping and plentiful car parking facilities (see Figure 3.28). Access to the motorway is direct, giving workers an easy journey to work. Their working environment is pleasant. A number of hotels have been built in the town Windsor Great Park, such as The Coppid Beach hotel which caters for company executives, many of which are TNCs, and offers conference facilities.

Figure 3.27 Leisure facilities in the Bracknell area

Figure 3.28 A hi-tech firm in Reading

ACTIVITIES

1 Describe the changes in the economically active age group between 1951 and 2001.
2 What problems might this population structure cause?
3 Use the information in Figure 3.26 to draw a line graph of Bracknell's population growth.
4 When was this growth greatest?
5 You are a member of Bracknell Forest Council in charge of increasing employment opportunities. Design a poster to attract more IT firms to Bracknell.

Extension

1 Why do you think major growth occurred in Bracknell between:
a 1951 and 1961?
b 1991 and 2001?

You will probably find the following website useful:
http://www.bracknell-forest.gov.uk

The nature of the formal and informal sectors

In MEDCs the majority of people are employed or self-employed and pay tax on their earnings. If they attempt to avoid paying their taxes, the inland revenue services fine them large sums of money. LEDCs are rather different to this. Although they have large numbers of people who are employed in the formal sector who work fixed hours for a certain wage and pay their taxes to the local government, there are also an increasing number of people who are employed in the informal sector. The informal sector in LEDCs is made up of jobs that people have found for themselves. These include jobs such as beach vendors, shoe shiners and the small businesses that set up to serve shanty town dwellers.

The jobs have much in common:
- They require little capital to set them up.
- They require few skills.
- Many of them are done from people's homes.
- They are labour intensive.
- They are small scale.

As urban areas in LEDCs continue to grow, this sector will also grow as there will not be enough jobs in the formal sector and people need to earn money. This robs the government of taxes, but as the money which is earned is generally re-spent immediately, the multiplier effect will apply (see Chapter 7).

The following case study on Fiat is an example of a formal sector employer.

ACTIVITIES

1. Look at these 3 figures and describe the work that is taking place and the nature of the jobs it involves.
2. Are they part of the informal or formal sector?
3. Make a list of 10 informal sector jobs. Describe their characteristics.

The economic world

Case Study: FIAT, A TNC, IN BRAZIL

A study of factors attracting one TNC to a particular country

Transnational companies (TNCs) are companies that operate globally. This means that although they tend to have their headquarters in their country of origin, they have branch plants all over the world.

One such TNC is the Italian company, Fiat, one of the world's largest industrial groups. It operates in 64 different countries around the world and its revenue is in excess of 48 billion euros, 39 per cent of which is generated outside of Italy.

A number of TNCs have located branches in Brazil: Volkswagen of Germany and Ford and General Motors of the USA have opened factories at São Paulo. Fiat opened a plant at Betim in 1976 that employs over 10 000 workers and produces 130 000 cars a year. Betim is part of the industrial belt of Belo Horizonte, the capital of Minas Gerais, a prosperous state in south-east Brazil (see Chapter 8, Figure 8.3 for its location). In the 1990s Fiat invested a further $1.5 billion in updating this plant and in developing the Palio and Tipo cars. The plant at Betim now employs 12,000 workers in producing 650 000 cars, a figure which is increasing each year.

Figure 3.30 Fiat plant in Brazil

Why did Fiat build a factory in Brazil?

- In the 1990s the Brazilian government decided to develop a motor industry in the hope that this would bring long-term employment. This led to the expansion of the market for cars in Brazil.
- The state of Minas Gerais offered loans, grants and cheap land which meant that Fiat could build and operate a modern factory at a low cost. The incentive package that Fiat received amounted to 50 per cent of its initial investment.
- Fiat would have a guaranteed market within Brazil and could supply the demands of other South American countries. The increase in demand for cars in Brazil has, in fact, been dramatic and has led to a growth in production.

Year	Production in thousands
1970	255
1990	1,000
1992	1,100
1996	1,800
2000	2,800

- There was a large pool of workers available who were prepared to work for low wages (although there has been some increase in wages due to the bad publicity received by the company for exploiting its workforce). They still only get the equivalent of $7 an hour. Workers on production lines in the UK get approximately £12 an hour.
- The car factory was set up when there was a strong military government, which meant that strike action was unlikely to happen. A Fiat manager, quoted in *The Economist* in 1997, 'Not a single hour has been lost to strikes in the last 14 years.' Even though there have been changes of government, the work ethic is

Figure 3.31 Workers on production line in Fiat factory

FIAT, A TNC, IN BRAZIL – continued

still good and the workers know that someone else will be happy to do their job. Metal mechanic Luizinho Rodrigues said, 'For every person hired, four others are waiting for a job.'

Why has Fiat expanded in Brazil?
In November 2000, Fiat opened a new $240 million plant at Sete Lagoas. This is a joint venture between Iveco which will make light trucks and Fiat Automoveis which will make Ducato vans. At present Fiat Iveco has a 9 per cent share of the light van market in Brazil; it hopes to increase its share of the market to 15 per cent by 2001.

One of the reasons for Fiat's decision to build another factory in Brazil was that the state of Minas Gerais gave Fiat $135 million towards the building of the new factory – over half of the construction cost. Fiat also believes that there will be a great increase in demand for these vehicles in Brazil over the next few years. Their predictions indicate that in 2003 2.2m cars and light vans will be sold. If these cars are produced within the country, Fiat will save on transport costs and import duties. At the same time, Fiat predict that the western European and North American markets will remain constant.

ACTIVITIES

1. What are the characteristics of a TNC?
2. Why did Fiat locate in Brazil?
3. Choose one other TNC in another industry, such as Nike. Try to find out which countries in the world it is located in. What might be the reasons for this global location in the case of your chosen TNC?

Sample Examination Questions

Higher tier

1. Name the physical features found at the following grid references. The aerial photograph in Figure 1.1 may help your answer.
   a 055 825   b 041 786   c 032 798   (3 marks)
2. a Which primary activity is found at grid reference 968 784? (1 mark)
   b Give the grid references of three other primary activities located on the map. (3 marks)
3. The map is of an area known as the Isle of Purbeck, a popular tourist area. Use map evidence to show why. (4 marks)
4. Woodland is being managed in the area of the map north of grid line 83. How does the map show that the woodland is being managed? (2 marks)
5. What type of farming is mainly practised in the area of the map extract? Give one reason for your answer. (2 marks)
6. How have the communication links been affected by the relief of the area? (5 marks)

Total 20 marks

Foundation tier

1. Name the physical features found at the following grid references. The aerial photograph in Figure 1.1 may help your answer.
   a 055 825   b 041 786   c 032 798   (3 marks)
2. Which primary activities are found at the following grid references: (4 marks)

Grid reference	Primary activity
00 84	
972 854	
968 784	
987 808	

3. The map is of an area known as the Isle of Purbeck which is a popular tourist area. Use map evidence to show why. (4 marks)
4. The woodland north of grid line 83 is being managed. How does the map show that the woodland is being managed? (2 marks)
5. What type of farming is mainly practised in the area of the map extract? Is it arable or pastoral? Give one reason for your answer. (2 marks)
6. How have the communication links (roads and railways) been affected by the relief of the area? (5 marks)

Total marks 20

The economic world

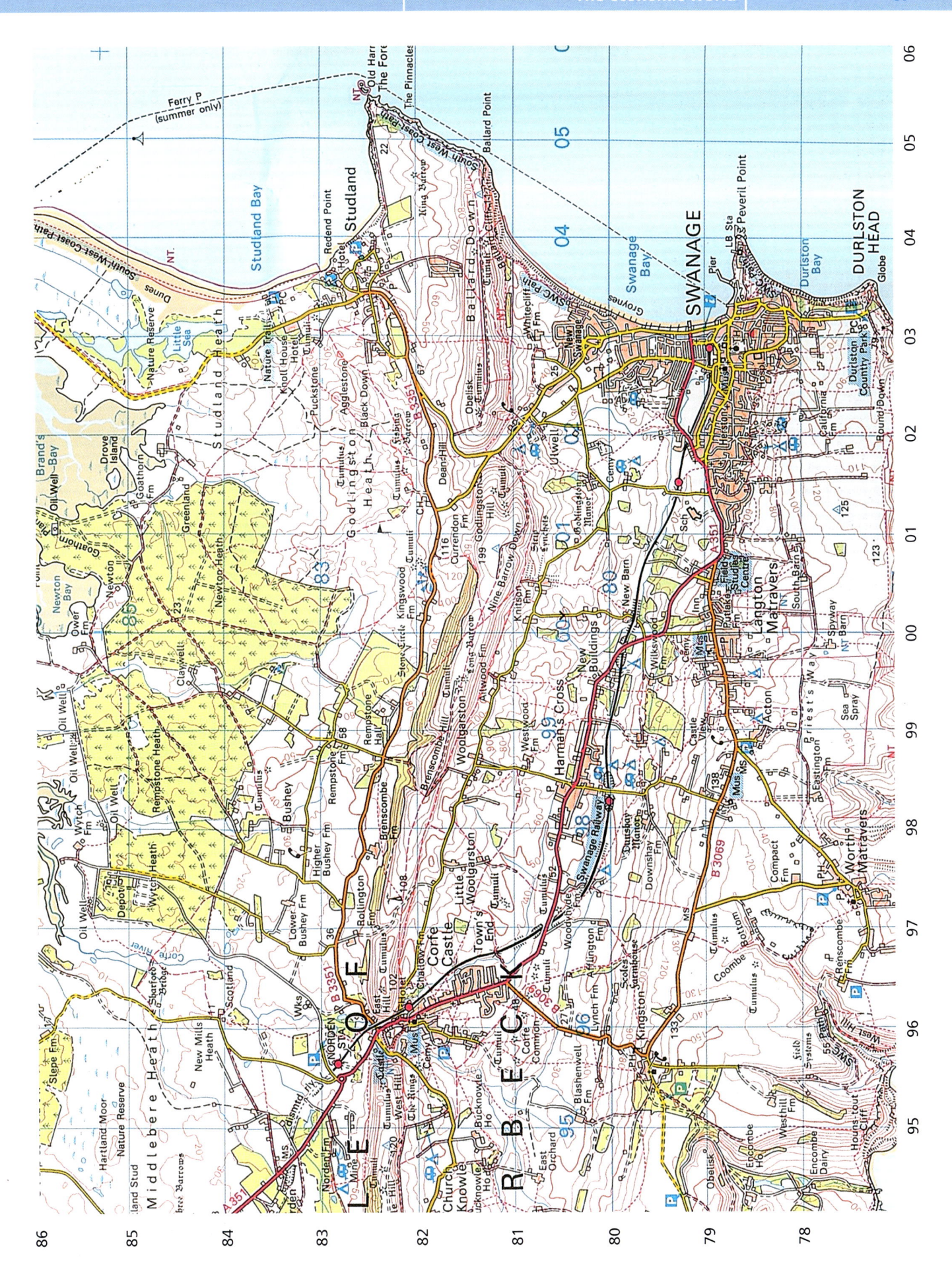

67

4 The natural world

Air masses lead to changes in the UK weather

What are air masses?

An air mass is a large body of air that has similar temperature and moisture properties. Air masses originate at source regions, which are large, usually flat, areas of water or land, where air can be stagnant long enough to take on the characteristics of the surface below. They move over long distances and the bodies of water and land from which they started will affect the weather of the areas to which they travel.

Air masses are defined according to their origin and the course they travel. The names of the air masses hold clues as to their place of origin and, consequently, the weather they will bring. Tropical air masses will bring warm weather; Polar and Arctic masses will bring cold weather. Continental air masses travel over land and will bring dry weather as they have not picked up much moisture on the way. Maritime air masses travel over the sea so will bring wet weather.

What air masses affect the UK?

The map in Figure 4.1 shows the source regions and the direction of movement for the five main air masses that affect the UK.

Tropical maritime (Tm) – The source region for this air mass is the Atlantic Ocean between Bermuda and the Azores. Large amounts of moisture are characteristic of this air mass as it travels long distances over the warm sea. It brings warm weather to the UK, but also low cloud which results in wet weather with long periods of drizzle and fog over coastal areas.

Tropical continental (Tc) – The source region for this air mass is northern Africa. The UK's highest temperatures (reaching over 30 °C in the day and around 15–20 °C at night) are associated with this air mass. It usually brings very dry weather. Occasionally it produces coloured rain from the sand from the Sahara Desert and leaves cars covered in a thin layer of orange dust.

Figure 4.1 Air masses affecting the UK

Polar continental (Pc) – This air mass usually forms in Scandinavia or Russia. Typically Polar continental air is cold and dry. The air is particularly dry as it has travelled only a short distance across the English Channel, but is more moist if it has crossed the North Sea before reaching Britain. In winter, Pc brings very cold temperatures, often bringing snow or hail to the east coast of England. In summer, it is associated with warm, stable conditions.

Arctic maritime (Am) – The source of this air mass is over the Arctic Ocean and brings very cold conditions in winter and spring. It is rare in the summer. It heats up as it moves south, collecting moisture that causes heavy snow and strong winds in northern Scotland, at which point the rest of the UK could also experience snow and very cold temperatures. Even in southern England temperatures can stay below freezing for several days.

Polar maritime (Pm) – This is one of the most common air masses to reach the UK. It usually arrives from a westerly direction, originating in Canada or Greenland.

It brings cool conditions throughout the year. The very cold polar air warms slightly as it crosses the Atlantic, causing clouds and showers along the west coast in winter – the east is sheltered by hills and mountains (see relief rainfall on page 70). In the summer it is commonly associated with showers and thunderstorms.

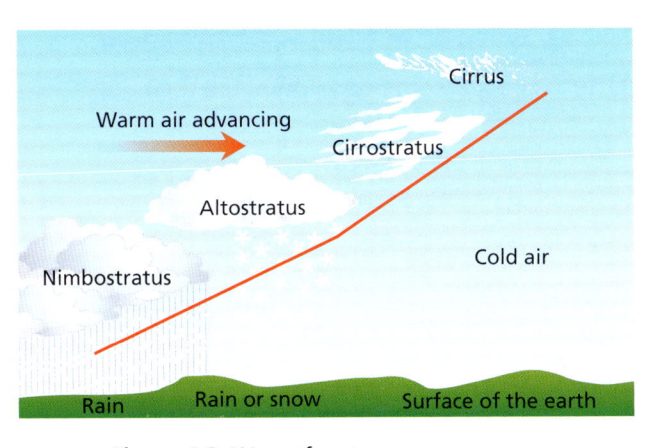

Figure 4.2 Warm front

Why is the weather in the UK so changeable?

The UK lies in an area where warm tropical air meets cold polar air. When two air masses meet, they do not mix readily due to differences in temperature and density. A front is an imaginary line separating two contrasting air masses. Fronts are areas where rainfall takes place.

Figure 4.3 Cold front

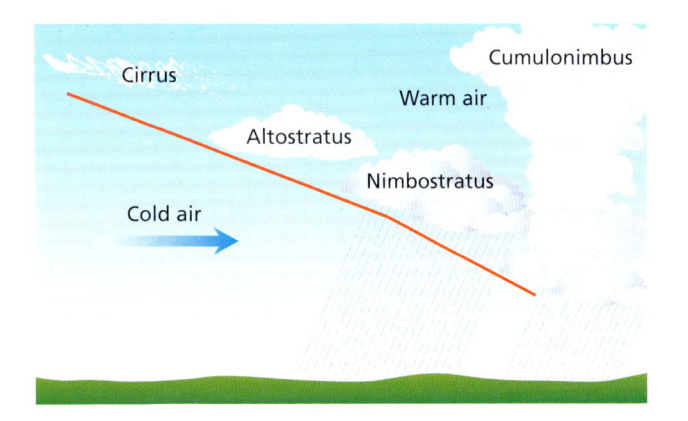

A warm front is found when warm air is advancing and is forced on top of cold air, which is denser. As the warm air rises it is cooled and therefore holds less moisture. Condensation takes place which is the changing of air from a vapour to a liquid.

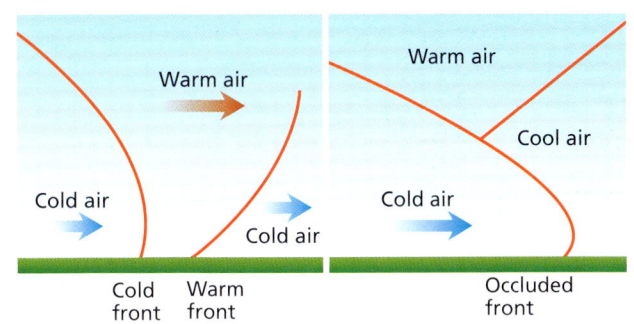

Continued uplift leads to the coalescing of water droplets which when heavy enough fall as rain. A cold front occurs when cold air is advancing and is forced beneath a body of warm air. The name of the front is specified by the temperature of the moving air.

An occluded front occurs when a cold front catches up and overtakes a warm front forcing the warm air to rise up.

Figure 4.4 Occluded front

As well as frontal rain, the UK is also affected by relief rain and, to a lesser extent, convectional rain.

Figure 4.5 Rainfall map of the UK

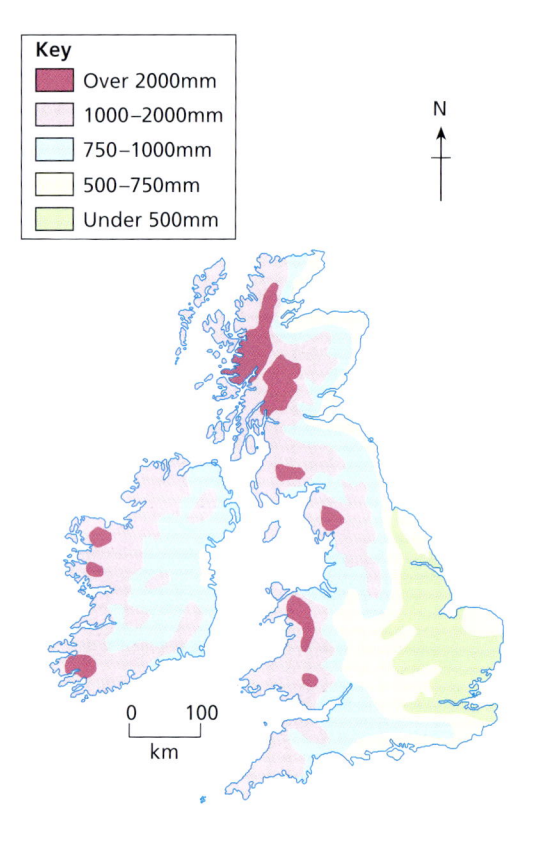

Key
- Over 2000mm
- 1000–2000mm
- 750–1000mm
- 500–750mm
- Under 500mm

Relief rain – Relief rain is formed when air is forced to cool when it rises over relief features in the landscape such as hills or mountains. Figure 4.5 shows that the highest rainfall totals of over 1,600 mm per year occur in the mountain areas along the west coast of England, Scotland and Wales. Figure 4.6 shows how relief rain operates in northern England.

1. South-west prevailing (most common) winds are saturated with moisture picked up as they cross the Atlantic.
2. Air is forced to rise over the hills. As air rises it cools by 1 °C for every 100 metres.
3. As the water vapour in the air rises, it condenses to form clouds and rain. Air that has cooled cannot hold as much water as warmer air.
4. The air starts to descend the hill and begins to warm up again.
5. As air warms up it can hold more water, but as it has already rained the air is dry and clouds disappear and rain stops. This area is known as a rainshadow.

Convectional rain – On hot summer days, the ground becomes heated, which causes the air above to be warmed. This warm air rises in thermals at over 20 m/sec. As it rises, it cools and condenses to form clouds, which may result in heavy rainstorms with thunder and lightning in the afternoon. This is not common in the UK, occurring most frequently in the warmer south east of England. This is one reason why some places in East Anglia have higher summer than winter rainfall.

Figure 4.6 Diagram of relief rain in northern England

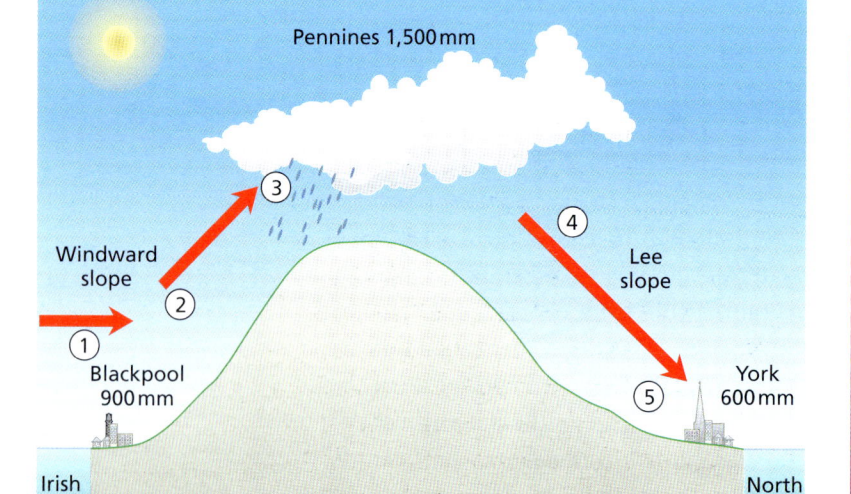

Pennines 1,500mm
Windward slope
Lee slope
Blackpool 900mm
York 600mm
Irish Sea
North Sea

ACTIVITIES

1. On a map of Europe, mark the major air masses and add labels to summarise the weather conditions that each one brings to the UK.
2. Explain what is meant by:
   a. warm front,
   b. cold front,
   c. occluded front.
3. Why does the west of Scotland have a high annual rainfall?

The natural world · 71

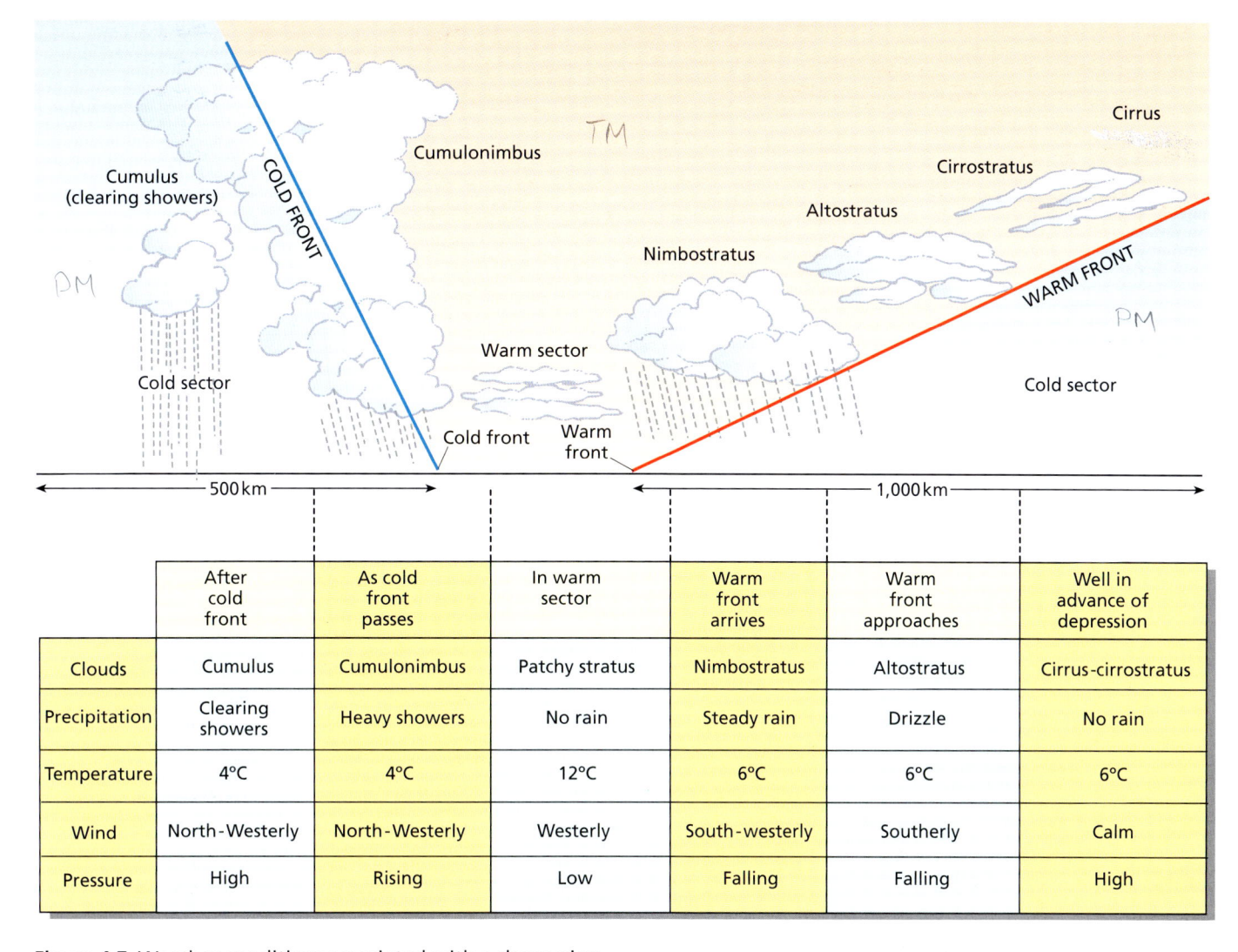

	After cold front	As cold front passes	In warm sector	Warm front arrives	Warm front approaches	Well in advance of depression
Clouds	Cumulus	Cumulonimbus	Patchy stratus	Nimbostratus	Altostratus	Cirrus-cirrostratus
Precipitation	Clearing showers	Heavy showers	No rain	Steady rain	Drizzle	No rain
Temperature	4°C	4°C	12°C	6°C	6°C	6°C
Wind	North-Westerly	North-Westerly	Westerly	South-westerly	Southerly	Calm
Pressure	High	Rising	Low	Falling	Falling	High

Figure 4.7 Weather conditions associated with a depression

Depressions – Depressions affect the weather in the UK for much of the year. These are areas of low pressure, bringing cloud, rain and wind. They form over the Atlantic Ocean where warm tropical air meets cold polar air. Fronts occur where these two different air masses meet and are unable to mix.

The depression becomes more extensive as it moves eastwards towards the UK. By the time a depression reaches the UK it has a warm and cold front. The cold front travels faster than the warm front squeezing the warm sector air upward between the fronts. Eventually the cold front will catch up with the warm front and, as the warm sector disappears, form an occluded front. The depression dies out when the warm air has completely risen and cooled. It now has underlying cold air and the temperature differences have equalled out.

Mature depressions pass across the country from west to east and produce a sequence of weather patterns (shown in Figure 4.7).

Figure 4.10 is a synoptic chart showing a depression over the UK. A synoptic chart is a map that shows the weather at a particular time and place using weather symbols to show the weather conditions. Look for Dover in Figure 4.10. It shows that the weather in Dover has a temperature of 25 °C with 1 okta of cloud, no rain and a light southerly wind of 15 knots. Remember winds are named after the direction that they are coming from.

The natural world

Figure 4.8 Air masses meeting

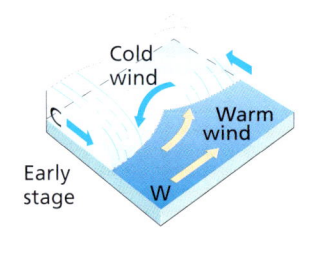

Figure 4.9 What is a depression?

- Cold polar air meets warm tropical air

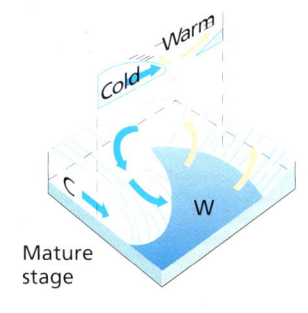

- Warm air rises over cold air. The boundary between the two forms the *warm front*. The colder air to the west is denser and undercuts the warmer air. The boundary forms the *cold front*.

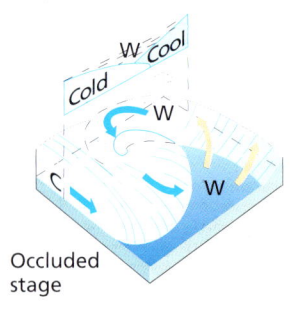

- The cold front moves faster than the warm front and eventually catches it up and lifts it away from the ground, forming an *occluded* front.

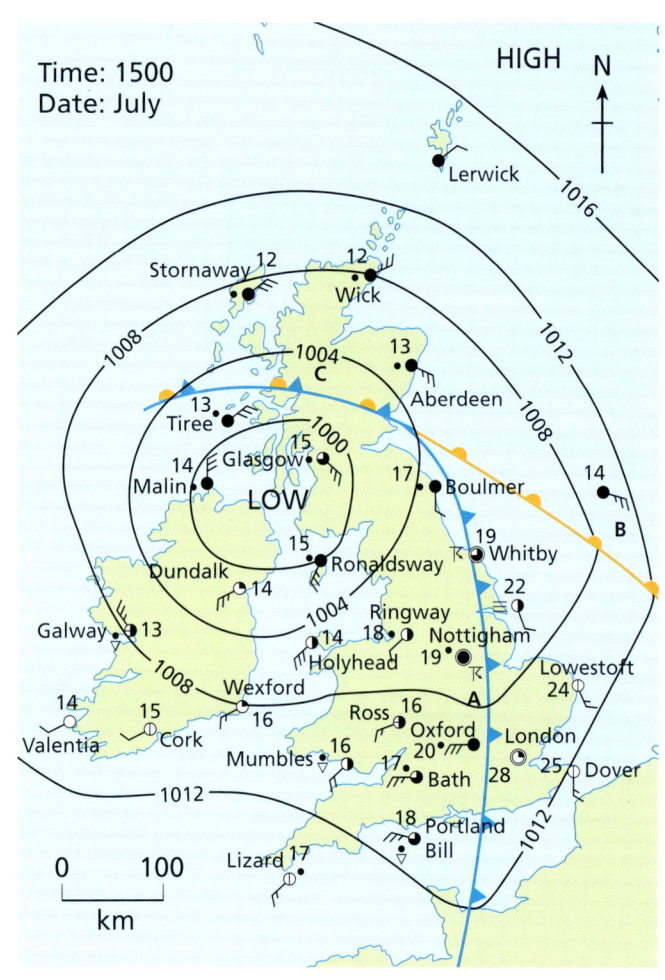

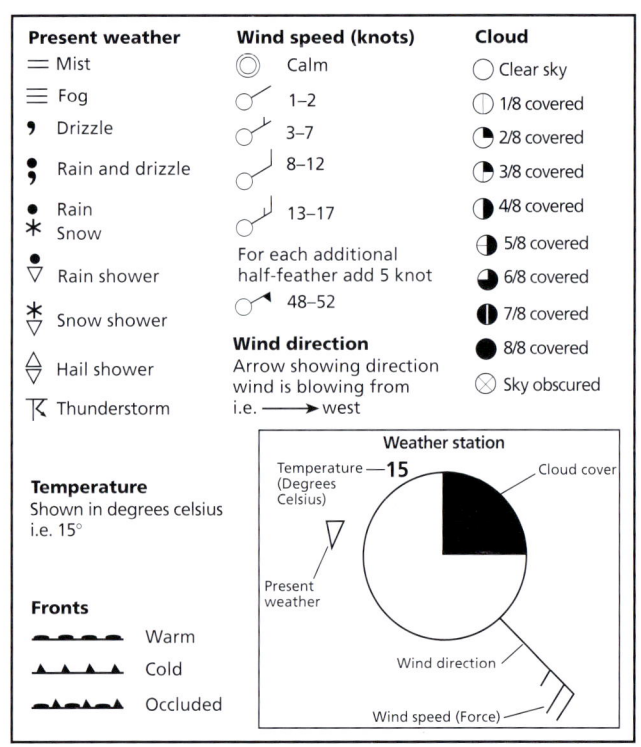

Early stage

Mature stage

Occluded stage

Time: 1500
Date: July

Figure 4.10 Synoptic chart and weather symbols

Present weather
- ═ Mist
- ≡ Fog
- 〉 Drizzle
- 〉• Rain and drizzle
- • Rain
- ✱ Snow
- ▽ Rain shower
- ✱̇ Snow shower
- ⌂ Hail shower
- ⎇ Thunderstorm

Wind speed (knots)
- ◎ Calm
- 1–2
- 3–7
- 8–12
- 13–17

For each additional half-feather add 5 knot

48–52

Wind direction
Arrow showing direction wind is blowing from
i.e. ⟶ west

Cloud
- ○ Clear sky
- ◔ 1/8 covered
- 2/8 covered
- 3/8 covered
- ◐ 4/8 covered
- 5/8 covered
- 6/8 covered
- 7/8 covered
- ● 8/8 covered
- ⊗ Sky obscured

Temperature
Shown in degrees celsius
i.e. 15°

Fronts
- ⌒⌒⌒ Warm
- ▲▲▲ Cold
- ▲⌒▲⌒ Occluded

Weather station

Temperature (Degrees Celsius) — 15
Cloud cover
Present weather
Wind direction
Wind speed (Force)

The natural world

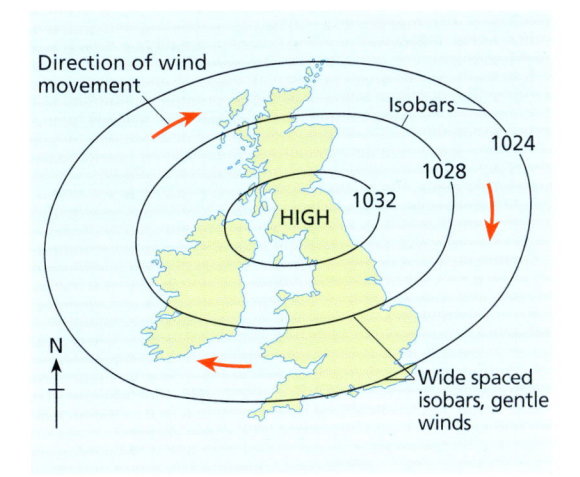

Figure 4.11 Synoptic chart of an anticyclone

Anticyclones – In contrast to depressions, anticyclones only involve one type of air mass which usually cover large areas and do not have any fronts. They are high pressure systems in which the air moves downwards towards the earth's surface. As the air descends, it warms. When air is warming, no clouds can form so the sky is clear. Anticyclones can be very large, typically at least 3,000 km wide. Once they become established, they can give several days of settled weather. Winds are gentle in an anticyclone and this is shown on a synoptic chart by wide spaced isobars (see Figure 4.11)

British anticyclone weather – In Britain in summer an anticyclone will mean heatwaves during the day. At night, however, as there are no clouds, mist or heavy dew may form which will clear rapidly the following morning. After a few days, a layer of hot air builds up at ground level, which eventually will give rise to thunderstorms, ending the anticyclone.

In winter the longer nights mean an increased risk of dew, frost and thicker, more extensive fog patches which may be slow to clear or even persist.

Under certain conditions, both frost and fog may persist for several days. An anticyclone's very stable conditions means that pollution is trapped at low levels, resulting in very poor air quality such as smogs.

Figure 4.12 Typical anticyclonic conditions in the winter

Figure 4.13 Satellite photo of western Europe

The natural world

Figure 4.13 is a satellite image of western Europe and clearly shows a depression marked with an X centred over the Atlantic Ocean and an anticyclone at Y. Most of the British Isles is experiencing bright sunny conditions. The temperature range is from 20 °C to 24 °C, and the winds are very light, peaking at 7 knots.

ACTIVITIES

Higher

1 Study the synoptic chart in Figure 4.10. What are the weather conditions in:
   a London,
   b Bath,
   c Galway.
2 Explain why the weather is different at these three locations.
3 What do you notice about wind directions in an anticyclone and a depression?
4 Study Figure 4.14. Construct a table comparing anticyclones and depressions. Use the following column headings: winds, pressure, size, air masses, summer weather and winter weather.
5 Study Figure 4.13 which was taken in the winter.
   a Name the weather systems at X and Y.
   b What are the weather conditions likely to be over Northern France?

Foundation

Look at the weather map (Figure 4.10).
1 What is the name given to this type of map?
2 Name the fronts at points A, B and C
3 What is the pressure at points A, B and C?
4 What direction does the wind blow in a depression and an anticyclone?
5 London is in the warm sector. What are the weather conditions at London?
6 Bath is in the cold sector behind the front. What are the weather conditions at Bath?
7 How can anticyclones affect people's health?

Comparison of anticyclones and depressions

Anticylones
There is only one air mass and so there are no fronts. Winds are light so the isobars are wide apart. Winds blow clockwise. Anti-cyclones bring stable, calm weather. In the UK they cause heatwaves in summer and cold frosty days in winter.

High pressure
1012
1008
1004

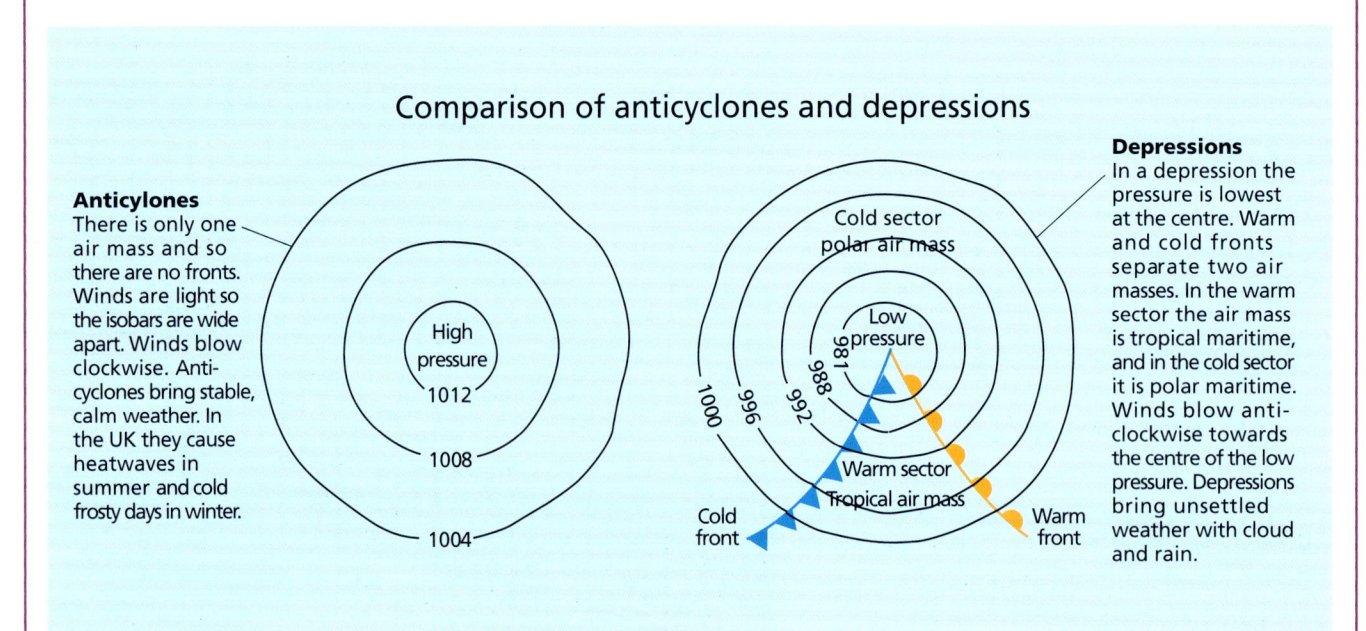

Cold sector polar air mass
Low pressure
981
988
992
996
1000
Warm sector
Tropical air mass
Cold front
Warm front

Depressions
In a depression the pressure is lowest at the centre. Warm and cold fronts separate two air masses. In the warm sector the air mass is tropical maritime, and in the cold sector it is polar maritime. Winds blow anti-clockwise towards the centre of the low pressure. Depressions bring unsettled weather with cloud and rain.

Figure 4.14 Diagram comparing anticyclones and depressions

Average long-term weather patterns lead to distinct climatic types

Climate is the seasonal pattern of weather that we can expect on the basis of records going back at least 30 years. The main features of a place's climate can be summarised on a climate graph. Climate graphs plot the mean monthly temperatures as a line graph and the mean monthly precipitation as a bar graph.

What are the characteristics of the west European maritime climate?

In Europe, areas with this type of climate are located between 40° to 60° north of the equator. This climate area spreads from the UK at the extreme west through the lowland areas of west Europe, including the coastal fringe of Scandinavia, to upland areas such as the Alps which act as a natural barrier to the eastward spread. Figure 4.15 shows the main characteristics of a West European maritime climate.

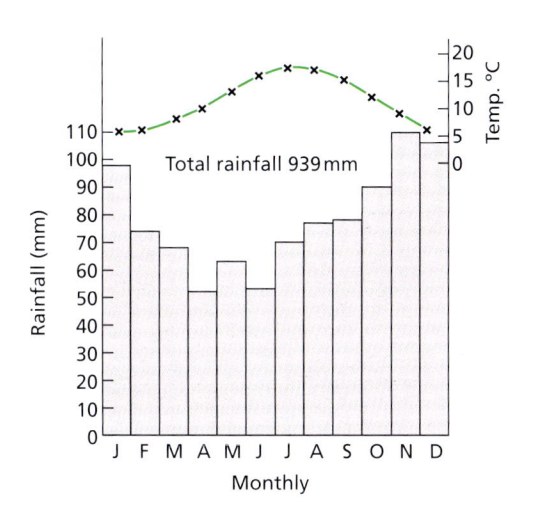

Figure 4.15 Climate graph for Plymouth 50° N

1 Extremes of temperature are very rare and the annual temperature range is small. For Plymouth, the maximum monthly temperature in July is 17 °C and the minimum temperature in January is 6 °C. This means that the annual range is only 11 °C.

2 There is a gradual monthly change in temperature with no month being more than 3 °C different to the next.
3 Summers are usually described as warm, with the mean temperature for the warmest month lying between 14° and 20 °C, depending upon latitude. Winters are cool or mild rather than not cold. Although winter temperatures on some days may never rise above freezing, the effect of the sea means that the average temperature of the coldest month is typically a few degrees above freezing point.
4 Rainfall is regular but very rarely torrential. There can often be, particularly in rain shadow areas, little difference between the wettest and driest months. In the UK rainfall totals are heavily influenced by relief (see relief rainfall).

East European continental interior climate

Areas experiencing this type of climate are situated inland between 35° and 60° north of the equator. Figure 4.16 shows a climate graph for Kiev, 50 °N. Kiev is in the Ukraine at the same latitude as Plymouth. It shows the main characteristics of an east European continental interior climate.

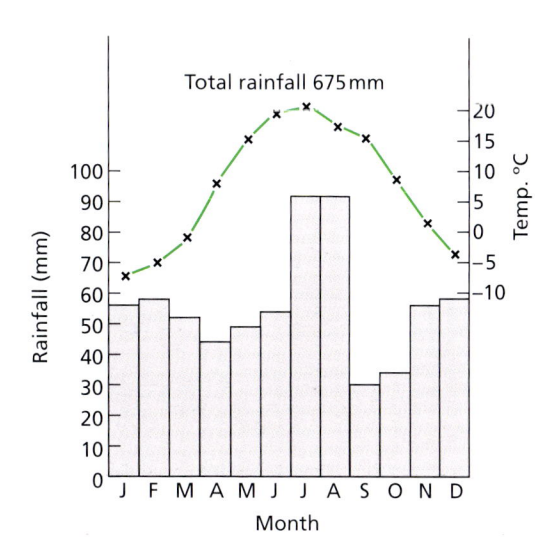

Figure 4.16 Climate graph for Kiev 50 °N

1 There is a large annual temperature range: it is 27 °C for Kiev, although in central Russia it can be as much as 40 °C, with winter temperatures dropping to 20 °C below freezing point.
2 Monthly changes in temperature can be quite large, up to 8 or 9 °C.
3 Summers are generally warm or hot with temperatures in the range of 15 °C to 23 °C, depending on latitude. Winters are exceptionally cold, with mean monthly temperatures falling below zero for 3 to 6 months.
4 Precipitation is low particularly in the centre of the continent. Kiev's precipitation is 650 mm, which is reasonably high for this climate (the average is about 500 mm)
5 In the winter months, much of the precipitation falls as snow as a result of the cold temperatures.
6 In the summer, maximum precipitation, in the form of thunderstorms, occurs due to convection.

> **Examiners' tips**
> Reading a climate graph
> Look out for:
> - Total rainfall.
> - Seasonality – does most of the rain fall in one season?
> - Maximum temperature.
> - Minimum temperature.
> - Range of temperature.
> - Does the temperature fall below zero?
> - Are there any anomalies – months that are different to the rest?

ACTIVITIES

1 Use the data in the table below to draw a rainfall and temperature graph for Norwich.
a What is the annual range of temperature for Norwich?
b Why does Plymouth have more precipitation than Norwich?
c When does Norwich have the most rain?
d Why is this?

Climate data for Norwich

	J	F	M	A	M	J	J	A	S	O	N	D
rain (mm)	52	48	40	48	42	46	80	54	60	64	64	52
temp (°C)	4	6	8	10	14	17	18	18	15	13	10	6

What are the factors that influence these climates?

Latitude – Places near to the equator are much warmer than places closer to the poles. At the equator the land heats up rapidly because the sun's energy is far more concentrated than it is at higher latitude. Further away from the equator the solar energy is spread out over a wider area and is therefore less concentrated, leading to lower temperatures. The sun's rays also have to pass through the earth's atmosphere. The atmosphere surrounding the earth contains dust, smoke and other solid particles. These particles absorb heat. At the equator the sun's rays pass through the

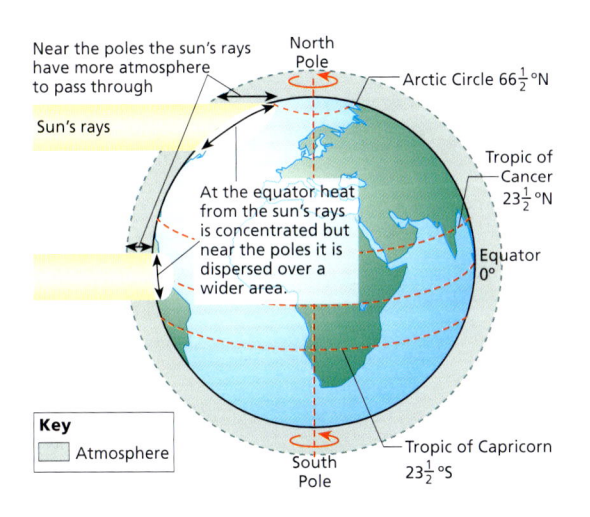

Figure 4.17 How latitude affects temperature

atmosphere at a more direct angle and, therefore, more quickly than nearer the poles. Because of this, less heat will be lost.

Latitude also affects temperatures by influencing the length of the days. In the UK during the winter, day length is short. Fewer hours of sunlight contribute to lower temperatures.

Distance from the sea – A town or city's distance from the sea has an effect on its climate. The temperatures of places that are close to the sea are moderated by its effect. In winter, places that are close to the sea will be warmer than places that are further inland. During the summer, the reverse happens,

places that are close to the sea are cooler than places that are inland. This is because land and sea respond differently to temperature. The land heats up quickly but also loses heat quickly. In contrast, the sea heats up and cools down much more slowly. The reasons for this are:

- The sea is in constant motion and water heated at the surface circulates to a great depth. Therefore heat is lost and gained slowly.
- The land is a solid and is heated to a depth of no more than 30 cm, so heat is lost and gained rapidly.

This is why places that are near to the coast are much cooler than places inland in summer, but are warmer than places inland in winter. This is what gives rise to the great annual temperature range in continental interiors (see Figure 4.18).

Figure 4.19 shows the effect of distance from the sea on temperatures in Europe.

Ocean currents – The effect of an ocean current depends upon whether it is a warm current or a cold current. Warm currents move away from the equator, whereas cold currents move towards it. Ocean currents can either raise or lower the air temperature in maritime environments. Figure 4.20 shows what effects the cold Labrador current and the warm North Atlantic Drift have on coastal temperatures in Europe and North America.

Figure 4.18 The continental influence on temperatures in Spain

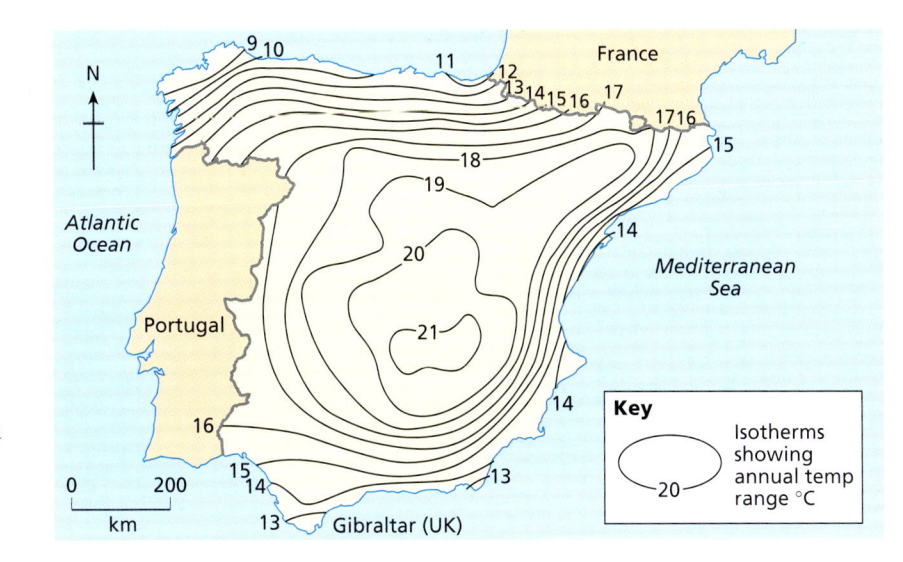

78　The natural world

Figure 4.19 Temperatures in Europe

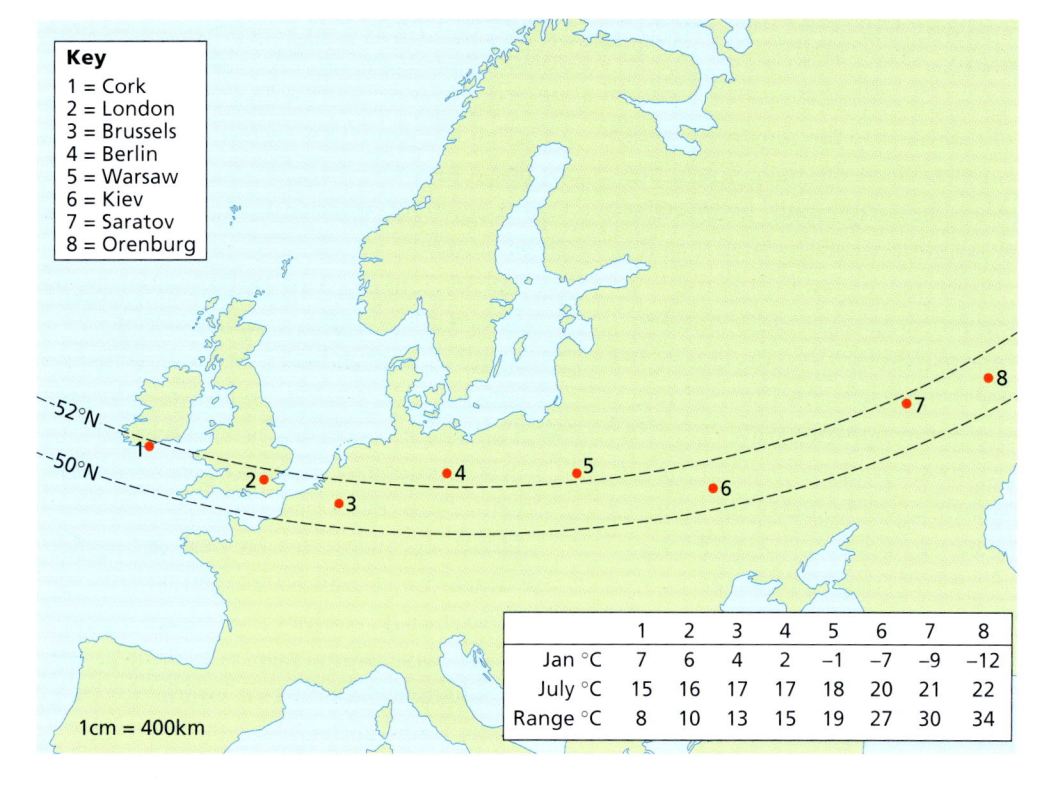

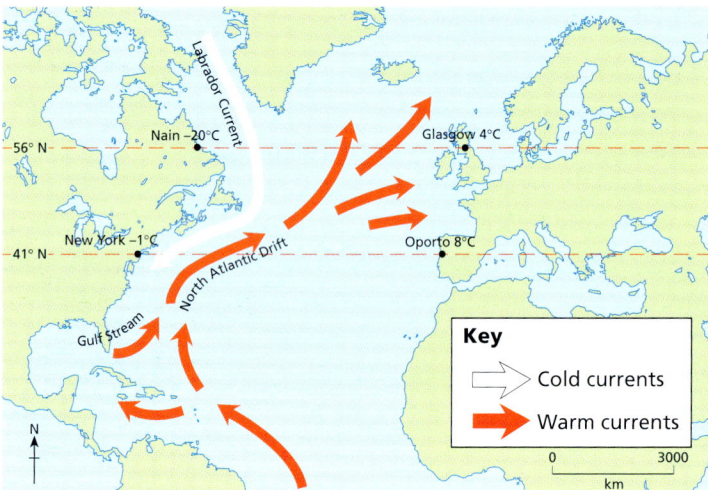

Key
1 = Cork
2 = London
3 = Brussels
4 = Berlin
5 = Warsaw
6 = Kiev
7 = Saratov
8 = Orenburg

1cm = 400km

	1	2	3	4	5	6	7	8
Jan °C	7	6	4	2	−1	−7	−9	−12
July °C	15	16	17	17	18	20	21	22
Range °C	8	10	13	15	19	27	30	34

Figure 4.20 How the Atlantic Ocean currents affect temperatures

Key: Cold currents, Warm currents

Nain −20°C, Glasgow 4°C, New York −1°C, Oporto 8°C
Labrador Current, Gulf Stream, North Atlantic Drift

Prevailing winds – Prevailing winds are the dominant winds in an area. The prevailing winds affecting the UK come from the south west and are warm and moist. In contrast, the dominant winds affecting much of continental Europe are cold, dry easterlies.

ACTIVITIES

Higher

1 Look at Figure 4.19:
a Draw a scattergraph to show how the annual range of temperatures varies with distance from the sea.
b Describe and explain what your graph shows.
2 How does latitude effect the temperature of places in the UK?

Foundation

1 Look at Figure 4.19.
a Which place has the highest temperature in summer? Is it on the coast or inland?
b Which place has the lowest temperature in summer? Is it on the coast or inland?
c Explain your answers.
2 Temperatures in the north of Scotland are usually cooler than in the south of England. Why is this?

Distinct forest communities develop in particular conditions

How are forests distributed throughout the world?

Figure 4.21 shows the distribution of the three major forest types.

The tropical rainforests are all found between the Tropic of Capricorn and the Tropic of Cancer. The largest area is found in South America, mostly in Brazil but also to a lesser extent in the countries bordering it to the west and north. Most of central Africa used to be covered in tropical rainforests, but it is now confined to areas of west Africa, notably in Cameroon and Zaire. A small area is still left on the east coast of Madagascar. Most of the islands of Indonesia are well covered in rainforests, although large areas are still being lost due to logging. Rainforest also exists in the state of Queensland, north-east Australia and parts of south-east Asia.

Temperate coniferous forests are found in a wide band between 50 °N and the Arctic Circle. They stretch across Canada, northern Europe (Scandinavia) and Russia, which has the largest continuous forests in Siberia. There are no large-scale occurrences of temperate coniferous forest in the southern hemisphere because of the lack of land at the appropriate latitude.

Temperate deciduous forests are found on the continents of North America, Europe and Asia between 30° and 60° north of the equator. Europe is the continent with the furthest northern extent. They do not spread across the continents as much as the coniferous forest as the centre of the continental landmass is too cold in the winter. There are no large scale deciduous forests in the southern hemisphere because of the absence of land at the appropriate latitude.

Figure 4.21 Map showing the distribution of major forests

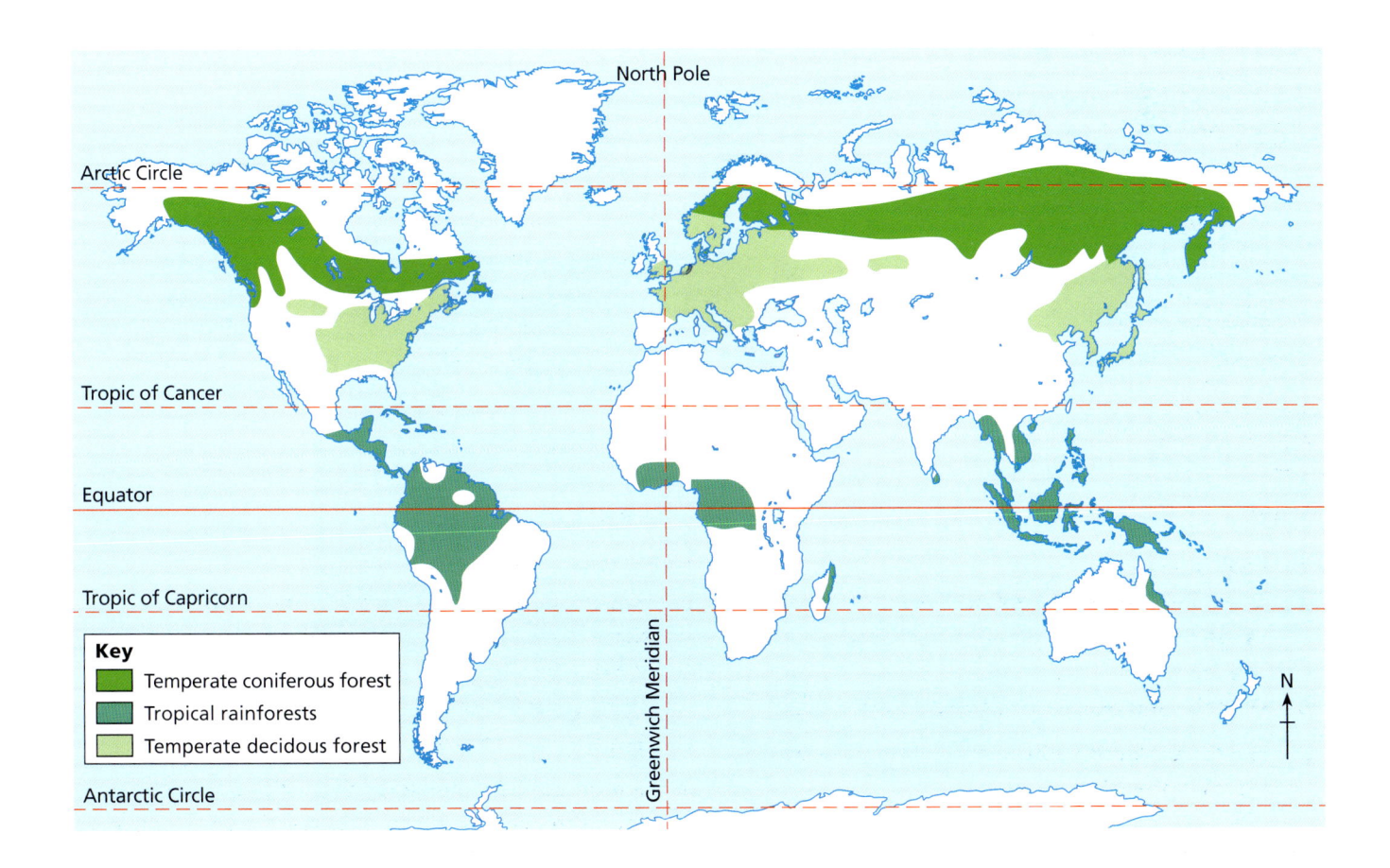

The natural world

Figure 4.22 Diagram of tropical rainforest

How have trees in the tropical rainforest adapted to the natural environment?

Figure 4.22 shows that a tropical rainforest has five separate layers. The vegetation has had to adapt to constant high temperatures and heavy rainfall. There are over 1,000 species of trees which must compete with each other to reach the sunlight. The tallest trees (the emergents) can grow to 50 metres in height. Their need to grow tall results in a tendency to straight trunks and few branches. The largest trees are anchored to the ground by buttress roots (see Figure 4.24) which the trees need as support because the soil is quite shallow in a rainforest and cannot support a deep root system. The main tree or canopy layer is typically 35 to 40 metres high and provides a dense unbroken cover. Lianas, which are vine-like plants, climb around the trees to reach the sunlight. The canopy receives most of the heavy rainfall so the leaves have adapted with drip tips that allow the water to run off the leaves. It is very dark under the main canopy and plants growing here have had to adapt to the lack of light, with the result that large frond-like leaves are common. There is very little vegetation at ground level due to the lack of sunlight: as little as one per cent of the sun reaches the forest floor. Only bacteria and fungi thrive here to rapidly rot the fallen leaves. However, near rivers or clearings where sunlight can penetrate, a dense undergrowth of ferns and shrubs develop.

Figure 4.23 Temperate coniferous forest

The natural world

How have trees in the taiga adapted to the natural environment?

The forests consist of conifers such as spruce, Scots pine and Douglas fir, growing to heights in excess of 30 metres. Each forest usually contains only one main type of tree and ground vegetation is limited because it is very dark and the soil is very acidic.

There are a number of ways in which temperate coniferous trees have adapted to the environment:
- The trees are evergreen (keep their leaves throughout the year). This allows them to photosynthesise when temperatures rise above 3 °C.
- Leaves are needle shaped and therefore have a small surface area and are waxy. Both of these adaptations reduce moisture lost by transpiration. This is important as these trees grow in low rainfall areas, often less than 500 mm per year.
- The conical shape of the trees gives them stability in high winds, common in these areas.
- Bendy trunks also protect them in high winds as they will not snap.
- The branches slope downwards to stop them breaking from the heavy snow which might collect on them.
- The seeds are protected in cones.
- The trees have wide, spreading roots to hold them in the shallow soil. The soil is shallow because of the slow decay of leaf matter in cold climates.

Figure 4.24 The Guatemala rainforest

ACTIVITIES

1. Draw a picture of a coniferous tree and add labels to show how it has adapted to the environment.
2. Describe the world's distribution of temperate deciduous forests. Use an atlas to help you.
3. Why are trees in the tropical rainforest so tall?

Case Study: PAPUA NEW GUINEA

Figure 4.25 Logging destruction

Papua New Guinea is located in the eastern half of the island of New Guinea and includes the surrounding islands. It is the last major island in a string of islands stretching from south-east Asia into the Pacific Ocean. The islands are surrounded by coral reefs and the land is covered in tropical rainforest. It is the third largest area of rainforest in the world. It is a very rich ecosystem with 9,000 species of plants, 250 species of mammals and 700 species of birds, including parrots, kingfishers and cockatoos. So far only 4 national parks have been created, including Varirata and McAdam. Greenpeace is working to have more of the country designated as national parks.

The population of 4.5 million is spread out around the country, with a concentration of approximately 750,000 in the capital Port Moresby. The majority of the population comprises subsistence farmers living in their tribal communities in the rainforest. This means that it is difficult to provide services to the population. Adult literacy rates are estimated at 70 per cent, although this is much lower in rural areas. There are 12,500 people per doctor although, again, this is higher in rural areas. A very small percentage of the country's GDP is spent on these areas.

For many years the world's community has been concerned about the exploitation of the tropical rainforests. The situation in Papua New Guinea mirrors those that are occurring in most countries with this rich resource. In 1996 the prime minister of Papua New Guinea Sir Julius Chan instigated a National Forest Plan in an attempt to legalise the logging that was going on in the forests and to show to the world that the country was in control of its forest resource. The plan was criticised by non-governmental organisations (NGOs) because:

- it prioritised the interests of industrial logging over the wishes of the local communities,
- it did not include conservation areas which had already been set up,
- it ignored the ideas that local landowners might have for the development of the land.

The plan allowed loggers to clear cut the forest as long as they had a permit from the government. Since then there have been many problems in the country as the loggers try to clear the forest and local groups attempt to stop them. In other areas of the country, NGOs have started to work with local community groups to manage the forest resource sustainably. Some areas of the forest are being conserved, although there have been many conflicts with the logging companies over particular areas of land.

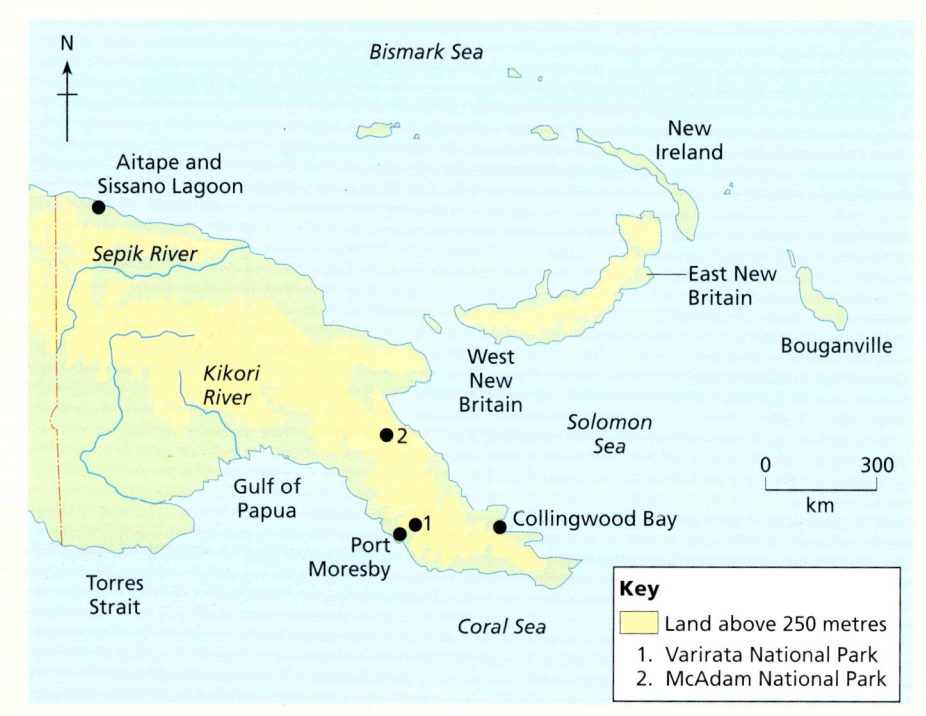

Figure 4.26 Map of Papua New Guinea to show case studies

Key
- Land above 250 metres
1. Varirata National Park
2. McAdam National Park

> **Conservation:** to manage the environment in such a way that it will be protected from change.
> **Sustainable development:** the development of an area using techniques and approaches that will help to preserve the environment for the future.
> **Exploitation:** when the environment is used in such a way that it is destroyed and will be of no use to future generations.

Figure 4.27 Definition of terms

How is the rainforest in Papua New Guinea being exploited?

The government of Papua New Guinea has mapped the rainforest and sells the logging rights to certain areas to transnational companies. The landowners are not consulted and are compelled to agree with the government's decisions. They are paid very little for giving up their right to the forest, for example, in July 1996 landowners were receiving 10 Kina per m³ while loggers sold the timber for 160 Kina per m³ (2 kina = £1). Many examples of this type of exploitation occur every year. Two other examples of the exploitation of rainforests and their communities are:

Aitape, Sanduan Province, West Sepik

In 1996 the government issued a timber authority (the right to clear the forest) to a Pia-Damansara, a joint venture company 85 per cent owned by a Malaysian company (Damansara) and 15 per cent owned by a local landowning company (Pia). The area to be felled was 5,000 hectares of rainforest just inland from Aitape. The intention was to clear-cut the forest and then to grow oil palm. The problem is that oil palm requires fertile soil and, once cleared, the rainforest soils are quickly leached of their nutrients which means that growing oil palm was not going to be very successful. The scheme started and approximately 1,000 hectares were cleared before there was a slump in the world market for hardwood logs. In 1998 the felling stopped and it seems unlikely to start again.

Sissano Lagoon

To the west of Aitape there is an area with a high priority for marine bio-diversity. It is also an important fishing ground for prawns and has a very fragile coral reef ecosystem. In 1996 the Lou Oil Palm Project was planned for its catchment area. This project involved moving the local Sissano community inland so that their tribal lands could be cleared for oil palm. This was both socially and environmentally unacceptable. The forest will be lost and the development of the catchment area of the lagoon will affect sediment levels which, in time, will kill the coral reefs.

Is the rainforest in Papua New Guinea being sustainably developed?

Many countries around the world have given aid to Papua New Guinea in an attempt to develop the country without destroying its rainforest. The projects have all had one thing in common: their commitment to sustainable development of the rainforest resource.

Figure 4.28 Logging operation at ground level

PAPUA NEW GUINEA – continued

Kikori Basin, Gulf Province 1993–2000

In the early 1990s Chevron Inc. discovered oil in the Kikori Basin area. A pipeline was built through the area and oil began to be exported in 1992. The company proposed a partnership with the Kutubu Joint Venture Project which was already working with the local community to protect the wide biodiversity of the Kikori Basin. The project also aimed to help local people to establish sustainable development that will not only protect the environment but also allow them to use the resources. The areas that are to be sustainably managed are: ecologically sound agriculture, such as the sale of butterflies, community based forestry, fish farming, nature based tourism, managing conserved areas and cottage industries. Technical assistance and training for local communities was also provided. As a result the lives of the 10,000 villagers and the environment in the area has improved.

Collingwood Bay Community Land Care Project, Oro Province 1996–2003

The aims of this project are to protect the natural and cultural heritage of the Collingwood Bay area. The idea is to help the local community (mainly the Maisin ethnic group) to plan for sustainable development. As this area is already a tourist destination, one of the ideas is to develop ecotourism.

Another idea is to develop the cottage industries. Tapa cloth production is already established and will be developed, although production will be kept to a small scale. Agriculture will also be developed, in particular nut harvesting. Greenpeace has already assisted the Maisin by developing markets in the USA for their cloth and artwork. The inhabitants have been given aid and technical assistance to start the projects.

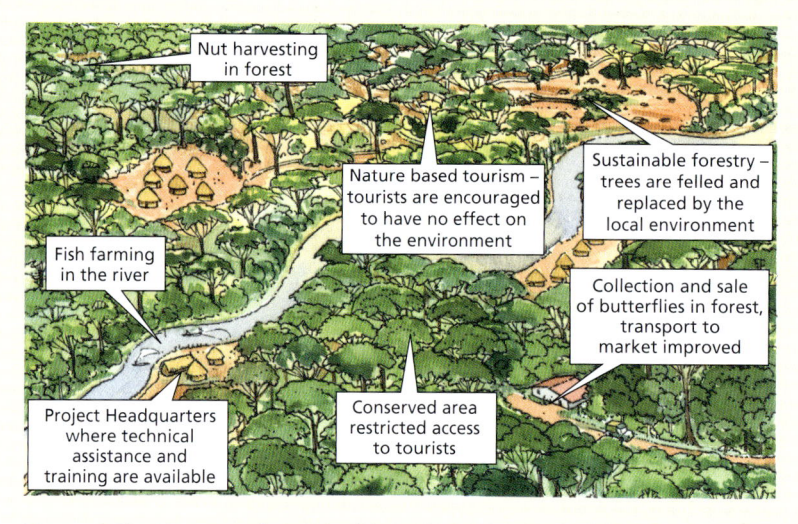

Figure 4.29 Diagram of sustainable techniques

How is the rainforest in Papua New Guinea being conserved?

One way in which the rainforests in Papua New Guinea are being conserved is through the development of ecotourism in areas like the rainforests of Crater Mountain. The Crater Mountain

Figure 4.30 Virgin rainforest at Crater Mountain

Wildlife Management Area was set up in the early 1990s and covers 2,600 square kilometres. Within this area there are 220 species of birds and 85 mammal species. Although the area at present has a low population density, it is threatened by activities such as logging, mining and oil drilling. By declaring the area a wildlife management area, it is hoped that the government will respect the environment and not grant any timber or mineral authorities. The project is establishing locally owned and run ecotourism businesses which provide guides and ecolodges for visitors interested in experiencing a nature-based holiday. The project has had to overcome a number of problems. The local communities have many rivalries and before the project began there was much fighting in the area between different clans. The project has helped to stop these conflicts. The other main problem, given that the guides must be able to speak to the tourists, is the level of illiteracy in the area. Resident field staff are available at present to help overcome this problem.

The natural world

'The forest is our livelihood. It is our inheritance from our forefathers.'
— Maisin landowner

'I cannot see what all the fuss is about; the new plantation will provide the area with lots of jobs.'
— Solicitor for the developers

'We are the rightful owners of the land. The lease is not worth the paper it is signed on because none of the elders of the tribe have signed it.'
— Tribal elder

'Timber companies quite often use devious methods to gain the rights to tribal lands which are being destroyed all over the country. If the Maisin win this case then other tribes might take their conflicts to court.'
— Conservationist from Greenpeace

'The sheer size of the country and the remoteness of some of the areas makes it easy for the timber companies to exercise their rights with a piece of paper that many of the remote tribes do not understand.'
— Environmentalist for WWF for Nature

'We have the correct authorisation from the government and a lease for this area of land, so surely we have the right to chop down the trees? It is our land now according to the government.'
— Malaysian logging company

Figure 4.31 People's opinions on Collingwood Bay

What conflicts have occurred as a result of the exploitation of the rainforest in Papua New Guinea?

Collingwood Bay, 1999

The Maisin have always defended their culture and land. In the past it was with spears; today, they are going to the court. A Malaysian company that intends to develop the tribal lands of the Maisin, claim that they have rights to clear cut the forest and grow palm oil. The Maisin do not recognise the developer's right to their land. They have taken the case to court and, for the present, the clearance has been halted. The case is dragging on, however, and the Maisin are running out of money. Remember that this is one of the areas that is being sustainably developed with the help of Greenpeace. Here are some of the viewpoints on the conflict.

Has the government of Papua New Guinea implemented sustainable policies?

In November 1999 Sir Mekere Morauta, the prime minister of Papua New Guinea, announced in his budget speech for 2000 that there would be no more logging licences, extensions to licences or conversions of licences granted. All existing licenses would be reviewed to ensure that practices being followed were sustainable. His comments were welcomed by all the main conservation groups in the world, including Greenpeace and WWF for Nature.

Unfortunately, carrying out these intentions in such a large country with such poor infrastructure was problematic. By May 2000 it seemed obvious that the government was not implementing its policy; at this point the World Bank threatened to withdraw funds from the country if it did not take control of the logging companies. The government immediately set up a review committee, chaired by Robert Igara, that was given three months to report back.

PAPUA NEW GUINEA – continued

A number of new initiatives have now been written into the National Forest Plan:

- Small, medium and large-scale logging operations will be encouraged. They must be owned by many different companies, who all have certified management models.
- Economically sustainable community based forestry will be encouraged as well as landowner-initiated conservation areas.
- As processed logs are worth much more on the world market, ways of processing the logs will be developed in Papua New Guinea rather than selling them unprocessed.

It is hoped that as a result of these new initiatives, the rainforest in Papua New Guinea will be sustainably developed or conserved for use by future generations.

> **Examiner's tip**
> When writing about conflicts, don't forget to name groups of people as well as their particular viewpoints.

ACTIVITIES

Higher

1. What percentage of the population of Papua New Guinea live in the capital?
2. Describe the problems that this creates for the provision of services.
3. What was the National Forest Plan and why was it criticised by NGOs?
4. Explain the difference between the terms 'sustainable development' and 'exploitation'.
5. The Crater Mountain scheme is trying to conserve this part of Papua New Guinea. Explain how.
6. Many conflicts are occurring in Papua New Guinea as local people fight for their land. The Maisin, for example, have taken their battle to court. Working in a group, choose one of the roles in Figure 4.31. Prepare your role for a courtroom scene that highlights the conflicts in the battle.
7. What do you think is going to happen in the next 50 years to the tropical rainforest in Papua New Guinea?

Foundation

1. What do most people do for a living on Papua New Guinea?
2. Where do most of the people live?
3. What percentage of people can read and write?
4. Why did NGOs criticise the National Forest Plan?
5. Match the following terms with their correct definitions.

Term	Definition
conservation	The development of an area using techniques and approaches that will help to preserve the environment for the future.
sustainable development	To manage the environment in such a way that it will be protected from change.
exploitation	When the environment is used in such a way that it is destroyed and will be of no use to future generations.

6. Describe 5 ways in which the rainforest in Papua New Guinea is being sustainably developed.
7. Many conflicts are occurring in Papua New Guinea as local people fight for their land. The Maisin, for example, have taken their battle to court. Working in a group, choose one of the roles in Figure 4.31. Prepare your role for a courtroom scene that highlights the conflicts in the battle.
8. What do you think is going to happen during the next 50 years to the tropical rainforest in Papua New Guinea?

Sample Examination Questions

Higher tier

1 Study the synoptic chart in Figure 4.32. It shows conditions at 12h00 in July.

   a Name the weather system shown on the map.
   (1 mark)

   b What is an isobar? (1 mark)

   c State the current wind speed and direction at B.
   (1 mark)

   d Describe the pattern of pressure and winds over the British Isles. (4 marks)

2 Study the climate graph for Plymouth (Figure 4.15).

   a Comment on the main features of the temperature. Use data in your answer. (3 marks)

   b Give reasons to explain why this graph displays the characteristics of a west European maritime climate. (4 marks)

   c Describe and explain the ways that trees in the taiga (east European continental climate) have adapted to the environment. (6 marks)

   Total 20 marks

Foundation tier

1 Look at the weather map (Figure 4.32). It shows the weather at midday in the summer.

   a Name the weather system shown on the map.
   (1 mark)

   b Cross out the wrong words in the following sentences:

      i An isobar is a line that joins places of equal pressure / rainfall.

      ii This is measured in millilitres / millibars. (1 mark)

   c Find the point marked B on the weather map. State what the weather conditions are at point B.

      i temperature: ii wind speed:
      iii wind direction: iv cloud cover:
      v precipitation: (5 marks)

4 Look at the climate graph for Plymouth (Figure 4.15). Plymouth has a west European maritime climate.

   a What is the maximum temperature at Plymouth?
   (1 mark)

   b What is the minimum temperature at Plymouth?
   (1 mark)

   c What is the temperature range at Plymouth?
   (1 mark)

   d Describe the rainfall at Plymouth. Use data from the graph. (4 marks)

   e Describe and explain the ways that trees in the taiga (temperate coniferous forest) have adapted to the environment. (6 marks)

   Total 20 marks

88 The natural world

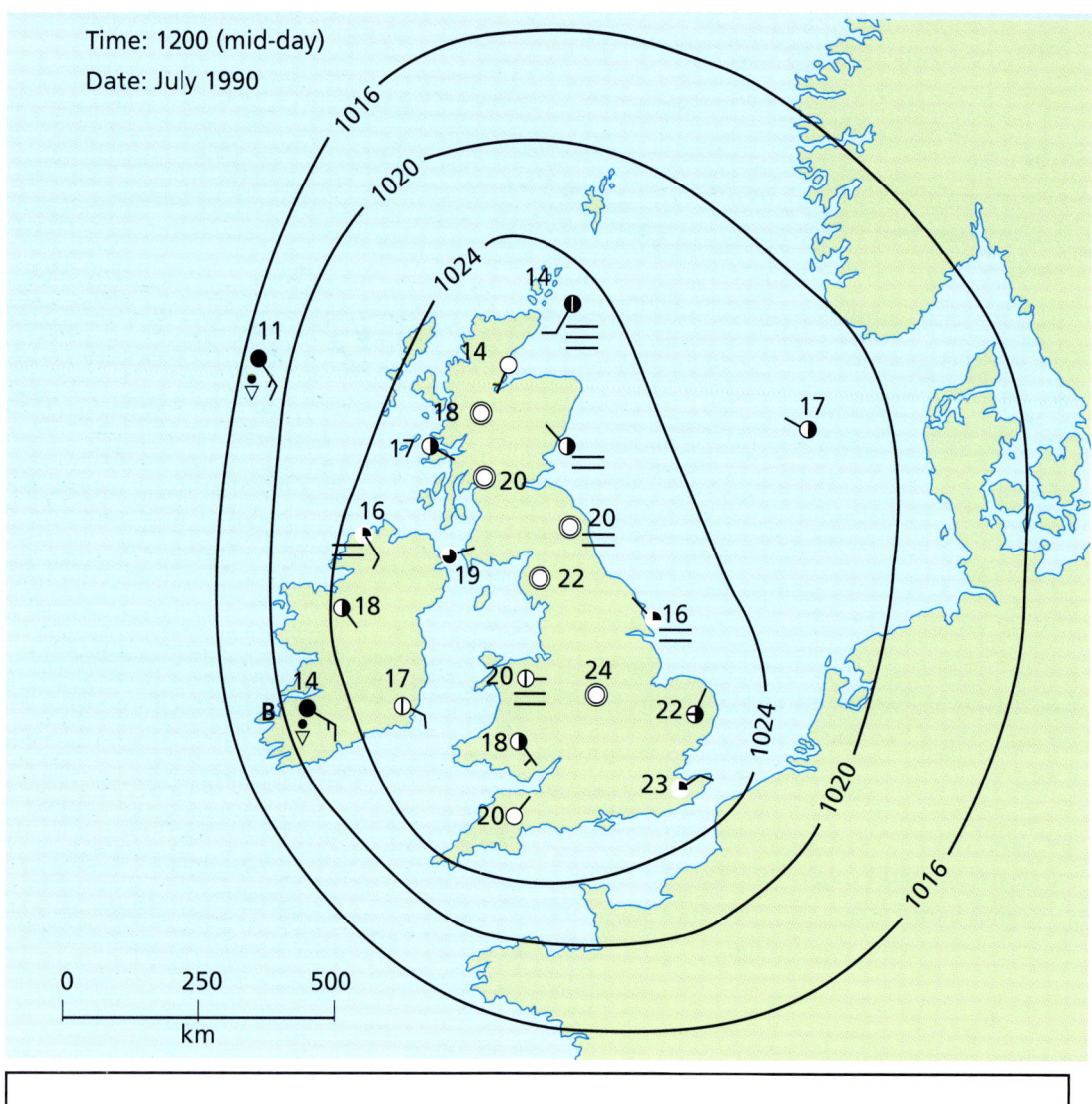

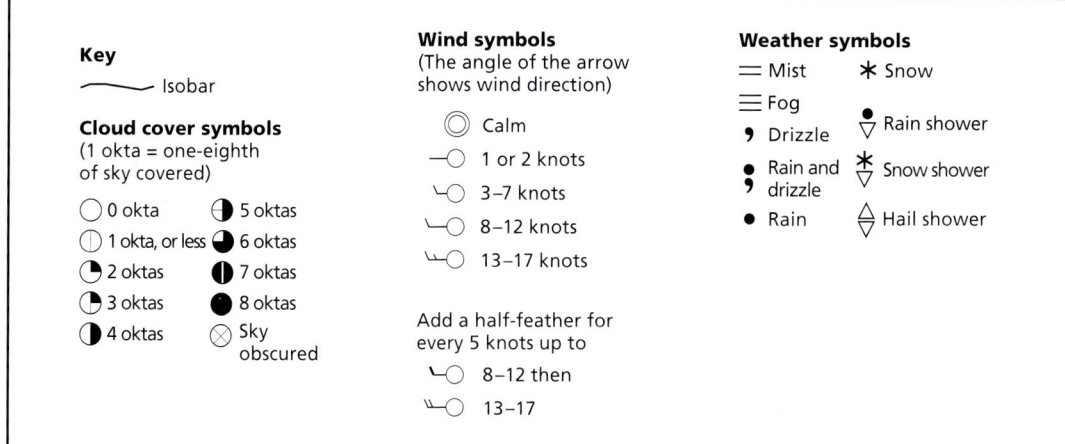

Figure 4.32 Synoptic chart of the British Isles

5 Managing the environment

Coasts are under threat and need to be managed

What causes cliffs to recede?

The coastline of Britain is made up of many different types of rocks which meet the sea in a number of ways: some are parallel to the sea, others lie at right angles to it. Cliffs are made of different rock types. Those made from less resistant rocks, like clay, recede faster than those made from resistant rocks like limestone. Other factors that cause cliffs to recede are the processes that occur on the cliff face, such as weathering and mass movement, and the processes of the sea which attack the foot of the cliff. (The causes of cliff recession are dealt with in more detail in Chapter 1.)

What are the effects of cliff recession?

If there is a settlement on a cliff top, then public awareness of the problems of cliff recession will be high because people's homes or businesses may be at risk. If the land is used for agriculture or leisure activities, the effects of cliff recession are considered less important and less is done in the way of coastal defences. In Figure 5.1, for example, Sue Earl's farm on the Holderness coast has been allowed to fall into the sea because her need for defence was seen to be minimal. Further down the coast, however, the Gas Terminal at Easington has been protected because it supplies large quantities of North Sea Gas to British households.

What are the options for the defence of coastal areas?

The defence of the British coastline has been a cause for concern for a long time. Many people, such as environmentalists and

Figure 5.1 Sue Earl's farm, Holderness coast

taxpayers in inland areas, believe that the coast should not be defended. There are a number of reasons for this:
- Sea levels are rising and inevitably some of the land near the coast will be below sea level in the near future. Would it not be more sensible to allow it to flood now?
- Building sea defences is very costly. As they are not indestructible, this is surely a waste of money?
- The environment that is created is not natural. Is this what we want for our coastline?

Although the sea erodes large areas of the British coastline every year, more is replaced by deposition than is removed. The problem lies in the fact that the areas which are being built up are not usually the areas that have been used by people for industry and settlement. Therein lies the dilemma.

Managing the environment

If we are going to spend millions of pounds defending the British coastline, what sort of coastal defences should we use? There are two options: hard or soft engineering.

Hard engineering options: this includes the traditional sea defences that have been used around the British coast for many years. Examples include sea walls in many different forms, groynes and revetments, newer ideas include rip-rap (rock armour), gabions, sea bees and off-shore reefs.

Soft engineering options: these have been used on the British coast more recently and includes managed retreat, beach nourishment, stabilising dunes and cliff regrading and, of course, doing nothing.

Hard engineering techniques – There are many different hard engineering techniques. The ones below are the most common around the British coasts.

Figure 5.2
Photographs a-d show coastal defences

a recurved sea wall
b groynes
c rip-rap
d gabions

Soft engineering techniques – Today soft engineering techniques are used more frequently around the British coasts.

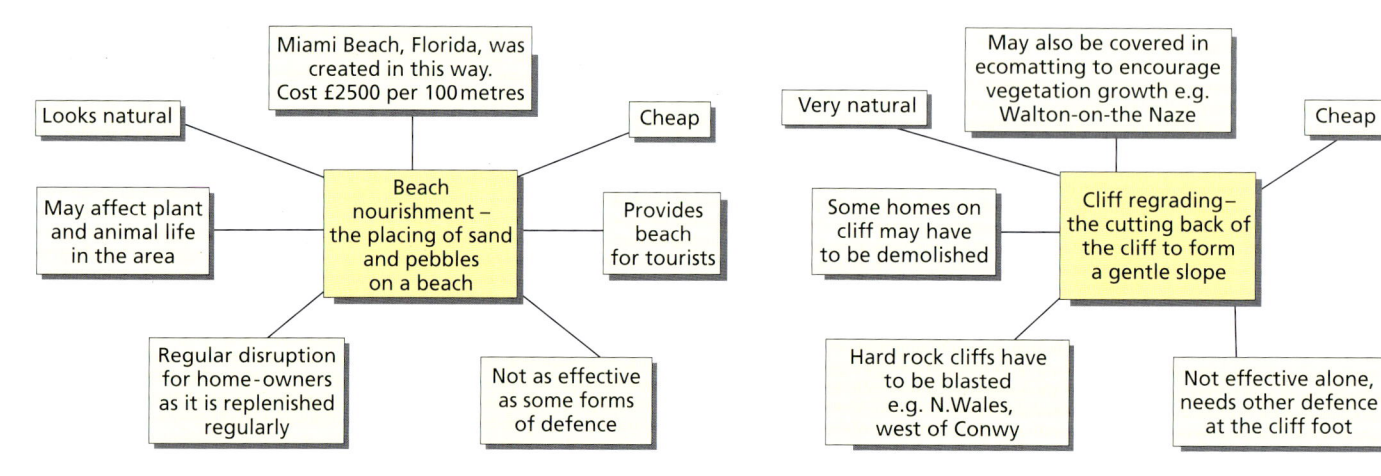

- Looks natural
- May affect plant and animal life in the area
- Miami Beach, Florida, was created in this way. Cost £2500 per 100 metres
- Cheap
- Provides beach for tourists
- Regular disruption for home-owners as it is replenished regularly
- Not as effective as some forms of defence

Beach nourishment – the placing of sand and pebbles on a beach

- Very natural
- May also be covered in ecomatting to encourage vegetation growth e.g. Walton-on-the-Naze
- Cheap
- Some homes on cliff may have to be demolished
- Hard rock cliffs have to be blasted e.g. N.Wales, west of Conwy
- Not effective alone, needs other defence at the cliff foot

Cliff regrading – the cutting back of the cliff to form a gentle slope

Figure 5.3 Spidergrams of soft engineering options

Managing the environment 91

Figure 5.4 *(left)* Swanage 1997

Figure 5.5 *(right)* Swanage 2000

ACTIVITIES

Higher

1 Explain the factors that cause cliffs to recede.
2 Why are settlements defended while agricultural land is left to the actions of the sea?
3 Some people are for coastal protection schemes and others are against. Explain these different opinions.
4 Copy and complete Table 1 to explain the advantages and disadvantages of coastal protection schemes.
5 Study the advantages and disadvantages of the coastal protection schemes in Figures 5.2 and 5.3.
a Do a cost-benefit analysis of the different techniques.
b Which, in your opinion, would be the best for: environmental reasons, economic reasons and social reasons.
6 Study the photographs of the coast at Swanage taken in 1997 and 2000 respectively (Figures 5.4 and 5.5).
a Spot the differences between the two photographs.
b Part of the cliff has been covered with a brown material. What is this brown material and why has it been put there?
c Explain what happened to this part of the cliff by the year 2000.
d Describe the other cliff protection techniques that are visible in the photographs. Why do you think that the cliff has been protected in different ways?

Foundation

1 Cliffs made of soft rock recede more quickly than cliffs made of hard rock. Why?
2 Which of the following land uses in coastal areas do you think should be protected? Give a reason for your answer:
farmland, housing, industry, golf courses, parks.
3 Would each group of people named below agree or disagree with coastal defences?
a home owners on a cliff,
b home owners inland,
c environmentalists,
d coastal defence construction firms.
4 Copy and complete Table 1 to show the advantages and disadvantages of coastal protection schemes.
5 Study the photographs of the coast at Swanage taken in 1997 and 2000 respectively (Figures 5.4 and 5.5).
a Spot the differences between the two photographs.
b Part of the cliff has been covered with a brown material. What is this brown material and why has it been put there?
c Explain what happened to this part of the cliff by the year 2000.
d Describe the other cliff protection techniques that are visible in the photographs. Why do you think that the cliff has been protected in different ways?

Table 1

Type of scheme	Hard: sea walls	Hard: groynes	Hard: rip-rap	Soft: beach nourishment
Advantages				
Disadvantages				

Case Study: RECESSION AT WALTON-ON-THE-NAZE

The Naze is a promontory that stretches northwards from the edge of Walton. It separates the inlet of Walton channel to the west and from the North Sea to the east. Part of the Naze is made up of a hill which is being eroded by the sea so that high cliffs, up to 20 metres, rise directly from the beach.

In 1977 large defence work, including a sea wall and breakwaters, were undertaken on the southern part of the Naze to protect the cliff-top properties.

The unprotected length of coastline runs from the tower breakwater northwards for approximately 1,000 metres to the start of the Anglian Water Authority flood wall. The cliffs decrease in height northwards from 20 metres to 4 metres. The cliffs are made up of sand and gravel deposits laid on top of London clay and it is because of this geological arrangement that the cliffs are so unstable. Water percolates through the permeable sand and gravel until it reaches the impermeable London clay. The water acts as a lubricant, causing the upper sections of the cliff to slip seawards. The sea is also eroding the lower sections of the cliff, leading to even greater instability.

The following two photographs clearly show the difference between the protected and unprotected cliffs. The protected cliff is stable and well vegetated with many varieties of shrubs and trees, such as hawthorn and alder. In contrast, the unprotected cliff has very little vegetation.

By looking at the 'pill boxes' on the beach, it is easy to see how rapid erosion has been at the Naze. These pill boxes were built in the Second World War to act as lookout positions and were placed on top of the cliffs. They are now about 35 metres from the cliff, a distance that must have been eroded since 1945.

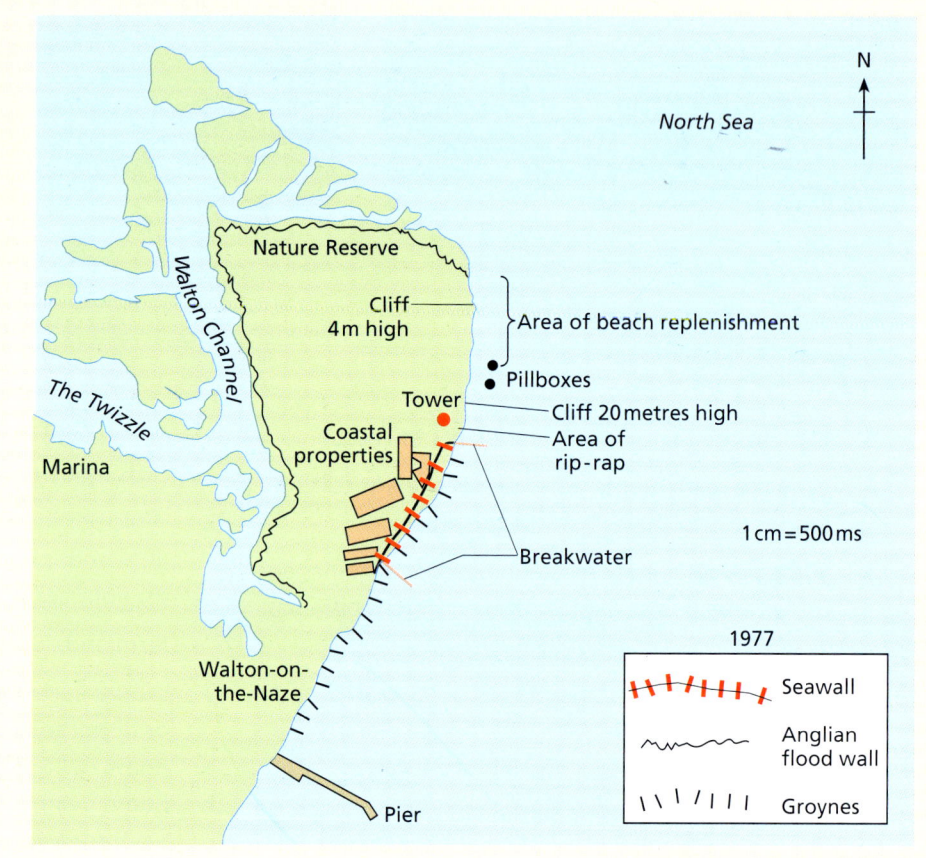

Figure 5.6 Map of Walton-on-the-Naze

Figure 5.7 Walton-on-the-Naze tower and cliff slumping

A group of students have taken measurements between 1994 and 2000 from the tower (seen on Figure 5.7) to the edge of the cliffs.

This shows that erosion is still occurring rapidly. The large amount of cliff lost in 1996 was due to a big slippage in September that year which removed the cliff edge footpath.

Year	Distance to cliff (m)
1994	71.80
1995	71.03
1996	69.52
1997	65.03
1998	63.64
1999	62.70
2000	62.20

Managing the environment

In the past the northern part of the Naze has not been protected because the Department of the Environment will only provide financial assistance if property is being threatened. Recently, however, engineering work has taken place. In November 1998 the local council paid £167 000 for 300 tons of Leicester granite to be placed around the tower breakwater. It is hoped that this rip-rap will stop the existing structure from being further undermined. In addition, millions of tons of sand and gravel from the dredging of Harwich harbour in 1999 have been deposited in front of part of the cliffs. This deposit extends the cliffs 25 metres seaward at a height of about 2 metres. Although this is being washed away initially, it is hoped that the beach will become stable and provide protection for the cliff.

The Naze Protection Society has also been set up and is bidding for funding from the National Lottery. A spokesperson for the Society said, 'We can't put the cliffs back where they were 50 years ago, but let us at least leave a legacy for future generations.'

Figure 5.8 Protected cliff

Figure 5.9 Unprotected cliff and WWII pill boxes

Figure 5.10 Rip rap

ACTIVITIES

1. Why are the cliffs at Walton receding so quickly?
2. The protected cliff has vegetation growing on it and the unprotected cliff does not. Explain why.
3. How much closer is the tower to the cliff edge in 2000 than it was in 1994? What is the average annual rate of erosion?
4. The photograph of the pill box at Walton (Figure 5.9) was taken in 2000. Draw a labelled sketch showing what the cliffs looked like at the end of the Second World War in 1945.
5. Using the information in the case study, describe how the area on the map (Figure 5.6) has been managed.

River floods are the result of human and physical factors

What causes rivers to flood?

The course of a river will flow through many different environments, both human and physical. These environments will have an effect on the river and determine whether it will flood or not.

There are both human and physical causes of flooding.

Physical	Human
If there are large amounts of rain day after day, the water will saturate the ground and flow more quickly into the river.	If vegetation has been removed, then there is less interception and water will move to the river more quickly.
During a cloudburst in a thunderstorm, the rain droplets are so large and fall so quickly that there is no time for the water to sink into the ground. Water runs very quickly into the river and causes flooding.	Similarly, if there is a town on the flood plain, storm drains will allow water to move into the river at a greater speed and so make flooding more likely.
If there is a sudden rise in temperature, a rapid thaw can happen. Rivers are unable to cope with the amount of water and flood.	Global warming may lead to the melting of polar ice caps and a rise in sea levels, flooding low-lying coastal areas.
River beds that have become silted up make the channel smaller and more likely to flood.	Dams may burst which will cause excess water in river channels and flooding of large areas.

Easter floods in the Midlands, 1998

Two people drowned and others were missing after torrential rain caused flooding across central England. The storm has cost £15m of damage and more than 1,500 people have had to be evacuated from their homes. A queue 40 miles long developed on the M40 as flood waters covered the road. A number of people are missing, including a 14-year-old boy who was swept from a van as it went off the road near Leamington Spa, Warwickshire.

Flooding has been particularly severe along the River Avon in Warwickshire, with water levels rising 5 metres in Evesham, which is more than during the great floods in 1947. Leamington Spa was also badly hit with flood waters so deep that only the aerials of cars could be seen. In Banbury the station was flooded and 200 people were forced out of their homes.

What are the effects of river flooding?

The effects of a river flooding are generally assessed in relation to the amount of damage that is caused. If the flood plain is densely populated, then its effects will be greater in terms of loss of property and human life. The newspaper articles show the difference between the effect of river floods on Somalia and the Midlands in the UK.

Figure 5.11 Easter floods

Managing the environment

Flooding in Somalia, November 1997

The United Nations estimates that over 1,265 people have died so far during the floods in Somalia. Up to 200 000 are stranded on diminishing banks of land while others are living in trees, as the worst floods in living memory hit Somalia. Livestock and food supplies have been destroyed; crocodiles and snakes are an added problem. Food aid is arriving from USA in watertight bags, but will it be enough and will it get to the victims who cling to the ever diminishing areas of dry land? Even when the waters recede, there will be little hope for the future, as precious food supplies and seeds have been ruined by the flood.

Figure 5.12 Somalia floods, November 1997

Figure 5.13 River management techniques

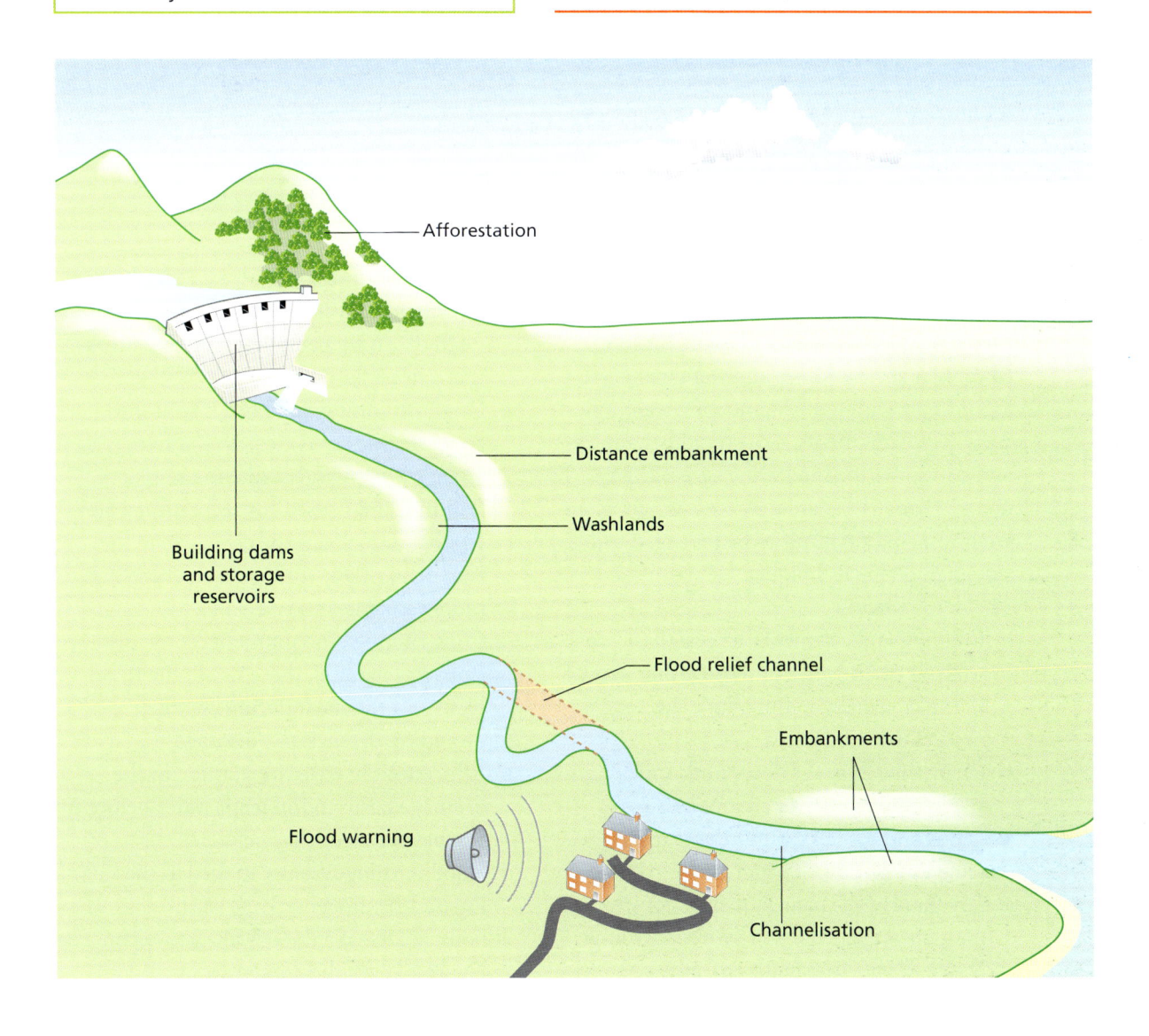

- Afforestation
- Building dams and storage reservoirs
- Distance embankment
- Washlands
- Flood relief channel
- Embankments
- Flood warning
- Channelisation

The effects of flooding can be split into short and long term:

Short term:
- loss of life of both people and livestock from drowning,
- bridges and roads can be washed away, destroying communication links,
- damage to people's homes and belongings due to water,
- lack of food due to crops being washed away,
- drinking water being contaminated by sewage.

Long term:
- dirty drinking water leading to ill health and disease,
- disruption to services such as gas and electricity,
- communication links disrupted which could lead to problems with relief campaigns,
- damage to crops resulting in shortage of food supplies.

Figure 5.14 Hard management techniques

Figure 5.15 Soft engineering techniques

What are the options for the management of rivers?

At one time the management of rivers was just that. Rivers were considered to be separate from their surroundings and were managed accordingly with hard engineering techniques such as embankments, new straight channels and dams. During the 1990s, a great change occurred and rivers are now seen as part of an environment that needs to be managed using soft engineering techniques.

The hard options:
- Building embankments/levees: these are walls or earth banks built on either side of the river, usually in built-up areas to protect the urban area.
- Channelisation: the deepening and straightening of river channels.
- Dams and barriers: built upstream to regulate the flow of water in the river.
- Dry flood relief channels may be constructed: these are only used if there are dangerously high levels of water in the channel.

The soft options:
- Washlands: these are parts of the flood plain that have been designated as areas that can be flooded.
- Land use zoning: land use is split into zones. Land that is close to the river is seen as having a low value due to the risk of flooding and is used for recreational areas. Further away from the river, where the land is less likely to flood, it is therefore more valuable and is used for housing.
- Constructing embankments some distance from the channel: these retain the flood plain and the meandering channel, providing defence at a distance.
- Afforestation: trees are planted in the drainage basin to intercept water before it reaches the river channel.
- Flood warning systems: in the UK the Environment Agency (EA) warns householders if a flood is likely to occur. (See Figure 5.16 for the flood warning codes.)

River management in the UK is the responsibility of the Environment Agency (EA) within an integrated catchment plan. It is developing Local Environment Action Plans (LEAPs) that have three main aims: to outline the future for the river basin, to identify conflicts, for example between flood defences and conservation, and to engage the public in debate about the uses of the land. In developing its plans the EA ensures an integrated approach to river basin management, with a particular emphasis on planning for environmental sustainability. This approach has been encouraged by the Rio Earth Summit (Agenda 21) which states that national action programmes for water management should integrate water resources planning with land use planning and other development and conservation activities.

Figure 5.16 Environment Agency flood warning codes

ACTIVITIES

Higher

1. Explain the physical factors that cause rivers to flood.
2. Look at the newspaper articles in the main text. Draw up a table showing the effects of flooding in an MEDC compared to the effects in an LEDC.
3. Draw two spider diagrams, one for hard engineering schemes, the other for soft engineering schemes. Include their advantages and disadvantages.
4. People have different opinions about flood management. Choose either the argument for or against hard engineering schemes and write a letter to *The Times* stating your case.

Foundation

1. Describe three climatic factors that can cause flooding.
2. Look at the comments below, which are taken from the newspaper articles on pages 94 and 95. Draw two spider diagrams labelled MEDC and LEDC. Put the comments around the correct diagrams:
200 000 stranded on earth banks, 1,265 died, problems with crocodiles, £15m damage, only car aerials can be seen, 2 drowned, 200 evacuated, railway stations flooded, food and seeds destroyed.
3. Complete the table below to show the advantages and disadvantages of the different engineering techniques.

Type of technique	Advantages	Disadvantages
Hard: embankments		
Hard: channelisation		
Hard: dams		
Soft: washlands		
Soft: land use zoning		
Soft: afforestation		

Case Study: THE MISSISSIPPI RIVER FLOOD, 1993

The Mississippi River flows through 10 states of the USA, from its source in Minnesota, just south of the Canadian border, to its mouth 6,000 kilometres away in Louisiana. The 1993 Mississippi flood was the most devastating in US history. The Mississippi River at St Louis was above flood stage for 144 days between 1 April and 30 September.

What caused the flood?

Exceptionally heavy rainfall was experienced over a large area of the Mississippi drainage basin during the first half of 1993. North Dakota, Kansas and Iowa received more than double their typical rainfall. Individual storms frequently delivered large downpours that could not be held in local streams. Over 160 mm of rain fell in parts of southern Iowa on the 4 and 5 July, which is over 150 per cent of the average July monthly total. The ground was already saturated with the spring rainfall and when it continued to rain in the summer months, the soil could not absorb the water which consequently ran off into streams.

The unusually heavy rainfall was caused when warm moist air from the Gulf of Mexico met cold dry air from Canada. When the warm Gulf air cooled, it released the moisture it carried as rain. A high pressure system over the south-east USA blocked the movement of this weather system and caused a constant stream of storms over the Midwest states.

The flooding was made worse because 80 per cent of the original wetlands along the river have been drained since 1940. Wetlands act as natural storage reservoirs for floodwaters; they absorb water during heavy rainfall and release it slowly as throughflow. As run-off is reduced, so is the likelihood of flooding. The problem was made worse because the Mississippi flood plain is closely settled (urbanised) which allows little throughflow.

Figure 5.17 Region affected by flooding in 1993

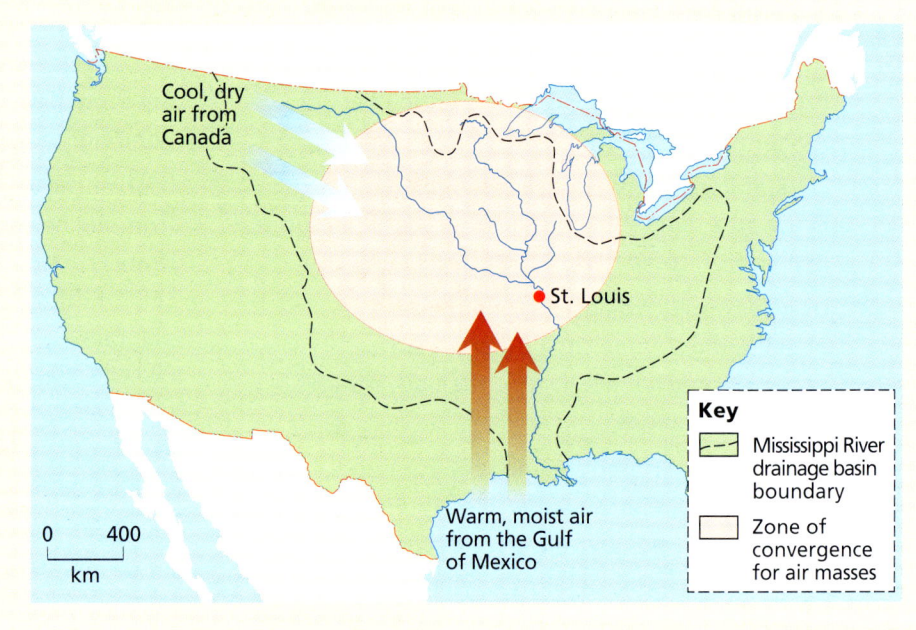

Figure 5.18 Weather conditions which contributed to the Mississippi floods in 1993

What was the damage caused by the 1993 flooding?

The river flooded an area the size of the UK and affected parts of nine states (North Dakota, South Dakota, Nebraska, Kansas, Missouri, Iowa, Wisconsin, Minnesota and Illinois).

Thirty two people lost their lives in the floods and 30 000 people were evacuated. As many as 60 000

Managing the environment 99

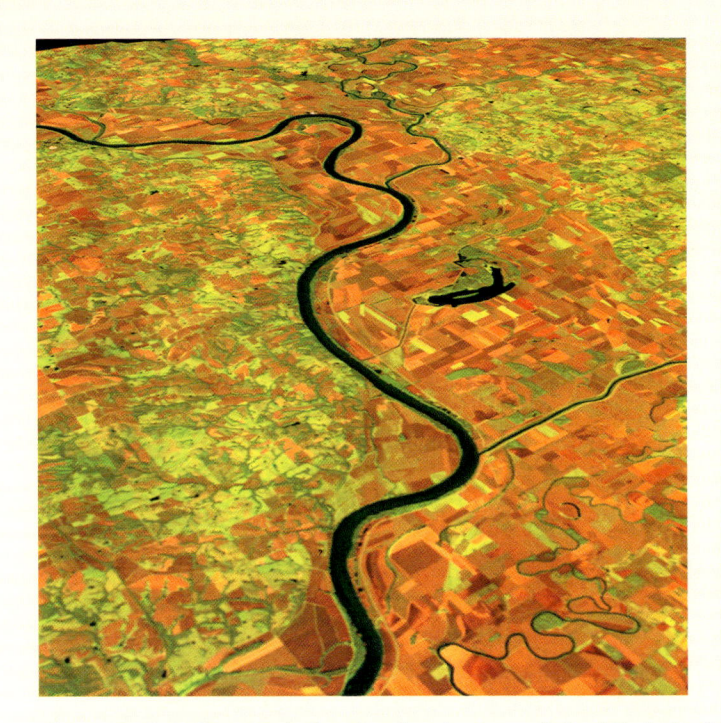

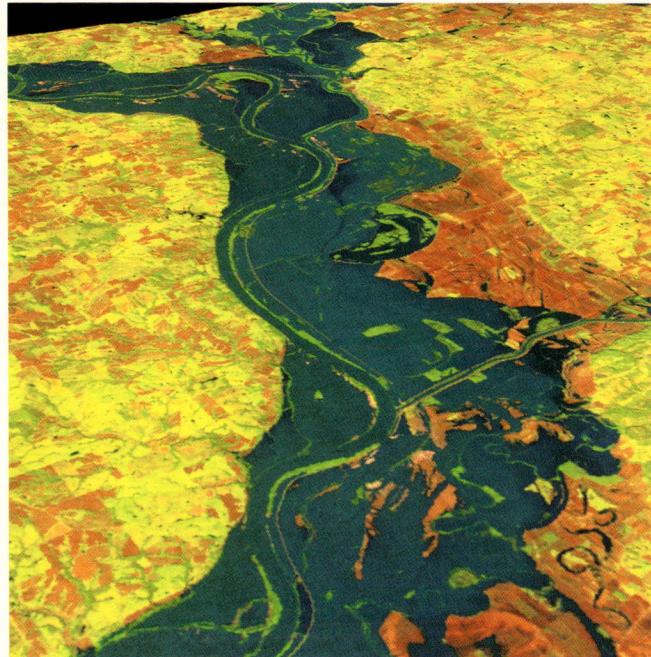

Figure 5.19 Before and after landsat images of the Mississippi flood

homes were destroyed or damaged, causing $10 billion of property damage. Only 10 per cent of residents had flood insurance; fortunately the Federal Emergency Management Agency (FEMA) declared the flood region a disaster area which made all the residents eligible for disaster relief. Four million hectares of farmland were flooded and, with corn production down 10 per cent, great losses were made.

The infrastructure of the Midwest was severely disrupted. St. Louis and Des Moines were the worst affected cities. Des Moines lost its water supply for 19 days. Barge traffic north of St Louis was halted for two months. Barges carry vast amounts of coal, petroleum and grain down the river. The barge owners lost an estimated $1 million per day. Hundreds of miles of roads were closed and most of the road and railway bridges over the river were also closed.

Figure 5.20 The effects of the 1993 flood

ACTIVITIES

1. Describe the location of the Mississippi River.
2. Draw an annotated map to show the extent of the Mississippi flood.
3. Explain the causes of the 1993 flood. Refer to physical and human causes in your answer.
4. What were the effects of the flood on the people living in the affected areas?

Fragile environments require sustainable management

Fragile environments are those in which links in the food chain can be easily damaged, or even destroyed, by human actions. An example is the oil tanker disaster which occurred in January 2001 close to the Galapagos Islands, where the tanker Jessica spilt 250 000 gallons of oil into the ocean. Although disaster was avoided, the oil could have washed up onto rocks and beaches of the Galapagos islands, killing seaweed. This would have caused a break in the food chain. The marine form of the giant iguana lizard which lives on the island of Sante Fe feeds on this seaweed and finding it increasingly difficult to find food, would have died. As the Galapagos Islands are the only place in the world in which these giant iguana lizards are found, the spill might have caused the extinction of a species.

Environments can be damaged by many different human actions. In this section we will discuss agriculture and resource exploitation. In Chapter 7 we will look at how tourism impacts on the environment.

Figure 5.21 Damage to fragile environments

Agriculture

Modern farming techniques have had a major effect on the environment. As farmers use their land more intensively to increase profits, so the environment has suffered:

1. The increased use of fertilisers containing large amounts of nitrogen has led to the process of eutrophication occurring in a number of areas in the UK and other MEDCs (see Figure 5.22). A number of areas, for example Cambridgeshire, have been designated nitrogen sensitive areas where farmers are being encouraged by the use of grants to reduce their use of chemicals.
2. Many farmers spray their crops with pesticides and herbicides to ensure a healthy crop that will bring the maximum price. These chemicals work their way into local ecosystems and kill insects which are essential to the working of local food webs.

3   Farmers in the UK and other MEDCs have removed hedgerows to make more space for crops and enable them to use large machinery. This has caused major problems. The hedgerows were useful windbreaks and provided homes for many animals and insects. If the hedgerows are removed, the wind gathers speed and becomes more powerful. The wind picks up pieces of dry soil and carries it great distances. Removing hedgerows, therefore, can cause soil erosion. Over the last 20 years many fields in East Anglia have lost a great deal of top soil due to this type of erosion.

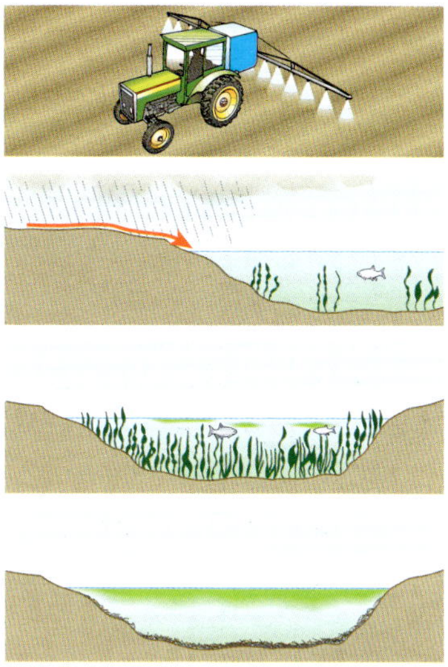

Resource exploitation

The exploitation of resources has had a major effect on environments. As countries become more wealthy, their need for resources has increased. This has destroyed environments, many of which will never recover.

1   The extraction of resources from the environment has had a major effect on the plants and animals which live in those environments. It generally involves the complete destruction of large areas, and there is no attempt to put right some of the damage that has been caused.

   An example is gold mining in the Amazon in Brazil. Problems also occur if there are leakages of toxic materials into local ecosystems during mining. This happened in the Doñana National Park in Spain.

2   Damage to fragile environments can also occur when resources are transported. The Exxon Valdez oil spillage disaster in 1987, for example, damaged large areas of the Alaskan coastline. The disaster also had an impact on fish stocks which, in turn, had a major effect on the local community.

3   Using resources can also damage the environment. When fossil fuels are burnt, they release carbon dioxide into the atmosphere. This increase in the levels of carbon dioxide in the atmosphere is thought to be heating up the world's temperature which could destroy many environments.

   The Chernobyl disaster in 1986 released a cloud of radiation into the world's atmosphere. This caused many environmental problems, locally, nationally and internationally.

If we are not to destroy the environment in which we live, more care must be taken. We need to develop strategies that are more sustainable. This means we should not exploit the environment for short-term gain, but use it sensibly so that its resources are still there for future generations.

Farmer sprays crops with fertiliser.

Rain washes the excess nitrogen into the river.

The nitrogen helps the river plants to grow and algae bloom, which use oxygen.

As the stream becomes covered by algae, other stream life dies due to lack of oxygen.

Figure 5.22 Eutrophication

ACTIVITIES

1   Describe ways in which farmers damage fragile environments.

2   Explain three different ways in which resource exploitation can damage environments.

3   Look at the photographs in Figure 5.21.
a   Describe how each fragile environment has been damaged.
b   Choose two of the photographs and say how the environment in each could be managed in a more sustainable way.

Case Study   THE BROADS: DAMAGE BY AGRICULTURE IN AN MEDC

The Broads are situated in eastern England in the counties of Norfolk and Suffolk. The area covers 303 square km with over 200 km of navigable waterways. The Broads are Britain's only wetland with a status equivalent to that of a national park. The Broads Authority was established in 1989 to manage conservation, recreation and navigation in the Broads. One of its aims must be to try to achieve an appropriate balance between these diverse areas.

What are the causes of damage to the Broads?

The damage suffered by this fragile environment comes from a number of different sources. The main contributors are:
- agriculture, both through eutrophication and irrigation
- sewage disposal
- tourism

When fertilisers are spread on the fields, some of the nitrates are washed by rain into streams and ditches and gradually work their way into the Broads. The increase in nitrates causes the growth of river plants which encourages algae bloom. This uses up oxygen and so life in the river or on the Broad dies. The problem is worse in Norfolk where the flat land causes the rivers to move slowly and so drop a lot of nitrate-rich sediment which comes from the surrounding, intensively cultivated land. An example is the Limpenhoe meadows in the Lower Yare. This unimproved fen-land is being polluted by agriculture, resulting in a decline in the diversity of the species. Barton Broad, the second largest of the broads, has also suffered extensive damage through agricultural pollution. Both the number of fish species and the age of the fish have declined, as have the variety of wildfowl.

Agriculture is also to blame for the low river levels. Farmers use the water to irrigate their crops because the rainfall in this area is low (only 625 mm annually). A typical 500 hectare arable farm would require approximately 8 million gallons of extra water a year. Sewage adds to the nutrient enrichment of the Broads and has caused a significant loss in water life.

The majority of the Broads are open to public navigation and congestion is a problem in the summer months. The main problem caused by the boats is erosion of the river banks. The resulting boat wash has caused a loss of vegetation. There has been a noticeable decline in fringing reed plants, especially around Barton Broad.

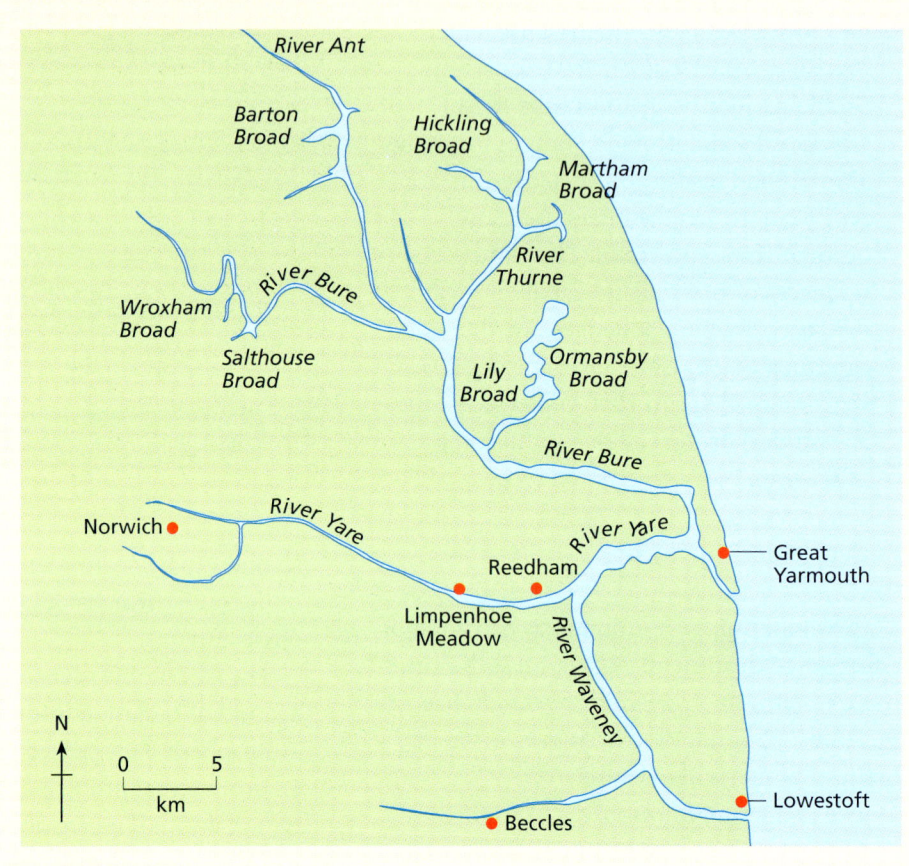

Figure 5.23 Map of the Norfolk Broads

Figure 5.24 River bank protection measure

How have these problems been managed?

1. Additional equipment has been installed in sewage treatment works to remove the phosphates from the sewage.
2. Farmers in nitrate sensitive areas are being more closely monitored. The move away from guaranteed prices to arable area payments should also help to extend farming activities (see Chapter 3). Grants have been made available for environmentally sensitive farming.
3. Tourism is being monitored by the Broads Authority. They have introduced speed limits to minimise damage to riverside fauna and flora, as well as zone arrangements in sensitive areas. The use of less damaging forms of boating is also being encouraged (speed boats are discouraged in favour of dinghies).
4. The most direct management is the restoration of Barton Broad. This is part of the Clear Water 2000 scheme. Barton Broad, on the River Ant, has been severely affected by decades of nutrient enrichment from phosphates and nitrates. This has led to the growth of algae, loss of water plants and a serious decline in the wildlife in the broad. The broad was murky and lifeless and mud had built up on the bottom, making it difficult to boat across. The scheme should return the broad to its (almost) original state. There is a range of work to be done at Barton, all of which will contribute to the success of the project, and it should be completed by April 2001.

- The whole broad is to be suction-dredged to remove 300 000 cubic metres of nutrient-rich mud.
- Biomanipulation is being used on part of the broad to balance the ecology of the water. (This is when small fish are removed in favour of the naturally occurring water flea.)
- The reed swamp fringe on the edge of the broad is being restored.
- Pleasure hill, a small island on the broad which had been almost eroded by motor boats, is being rebuilt.
- New facilities are being developed to provide information, education and access for tourists, including a walkway and boat trip.

This project has been funded mainly by a grant for over £2 million from the Millennium Commission.

ACTIVITIES

Higher

1. Why are the Norfolk Broads in eastern England so important?
2. Explain the process of eutrophication. Use diagrams in your answer.
3. Describe the problems that are faced by the Norfolk Broads.
4. Construct a management plan for the Norfolk Broads. Use Table 1 to help you. You should have a strategy for all the problems described in question 3.
5. People have different opinions about the management of fragile environments like the Broads. Discuss these opinions.

Foundation

1a. Where are the Norfolk Broads?
 b. Why are they being protected?
2. Farmers are causing problems to the Broads. One of these is eutrophication. Draw a series of diagrams to show the process of eutrophication.
3. The Broads are being damaged in a number of ways. Describe two.
4. How are farmers being encouraged to use fewer chemicals?
5. Describe how Barton Broad is being managed.
6. Tourists cause a number of problems to the Norfolk Broads. How are these problems being managed?

Table 1

Problem	Strategy	Timescale	Monitoring

Case Study: DESERTIFICATION IN THE SAHEL

Desertification is the process whereby a combination of human and climatic factors change fertile farming land into unproductive desert. It is a global problem affecting all the continents, with the exception of Antarctica, to varying degrees. About 3.6 billion hectares of the world's land surface area (a landmass equivalent to the size of India) has been affected by desertification. The lives of approximately 300 million people have been affected by desertification.

What causes desertification?
Climatic factors
1. Droughts (periods of below average rainfall) have lasted for many years in certain parts of the world. Only once in the last three decades of the twentieth century was the annual rainfall in the Sahel greater than the long-term average.
2. High temperatures cause a high rate of evapotranspiration and, therefore, a high rate of moisture loss from soils. Scientists believe that increasing amounts of dust in the atmosphere prevent air from rising freely to form convection clouds.
3. Rainfall is infrequent and intense. Heavy showers cause soil erosion. In these areas, rainfall is not spread evenly throughout the year. Timbuktu in Mali receives 70 per cent of its annual rainfall in just two months.

Human factors
1. Overgrazing occurs where animal herds are too large. The cattle graze continually on the same piece of land, eating not only the grass but also the roots which means that the grass is unable to re-grow. The land is not being sustainably managed.
2. As populations increase, overcultivation (the continual use of the soil leading to loss of fertility) occurs.
3. A growing population requires more fuel wood; this leads to deforestation of the land which causes the soil to become more vulnerable to erosion.

The Sahel in Africa
This is an area of the world that has been seriously affected by desertification. It is a belt running across Africa south of the Sahara desert and includes the countries of Senegal, Mauritania, Burkina Faso, Mali, Niger, Chad, Sudan, Ethiopia and Somalia. It takes up an area of 650 000 square kilometres, an area twice the size of Great Britain.

Dalli is a village in Central Niger on the edge of the Sahara Desert. Forty years ago Malam Garba and his brother harvested 700 baskets of millet from their field which was enough to provide a surplus for both families. The village was surrounded by many varieties of shrubs and trees in which they could hunt antelope, monkey and squirrel. The villagers did not need to cut down trees for firewood because enough dead wood was available.

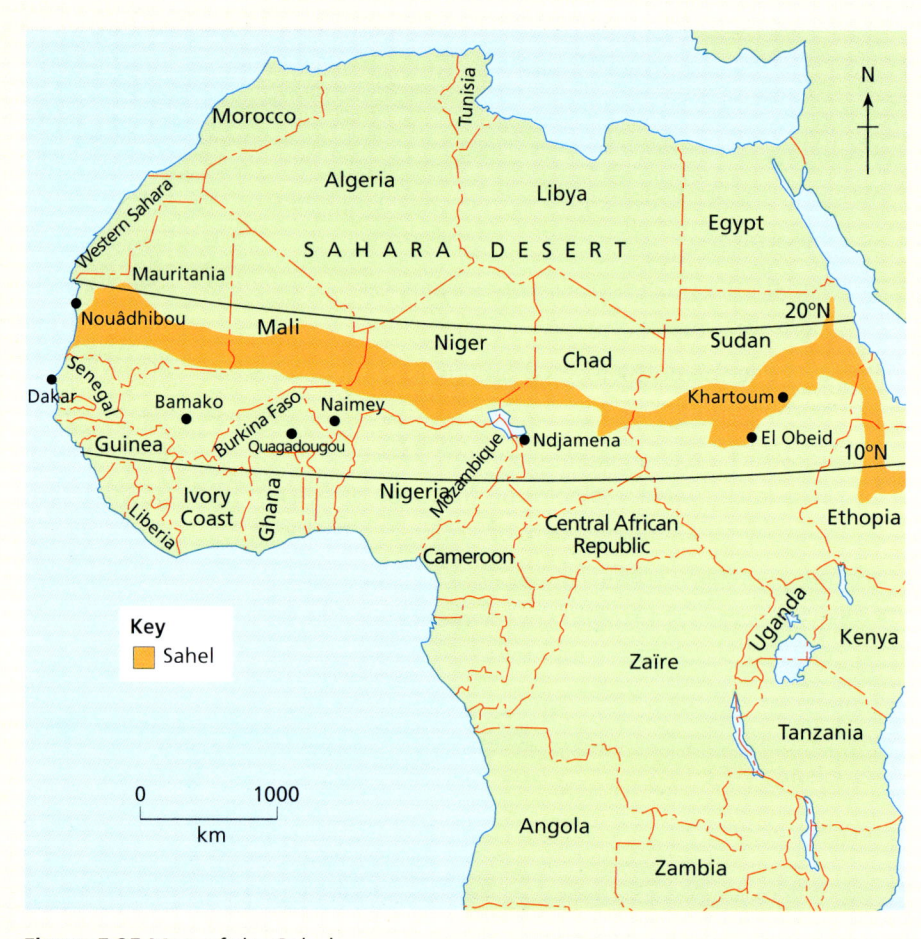

Figure 5.25 Map of the Sahel

Managing the environment   105

Figure 5.26 Desertification in the Sahel

Nowadays, the wind easily erodes the soil because there is little vegetation and the landscape is brown and desolate for most of the year. The rain is lighter and more erratic than it used to be. Frequent daily showers have now ceased. Malam Garba now farms an area 3 times greater than he did 40 years ago, but his harvest of millet is only 1/7 of what it used to be. The low yields have been caused by the destruction of shrub and woodland that used to shelter the crops and contribute to soil fertility.

The director of the National Department of the Environment in Niger said that 250 000 hectares (an area the size of Luxembourg) are being lost each year in Niger through desertification.

Population growth in the Sahel has been identified as a major cause of overgrazing, overcultivation and deforestation. The population of Ethiopia and Sudan increased by over 300 per cent in the second half of the twentieth century, primarily as a result of the decreasing death rate and the high birth rate. Where population density is high, woodland is cleared for crops and the demand for firewood increases. In the countries of the Sahel, over 80 per cent of domestic energy comes from firewood. Firewood for Zinder, a village in Niger, is collected up to 200 km away. In some areas of the Sahel, rural people have been encouraged to grow cash crops for sale in city markets and for export. Growing the same crop year after year, without any rest or fallow years, leads to rapidly declining soil fertility. This has happened in Chad where the government forcibly tripled the area of cotton cultivation.

ACTIVITIES

Higher

1   What are the causes of desertification?
2   Why is the Sahel increasing in size?
3   How is human activity affecting the climate of the Sahel?

Foundation

1   Fill in the boxes to explain the causes of desertification.

Climatic	Human

2   Where is the Sahel?
3   How much of the Sahel is being turned into desert each year?
4   Why are trees cut down in the Sahel?
5   How does population growth lead to desertification?

Examiners tip
Grade A answers will be expected to focus on specific case study material and show a thorough understanding of the interaction between natural and human factors.
Grade C answers will also require some focus on case study material, but not in such depth. They will need to show clear understanding of some climatic and human factors.
Grade F answers will be more generalised and will often not refer to an actual located study, but will make some relevant comments about the theme of the question.

Managing the environment

Case Study: DOÑANA NATIONAL PARK

Doñana National Park is located in Andalucia, southern Spain. It is Europe's largest nature reserve, amounting to 78 000 hectares around the mouth of the Guadalquivir River. The area consists of duneland (*corrales*), marshes (*lucios*) and canals (*canos*). It has a rich variety of wetland flora and fauna, including some species in danger of extinction, such as the Spanish lynx, the Egyptian mongoose and the Imperial eagle, which had been reduced to only 14 pairs in 1999.

The park was declared a Ramsar site in 1990 and a World Heritage site in 1994. It is protected by law from hunting, drainage, forestry plantation and excessive tourist exploitation.

This fragile ecosystem is vulnerable to attack by farming activities. Chemicals used on nearby farms run off into the streams, leading to increased growth of algae and destruction of the local waterplants. In 1986 the uncontrolled use of pesticides led to the poisoning of 30 000 birds. Agricultural development to the north of the park has diverted some of the natural canals for irrigation. If this carries on unchecked, it could lead to large areas of the park drying up.

In 1991 the park was threatened by the proposed construction of a 32 000-bed holiday resort on its borders, but the development was successfully contested by environmentalists. Tourist development continues to be a problem, however, as developers are always searching for new areas away from the overdeveloped Costa del Sol.

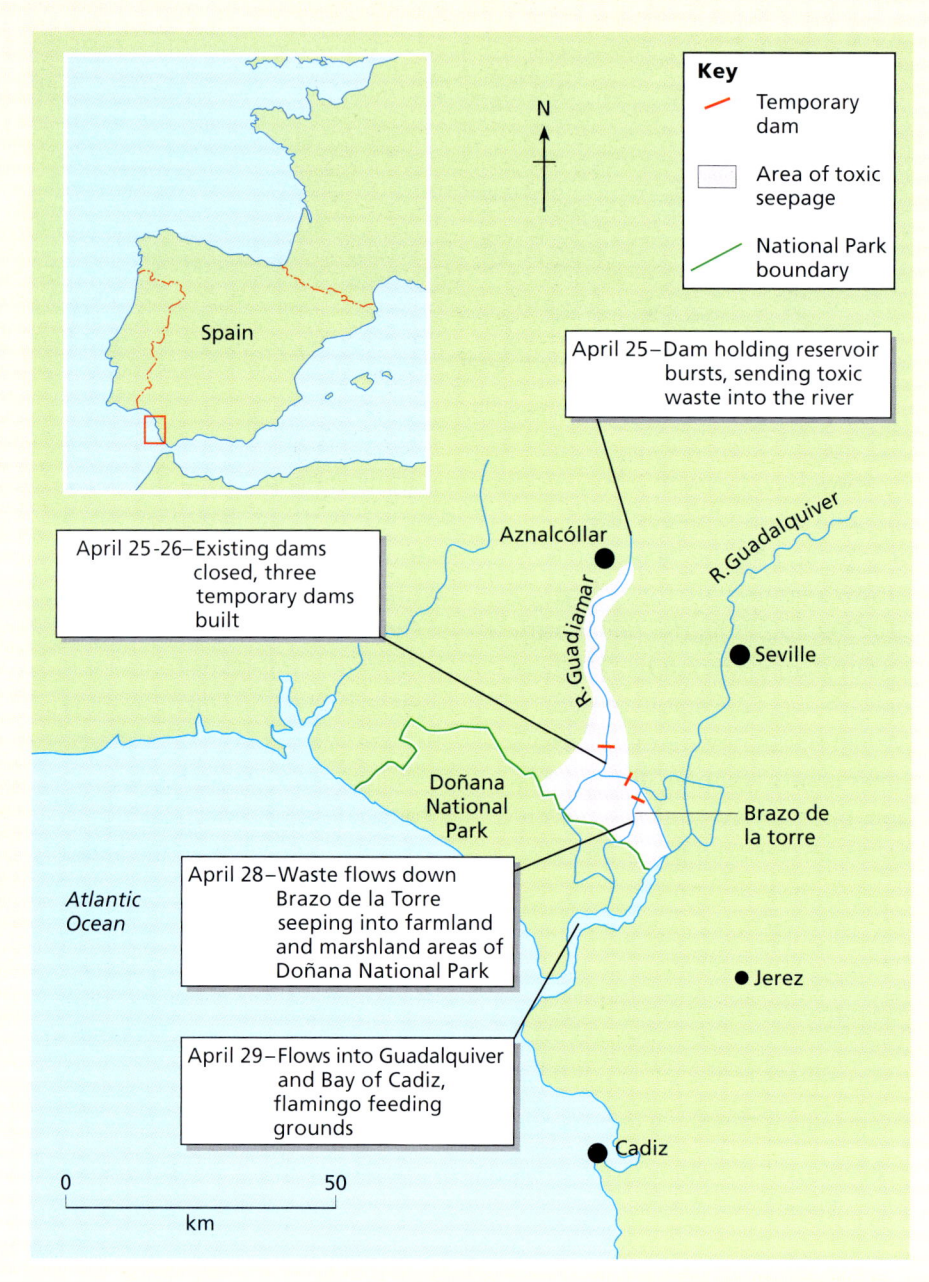

Figure 5.27 Map of Doñana National Park

However, the biggest threat to the park occurred in April 1998 when a toxic waste spillage from the Boliden iron ore mine at Aznalcollar flowed into the water system for five days.

Billions of gallons of sludge, containing cadmium, zinc, lead and chromium, flowed down the Guadiamar River, leaving a slick up to two feet deep on the banks. The acidity of the river immediately began to rise. Martin Barajas from the Organisation for the Defence of the Environment said that, 'the spillage was of an acidity somewhere between vinegar and sulphuric acid and had killed all the vegetation along the river banks'.

Figure 5.28 The devastation caused by the leakage

of tons of contaminated top soil. An estimated 350 000 lorry loads of sludge were dumped into a disused mine.

In total, the RSPB estimated that 1,500 hectares of protected area and 8,000 hectares of important wetlands had been contaminated. Large numbers of birds died, including storks, teal, avocets and flamingos. Many more would have died had it not been for the sanctuary warden, Placido Rodriguez, and a group of volunteers who helped rescue live birds and the eggs of several rare species which were incubated.

The Spanish government was chastised by environmental groups such as Greenpeace and World Wide Fund for Nature for not acting quickly enough. The director of the Spanish Ornithological Society said, 'What is the point of having an environment minister and a regional authority if they cannot co-ordinate in an emergency?'.

'The ecological disaster in the Doñana National Park will endure for several decades', stated *El Mundo*, a Spanish daily newspaper.

Emergency operations were put into action to try to protect the park. Dams on the river were closed, three new containing dams were rapidly built and earth-moving vehicles dumped rock to reinforce the leaking dam at the mine. Masked council workers picked out dead fish and placed them in plastic bags to prevent birds from eating them. Unfortunately, they were unable to collect dead fish in the lagoons where storks, egrets and herons wade and feed.

It was nine days before the toxic sludge began to be scraped up by earth-moving machines. The clean-up operation, which was carried out by the company responsible for the spillage, eventually removed millions

ACTIVITIES

Higher

1. How was the fragile environment of the park threatened?
2. What was done to limit the effects of the disaster?
3. What were the short and long-term effects of the Doñana disaster?
4. You have been asked by the Spanish tourist authority to promote this area of Spain. Prepare a speech outlining the tourist potential of the area.

Foundation

1. What caused the disaster in April 1998?
2. Which animals died in the National Park?
3. What was done to clean up the Park?
4. Draw a poster advertising the tourist possibilities of the Doñana National Park.

Case Study   OIL EXTRACTION IN THE AMAZONIAN RAINFOREST

Texaco were the first oil company to arrive in Ecuador in 1964. Until then the Oriente, Ecuador's Amazon forest, was inaccessible. Its native people, like the Secoya, Quichua and Huaorani, had lived there virtually undisturbed for centuries. Along with the oil pipelines came roads that enabled thousands of Ecuador's poor people to migrate to this area. These newcomers to the forest, the *colonos*, were encouraged by the government's Living Frontiers policy to cut down thousands of hectares of forest to make farms.

In the past 30 years, 16.8 million gallons of crude oil have been spilled into the Ecuadorian Amazon – in one incident in August 1992, 275 000 gallons of oil spilled out into the Oriente region of Ecuador. In the 20 years that Texaco has drilled in this area, it has dumped 20 billion gallons of waste water containing toxic hydrocarbons and chemicals into the region's waterways.

The drilling has also led to the deforestation of one million hectares of rainforest. Ecuador's rainforest is being cut down at the rate of 340 000 hectares a year. The wood is used for construction, roads, fuel and furniture.

The numbers of many of the indigenous tribes have been drastically reduced as a direct result of the pollution produced by the oil companies. Their drinking, bathing and fishing water contains toxins many times higher than the safety limits set by the US Environmental Protection Agency. Water contamination has led to increased risks of cancer, miscarriage, dermatitis and fungal infection. The tribes rely on the forest and its animals for their food, but oil pollution has meant that the feeding and reproductive processes of many animals, especially marine creatures, has been disrupted and this had led to population decline. Many of the toxins are passed up the food chain and accumulate in greater quantities in the top carnivores, such as the anaconda.

Figure 5.29 Oil mining in Ecuador

Ecuador relies heavily on oil production: 50 per cent of their Gross National Product is based on the oil industry. As a result of its dependence on foreign capital, the government has exerted very little environmental control and has encouraged oil exploration.

> **Examiner's tip**
>
> If a question asks how different groups of people have been affected by an event, always be specific. For deforestation, for example, don't use phrases like 'some people' or 'a tribe in the forest', use the tribe's proper name, like the Huaorani.

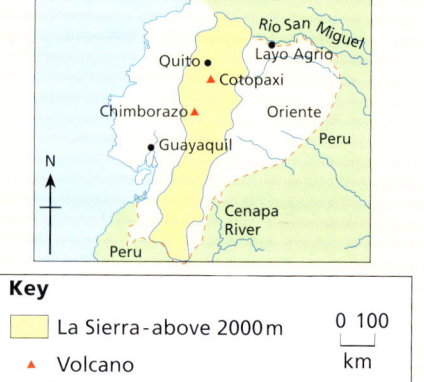

The oil companies have recently made some attempts to clean up the pollution that they have caused. The Maxus Energy Corporation has constructed an underground pipeline passing through the territory of the Huaorani and Quichua tribes and the Yasuni National Park. However, a great area of forest was destroyed to lay the pipelines and there is still the possibility of oil leakage.

Figure 5.30 Map of Ecuador

Managing the environment   109

Ecuador's Minister of Trade: 'We need to invest in oil exploration. It has opened up new areas of our country to investment. How could we survive as a country if we lost the oil revenue?'

Angel Armijus, a *colono*

A Huaorani leader: 'They have destroyed our forest and our culture. They have divided our people by offering them bribes of food, money and clothes in exchange for the use of our land. The Americans have brought in diseases that we have no resistance to.'

Celso Granada, a *colono*: 'When I was nine years old, I was walking home from school one day when I found some dynamite (used by the oil company) by the side of the road. I picked a stick of dynamite up and started playing with it. I didn't know what it was. Suddenly it exploded and my left arm was blown off.'

'Ever since I arrived in 1988 companies have been coming to drill wells and extract oil and all the time they've been causing damage to the area and making our lives harder. First they pollute the water, then the products that we grow, and in the end the whole environment suffers.'

A representative from the Maxus Energy Corporation: 'We have tried hard to protect the environment. The colonos have cleared more forest than us. We have invested $60 million on environmental protection. We have built schools for the natives.'

Figure 5.31 People's opinions on oil extraction in Equador

ACTIVITIES

Higher

1. Comment on the advantages and disadvantages of oil extraction in the Amazon rainforest.
2. How is the life of the Huaorani changing?
3. If the forest is to be sustainably developed, is oil extraction a feasible option?
4. In groups of four, imagine that you are either a *colono*, a member of the Ecuadorian government, the chief of the Huaorani or an oil executive. Devise a short play that highlights the conflicts in the forest.

Foundation

1. In the case study several groups of people are mentioned. Which groups of people are:
    a. for oil extraction,
    b. against oil extraction.
2. Name three ways in which the environment has been damaged by the oil companies.
3. What are the oil companies doing to protect the forest?
4. The life of the Huaorani is changing because of their contact with outsiders. In what ways are their lives changing?

Sample Examination Questions

Higher tier

1 a i   Name three causes of cliff recession. (3 marks)
   ii How do groynes protect cliffs from erosion by the sea? (4 marks)
   iii Explain the soft engineering techniques which are now being used to protect coastlines. (5 marks)
   b i   Study Figures 5.14 and 5.15 on river management techniques on page 96. Complete the box below with two soft and two hard management techniques.

Hard engineering techniques	Soft engineering techniques

   (4 marks)

   ii Choose *one* soft and *one* hard engineering technique. Describe and explain the advantages and disadvantages of each technique. (6 marks)
   c Many fragile environments in the world are being damaged by people's actions. Choose a case study of an environment that has been damaged by farming.
      i   What are the effects of the damage?
      ii Some people are in favour of the farming techniques that damaged the environment, others are against them. Explain the opinions of both groups. (8 marks)

   Total 30 marks

Foundation tier

2 a i   Which *two* of the following are causes of cliff recession? Circle the correct answers.
   Weathering, Corrasion, Eutrophication, Attrition
   ii Two ways of protecting coasts are with groynes and gabions. Give *one* advantage and *one* disadvantage of each technique. (4 marks)
   iii The following are soft engineering techniques used to manage coastlines. Draw a line between the correct soft engineering technique and its description.

Soft engineering techniques	Description
Beach nourishment	The coastline is built up with sand and pebble from elsewhere.
Managed retreat	The sea is allowed to flood areas which were once defended.
Cliff regrading	The land by the sea is made into a gentle slope instead of a steep one.

   (3 marks)

   iv Choose *one* soft engineering technique. Describe the advantages and disadvantages of this technique. (5 marks)
   b i   What does the term 'afforestation' mean? (2 marks)
   ii Look at Figure 5.13 on page 95 which shows river management techniques. Complete the box with three soft and three hard engineering techniques.

Soft engineering techniques	Hard engineering techniques
1	1
2	2
3	3

   (6 marks)

   c Many fragile environments in the world are being damaged by the actions of people. Choose a case study of an environment which has been damaged by farming.
      i   What are the effects of the damage? (3 marks)
      ii Some people are against modern farming techniques which can cause damage to the environment. Why is this? (5 marks)

   Total 30 marks

6 Managing hazards

Some places are more hazardous than others

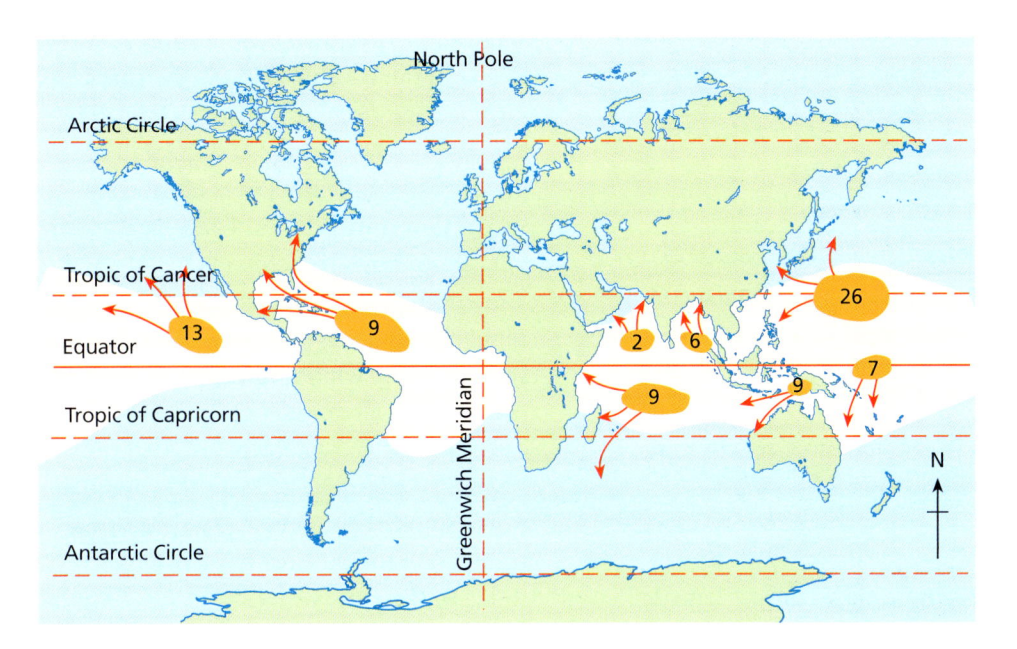

Figure 6.1 World's distribution of tropical storms

What is a tropical storm?

Tropical storms are intensive, low pressure weather systems known in different parts of the world as hurricanes, cyclones, typhoons or willy-willies. Their source regions are in the major oceans between the tropics of Cancer and Capricorn. They originate here because they need a sea temperature of over 27 °C in order to form. They only occur for a few months in the summer when sea temperatures are highest. There are an average of 84 tropical storms a year throughout the world, the highest number occurring in the North Pacific Ocean.

As there can be more than one storm at a time, tropical storms are given names to distinguish them. Since 1979 the names of women and men have been used for Atlantic tropical storms; each letter of the alphabet is selected in turn, except for Q, U and Z. The World Meteorological Organisation uses six lists in rotation. The same lists are reused every six years. If a hurricane has been particularly large and destructive, then its name is retired and a new name is chosen. Both Mitch and Floyd will be replaced with new names in 2004 and 2005 respectively.

This is the six-year list of hurricane names for Atlantic storms:

2002	2003	2004	2005	2006	2007
Arthur	Ana	Alex	Arlene	Alberto	Allison
Bertha	Bill	Bonnie	Bret	Beryl	Barry
Cesar	Claudette	Charley	Cindy	Chris	Chantal
Dolly	Danny	Danielle	Dennis	Debby	Dean
Edouard	Erika	Earl	Emily	Ernesto	Erin
Fran	Fabian	Frances	Floyd	Florence	Felix
Gustav	Grace	Georges	Gert	Gordon	Gabrielle
Hortense	Henri	Hermine	Harvey	Helene	Humberto
Isidore	Isabel	Ivan	Irene	Isaac	Iris
Josephine	Juan	Jeanne	Jose	Joyce	Jerry
Kyle	Kate	Karl	Katrina	Keith	Karen
Lili	Larry	Lisa	Lenny	Leslie	Lorenzo

What are the characteristics of tropical storms?

Tropical storms have three major effects which together can have huge human, economic and environmental impacts on an area.

1 Strong winds: hurricanes can be split into five categories according to their wind speed.

Category	Wind speed (km/h)	Amount of damage	Example
1	120–149	minimal	Allison (1995)
2	150–179	moderate	Bob (1991)
3	180–209	extensive	Alicia (1983)
4	210–249	extreme	Floyd (1999)
5	over 250	catastrophic	Camille (1969)

Winds this strong can blow cars over and uproot trees and areas of poorly constructed housing will be badly affected. It is impossible to walk in winds this strong. In the twentieth century Category 5 hurricanes have hit the USA only twice. In the 1935 hurricane, the winds were so strong that entire communities were flattened in the Florida Keys.

2 Heavy rain: the highest rainfall in 24-hour was measured at 1,825 mm on the island of La Réunion during tropical storm Denise in January 1966. Heavy rainfall can lead to severe flooding as rivers swell and burst their banks, causing crop damage and contaminating water supplies. Two hundred people died during Hurricane Diane in the USA in 1955. As the surface layers of soil become saturated, landslides can also occur. Pressure and the pull of gravity causes the top layers of saturated soil to flow down slopes. These can destroy villages and bury inhabitants.

3 Storm surges: this happens when there is a rapid rise in sea level caused by the tropical storm's strong winds blowing the sea onto the land. A wall of water several metres high can demolish coastal towns and harbours. In 1999 winds of 200–225 km/hr caused a storm surge of 5 metres above the normal tide level in the state of Orissa in eastern India. In the same year a storm surge hit the coastal region of Thatta in Pakistan causing 15 000 cattle and sheep to lose their lives. Ninety per cent of all deaths from tropical cyclones are attributable to storm surges.

Figure 6.2 The effects of a storm surge

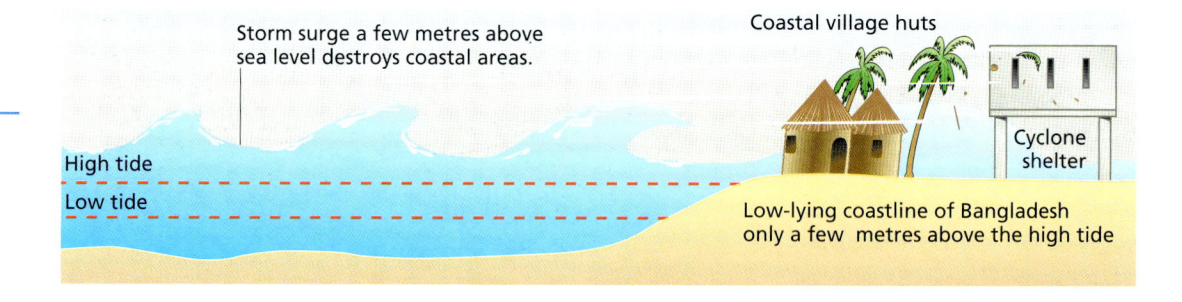

ACTIVITIES

1a What is a tropical storm?
 b What is a source region?
2 Look at Figure 6.1 which shows the distribution of tropical storms.
a Describe the distribution of tropical storms.
b If a tropical storm occured in the following countries: Pakistan, Madagascar, Japan and Costa Rica where would its source region be?
3 Why do storm surges cause so much damage?
4 Can you make a list of hurricane names using the names of pupils in your year?

Managing hazards   113

Case Study: MEDC HURRICANE FLOYD IN THE USA, SEPTEMBER 1999

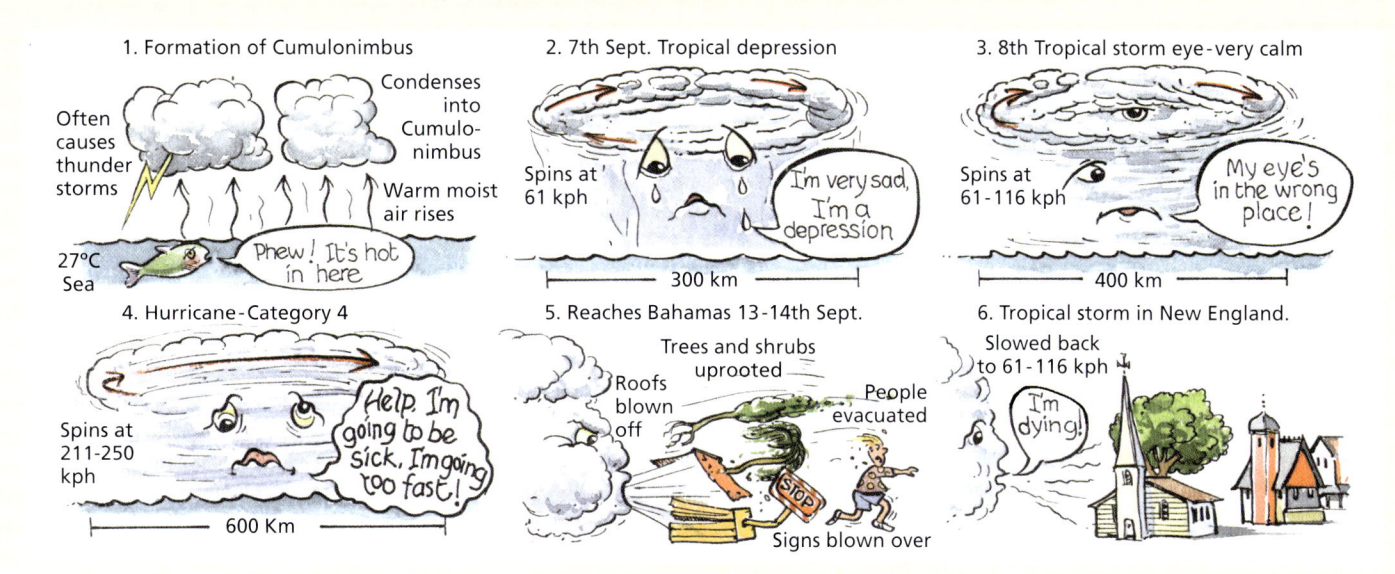

Figure 6.3 Diagram showing the stages of a hurricane

What are the impacts of a tropical storm?

Hurricane Floyd formed in the Atlantic Ocean off the coast of Africa on 2 September 1999. Increasing in intensity, it became a tropical depression on 7 September and a tropical storm on 8 September, located 1,350 km east of the Lesser Antilles.

It intensified further into a Category 4 hurricane as it moved towards the Bahamas, which were ravaged on 13 and 14 September. Slowly weakening, Floyd took a more northerly course and eventually hit the US mainland near Cape Fear, North Carolina on 16 September. It then moved up the coast, weakening to a tropical storm as it entered New England.

Figure 6.4 Radar image of Hurricane Floyd, September 1999

What were the effects of the cyclone?

- 14 states from Florida to Maine were affected, with North Carolina being the most seriously hit.
- 79 deaths and thousands of injuries were attributed to Floyd.
- 47 people died in North Carolina after the storm dumped over 500 mm of rain and flooded an area of 30 000 square kilometres.
- 4 million people were evacuated in North Carolina, South Carolina, Georgia and Florida.
- 1 million people had no electricity or water supplies.
- 4,000 people in Pennsylvania were left homeless.
- Flood insurance claims from Hurricane Floyd were the second highest ever: 25 000 claimants received payments totalling $460 million.
- 42 973 homes sustained some degree of damage due to Floyd. Of that total 11 779 dwellings were either destroyed or heavily damaged.
- 144 854 people in 9 states registered for state and federal assistance.

Managing hazards

MEDC HURRICANE FLOYD IN THE USA, SEPTEMBER 1999 – continued

- Unemployment offices saw a huge surge in applications for benefits. Rocky Mount in Alabama alone saw a tenfold increase.
- 105 580 people received shelter.
- Agricultural losses were estimated at $1 billion.
- 10 per cent of North Carolina's tobacco crop was lost.
- Farms in several states were heavily affected with 14 per cent of farmers stating that their losses were so great that they would have to find other employment. Doug Lewis, a farmer from Tarboro, lost all his corn, cotton and soy beans and stated the problem facing many other farmers, 'The government is talking about loans. I've got all the loans I need. I can't pay back what I've got.'
- In North Carolina, 250 roads were listed as impassable including the major highways Interstate 95 and 40.
- The St. James Street bridge in Tarboro was washed away.
- A storm surge in Nassau, Bahamas, caused a number of boats to be beached or sunk.
- Homes, offices and hotels had their windows blown out and structural damage was experienced throughout the Bahamas.
- Large areas of dunes and beaches were destroyed. Oak Island lost 20 metres of beach and Wrightsville Beach on the barrier island suffered considerable erosion with over 1 metre of sand being blown onto the beach roads.

Figure 6.5 Effects of Hurricane Floyd at Tarboro (taken from television footage)

Figure 6.6 Housing destruction in North Carolina (taken from television footage)

What was done to lessen the impact of Hurricane Floyd?

Predictions and warnings

The National Hurricane Centre (NHC) in Miami, Florida is a government-funded warning service.

Geostationary satellites constantly provide data so that meteorologists can give early warnings of tropical storms developing. Interpreting the data is very difficult and can lead to wrong warnings and if too many of these are given, the population may ignore the alert. Wrong warnings can also lead to economic losses if the population is evacuated.

However, evacuation in the event of a hurricane is vital: the death toll from Hurricane Floyd was reduced because 2.5 million people were evacuated. In South Carolina alone Governor Jim Hodges ordered the evacuation of 800 000 people. This lead to bumper to bumper traffic along Interstate 26, causing a 150 km journey to take 10 hours, but the evacuation was effective and fatalities were low.

By June 2000 new highway renovation and preparedness strategies for Interstate 26 were all in place.

Preparing the community

The Federal Emergency Management Agency (FEMA) provides a free consumer guide offering tips on how families, businesses and communities can protect themselves against hurricanes. 'Being prepared is the key to dealing with any potential disaster', says FEMA director James

Managing hazards

Figure 6.7 Volunteer workers in North Carolina

Figure 6.8 Disaster housing programme (video still)

Lee Wiff. These tips include how to prepare a family disaster plan and how to assemble a disaster supply kit.

Building hurricane proof buildings

Hurricanes work at weaknesses such as windows, doors and roofs. If winds rush into a house through a door or a window, it creates pressure inside the house which in turn exerts an outward force on the walls and roof. This can cause the house to collapse. Windows and, if possible, doors should be covered with wood and firmly nailed down. Houses can also be fitted with storm shutters and shatter-resistant windows. All hurricane-prone states in the USA have building codes to construct hurricane-proof buildings. However, not all builders follow these codes, as was discovered after Hurricane Andrew ploughed through Dade County in Florida. Many of the most recently constructed houses that were destroyed had not been built in accordance with the South Florida Building Code.

Land-use planning

Land-use planning is most effective in coastal zones at risk from tropical storms or the associated storm surge. Past data can be used to identify areas of high risk. Its aim is to limit development in these areas to uses more compatible with flooding such as beaches and other recreational areas. This is a difficult aim to achieve. In LEDCs, the need for land and in MEDCs, the desire for a beach front location are likely to outweigh the risks involved, even if people are aware of them. Nevertheless, the US government is limiting the building of new developments in high risk coastal and river flood plain areas.

Date	Latitude	Longitude	Max wind km/h
9/8/99	15.6	50.0	65
9/8/99	16.6	51.7	80
9/9/99	17.3	54.6	100
9/9/99	18.2	56.9	120
9/10/99	18.9	58.7	120
9/10/99	20.5	60.0	140
9/11/99	21.7	61.6	170
9/11/99	22.7	63.5	180
9/12/99	22.8	65.9	180
9/12/99	23.4	68.2	200
9/13/99	23.7	70.6	255
9/13/99	24.2	73.7	255
9/14/99	25.1	75.9	255
9/14/99	26.5	77.4	225
9/15/99	28.8	78.8	225
9/15/99	31.3	79.0	190
9/16/99	34.5	77.6	170
9/16/99	39.3	74.6	110

Figure 6.9 Positions of Hurricane Floyd

Managing hazards

MEDC HURRICANE FLOYD IN THE USA, SEPTEMBER 1999 – continued

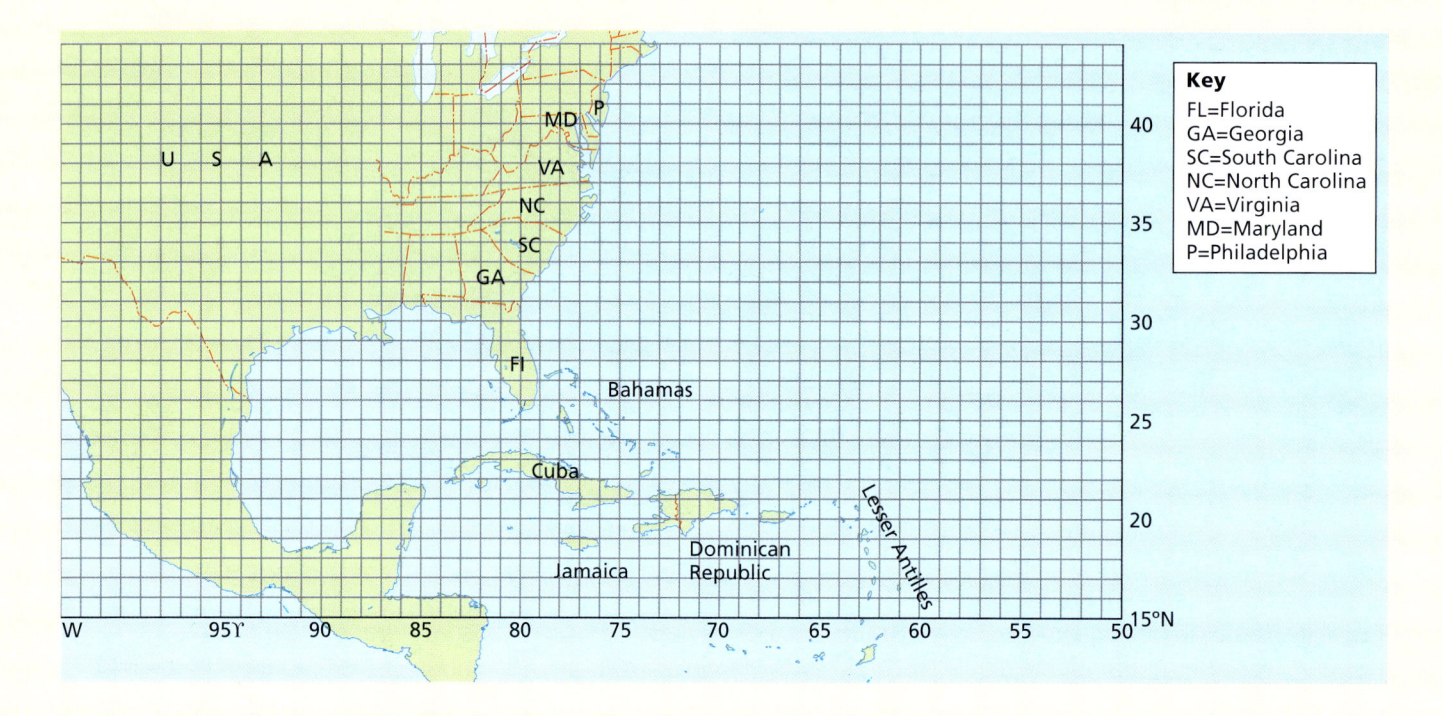

Key
FL=Florida
GA=Georgia
SC=South Carolina
NC=North Carolina
VA=Virginia
MD=Maryland
P=Philadelphia

Figure 6.10 Base map for Hurricane Floyd

ACTIVITIES

1 Plot the course of Hurricane Floyd.
a Lay a sheet of tracing paper over Figure 6.10 and draw the outline of the USA, Central America and the Caribbean Islands.
b Carefully plot the course of the hurricane using the 18 positions given in Figure 6.9
c Join up the points that you have plotted using different colours to show the intensity of the hurricane. Use the hurricane categories on page 112 to help you.
d Add labels to the map to show:
   i direction of movement
   ii dates and times
   iii areas of greatest damage
e Work out the average speed of the hurricane (in km/ hour) from 5 pm on 12 September to 5 pm on 14 September. (To do this work out the total distances in kilometres and divide by the total time taken in hours.)

2 Make a table with three columns. Label it 'Impacts of Hurricane Floyd'. Label the three columns 'human impacts', 'economic impacts' and 'environmental impacts'. Use information from the case study to complete the table.

3 Why do people still live in areas like South Carolina even though they know that hurricanes will happen? Can development here be sustainable?

4 Use the FEMA website given at the end of this chapter to help you to prepare your own family disaster plan.

Case Study: LEDC CYCLONE ONE BRAVO, BANGLADESH, MAY 1997

The severe tropical cyclone known as One Bravo gathered intensity in the Bay of Bengal and struck the south-eastern coast of Bangladesh on Monday, 19 May 1997, crossing the Chittagong-Feni coast north of Chittagong at around 6.30 pm. Wind speeds of up to 250 kilometres per hour were recorded and the cyclone caused serious damage and flooding in the eastern coastal belt area of Bangladesh which is home to approximately 4 million people.

The effects of the cyclone were felt mostly along the 200 kilometre coastal area between the port city of Chittagong and Teknaf at the southern tip of Bangladesh. The cyclone's winds continued northward, bringing torrential rain and high winds to the Himalayas and trapping eight Mount Everest expeditions in base camps. A tornado hit Maheshkhali Island near the city of Cox's Bazaar about six hours after the cyclone passed.

The power of Cyclone Bravo One was similar to that of the cyclone that hit the same coastal area in 1991 and killed 140 000 people. This time, however, the death toll was considerably lower. This was due mainly to the Bangladesh Red Crescent Society's Cyclone Preparedness Programme.

Effects of the cyclone:
- 111 people died, 7,000 were injured.
- 2-metre high tidal surges covered the low-lying islands in the Bay of Bengal destroying the crops.
- The storm cut communication lines with islands along the coasts, making it difficult to receive damage and casualty reports.

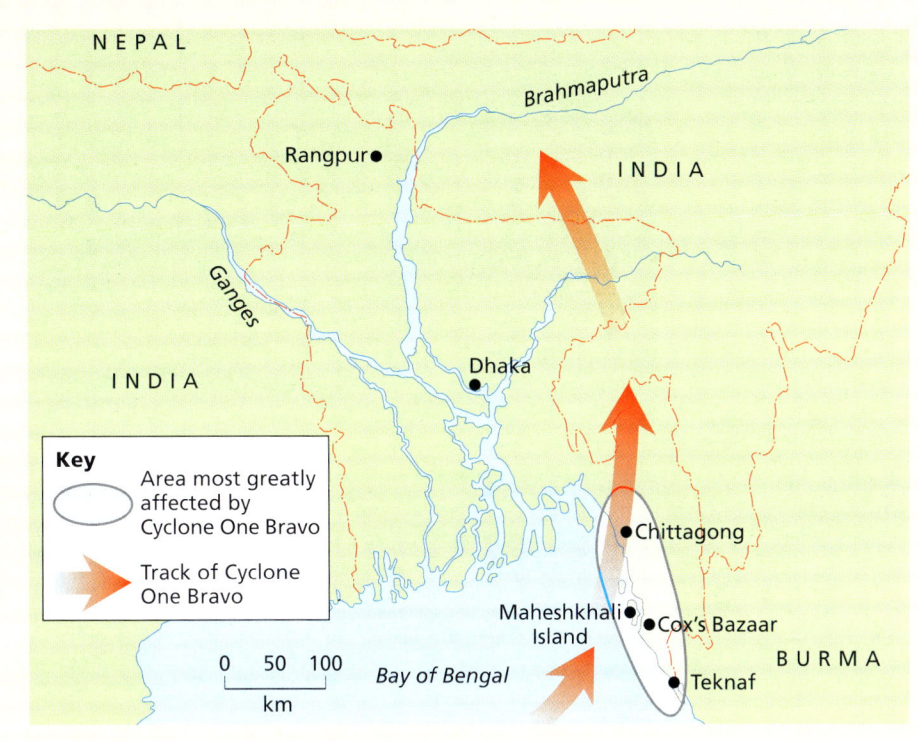

Figure 6.11 Map of places affected by Cyclone One Bravo

- 500 000 people were left homeless as the mud, brick and thatch houses that crowd the coast were completely flattened. Most of these houses had been built outside the embankment which had been strengthened after the 1991 cyclone.
- 608 educational institutions were damaged.
- Fish ponds and tube wells were contaminated by salt water, leaving over 1 million people with no access to fresh water.
- Large numbers of fishing boats and nets were destroyed.
- 30 000 hectares of crops were damaged and 2,000 cattle were lost. Cash crops were lost as betel leaves crops were flattened and the betel nuts were blown off the trees. Much of the year's harvest in storage was destroyed.

- The electricity supply was disrupted in most affected areas and was only partially restored in the largest towns after a week.
- Outbreaks of diarrhoea affected thousands of people.
There was widespread destruction of the infrastructure, including roads, bridges and cyclone shelters.
- Some families in poverty, without insurance, went to desperate lengths to save their possessions. After the storm CARE staff (see glossary) learned of one woman who had increased the height of her bed by tying bamboo to its legs when the water level was over 1 metre. She cooked, slept and essentially lived in her bed, the unsanitary conditions leaving her vulnerable to disease. She would not leave as she feared that her possessions would be stolen.

Case Study

LEDC CYCLONE ONE BRAVO, BANGLADESH, MAY 1997 – continued

Figure 6.12 The destructive power of Cyclone One Bravo

Figure 6.13 Aftermath of Cyclone One Bravo

Limiting the impact of the cyclone

'Two factors were responsible for the low numbers of deaths in 1997 compared with 1991: the government's quick response and the low tide', said CARE's regional manager for Asia. (CARE is the world's largest private international relief and development agency.) After years of repeated storms, the Bangladeshi government has become expert at lessening the death toll from cyclones.

Relief

National aid – The prime minister established a Relief Fund in 1997 to cover relief and rehabilitation needs. The government decided that 500 families in each of the affected areas would be given 32 kg of rice over 2 months. The food was given to the poorest families, regardless of whether they were directly affected by the cyclone or not. An action plan to give one bundle (72 running feet) of corrugated iron sheets to each family with a totally damaged house was also established.

The Red Crescent chartered a plane to conduct an aerial survey of the eastern coastal belt between Chittagong and Teknaf. The survey formed the basis for a fuller assessment of damage and provided much-needed information about the immediate needs of the population.

Koinonia, formed in 1983, is part of the National Christian Fellowship of Bangladesh. They distributed 14 pieces of corrugated iron and 3 pieces of ridging as house building materials along with 500 taka (approximately £6.50) to 1,000 families.

On 20 May 2000 the Bangladesh Red Crescent sent two relief trucks from its national headquarters to its branches in Chittagong and Cox's Bazaar. Branch volunteers distributed 400 tarpaulins, 20 rolls of plastic sheeting, 100 jerry cans, 500 mugs, 500 pieces of crockery, 500 aluminium plates, 5,000 pieces of second-hand clothing, 50 bars of soap, 1 ton of compressed rice and 120 kg of ghur. Six medical teams with first aid volunteers were also sent to the area.

Figure 6.14 Relief aid in Bangladesh

Managing hazards

International aid – The following section uses contemporary reports to help explain the efforts that were made to limit the impact of the cyclone.

> The government and NGOs set into motion plans to assist in rehabilitating the water sources for fish and drinking water. In some areas, new tube wells were installed and old ones were repaired as a rehabilitation measure. The government gave indications that international assistance would be welcome in this area. 'It's likely that the damage to property is high, so the need for assistance from the international community is more likely to be for medium to long-term recovery rather than for emergency relief', said UN Resident Co-ordinator David Lockwood.

> The European Commission approved emergency humanitarian aid worth ECU 350 000 for victims of the cyclone. The aid, managed by the European Community Humanitarian Office (ECHO), enabled the International Federation of the Red Crescent (IFRC) to carry out an emergency programme. CARE immediately began distributing food and survival kits, as well as water purification tablets. 'We're ready to work with the Government to begin putting this storm in the past, and help people start rebuilding their lives', a spokesman for CARE said.

> The following contributions were announced at a meeting in Dhaka and were administered through NGOs working in the affected areas:
> Australia $77 000
> Canada $100 000
> France $35 000
> Sweden $240 000
> UK $160 000
> USA $640 000

Figure 6.15 Cyclone shelter in Bangladesh

Protection schemes

- Earth embankments have been constructed and are continually being strengthened but are often not high enough or strong enough.
- Cyclone shelters, many made of concrete and constructed above floodwater levels, have been built in the most frequently affected areas.
- Education programmes have been implemented so the inhabitants know what to do if there is a storm alert.

ACTIVITIES

1. Where was the source region of Cyclone One Bravo?
2. Use an atlas to draw a sketch map to show the path of the cyclone. Shade the area that experienced the greatest damage.
3. Make two lists showing the short-term and long-term effects of One Bravo. Include specific detail in your answer.
4. Research the April 1991 cyclone that hit Bangladesh. Why were the deaths and damage caused by One Bravo less than the 1991 cyclone?
5. Compare two tropical storms, one from an LEDC and one from an MEDC. How does the state of development of the country influence the storm's impact?

Managing hazards

Plate tectonics

Plate tectonics explains why natural hazards, such as earthquakes and volcanoes are found where they are. According to the theory of plate tectonics, the earth's crust is divided into seven large and twelve smaller plates.

The earth's crust is between 10 and 100 km thick and consists of cooler solid rock 'floating' on the hotter molten rock of the mantle.

If you boil an egg and then tap the shell it will break into jigsaw bits. These are much like the earth's plates, although in terms of scale, the egg's shell is much thicker than the earth's plates. In terms of scale, the plates are like postage stamps stuck on a football.

The earth's plates consist of two types of crust:
1. Oceanic crust is between 5 and 10 km thick, denser (heavier) than continental crust and continually being renewed and destroyed.
2. The continental crust which is between 25 and 100 km thick, is less dense (lighter) than oceanic crust and does not sink. It is not destroyed.

Most plates move a few centimetres a year and, in the course of the earth's history, cause the continents to move, split apart and collide. The relative positions of the continents are still changing. This movement is known as continental drift.

There are three different types of plate movement:
1. Some plates move towards each other (convergent or destructive), e.g. Nazca and South American plates.
2. Some plates move away from each other (divergent or constructive), e.g. Nazca and Pacific plates.
3. Some plates slide past each other (conservative or transform), e.g. Pacific and North American plates.

The plates meet at plate boundaries or plate margins which are areas of great crustal stress. These meeting points are where most of the world's earthquakes and volcanoes and other structural features such as fold mountains, rift valleys and ocean trenches occur.

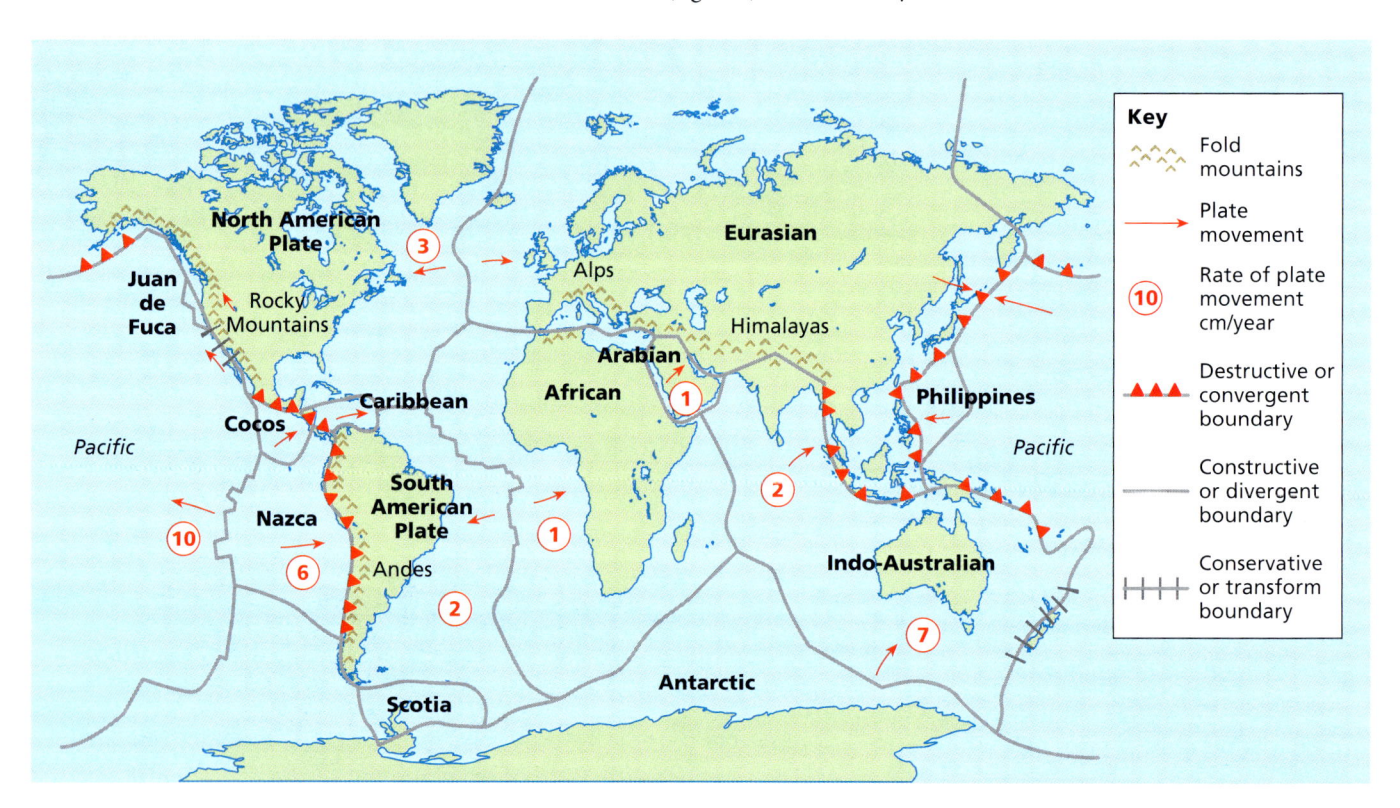

Figure 6.16 World map of plate boundaries

Types of plate margin

1 Convergent or destructive margins – At a destructive plate margin, two plates move towards one another. Where they meet, one plate is subducted (slides) below the other. The cause of this subduction is the difference in density between the two plates, with the heavier one being subducted below the lighter one.

Three types of destructive plate margin have been identified:

a Ocean – continent margin – Figure 6.17 shows the Nazca plate being subducted below the South American plate. As the oceanic plate is being subducted, a deep oceanic trench forms. These oceanic trenches are the deepest part of the ocean. If it were possible to drop Mount Everest into the Marianas Trench, part of the Pacific Ocean close to the Philippines, it would be completely covered.

The heat from the mantle and friction from the contact between the two plates causes the oceanic plate to be destroyed. At the same time, this friction and pressure causes earthquakes to occur along the subduction zone. The melting plate creates liquid magma that rises towards the surface to form volcanoes such as Aconcagua, the highest peak in the Andes (6960 m). The collision of the plates also causes severe folding and uplift of the rocks. This process has contributed to the growth of the Andes.

b Ocean – ocean margins – The Ryuku Islands, just to the south of the Japanese island of Kyushu, are a direct result of destructive plate activity in the western Pacific. The Philippine plate to the east is subducting beneath the Eurasian plate to the west. As it subducts, the tremendous pressures that are released cause earthquakes. At about 100 km below the surface, the subducting plate begins to melt and magma escapes to the surface to form volcanoes. After several eruptions, these volcanoes break the ocean surface to form islands. When several of these islands form together they are called an island arc. The Ryuku Islands are an example.

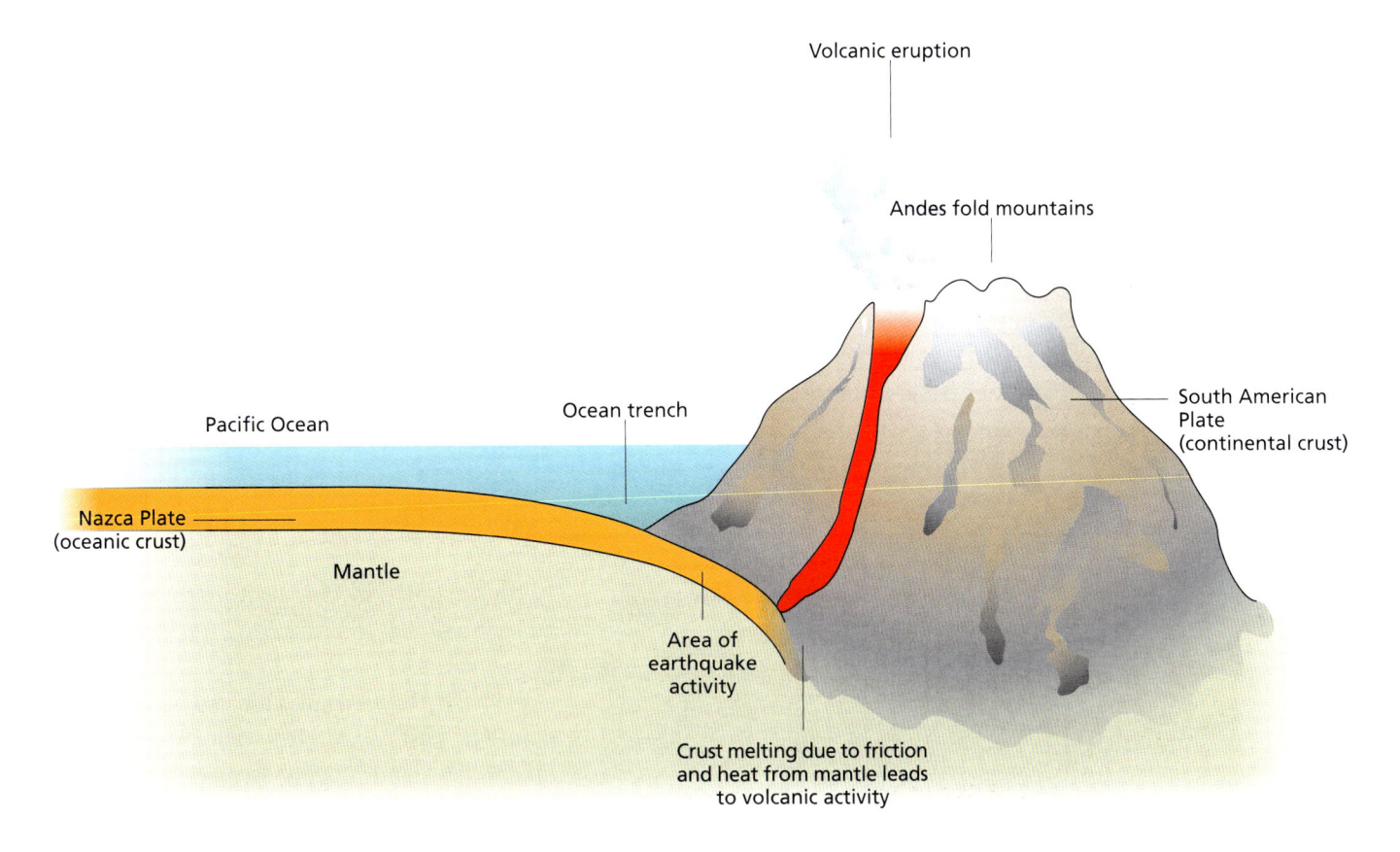

Figure 6.17 Convergent plate boundary of Nazca and South American plates

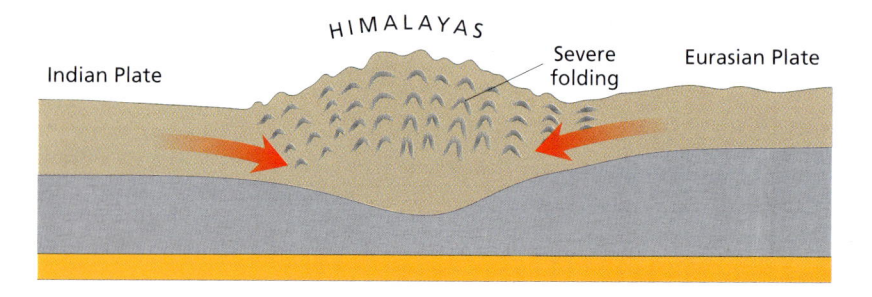

Figure 6.18 Ocean to ocean convergent plate boundary

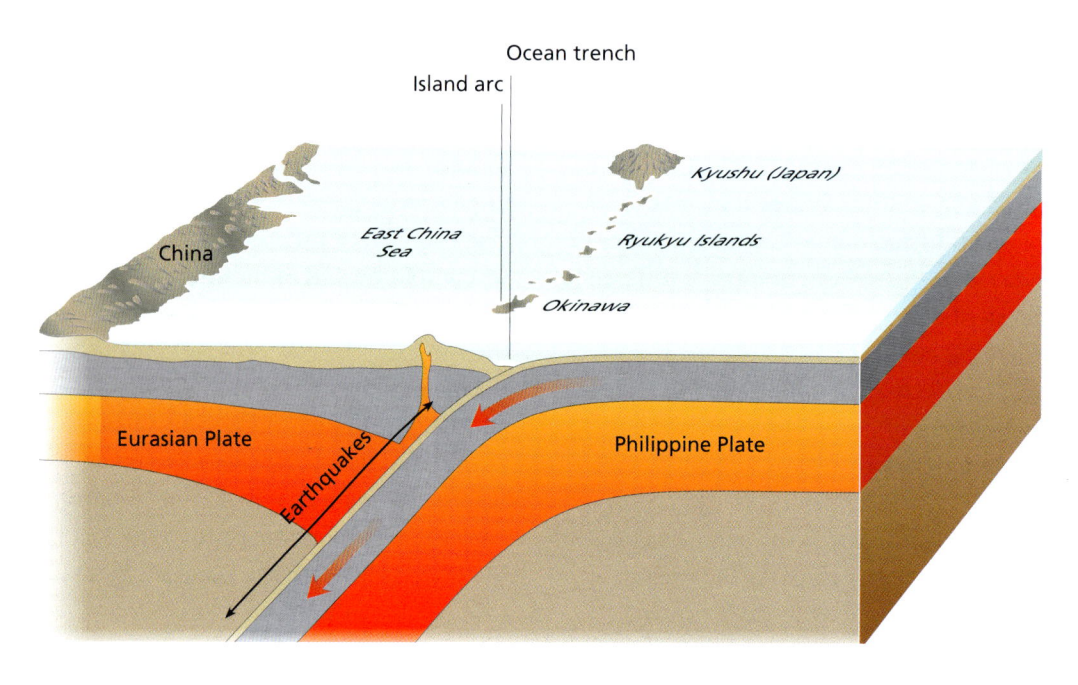

c Continental – continental margin – Continental crust is less dense than oceanic crust and so, when two continents meet at a destructive plate margin, a slow collision rather than any marked subduction takes place. This results in intense folding, faulting and uplift and leads to the formation of mountains. As there is very little, if any, subduction at this plate margin, there are few earthquakes and no volcanoes.

Figure 6.19 shows the movement of India. About 100 million years ago the Indian plate started to converge with the Eurasian plate. Gradually, the ocean between them narrowed until the two continental land masses collided. The thick layers of sediments between the two continents were carried into the sea by rivers which had eroded them from the land. As the plates collided, these sediments were squeezed and folded to form the Himalayas. The process continues today, with the Indian plate grinding into the Eurasian plate at a rate of 5 cm a year.

2 Divergent or constructive margins – Constructive margins occur where two plates move away from each other and create a new crust. This occurs most commonly in the middle of oceans. Figure 6.20 shows how the North American plate is moving apart from the Eurasian plate, causing the Atlantic Ocean to widen by about 3 cm a year. The convection currents that are causing this movement are creating a gap called a mid-oceanic ridge. Magma rises to fill the gap, thus forming new land.

Where the magma builds up above the surface of the ocean, volcanic islands form. Iceland, which is a volcanic island, did not exist two million years ago when Britain entered its last Ice Age. Iceland's location on the Mid-Atlantic ridge means that it is a major site of volcanic and earthquake activity. The island of Surtsey to the south west of Iceland was a volcano under the sea that erupted in 1963. Within four years an island of 2.8 square kilometres had been created.

Constructive margins can also be found on land. The East African Rift Valley is opening up and new land is being formed in the bottom of the valley.

Figure 6.19 The formation of the Himalayas

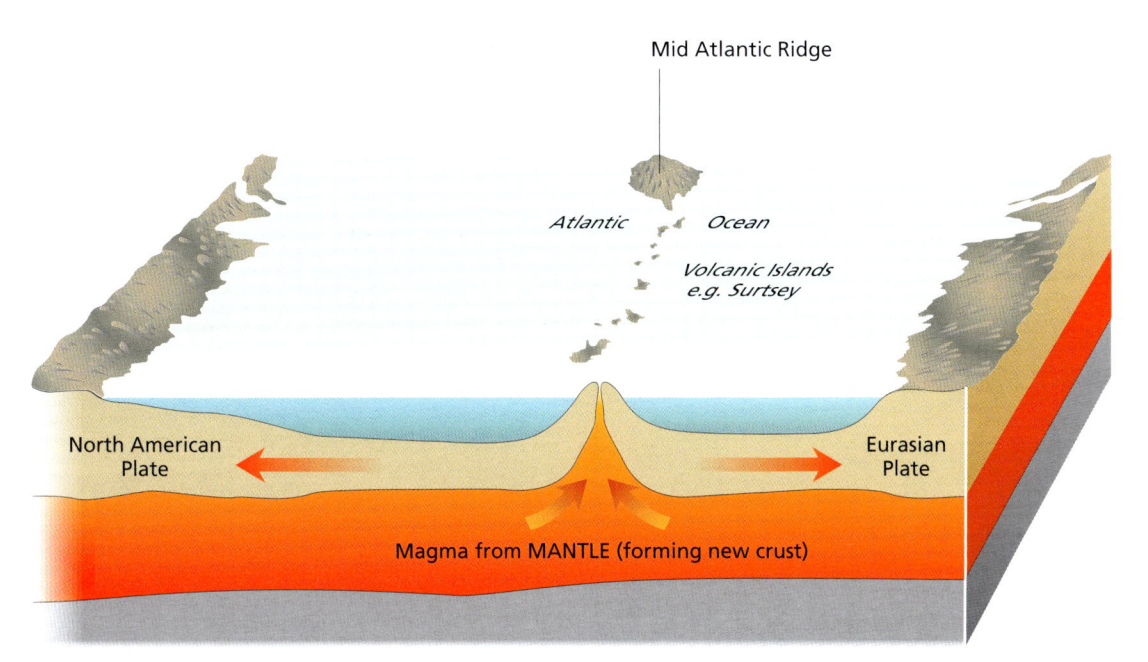

Figure 6.20 Landforms at a divergent plate boundary

3 Conservative or transform margins – Conservative margins are where plates move alongside each other. No new crust is created nor is any destroyed and no new landforms appear. However, these can be sites for violent earthquakes. The San Andreas Fault in California marks the junction of the North American and Pacific plates (see Figure 6.21). Both plates are moving north west but at different speeds. Instead of slipping smoothly past each other, they tend to 'stick'. The pressure builds up until suddenly the plates jerk forward, sending shock waves to the surface and triggering a sudden earthquake. There is no volcanic action because the crust is not being destroyed at conservative margins.

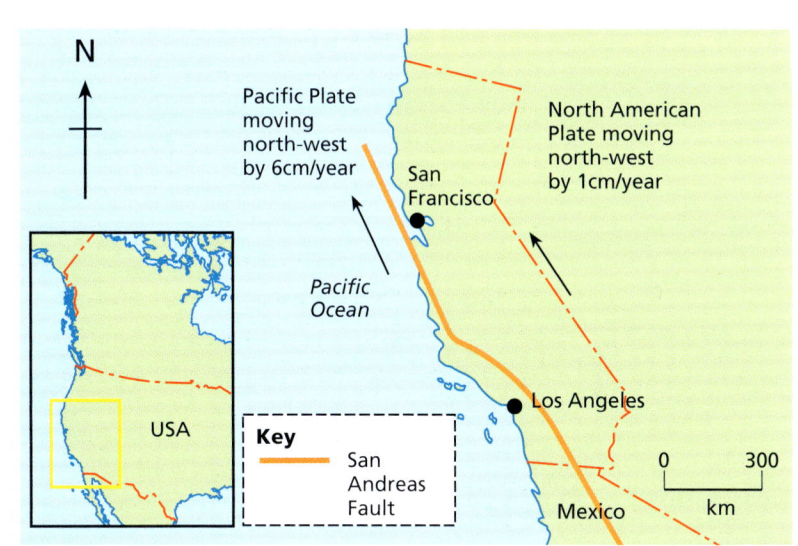

Figure 6.21 The San Andreas Fault

The global distribution of volcanoes and earthquakes

The distribution of the world's main earthquakes and active volcanoes is shown in Figures 6.22 and 6.23. If you compare Figures 6.16, 6.22 and 6.23, you will see a clear pattern emerging between the distribution of volcanoes, earthquakes and the world's plate margins. Earthquakes occur in long narrow bands on all three types of plate margin, both on the land and in the sea. The largest belt runs around the Pacific Ocean. Other major belts travel along the middle of the Atlantic Ocean and through the continents of Europe and Asia from the Atlantic Ocean to the Pacific Ocean.

Volcanoes also occur in long narrow bands. The largest band, called the Pacific Ring of Fire, goes around the entire Pacific Ocean. They are found at constructive and destructive plate margins, occurring both on the land and in the sea. They are sometimes found away from plate margins at 'hot spots' where the crust is particularly thin. The best example of a hot spot is Hawaii.

124　　Managing hazards

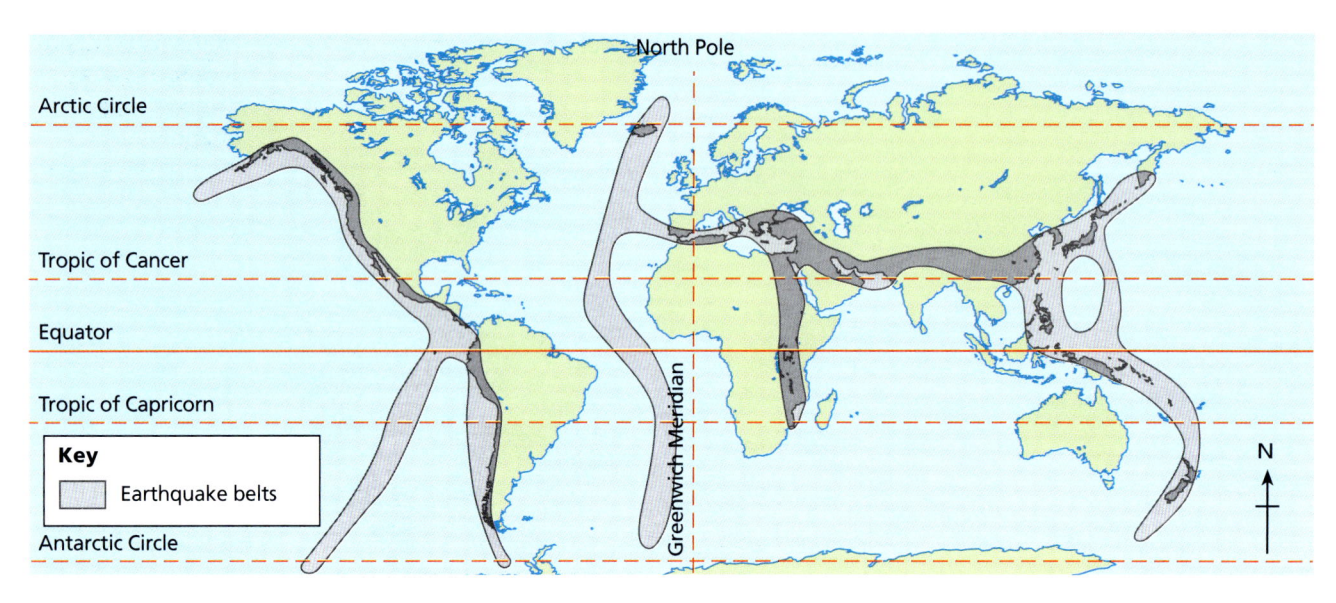

Figure 6.22 The world's distribution of earthquakes

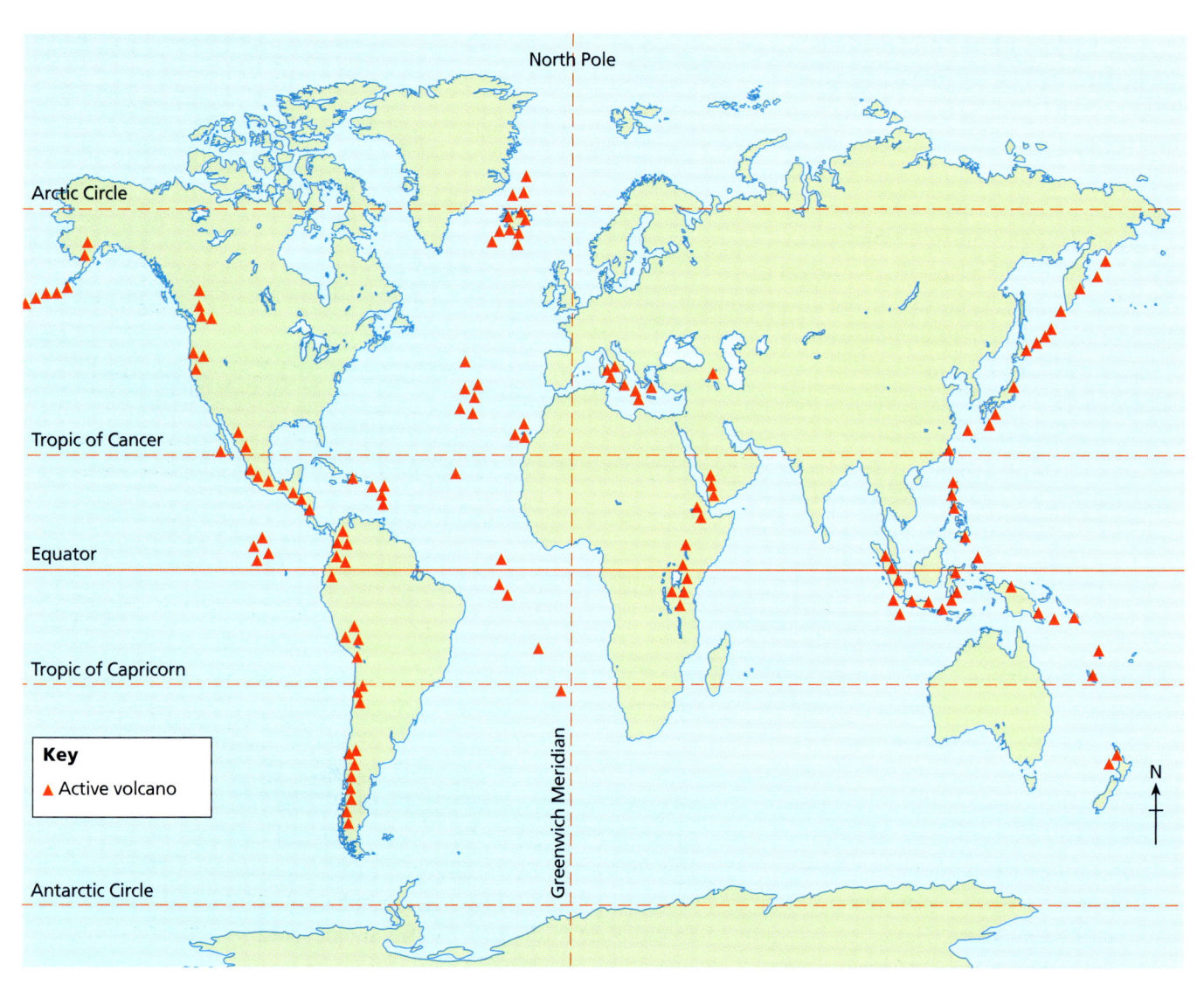

Figure 6.23 The world's distribution of active volcanoes

Managing hazards 125

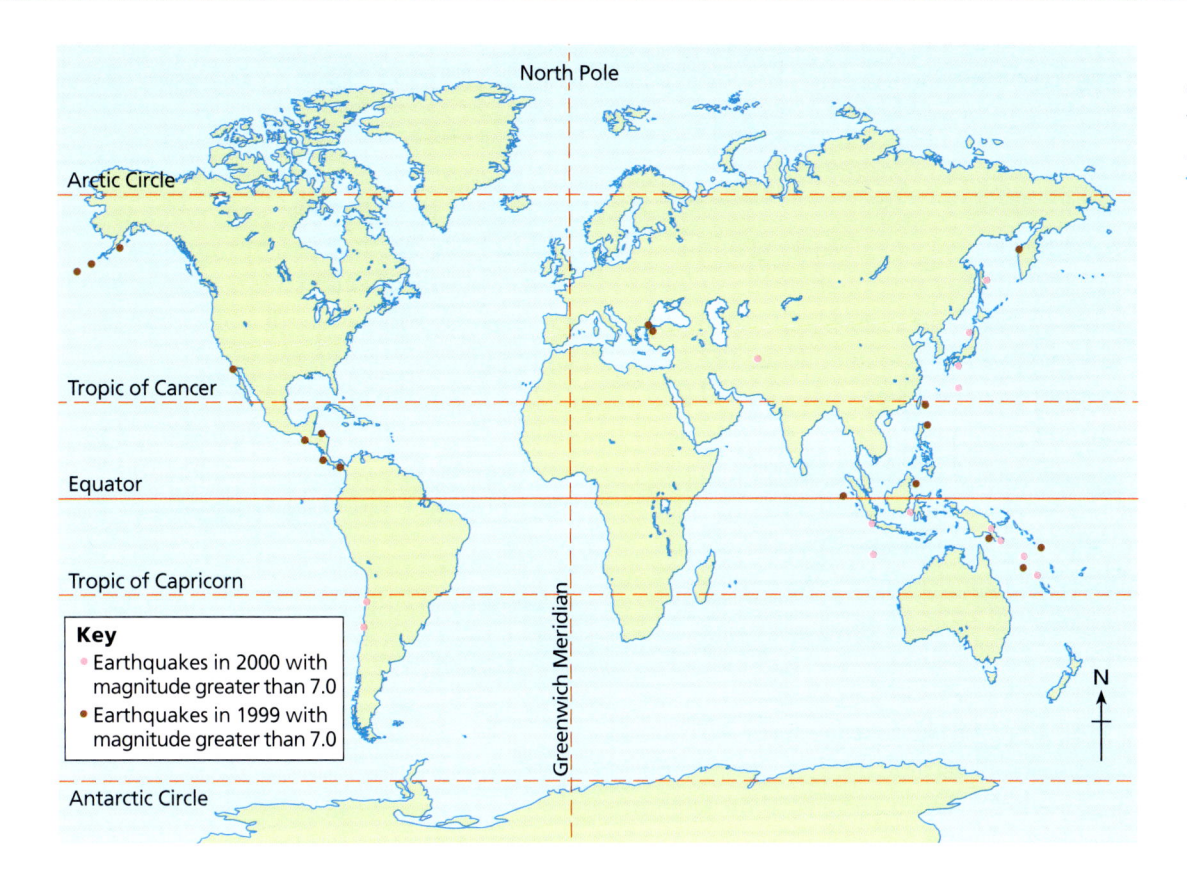

Figure 6.24 Major earthquakes for the years 1999 and 2000

Key
- Earthquakes in 2000 with magnitude greater than 7.0
- Earthquakes in 1999 with magnitude greater than 7.0

ACTIVITIES

Higher

1a What are plates?
b What are the differences between oceanic and continental crusts?

2 Draw simple annotated diagrams to show the main features of:
a convergent
b divergent,
c conservative plate margins.

3 Describe the distribution of earthquake activity. Use specific place names.

4 Explain why no volcanoes exist along conservative plate margins.

Foundation

1 Name two plates that:
a move away from each other,
b move towards each other,
c move alongside each other.

2 Name three differences between oceanic and continental crusts.

3 a Make a copy of Figure 6.25. Add the following labels in the correct place: continental crust, oceanic crust, ocean trench, fold mountains, volcano, area of earthquakes, crust being destroyed.

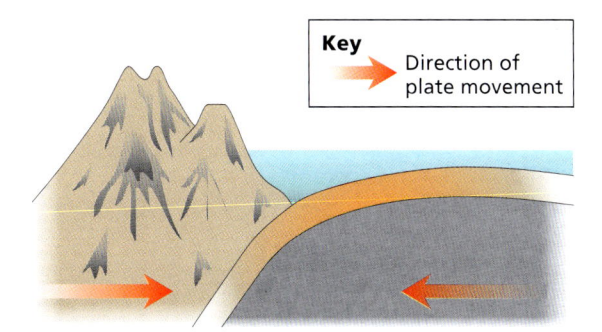

Key
→ Direction of plate movement

Figure 6.25 Plate margin

b What type of plate margin is this?
c Draw and label a similar diagram for a divergent (constructive) margin.

Managing hazards

People can prepare for hazards and they respond to events in different ways

What is an earthquake?

An earthquake is a violent shaking of the earth's crust. They are caused by the sudden release of enormous stresses and lead to the crust snapping. The point at which the snapping occurs is called the focus and is below the surface of the earth and may be many kilometres deep. The point on the ground surface immediately above the focus is called the epicentre and this is where the greatest damage usually occurs.

What is an earthquake hazard?

There are several earthquakes recorded every day, but not all earthquakes have devastating results. What factors turn an earthquake into a disaster?

1 The power of the earthquake – The strength of an earthquake is measured on the Richter scale. Earthquakes measuring more than 6.0 on the Richter scale usually result in some damage. But strength alone is not always the most important criteria.

An earthquake measuring 6.4 in Latur, India killed 25 000 people whereas the 1994 Los Angeles earthquake, which was more powerful (6.6), killed only 40 people.

2 Geology – The effect of an earthquake is less on solid rock and greater on weak sands and clays. The worst damage in the 1989 San Francisco earthquake was on property built on an unstable landfill site.

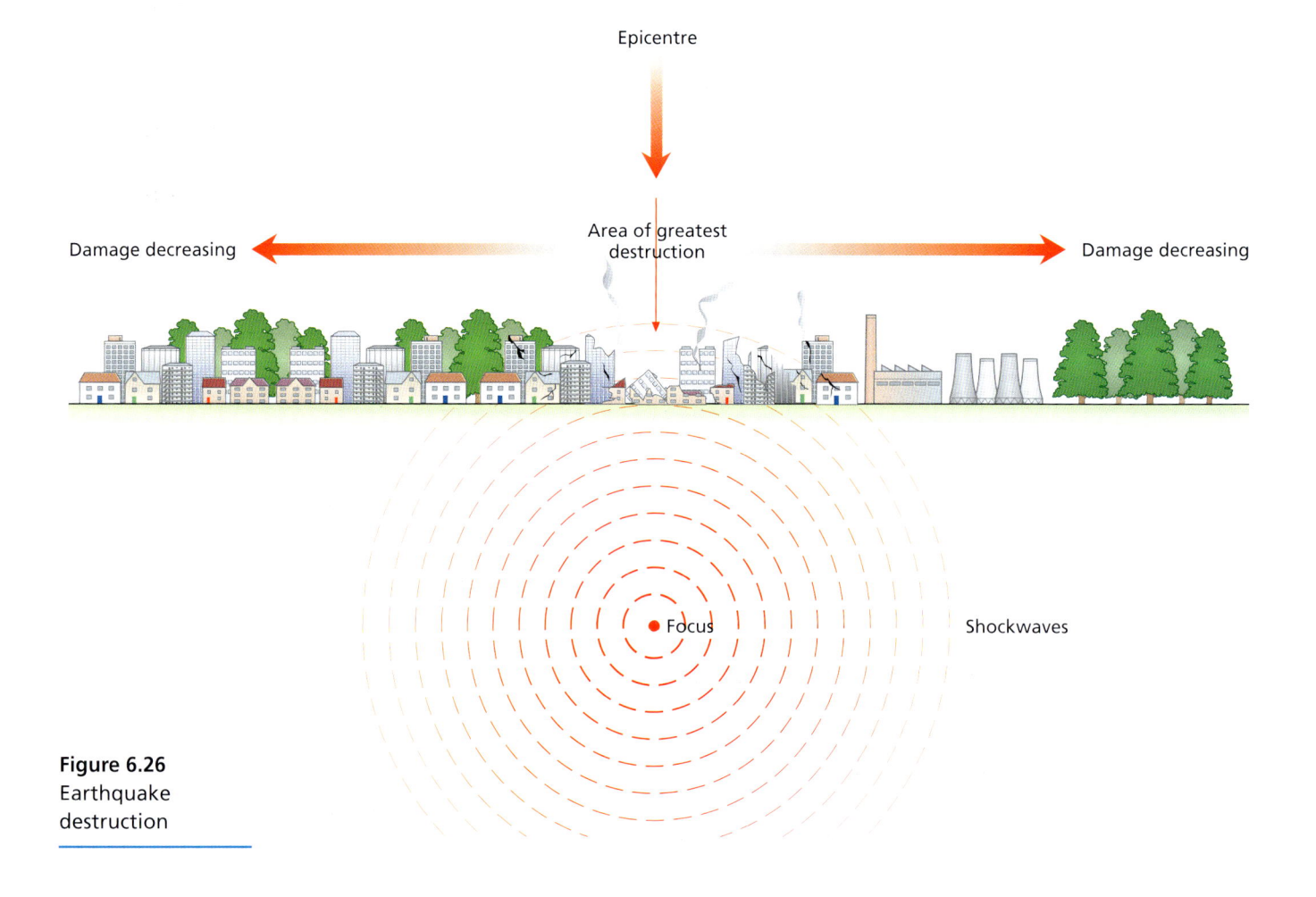

Figure 6.26 Earthquake destruction

Figure 6.27 Earthquake proof structures: (a) buildings and (b) bridges

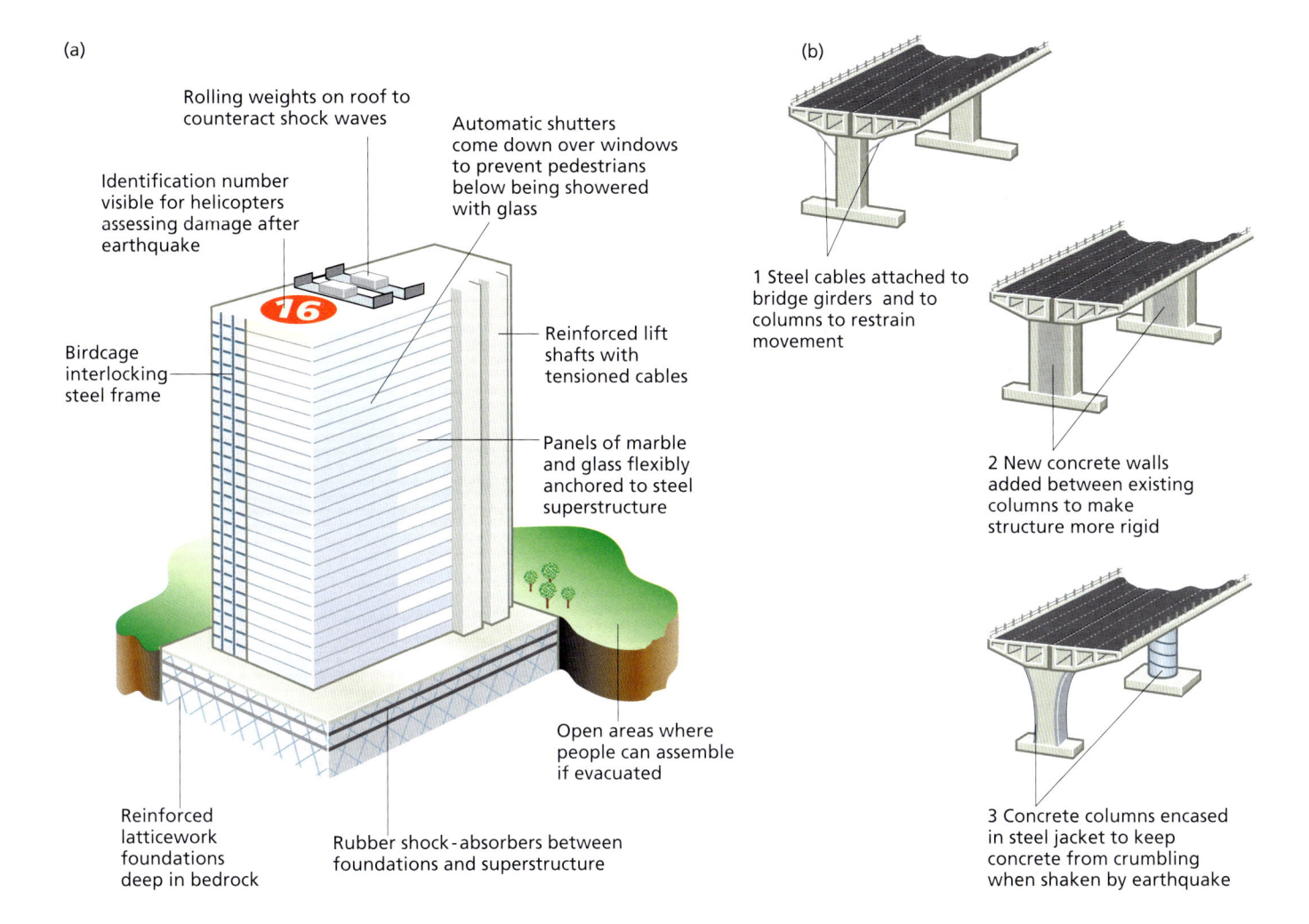

(a)
- Rolling weights on roof to counteract shock waves
- Automatic shutters come down over windows to prevent pedestrians below being showered with glass
- Identification number visible for helicopters assessing damage after earthquake
- Birdcage interlocking steel frame
- Reinforced lift shafts with tensioned cables
- Panels of marble and glass flexibly anchored to steel superstructure
- Open areas where people can assemble if evacuated
- Reinforced latticework foundations deep in bedrock
- Rubber shock-absorbers between foundations and superstructure

(b)
1. Steel cables attached to bridge girders and to columns to restrain movement
2. New concrete walls added between existing columns to make structure more rigid
3. Concrete columns encased in steel jacket to keep concrete from crumbling when shaken by earthquake

3 Depth of the earthquake – Generally the closer the earthquake's focus is to the earth's surface, the greater the damage.

4 Population density – Many of the world's greatest cities are located close to plate margins. Tokyo, Mexico City, San Francisco and Los Angeles are all particularly vulnerable. Obviously if an earthquake hits a densely populated urban area, there are likely to be more deaths than if an earthquake hits a sparsely populated rural area.

5 Building design – Very often the number of deaths resulting from an earthquake is the consequence of poor building design. It is possible to build houses that withstand shaking, but often building regulations are not followed.

6 Wealth of country – Wealthy countries like the USA have good communications and can afford to stockpile emergency supplies of water, food, medicines and shelter. There is more money available to build earthquake-proof buildings, and to spend on research, prediction and prevention. Much work on earthquake prediction has been done in California on the San Andreas Fault. As we have seen, earthquakes are plotted along fault lines. Where gaps appear, it is possible that pressure is building up in these areas and that when this pressure is released, it will trigger an earthquake. This is called the seismic gap theory. The 1989 San Francisco earthquake was anticipated, to some extent, as it occurred in a seismic gap at Loma Prieta.

Managing hazards

Case Study   **LEDC EARTHQUAKE IN TURKEY, 1999**

On 17 August 1999 at 3 am, western Turkey was hit by an earthquake measuring 7.4 on the Richter scale. Its epicentre was close to the industrial centre of Izmit, which was devastated by the earthquake. The effects were also felt in many other large towns, including Golcuk, the coastal resort of Yalova and Istanbul, the largest city in Turkey.

The earthquake was caused by violent movements of the Eurasion and African plates.

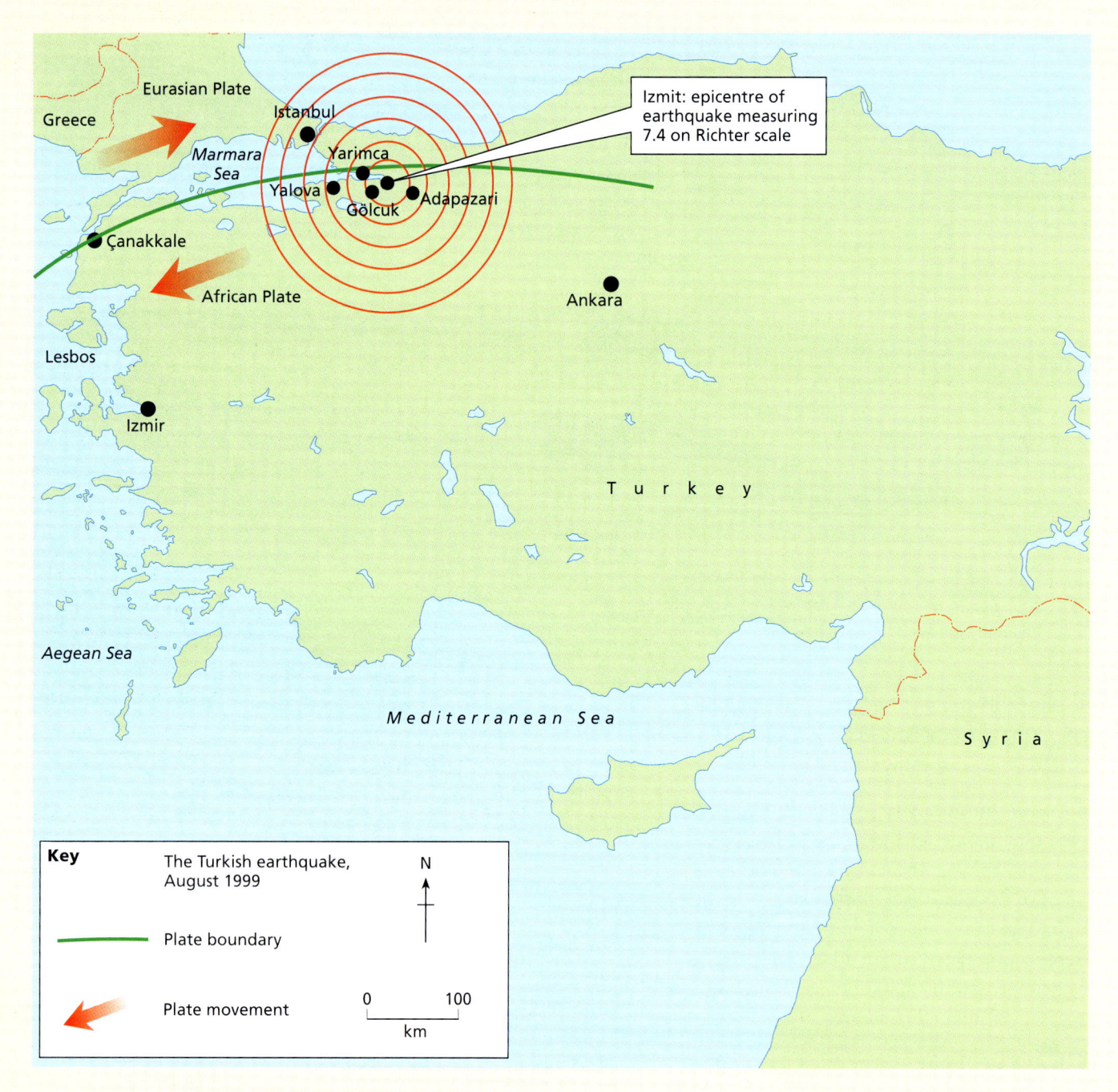

Figure 6.28 The Turkish earthquake

On the following pages are reports about the Turkish earthquake. They explain the human and environmental impacts and the aid that was given to the local people.

Human impacts of the earthquake

The scene unfolding around the collapsed apartment building shown in Figure 6.29 was being repeated all over the devastated city of Izmit. Eighty people lived in this particular apartment complex. To date, only two survivors have been found.

Turkish officials on Tuesday were calling it 'the disaster of the century' as they broadcast appeals for bulldozers, body bags and tents to help deal with the destruction from last week's 7.4-magnitude earthquake, which left more than 14 000 people dead and 200 000 homeless.

Golcuk, a city on the Marmara Sea that's characterised by its military base and a large population of working-class factory workers, is located at the earthquake's epicentre. Today it is a wasteland of crumbled buildings, dead bodies and human suffering. Officials estimate that the earthquake damaged or destroyed as much as 80 per cent of the buildings, burying thousands under tombs of wreckage. And as volunteers and relief workers from around the country and the world arrive here, it is becoming increasingly clear that hope of pulling survivors from the rubble has nearly vanished.

Adapazari, 100 miles east of Istanbul, lies directly along the North Anatolian fault line. Before 17 August it was a bustling industrial centre. Now an estimated 65 000 buildings are destroyed or so damaged as to be unusable. Rubble litters the streets and tens of thousands of people are living in tents and makeshift shelters. The death toll stands at more than 2,500 but hundreds more bodies are believed still to be buried in the destruction.

Figure 6.29 Collapsed buildings in Izmit

Environmental impacts of the earthquake

Concern centres on the Tupras refinery, set ablaze by the quake. The refinery was stocked with 700 000 tonnes of oil. The fire is likely to burn itself out, but by then it will have poured out large quantities of pollution into the air, the water and onto land.

Oil industry experts say the outcome depends partly on how much of the crude oil had been refined, as crude burns more dirtily.

They say the smoke will cause pollution and possible health problems for as long as the fire burns.

The oil can be dispersed over a wide area if it gets into the water. However, there is a team from a UK-based Oil Spill Response Company in Turkey carrying booms, absorbent material and other equipment for containing and clearing up the oil.

The part of north-west Turkey affected by the earthquake contains about a third of the country's industry, and there are reports of extensive damage to factories in Izmit and the surrounding area.

Greenpeace activists in Turkey are concerned about the potential for further pollution. 'The toxic waste dump at Petkim has large cracks and the waste which has been dumped there for years is now exposed', said Melda Keskin, a Turkish member of Greenpeace's Mediterranean branch. 'It is possible there is also damage to the nearby PVC factory, to the waste treatment plant and to the incinerator', she told BBC News.

She went on to say that near Yalova is a chlorine plant, which appeared to be deserted. Next door to it is a factory producing synthetic fibres, where there was some chemical leakage, though it was brought under control.

Figure 6.30 Tupras oil refinery on fire

LEDC EARTHQUAKE IN TURKEY 1999 – continued

Help and aid given to the earthquake zone

The American Red Cross announced that it has established a new 24-hour record for online disaster relief donations through its Internet portals in the wake of last Tuesday's devastating earthquake in Turkey. On Friday, 20 August, donations through redcross.org totalled $138 508. It stated that The Lincy Foundation had made a $1 million donation to support the Red Cross's disaster relief efforts.

The International Red Cross and Red Crescent Movement is rushing technical expertise, disaster relief supplies and financial assistance in response to the devastating earthquake. The American Red Cross is sending 4 members of its International Emergency Response Unit to Turkey to assist the Turkish Red Crescent Society in their relief efforts for victims of the devastating pre-dawn earthquake. The American Red Cross will also provide a donation of 25 000 high-protein biscuits and 25 000 comfort kits to aid the victims of this earthquake.

Within five days of the enormous earthquake which devastated towns and cities around the Marmara Sea, two field hospitals – supplied by the German and Norwegian Red Cross Societies – have not only been transported to the earthquake zone but are up and running and treating patients.

'We have 150 beds but we can go up to 200 and even more if need be', says Dieter Jakobi, director of the German Red Cross field hospital, a series of large tents on a gravel field outside Golcuk.

Figure 6.31 A tented village in the affected area

'We started setting up tents on Friday afternoon', says Attila Demirtas who is running the Turkish Red Crescent operations in Yalova. 'We are now setting up a field kitchen, but we need sanitary facilities such as mobile toilets and showers in order to prevent an outbreak of disease.'

As he speaks, Red Crescent volunteers are mixing cement at one edge of the tent camp to create a platform for a soup kitchen. Other volunteers are setting up the remaining tents. In all, there will be 1,300 Red Crescent tents in the camp and a further 2,700 have been erected around Yalova, but more are needed. 'We need another 10 000 tents if we are to provide shelter for all those who are staying in the streets now,' says Yalova governor, Nihat Ozgun.

The danger of epidemics is ever-present in people's minds. 'Our kids have started to get diarrhoea', says one lady. 'I haven't had a bath or change of clothing since the earthquake struck', she adds.

The factors that contributed to the disaster

Downed bridges, blocked roadways and telecommunications failures in Turkish provinces most devastated by last week's 7.4-magnitude earthquake slowed response to the disaster, Turkish prime minister, Bulent Ecevit admitted. The Turkish leader also promised stricter building rules to prevent the shoddy construction blamed for the thousands of deaths caused by the massive quake.

While older buildings made of solid materials had remained intact, much of the modern housing in poorer urban areas was constructed from mud brick and was unable to withstand the impact of such a tremor and crumpled like packs of cards. 'Cheaply-built, illegal housing lies at the heart of this disaster', said engineering experts. The problem was compounded by the huge influx of people from rural areas into Istanbul and Izmit.

Thirty years ago, three-quarters of the population lived in the countryside and a minority lived in major cities. Now, the opposite is true. This migration has encouraged a growing housing and land Mafia to whom officials have turned a blind eye. The large migrant quarters have grown on public land on the outskirts of these large cities where regulations are frequently flouted. Contractors use the cheapest materials, despite the fact that much of the region lies on an active faultline.

Case Study · MEDC TOTTORI EARTHQUAKE, JAPAN, OCTOBER 2000

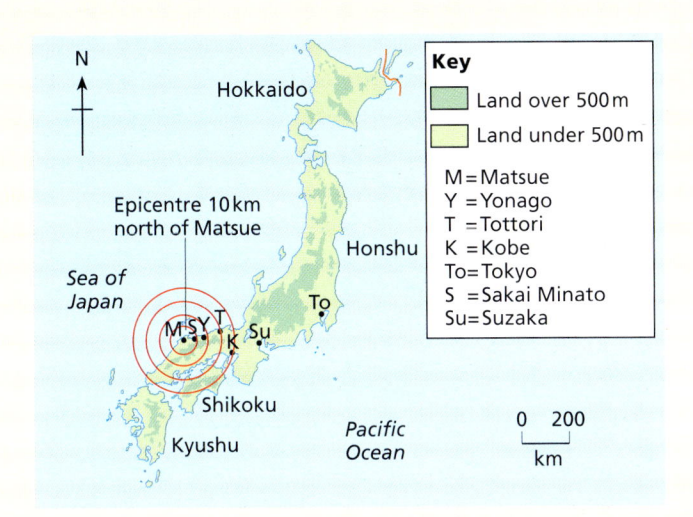

Figure 6.32 Location map of Japanese earthquake

On 6 October 2000 at 1.30 pm an earthquake measuring 7.3 on the Richter scale shook the western coast of Honshu, the largest island of Japan. The focus was 10 km below ground. It was the most powerful earthquake to hit Japan since Kobe in 1995 in which 6,000 people were killed.

Hardest hit were the mainly rural coastal and mountain areas in Tottori about 500 km west of Tokyo: 130 people were injured (there were no fatalities), 2,230 homes were damaged of which 104 were totally destroyed. Two people were rescued after being buried by landslides at two construction sites in Shimano prefecture on the coast of the Sea of Japan.

The cities of Yonago and Sakai Minato were the worst hit. Here water mains, electricity supplies and roads suffered damage, severely disrupting the inhabitants' lives. Display cases in shops were knocked to the ground and white foam from ceiling sprinklers flowed out of buildings. The Shinkansen bullet train services were halted and some small airports were closed for checks.

The earthquake was strong enough to shake the Suzuka racetrack 250 km away where drivers were practising for the Formula One Grand Prix race. It was even felt in Tokyo. No tidal wave warnings were issued. Companies with factories in the area suffered no major damage, but many were temporarily closed for inspections. Experts said that the deep focus of the earthquake, its location offshore and away from densely populated urban centres would have helped to lessen its impact.

Figure 6.33 Devastation in Yonago city

Figure 6.34 Shop damaged by the Tottori earthquake

ACTIVITIES

1   The movement of which plates were responsible for:
a   the Turkish earthquake,
b   the Japanese earthquake.

2   The two earthquakes were very similar in magnitude. However, their effects were very different.
a   In the form of a table, compare the effects of the two earthquakes.
b   Suggest reasons for the differences you have identified.

3   Were short- or long-term effects more damaging in the worst affected areas in Turkey and Japan?

4   Research designs for earthquake-proof buildings. Design your own building to withstand an earthquake.

Managing hazards

Case Study — **LEDC MOUNT PINATUBO, PHILIPPINES, JUNE 1991**

Having remained dormant for 600 years, Mount Pinatubo on the island of Luzon in the Philippines exploded into life in June 1991. Mount Pinatubo is one in a chain of volcanoes known as the Luzon volcanic arc. The arc is the result of the oceanic crust of the Philippines plate being subducted under the lighter continental crust of the Eurasian plate. As it is pushed deep under the earth's surface, the oceanic crust melts resulting in an area of considerable volcanic unrest.

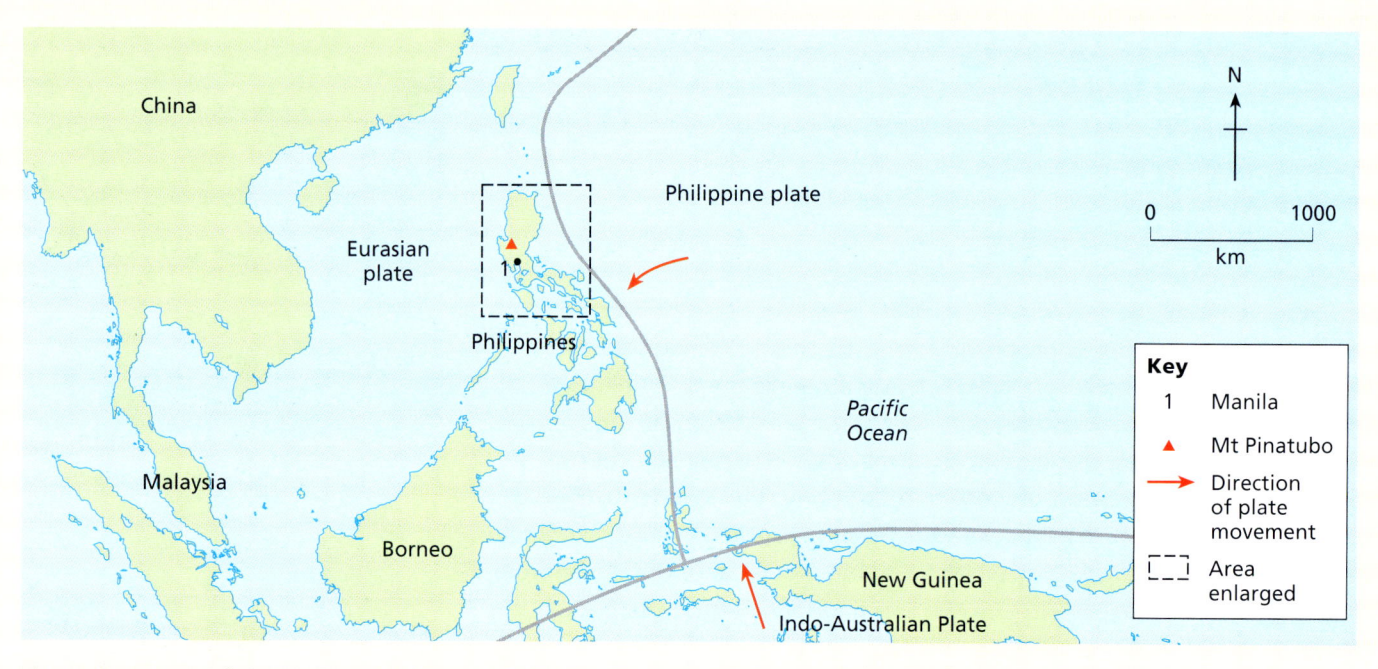

Figure 6.35 Map of the plates causing the eruption of Mt Pinatubo

Figure 6.36 Mt Pinatubo erupting

Stages in the eruption of Mount Pinatubo:

Date (1991)	Volcanic activity	Monitoring	Effects
2 April	Steam explosions form a 1.5 km line of vents near the summit.		A new line of craters formed, vegetation killed, several villages dusted with ash.
3 April	Several new vents formed on the north-west slope.	Philippine Institute of Volcanology and Seismology (PHIVOLCS) called in.	5,000 people evacuated in a 10 km zone around the volcano.
5 April	40 earthquakes recorded.	PHIVOLCS install portable seismographs.	
23 April	Continuing earthquakes and steam emission.	US Geological Survey team set up 7 seismometers at Clark Air Base.	
24 April to 5 June	Some small ash explosions.	Sulphur dioxide emissions measured.	Alert system put into operation.
7 June	Explosion causes a column of steam and gas 7 km high.	Seismic monitoring continued.	Villages on north-west slopes evacuated again.
9 June	Eruption lasting eight hours, causes pyroclastic (rock) flows into the Maraunot and Morazu rivers 4 to 5 km from the centre of activity.		Alert Level 5 (eruption in progress) was issued. Radius of evacuation extended to 20 km.
10 June		14 000 US military evacuated from Clark Air Base.	
12 June	Major explosions eject a grey mushroom-shaped cloud that reaches 20 km into the air. Ash and pumice hurled from the volcano.		Evacuation radius extended to 30 km. 58 000 people now evacuated. Rivers overflow because of blocking by pyroclastic flows.
13 June	Another violent eruption.		Heavy ashfalls cover most of Zam Bales, Torlac and Pampanga. Winds blow volcanic ash hundreds of kilometres in all directions.
14 June	Eruption produces a column of volcanic debris 30 kms high.		Pyroclastic flows run 15 km down the Maraunot River. Up to 50 cm of ash deposited.
15 June	Most violent eruption produces 40 km high column of ash; pyroclastic flows moving at 80 km/hr.	PHIVOLCS record 19 eruptions.	Volcano's original summit collapses. Typhoon Yunga produces heavy rainfall which causes the ash to become saturated, causing buildings to collapse. Manila airport closed. Fast flowing lahars (mudflows) severely erode river channels, undercutting banks and destroying houses and all of the bridges connecting the north and south parts of the city of Angeles.
16 June onwards	Minor earthquakes.		Rivers diverted by lahars Farmland destroyed.

LEDC MOUNT PINATUBO, PHILIPPINES, JUNE 1991 – continued

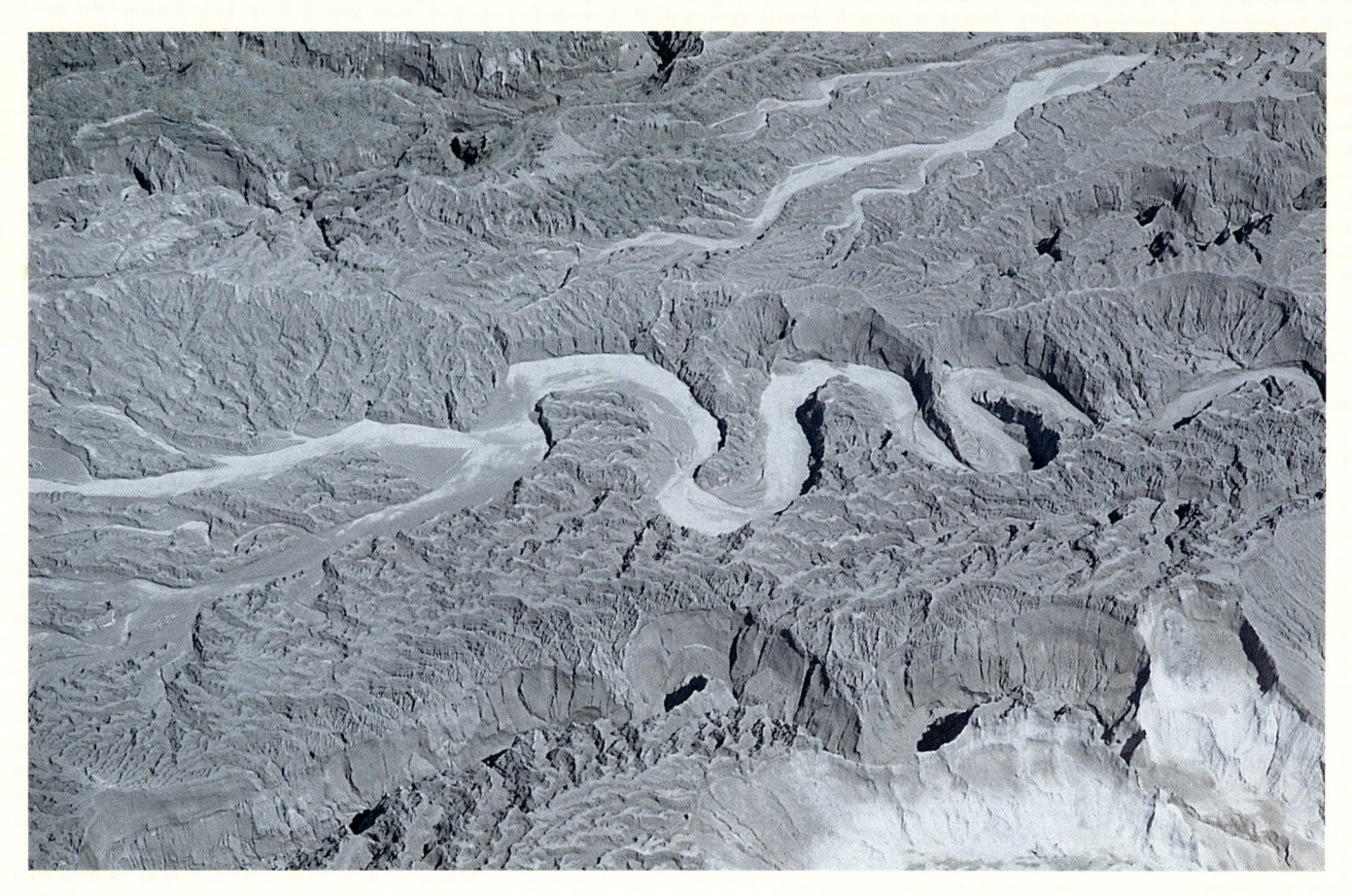

Figure 6.37 Effect of eruption

Final effects of the eruption
- 847 people lost their lives: 300 were killed by collapsing roofs and over 100 by lahars. However, most deaths occurred in evacuation centres. The most vulnerable were the tribal Aetas people who lived as subsistence farmers on the slopes of Mount. Pinatubo. Some of them refused to leave their holy mountain and died during the eruptions, but many died in evacuation centres in the months following the eruption because they became susceptible to disease and were unwilling to take medicines. Measles, respiratory and gastric diseases killed several hundred, most of whom were children.

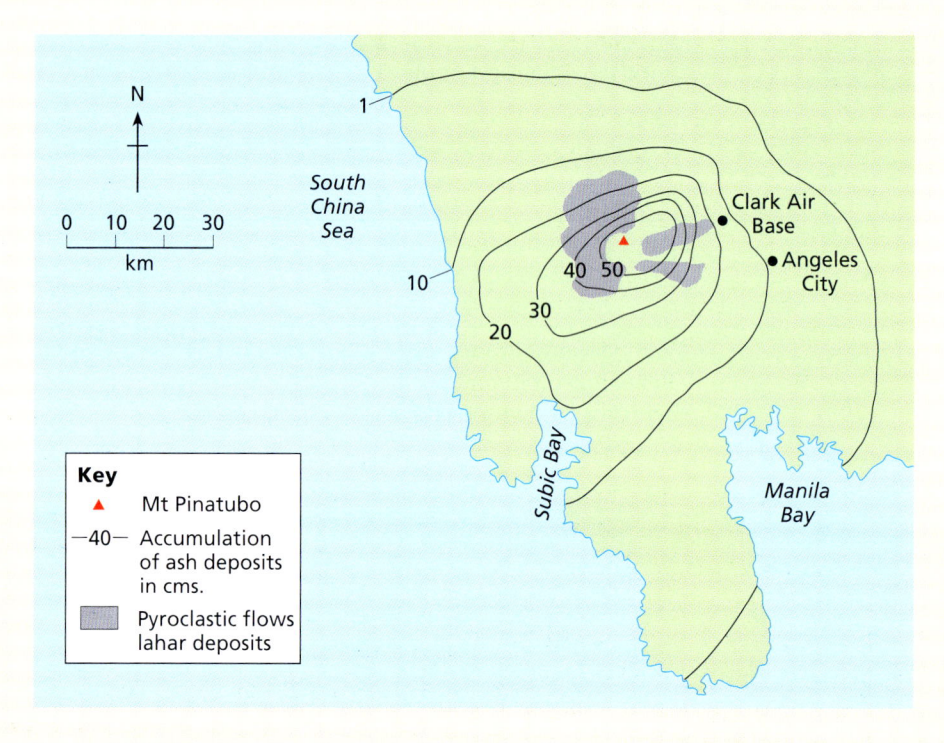

Key
- ▲ Mt Pinatubo
- —40— Accumulation of ash deposits in cms.
- Pyroclastic flows lahar deposits

Figure 6.38 Map showing impact of the eruption

- 1.2 million people lost their homes in settlements up to 40 kilometres way from the centre of activity. 500 000 people migrated to the already overcrowded capital city of Manila. 650 000 workers lost their jobs due to the destruction of farms, shops and factories. 80 000 hectares of cropland were destroyed. The 1991 harvest was destroyed and planting for 1992 was impossible. Over 1 million farm animals died.
- Supplies of electricity were cut off for over 3 weeks. Water was contaminated and roads and telecommunication links were destroyed. Total losses amounted to over $700 million. 5 cubic kilometres of rock, ash were ejected into the atmosphere, causing a global cooling of approximately 0.5 °C.

Planning for volcanic activity

There are several measures that can be taken to reduce the loss of life and limit damage to buildings. Most volcanic events are preceded by clear warnings of activity from the volcano such as gas emission and bulges on the side of the mountain. If these warnings are heeded, then evacuations can take place. Evacuation of the villages around Mount Pinatubo undoubtedly saved thousands of lives. However, if evacuation becomes long term, then strategies need to be in place to house and feed the evacuees. Most of the Mount Pinatubo deaths were caused by disease spreading in the evacuation centres.

Aid is extremely important both in the short term to provide food and blankets, but also in the long term to help rebuild the country's infrastructure. Aid can also come in the form of monitoring and forecasting. This is usually supplied by MEDCs and involves the use of high-cost monitoring equipment and expertise to try to forecast events. Simple monitoring can also be useful. In the Philippines, for example, the local people are trained to look out for early warning signs such as steam releases or the smell of sulphur in the air.

Figure 6.39 Victims being carried on makeshift stretcher

ACTIVITIES

1. Why did Mount Pinatubo erupt?
2. Draw a timeline from the 2 April to 16 June. Mark the changing activity of Mount Pinatubo on the timeline.
3. What is a lahar and a pyroclastic flow? Use Figure 6.38 to describe the area affected by lahars and pyroclastic flows.
4. Outline the short-term and long-term effects of the eruption.
5. Imagine that you were living in an evacuation centre. Make a diary for a week describing the conditions, what happened to you and how you felt.
6. Using newspapers and the Internet, research a current active volcano in an MEDC.
a. What damage was done?
b. Were there many deaths?
c. Was there any aid given?
d. Was the volcano being monitored?

Sample Examination Questions

Higher tier

1 Study Figure 6.24 on page 125 which shows major earthquakes in 1999 and 2000.

   a Which continent did not have any earthquakes?
   (1 mark)

   b Describe the distribution of the earthquakes.
   (3 marks)

   c Explain why there was earthquake activity on the west coast of South America.
   (4 marks)

   d Outline the attempts that have been made to predict earthquakes and say how successful these attempts have been.
   (5 marks)

2 Read the following passage.
   Mount Etna has a long history of frequent eruptions, yet over 1 million people live on its slopes. This is because of fertile soils, rich orchards, vineyards and orange groves. There is also a thriving tourist industry, including skiing, which is a source of employment for many inhabitants. When the volcano erupts the lava has been diverted away from villages by digging channels and erecting dams.

   a Give three reasons to say why so many people choose to live close to Etna?
   (3 marks)

   b In 1985, 23 000 people were killed by a volcanic eruption in Colombia. In 1980, 70 people were killed by a volcanic eruption in the USA. with reference to specific examples, explain why some volcanic eruptions cause more deaths than others.
   (6 marks)

3 Tropical storms occur in many parts of the world. Evaluate the impact that the storm that you have studied has had on a community and the environment.
   (8 marks)

   Total 30 marks

Foundation tier

1 Look at Figure 6.24. It shows the distribution of large earthquakes in 1999 and 2000.

   a In which year – 1999 or 2000 – were there more large earthquakes?
   (1 mark)

   b Which continent did not have any earthquakes? Circle the correct answer from the list below.

   South America   Asia   Africa   North America
   (1 mark)

   c Describe the distribution of earthquakes.   (3 marks)

   d Earthquakes commonly occur at plate boundaries. Explain why.
   (4 marks)

   e Give two ways that scientists try to predict earthquakes.
   (2 marks)

   f How successful are scientists at predicting when earthquakes will happen?
   (3 marks)

2 Read the following passage.
   Mount Etna has a long history of frequent eruptions, yet over 1 million people live on its slopes. This is because of fertile soils, rich orchards, vineyards and orange groves. There is also a thriving tourist industry, including skiing, which is a source of employment for many inhabitants. When the volcano erupts the lava has been diverted away from villages by digging channels and erecting dams.

   a Give three reasons to say why so many people choose to live close to Etna.
   (3 marks)

   b In 1985, 23 000 people were killed by a volcano in Colombia an LEDC. In 1980, 70 people were killed by a volcano in the USA an MEDC. With reference to specific examples, explain why some volcanoes cause more deaths than others.
   (5 marks)

3 Tropical storms happen in many parts of the world. For a tropical storm that you have studied say:

   a what effect it had on the local people.   (4 marks)

   b how it affected the environment.   (4 marks)

   Total 30 marks

7 Managing tourism

The global tourist industry has grown rapidly

Figure 7.1 Different types of holidays

The three main sectors of employment are primary, secondary and tertiary. The primary sector deals mainly with the extraction of raw materials from the earth. The secondary sector is the manufacture of these materials into something more useful. The tertiary industry deals with services, tourism is therefore a tertiary industry.

As tourism develops in a country it provides many jobs; in many LEDCs, tourism can become the main employer and source of income. Tourism not only creates jobs in the tertiary sector, it also encourages growth in the primary and secondary sectors of industry. This is known as the multiplier effect. In its simplest form, the multiplier effect is how many times a dollar injected into the tourist destination's economy circulates through that economy. For example, US$500 spent at a hotel is then re-spent by the hotel to purchase produce from the local farmers or to clean linen. In this way, the US$500 has an indirect impact on the economy of the country. When the farmers use the money, they are paid by the hotel to buy their supplies and this means another round of indirect impact. This is a very positive impact of tourism. The multiplier effect continues until the money is lost through leakage, for example, T-shirts bought from another country which are then printed and sold within the country. The money that is spent on buying the T-shirts has 'leaked' from the country's economy.

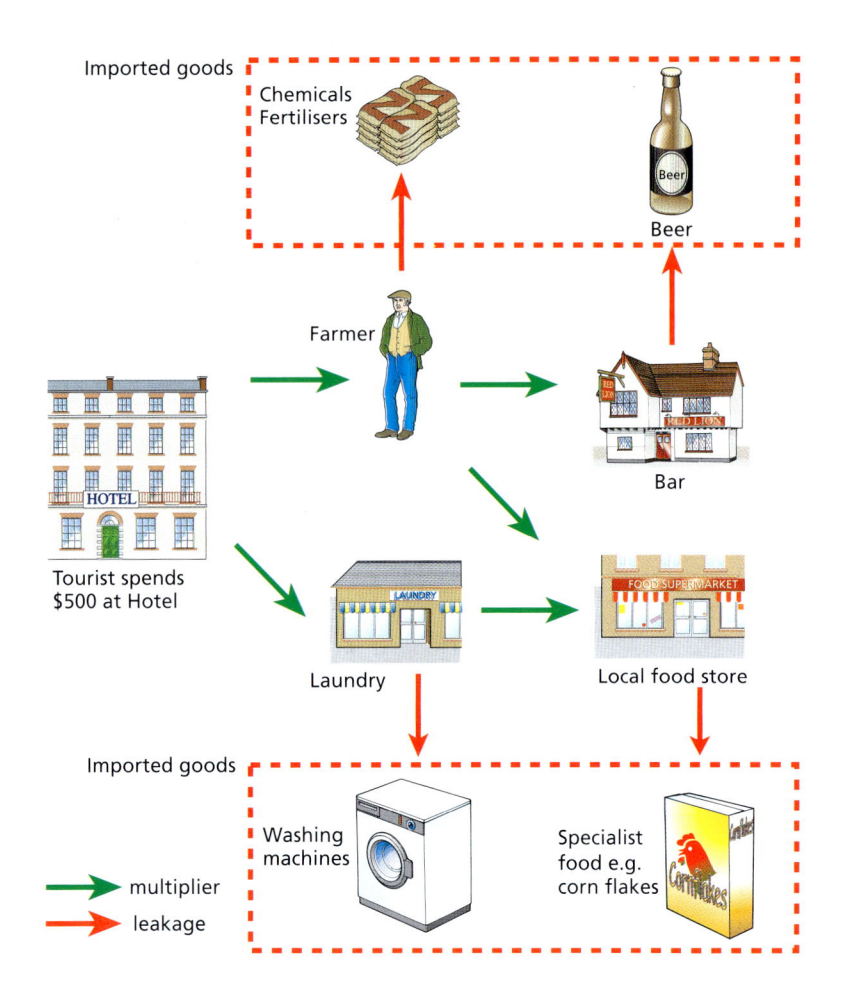

Figure 7.2 The multiplier effect

Thus when tourism develops in an area, it also provides a market for local farm produce, which provides more jobs and revives the primary industry. The demand for local products increases as tourists usually wish to buy souvenirs, which increases secondary employment.

Causes of the rapid growth in tourism

Tourism is one of the fastest growing industries in the world. It is becoming an important sector in both developed and especially developing world economies. Why is the industry growing at such a fast rate?

The growth can be attributed to a number of factors:
- changing socio-economic circumstances,
- technological developments,
- product development and innovation,
- changing consumer needs, expectations and fashions.

Changing socioeconomic circumstances – 'Socioeconomic' is the term used to describe all the factors to do with people and their economic circumstances. It can be split into three categories:

Time – The amount of leisure time available to people has increased dramatically over the last 40 years. This is because jobs come with a holiday entitlement which is paid for. In the UK we are also working shorter weeks – in the 1950s, a 50-hour week was the norm. Most office workers now work between 35 and 40 hours a week. Some people now work flexitime which enables them to work longer days but have more time off at the weekend.

The number of people who are retired and are receiving pensions is also increasing in the developed world. This is a growth market for the tourist industry and is being exploited by many holiday firms.

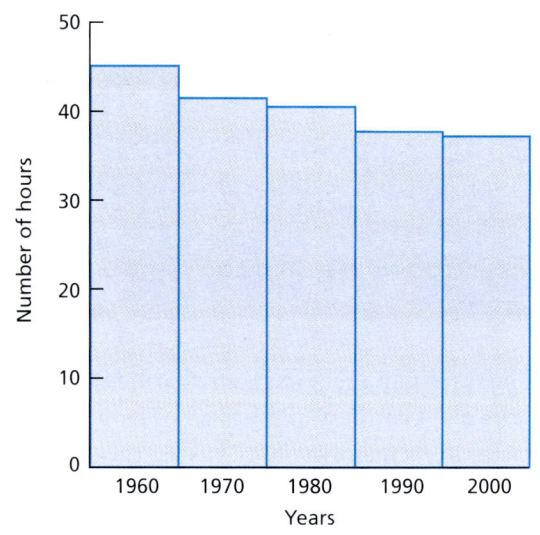

Figure 7.3 Working week hours table

Greater wealth – The populations of most of the countries in the developed world are becoming increasingly wealthy. Although there are large numbers of unemployed people, those who are employed receive good incomes that enable them to afford holidays. Most people also have fewer children, which gives them more disposable income and allows for the possibility of more frequent holidays or travel to more exotic places.

Greater mobility – The increase in car ownership has given people more freedom to choose where they go on holiday. Road networks have also improved – in the 1950s, there were no motorways in the UK. This means that places become closer in time distance and thus more accessible to the population. The development of air travel has increased access to foreign countries.

Year	No. of cars
1920	250 000
1930	1.5 million
1940	1.6 million
1950	2.0 million
1960	5.0 million
1970	10.1 million
1980	15.3 million
1990	20.2 million
2000	24.3 million

Figure 7.4 Car ownership

Technological developments – Technological developments can be split into the developments in transport and developments in communications and information technology.

Developments in transport have revolutionised the travel industry. Aircrafts, ships and trains can now take large numbers of people to their destination safely and quickly. This has opened up areas of the world for the average person with just two weeks' holiday in the summer.

Computer reservation systems have totally changed the sale of air tickets and hotel accommodation. Global distribution systems such as Sabre, Galileo, Amadeus and Worldspan have made it possible for companies such as Thomson to operate commercially on a world scale. These systems make it possible to obtain the latest information on an enormous range of travel and tourism products and services. Many customers now use Teletext and the Internet to book holidays from their own homes. Many airlines and tour operators have recognised this potential and have developed on-line booking services.

Figure 7.5 Advert for holidays in Florida

Product development and changing consumer needs, expectations and fashions – The travel and tourism industry has to continually come up with new products due to changing consumer tastes. One of the first products to be developed were the Butlin's holiday camps in the 1950s. At the time, these were very successful, as they appealed to the British holidaymakers. More recently, there has been the development of theme parks, led by the Disney parks in the USA.

One of the most important product developments has been the package holiday which involved a tour company providing travel, accommodation and sometimes holiday activities. These evolved in the 1950s and were first run by Horizon Holidays. The most recent product developments include long-haul holidays to places like the Maldives and the specialist package holiday which can include getting married!

Many of these product developments are led by changing consumer needs, expectations and fashions.

Managing tourism

Figure 7.6 Example of a holiday offer

holidays which involves them in a particular sporting activity. Perhaps the most popular are skiing holidays. Other types of activity holidays involve scuba diving in the Caribbean or golf holidays in Spain. Passive holidays usually involve sightseeing or just relaxing on a beach in the sun.

Location preference – Some tourists prefer to take their holidays at coastal resorts where they can take advantage of the sea and beach. Other tourists prefer holidays in the mountainous areas where they can hike or ski.

Duration of trip and distance travelled – These categories are dictated by social and economic circumstances. People now have the time and can afford to take both long and short break holidays each year. They may go locally within their own country for a weekend trip: 70 per cent of visitors to the Yosemite National Park in California are on weekend breaks and come from California, for example. Longer holidays tend to be the main holiday of the year. Holidaymakers are likely to stay there for one or two weeks and travel further. Many Britons go to Spain for their annual holiday each summer, for example.

Classifying tourists

There are many different types of tourists, which can be classified in a number of ways:

Nature of activity – Tourists can be either active or passive. Active tourists go on

ACTIVITIES

1. What is the multiplier effect?
2. Draw a suitable graph to show the increase of car ownership in the UK (see Figure 7.4).
3. Research what it was like at holiday camps such as Butlin's in the 1950s compared to the 1990s. Use the table below to help you.

Category	1950s	1990s
Accommodation and catering		
Activities		
Facilities provided		

4. Choose one theme park and describe a day out there. Be sure to include a range of the different products and facilities that are provided.
5. Look at the four pictures in Figure 7.1. Describe and explain two of the photographs in terms of: nature of activity, location preference, duration of trip and distance travelled.

Managing tourism

Case Study — THE IMPACT OF TOURISM ON AYIA NAPA, CYPRUS

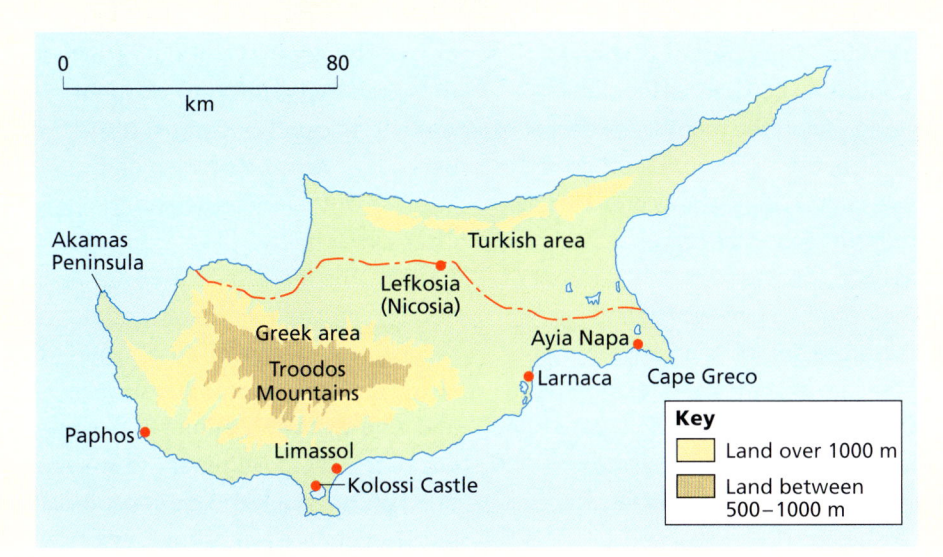

Figure 7.7 Map of Cyprus

Cyprus is the third largest island in the Mediterranean. It has been divided politically since 1974, when the Turks occupied the northern third of the island. The Greek-Cypriot territory in the south has built up a strong tourist industry.

The present employment structure on Cyprus shows a bias towards the tertiary sector (see Figure 7.8).

The numbers of tourists has risen dramatically since the mid 1970s (see Figure 7.9). In 1998 it was estimated that tourism brought £879 million to the country. The Cyprus Tourism Organisation (CTO) has encouraged this growth and certain areas of Cyprus have become known for particular types of holidays. An example of this is Ayia Napa which is seen to be taking over from Ibiza as the capital for young people's holidays.

What are the physical and human attractions of the area?

The climate of Cyprus is typical of the eastern Mediterranean (see Figure 7.10). The summers are long and hot with average August temperatures of 30 °C and 10 mm of rainfall. In December average temperatures are 17 °C with a rainfall average of 75 mm.

There are many physical attractions of the islands; one of these is the Akamas peninsula. This is one of Europe's last unspoilt forests, home to unique species of fauna and flora and the beaches of which are perfect breeding grounds for turtles. Greenpeace are working to make this area into a national park to preserve it, rather than allow it to be exploited for tourism. In the centre of the island are the Troodos mountains which are covered in pine forests. Closer to Ayia Napa is the Greco peninsula with spectacular cliffs dotted with caves. Nissi beach near the town of Ayia Napa is one of the best beaches on the island. There is also a small natural harbour which used to provide the main source of income for Ayia Napa. The harbour is now deserted and the only fishing trips are for tourists. Cruise ships also use the harbour, taking tourists to sea for the day or to Egypt or Jerusalem.

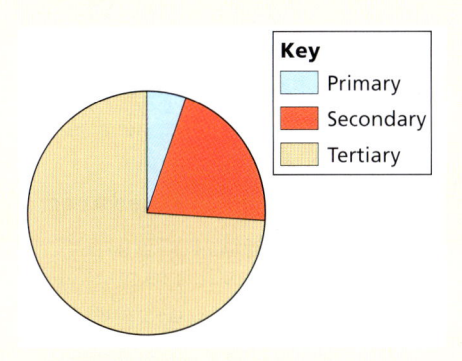

Figure 7.8 Employment structure of Cyprus

Year	No. of visitors
1975	47 085
1986	827 987
1988	1 000 000
1992	1 991 000
1996	1 950 000
1998	2 222 000
2000	2 223 000

Figure 7.9 Tourist numbers for Cyprus

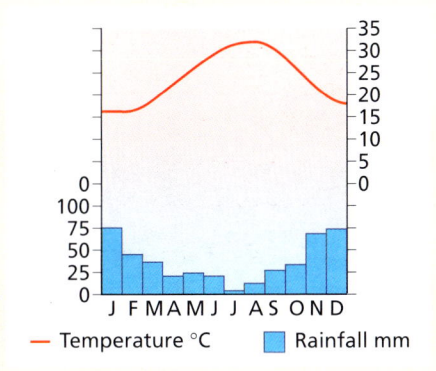

Figure 7.10 Climate graph for Cyprus

Figure 7.11 Ayia Napa

THE IMPACT OF TOURISM ON AYIA NAPA, CYPRUS – continued

As Ayia Napa is a purpose-built resort, there are many human attractions in the area. The resort has a reputation for catering for young people. There are many bars, clubs and discos which stay open for most of the night. There is a waterpark called Waterworld which opened in 1996 and has numerous slides, one of which is a four-track multislide which is ridden head first on a mat. The park has Greek mythology as its theme. Ayia Napa recently opened a marine park which has 4 performing dolphins and 2 performing seals. Tourists can watch the shows and swim with the dolphins under strict supervision. More peaceful human attractions are the Makronissos Tombs which were first discovered in 1872. Although they have been looted, it is agreed that they date back to the Roman period. In the main square of Ayia Napa, surrounded by a high wall, is the monastery dedicated to Our Lady of the Forests. This is one of the few remaining buildings from the original village.

What is the impact of tourism on the area?

The impacts of tourism on Cyprus and Ayia Napa in particular can be split into social, environmental and economic. Although some of the impact has been negative, if there was not also positive impact, the CTO would not have encouraged the development of tourism to such an extent. Cyprus was developing as a tourist destination in the early 1970s. The war with Turkey and the loss of the north-eastern part of the island with its developing tourist centres, was a great loss. Since the formation of the CTO in 1976 the tourist industry has grown dramatically. It now provides 20 per cent of GDP and employs 40 000 people in hotels alone. When the multiplier effect is applied, this figure is at least doubled (see page 138). The jobs provided by tourism tend to be seasonal, however, as hotels only let about 30 per cent of their rooms in the winter and therefore do not need the same numbers of staff. The CTO is trying to remedy this by marketing Cyprus as a holiday destination for all seasons.

The social impacts of mass tourism can be both beneficial and detrimental. On the positive side, the local youth in Ayia Napa have a much better night life as the provision of entertainment is much better than it would be without the tourists. There are more bus services to Larnica, the capital, than there would be if Ayia Napa was still a small fishing village. However, there are a number of negative impacts. The original inhabitants of the village have moved away and built themselves a new village on the hill. This is very distressing as many had lived and fished from the village all their lives, but were forced to move because of the noise and bad behaviour of the tourists.

Environmental impact has also been great. There has been a massive building programme with many new hotels being built right next to the beach. The beach was used by turtles to lay their eggs but they no longer come to this part of Cyprus. The beaches have to be cleaned daily because of their overuse and the litter which is left by hundreds of tourists. The increase in tourists has also put pressure on the essential services like sewage disposal. There is also a problem with power supplies and a new power station has become necessary. The government wants to build another oil-fired power station, but Greenpeace is putting pressure on them to build a solar-powered station which would be ideal given the climate.

What is the future for tourism in Cyprus?

The CTO say that if it is to continue to increase its share of the worldwide tourist market, it needs to diversify and change the image of Cyprus, but not Ayia Napa.

1. Agro-tourism is being developed in the Troodos mountains.
2. Paphos is being marketed as an upmarket resort.
3. The CTO is planning to market Cyprus as a golfing destination and has business consortiums and hoteliers queuing up to get involved.
4. Marinas are being built.

Figure 7.12 Ayia Napa harbour

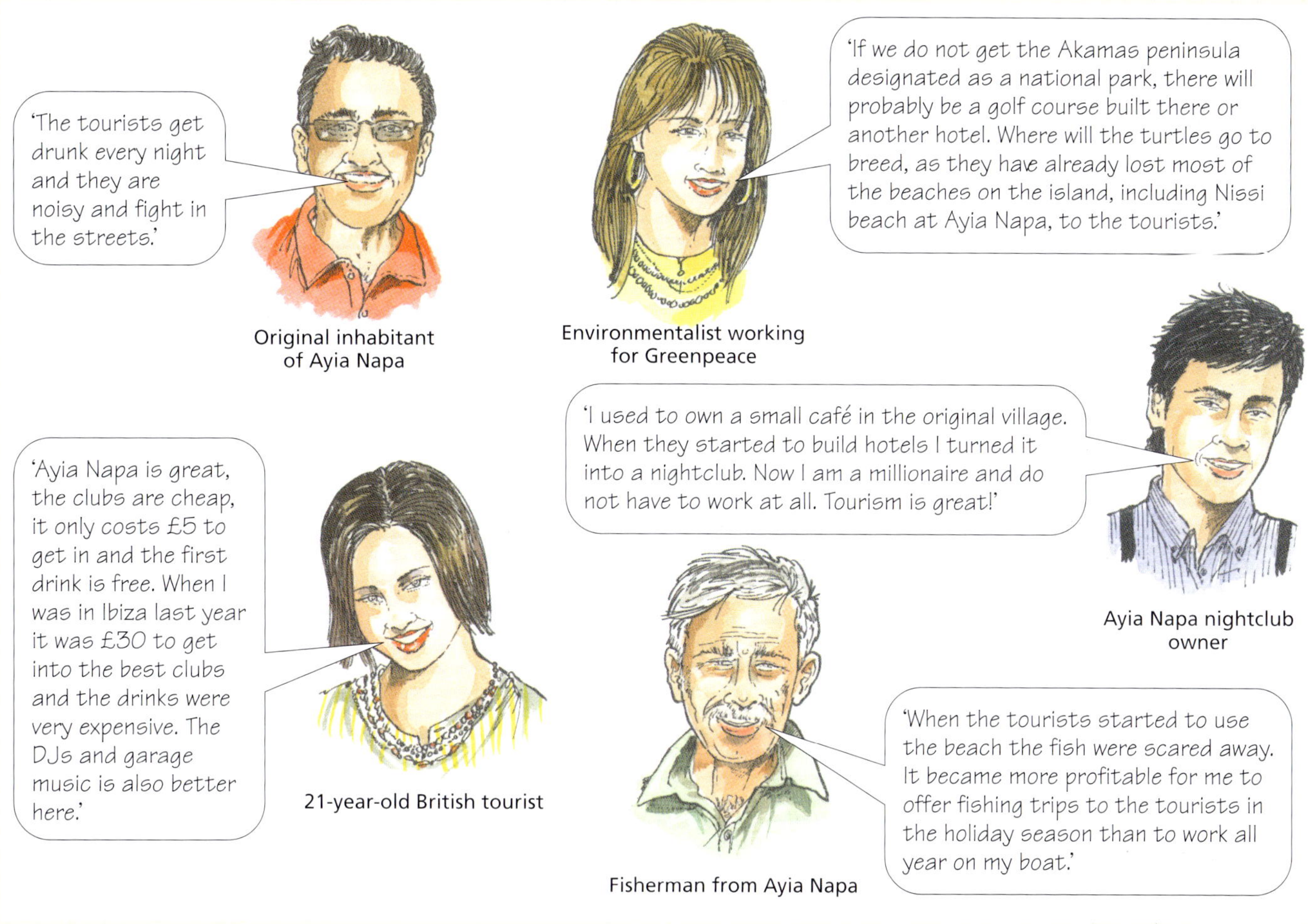

Managing tourism   143

'The tourists get drunk every night and they are noisy and fight in the streets.'
— Original inhabitant of Ayia Napa

'If we do not get the Akamas peninsula designated as a national park, there will probably be a golf course built there or another hotel. Where will the turtles go to breed, as they have already lost most of the beaches on the island, including Nissi beach at Ayia Napa, to the tourists.'
— Environmentalist working for Greenpeace

'I used to own a small café in the original village. When they started to build hotels I turned it into a nightclub. Now I am a millionaire and do not have to work at all. Tourism is great!'
— Ayia Napa nightclub owner

'Ayia Napa is great, the clubs are cheap, it only costs £5 to get in and the first drink is free. When I was in Ibiza last year it was £30 to get into the best clubs and the drinks were very expensive. The DJs and garage music is also better here.'
— 21-year-old British tourist

'When the tourists started to use the beach the fish were scared away. It became more profitable for me to offer fishing trips to the tourists in the holiday season than to work all year on my boat.'
— Fisherman from Ayia Napa

Figure 7.13 People's opinions on tourist developments at Ayia Napa

---

ACTIVITIES

Higher

1. Where is Ayia Napa?
2a. What is the CTO?
 b. Why is it important to the tourist industry of Cyprus?
3. Draw up a table which lists the physical and human attractions of Cyprus.
4. Do a cost–benefit analysis of the effects of tourism on Cyprus.
5. Discuss people's opinions on the development of Ayia Napa as a tourist resort.
6. Explain how the CTO is taking a more sustainable approach to tourism in the future.

Foundation

1. Where is Ayia Napa?
2a. What is the CTO?
 b. Why is it important to the tourist industry of Cyprus?
3a. List 3 physical attractions that Cyprus has for tourists.
 b. List 3 human attractions that Cyprus has for tourists.
4. Tourism has many effects on a country. Draw up a table to show the positive and negative impacts of tourism on Cyprus.
5. Some people are for tourist developments and others are against them. Give reasons for these different opinions.
6. Cyprus is developing new ideas for its tourist industry. Describe two of these ideas and explain how they are sustainable.

Managing tourism

Case Study: THE IMPACT OF TOURISM ON ZANZIBAR, EAST AFRICA

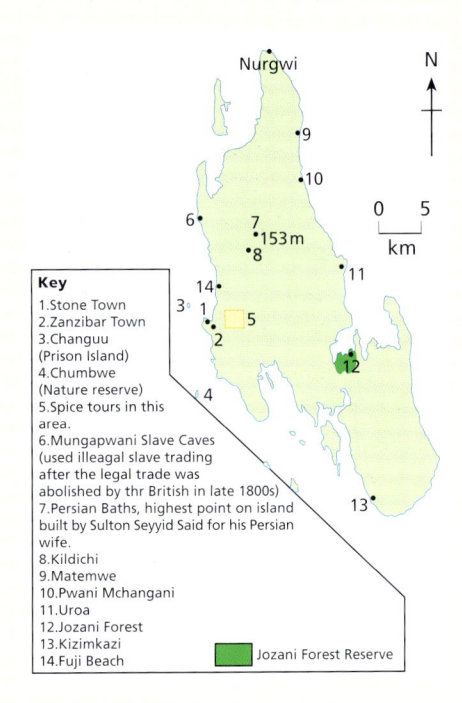

Figure 7.14 Map of Zanzibar

Key
1. Stone Town
2. Zanzibar Town
3. Changuu (Prison Island)
4. Chumbwe (Nature reserve)
5. Spice tours in this area.
6. Mungapwani Slave Caves (used illeagal slave trading after the legal trade was abolished by thr British in late 1800s)
7. Persian Baths, highest point on island built by Sulton Seyyid Said for his Persian wife.
8. Kildichi
9. Matemwe
10. Pwani Mchangani
11. Uroa
12. Jozani Forest
13. Kizimkazi
14. Fuji Beach

Jozani Forest Reserve

Zanzibar is an archipelago made up of Zanzibar (known locally as Unguja), the Pemba Islands and several islets. The most well-known is Chumbe, a nature reserve which won the British Airways Global Tourism for Tomorrow Award in 2000 for its commitment to sustainable tourism. The archipelago, which is 86 km long and 39 km wide, is located in the Indian Ocean about 37 km from the Tanzanian coast. The population of Zanzibar is estimated at 750 000 in 2000 and is expected to double by 2006.

Figure 7.15 Zanzibar population figures

Year	Population
1985	590 000
1990	660 000
1995	750 000
2000	950 000
2005 (projected)	1 600 000

Figure 7.16 Nungwi beach and hotels

The island is known for its exports of cloves and spices. However, a world slump in the markets for these products and others that are produced on the island has meant that agriculture on the island is declining. This, coupled with the growing population and very little industrial development, has meant that the economy of the island has many problems. The latest figures indicate that 35 per cent of the population is unemployed. It is clear that the island must develop in some way to cope with these problems. Could tourism be the answer?

What are the physical and human attractions of the area?

Zanzibar has the ideal weather for holidays as it is warm all the year round with temperatures that vary between 28 and 38 °C. The cool sea breezes to the east and north of the island offset the summer heat. However, there are long rainstorms in April and May and frequent showers in November. The island is fringed by coral reefs and there are unspoilt white sand beaches in the north of the island. Visitors are charged an entrance fee of US$50 to enter the village of Nungwi, where there are a number of hotels. The style of the present hotels at Nungwi fits in well with the local landscape (see Figure 7.16).

There are other beautiful undeveloped beaches along the west coast of the island at Matemwe, Uroa and Pwani Mchangani. The hotels along this coast are very simple and few have electricity, running water, swimming pools or any form of entertainment. The roads to this part of the island are no more than tracks. The sea is an ideal temperature of 27 °C, and so snorkelling and scuba diving are particularly popular around the island, as is swimming with the dolphins at Kizimkazi.

Figure 7.17 Scuba diving off the coast of Zanzibar

Jozani Natural Forest Reserve is 24 km south east of Zanzibar town. It is the home of the rare Red Colobus Monkey which is native to Zanzibar. The forest has an excellent nature trail and the guides are well trained and informative. Tours cost US$2 and take about half a day.

There are many human attractions on the island. The most famous is perhaps Stone Town, said to be the only functioning ancient town in east Africa. It has been designated a World Heritage Site. Within its walls there are many other places to visit, such as Dr Livingstone's House and the Palace Museum.

From Stone Town many tourists take a trip to Changuu, or Prison Island as it is also known. It was a prison for unruly slaves and the old buildings are still there. The island also has a superb beach, clear sea as well as a family of giant tortoises which came from the Seychelles in the early twentieth century and are now protected on the island.

Zanzibar is a Muslim country which was ruled by the Arabs for many years. There are many mosques to visit, including the ruins of Shirazi Dimbani at Kizimkazi on the southern tip of the island which dates back to the twelfth century. Just outside the town of Zanzibar are the plantations that produce the island's main agricultural products of cloves and spices. Many visitors go on walking tours of the wooded areas to spot the clove trees. Perhaps one of the most unique attractions is a visit to Chumbe Island off Zanzibar, a private nature reserve (only 14 people may visit at a time). The visitors have zero impact on the environment, hence the power is solar, there are compost toilets and the only air conditioning is the wind. Another trip which can be taken from Zanzibar is to fly to the mainland and take a safari to the Amboseli game reserve.

What are the impacts of tourism on the area?

The development of tourism on Zanzibar is small scale at present, but is growing rapidly and is already starting to have an effect on the local population. There were an estimated 64 285 tourists in 1995 and by 2000, numbers were still below 100 000.

Figure 7.18 Zanzibar Tourist numbers

Year	Tourist numbers
1980	15 678
1984	18 123
1988	37 650
1992	59 747
1996	65 000

The population of Zanzibar lives mainly on the coast and many of them are fishermen. For them, the development of tourism has meant a loss of fishing stocks as well as access to the beach area as a resource. An example of this is the east coast of Zanzibar, which in 1990 had no hotels but several small fishing communities. By 1997 there were 80 hotels, many of which had controlled access to the beach. The tourists and their leisure activities, such as snorkelling and wind surfing, come first and access for the local community to earn a living, second. On the other hand, the development of hotels has meant that there are other job opportunities in an area which previously relied on primary activities, such as farming and fishing. However, in many cases the jobs are menial and low paid. The improved infrastructure, such as roads, benefits the local population as well as the tourists, but the fresh water supplies that are provided are only for the benefit of the tourist hotels.

One of the main problems in Zanzibar is that there are no clear rules as to who owns the land by the coast and, as yet, the government has not taken a lead in this. In the meantime, local inhabitants are losing access to the coast as new hotels are built. In urban areas, increasing demand for food from hotels has raised prices so that local inhabitants are unable to afford a staple diet.

However, the picture is not all bleak. In designating Stone Town as a World Heritage Site, for example,

Figure 7.19 Palace museum and walls surrounding Stone Town

Case Study: THE IMPACT OF TOURISM ON ZANZIBAR, EAST AFRICA

the government has protected it from tourist development. This can now only take place as a concerted scheme to redevelop the town in keeping with its historic nature. The government needs to take further action to preserve the coastline as pressure is mounting on the breeding ground of turtles and the coral reef which surrounds the island.

The social effects on the people of Zanzibar must also be considered. Relative to the population of Zanzibar, tourists are wealthy and have different moral codes particularly as this is a Muslim country.

Economic problems can also develop if a country becomes too dependent on one industry. Tourism is very reliant on fashion and certain countries can go in and out of favour, which can create major problems for the country's economy. The government of Zanzibar is

Figure 7.20 Zanzibar

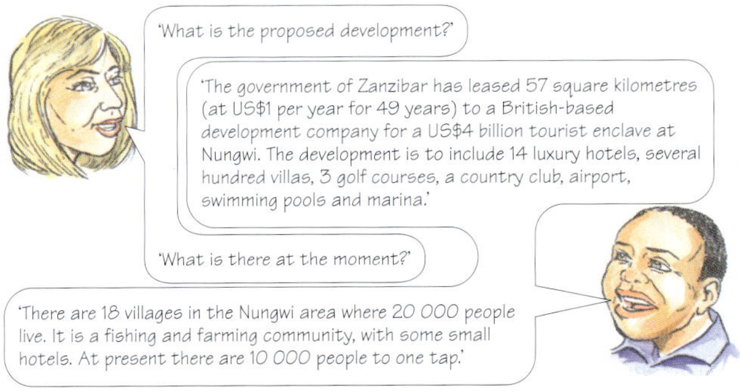

Figure 7.21a Nungwi development

'What is the proposed development?'

'The government of Zanzibar has leased 57 square kilometres (at US$1 per year for 49 years) to a British-based development company for a US$4 billion tourist enclave at Nungwi. The development is to include 14 luxury hotels, several hundred villas, 3 golf courses, a country club, airport, swimming pools and marina.'

'What is there at the moment?'

'There are 18 villages in the Nungwi area where 20 000 people live. It is a fishing and farming community, with some small hotels. At present there are 10 000 people to one tap.'

Figure 7.21b People's opinions on the proposed Nungwi development

Abdalla Said, who runs a development project in Nungwi: 'We have been assisting the villagers on income-generation activities for a number of years to help reduce poverty in the area. It will mean a loss of our money and energy.'

Sheha, the village head: 'We have not been consulted at all about this project.'

Maalim Khatib, a local villager: 'I have been living in this village for more than 10 years fishing for a living. I have a market for my fish at hotels in Zanzibar. How am I going to survive when the project denies me access to the beach?'

Athman, a local hotelier: 'This is unfair because we are not sure whether we will get any compensation.'

'Nungwi is being developed with the needs of the local people and environment being taken into consideration. Surely this type of development is more sustainable?'

A representative of an environmentalist group: 'We fear the outcome of a development of this size on the local communities and the local environment.'

A spokesmen for EADC, the development company: 'The villagers will not be displaced. Most will be employed by the company, while others can carry on farming on the outskirts of the complex.'

An environmental spokesperson: 'We are concerned that an environmental impact assessment has not been carried out.'

British tourist, Lucy Phipps: 'Nungwi is beautiful as it is. Why spoil it by building a resort complex? Surely there are enough of those in the world already?'

Local conservationist spokesperson

Managing tourism

trying to combat this by promoting upmarket tourism rather than mass tourism. There has also been an increase in the number of robberies and muggings on the east coast, but this is not yet a problem on the undeveloped west coast.

Zanzibar has no sewage treatment centres. Raw sewage and hospital waste flows straight into the Indian Ocean. This is already becoming a problem around Zanzibar town where trickles of sewage have to be avoided by those walking on the beach.

If the island continues to increase its tourist numbers, this problem will spread to other areas around the island. The government has foreseen this problem and brought in strict requirements for waste treatment and disposal at new out-of-town resort developments. However, the monitoring and enforcement of the rules is relaxed. Solid waste is dumped around the island with no control. There is growing concern that there will be serious contamination of water supplies. Most of the water comes from underground water supplies, due to the porous rocks. There is also concern about a lack of drinking water: in Nungwi, for example, one tap serves 10 000 people. What will happen when the proposed new resort complex is built (see Figure 7.21)?

ACTIVITIES

Higher

1. Where is Zanzibar?
2. Draw a table which lists the physical and human attractions of Zanzibar.
3. a. Study the photograph in Figure 7.16 of a hotel at Nungwi.
   b. Describe and explain how the hotel is appropriate in its setting.
4. Do a cost–benefit analysis of the effects of tourism on Zanzibar.
5. There has been a proposal to build a resort complex at Nungwi (see Figure 7.16). The details of the proposal are in Figure 7.21a. People's opinions are in Figure 7.21b.
   a. Describe the proposed development.
   b. Do an environmental impact analysis of the proposed development.
   c. People have differing opinions about these types of developments. Describe their different opinions.
   d. In your opinion, should Nungwi be developed?
   e. Is this method of development sustainable?

Foundation

1. Where is Zanzibar?
2. a. List 3 physical attractions that Zanzibar has for tourists.
   b. List 3 human attractions that Zanzibar has for tourists.
3. Look at the photograph of a hotel at Nungwi in Figure 7.16.
   a. Describe the hotel.
   b. The hotel seems to fit in with the local environment. Give reasons why.
4. Tourism has many effects on a country. Draw up a table to show the positive and negative impacts of tourism on Zanzibar.
5. There has been a proposal to build a resort complex at Nungwi (see Figure 7.16). The details of the proposal are in Figure 7.21a. Peoples opinions are in Figure 7.21b.
   a. Describe the proposed development.
   b. Complete the table below for the proposed development.
   c. People have differing opinions about these types of developments. Describe their different opinions.
   d. In your opinion, should Nungwi be developed?

Impact	Negative	Positive
Environmental		
Social		
Economic		

Case Study: THE IMPACT OF TOURISM ON THE PENNINE WAY AND MALHAM, UK

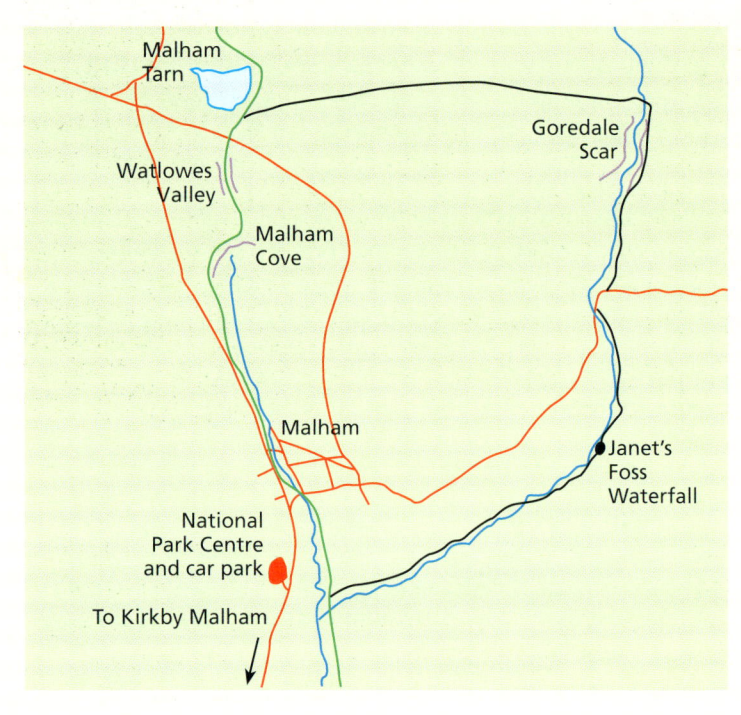

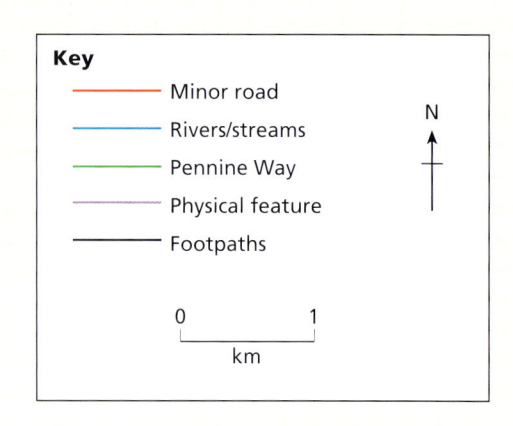

Figure 7.22 Map of the Malham area

The Pennine Way is Britain's first and best-known national trail. It runs from Edale in Derbyshire to Kirk Yetholm just over the Scottish border, a distance of 429 km. The Pennine Way was officially opened in 1965. It takes in some of northern England's finest scenery. The Malham area is one of the most popular locations for people who complete part of the trail, with between 75 000 and 100 000 walkers per year. Counters set up at Malham have been known to count 4,000 people a day on summer Sundays.

What are the physical and human attractions of the area?

The climate of the Malham area is typical of the Pennine region of northern England. It receives approximately 1,000 mm of rain a year. Its July temperatures average 14 °C and its January temperatures average 2 °C. Although tourists do not visit Malham for its climate, the area has many other physical attractions. It has a number of unique features which cannot be seen in any other area of the UK. These include Malham Tarn, Malham Cove, Watlowes Valley and Goredale Scar (these features can be seen on the annotated map in Figure 7.22).

Figure 7.23a Malham Cove

Figure 7.23b Watlowes valley

Managing tourism

The area also includes wide biodiversity, from wetlands around the tarn, to limestone pavements. Day visitors can be split into two categories: honeypotters, who walk for less than two miles and full, or part day walkers, who walk more than two miles.

The area has a number of human attractions and has been designated a honeypot area by the Yorkshire Dales National Park Authority. This means that a number of facilities have been provided for tourists. The National Park Centre, opened in 1974, provides information on the area such as local walks and places to stay. There is also a pay-and-display car park next to the centre. The area is well marked with signposts and footpaths which are maintained by the numerous authorities that manage the area. There are numerous cafes and public houses providing refreshments in the village of Malham. In the centre of Malham there is a former packhorse bridge, as well as many Dales stone houses dating back to the eighteenth century.

What are the impacts of tourism on the area?

Tourism has had both positive and negative impact on the area. Although it has been popular for centuries, it is only since the 1950s with the increase in car ownership, that tourism has increased greatly. The increase in tourists has meant that there are more cars on the narrow country lanes.

As many of the lanes are only wide enough for one vehicle, passing places have been provided. Some tourists park in these passing places which causes major congestion, especially during July and August. Although the National Park has provided a car park for the visitors, demand for spaces far exceeds its capacity for 105 cars and 8 coaches. Visitors tend to park in the narrow village streets causing further congestion. The local residents are prevented from going about their necessary activities and access for emergency vehicles is severely restricted.

Footpaths are provided in the area and are well marked and this has overcome the problem of trespass. However, the area has, with its many signposts and commercial boards, become over commercialised. Local businesses have been asked to cut down on the number of advertising billboards. It is hoped that this will bring back the atmosphere of a traditional English village.

Another problem associated with tourism is the decline of the traditional village shop. Newsagent and grocery shops now concentrate on crafts, souvenirs and speciality goods to cater for the tourists. However, without the tourists, shops would, more than likely, have been forced to close down. This is illustrated in the winter months

Figure 7.24 Malham village

Figure 7.25 Footpath erosion at Malham

THE IMPACT OF TOURISM ON THE PENNINE WAY AND MALHAM, UK – continued

when the newsagents in Malham only open for three days a week, but every day in the summer months. Traditional village public houses have become 'themed', destroying their authentic nature as well as discouraging the locals. The pubs also rely heavily on the tourist trade: between May and October one pub opens a bar for hikers.

Tourism can also be beneficial in creating more demand for local services such as banks and public transport. It also provides new employment opportunities in an area suffering from the depression in farming.

The increase in the number of tourists has also affected the environment of the area. The footpath from Malham village past Janet's Foss waterfall to Goredale Scar is particularly badly worn as this landscape feature is the closest to the village. Surface erosion to the path is particularly bad and continually widens as people seek to find easier routes. This has led to a loss of grazing in the area and the destruction of wildlife habitats. Litter is a constant problem which not only reduces the appeal of the area but also poses a risk to wildlife and local farmers' livestock. It is both costly and time consuming to remove the litter. Other problems that farmers face are damage resulting from visitors climbing walls, visitors' dogs disturbing farm animals and vandalism. Nevertheless, farmers in the area have benefited from tourism. Farmers who have opened campsites or self-catering accommodation benefit from the badly needed extra

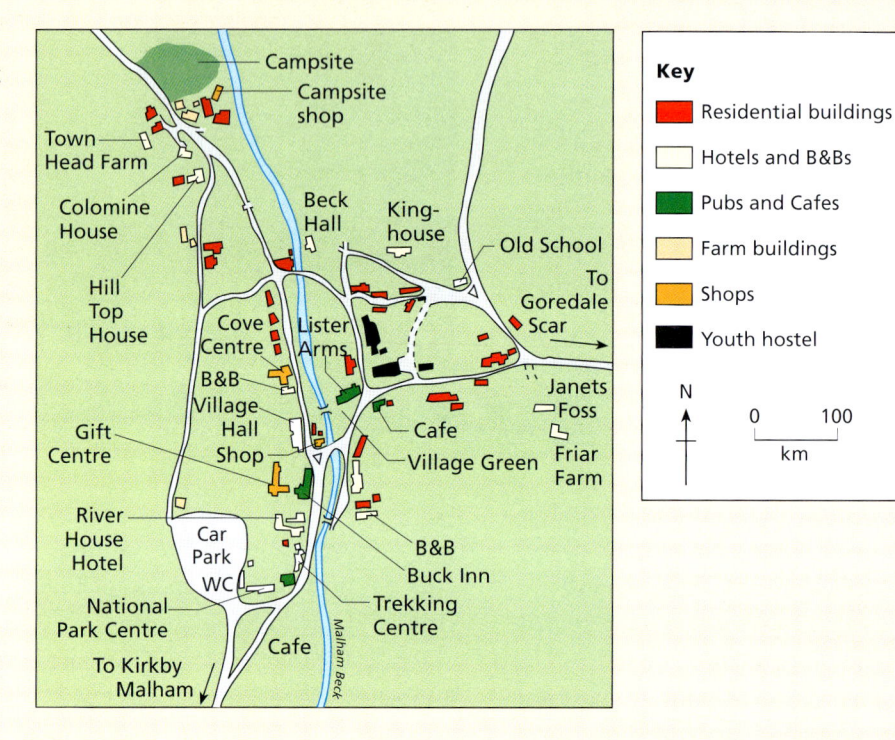

Figure 7.26 Land use in Malham village

income which this accommodation provides.

Tourists have also put pressure on housing in the area. In 1991, 55 per cent of the houses in Malham were used for holiday purposes. There is a trend towards buying holiday cottages rather than hiring accommodation. The demand for second homes has meant that the prices of houses in the area have risen dramatically. This makes it very difficult for the locals, especially young couples, to buy property in the area. This has resulted in a demand by locals to build new, cheaper housing. This could ruin the traditional nature of Malham.

What are the management issues?

It is the policy of all national parks in the UK to aim for sustainable management. This means that the quality of people's lives within the parks will be maintained or improved and visitor access will not be allowed to destroy the natural resources which should be preserved for future generations.

With this in mind, the National Park Authority, working with the National Trust who own 7,200 acres of land to the north of Malham, set up a steering group in 1977 to ensure that the area was not overdeveloped or ruined by visitor pressure. National Trust volunteers carry out some of the work and National Park Authority workers do the rest.

The following remedial works have been carried out.

The village of Malham seems to be adapting to the pressures of tourism and using the opportunities presented by the visitors to start new ventures.

Managing tourism

Date	Remedial measure
1976	Construction of first set of steps by Malham Cove.
1980	Restoration of eroded paths in Gordale Scar area, since this time most of the paths in the area have been resurfaced.
1984	Restoration of clapper bridge and pond in the village. Placing of parking restrictions in the village. Litter bins removed, Malham becomes litter free area.
1985	Start of tree planting projects in the area.
1994	Creation of open access area and additional footpaths through the Countryside Stewardship scheme in partnership with local farmers, landowners, English Nature and the Countryside Commission.
1995	Access improvements with remove of some stiles and the construction of kissing gates.
1996	Voluntary constraint on commercial signs.
1997	Tree planting in Cove area.

Local newsagent owner: 'Without the tourists I would have had to close many years ago. They provide a major part of my income for the year.'

English Heritage representative: 'The situation at Malham needs to be continually monitored. The numbers of tourists in the area must not be allowed to increase beyond the capacity of the area. This will lead to the area being destroyed by its own popularity.'

Owner of Town Head Farm: 'With the income from farming being so poor I need the extra money generated by the campsite to survive. We rely heavily on the income from tourism.'

National Park Centre manager: 'Most of the tourists that come into the centre show respect for the environment and are interested to find out more about what is here and how they can cause least damage.'

Figure 7.27 People's opinions on the impact of tourism on the Malham area

ACTIVITIES

Higher

1a What is the name of Britain's first national trail?
b What is a national trail?
c Where is Malham located in the UK?

2 Describe and explain why Malham is such a popular location for day visitors.

3 What advantages and disadvantages does tourism have for the residents of Malham?

4 There are a number of problems facing the steering group set up to protect Malham. Describe the problems and devise an action plan of how they should be resolved in a way that is sustainable.

5 Draw a field sketch of the photograph in Figure 7.23b. Include in your sketch: the land use, processes occurring (weathering), landform features (scree).

Foundation

1a What is the name of Britain's first national trail?
b How long is the trail?
c How many people visit Malham on Sundays in summer?

2 Many people visit Malham for the day. Describe the physical features that attract people to Malham.

3 List three problems that tourists cause the residents of Malham.

4 There are a number of problems facing the steering group set up to protect Malham.
a Describe the problems that the steering group faces.
b Suggest solutions for three of the problems.

5 Draw a field sketch of the photograph in Figure 7.23b. Include in your sketch: the land use, processes occurring (weathering), landform features (scree).

Case Study: THE IMPACT OF TOURISM ON THE INCA TRAIL TO MACHU PICCHU

The Inca Trail to Machu Picchu is in the south-west of Peru. It is 48 km long, starting at the local train track and ending at the ancient Inca site of Machu Picchu 2,400m above sea level. This area has attracted visitors ever since Hiram Bingham, an archaeologist from Yale University, rediscovered it in 1911. It is only in recent years that its popularity has started to threaten its beauty.

What are the physical attractions of the area?

The climate of the area does not vary greatly during the year, although during the night temperatures often fall below zero. The minimum temperature is 9 °C in June, July and August. The hottest temperature is 23 °C in November, December and January. Heavy rainfall occurs from November to March.

The area is in the Andes mountains. Scenery varies from glacier-topped mountains to deep, rich river valleys and, as people walk the Inca Trail, they experience a great variety of environments, from sub-tropical on the lower slopes to grassland and bare slopes 4,050 m above sea level. The forest is filled with cedar and laurel trees.

It is the decorative plants, such as the 90 species of orchids, that have made the area famous. The area contains many rare animals such as the Andean fox, puma and river otter. This variety of wildlife makes the area an ideal place for people who wish to watch or study the wildlife. In the 1980s the area was declared a national park to preserve this rare flora and fauna.

There are also impressive human features in the landscape. One of these are the terraced hillsides which were built by the Incas hundreds of years ago. These are still being farmed today with crops such as potatoes, cereals and lima beans. Perhaps the most important human features in the area are the Inca settlements. On the trail itself there are 18 archaeological sites, including Runkuracay and Sayacmarca, and of course at the end is Machu Picchu itself.

The stone roadway, built by the Incas over 500 years ago, comprising the Inca Trail, is a feat of engineering in itself. Other attractions in the area are the ancient Inca capital of Cuzco: at 3,400 m, it is one of the highest cities in the world and has ancient streets and buildings of Inca stonework.

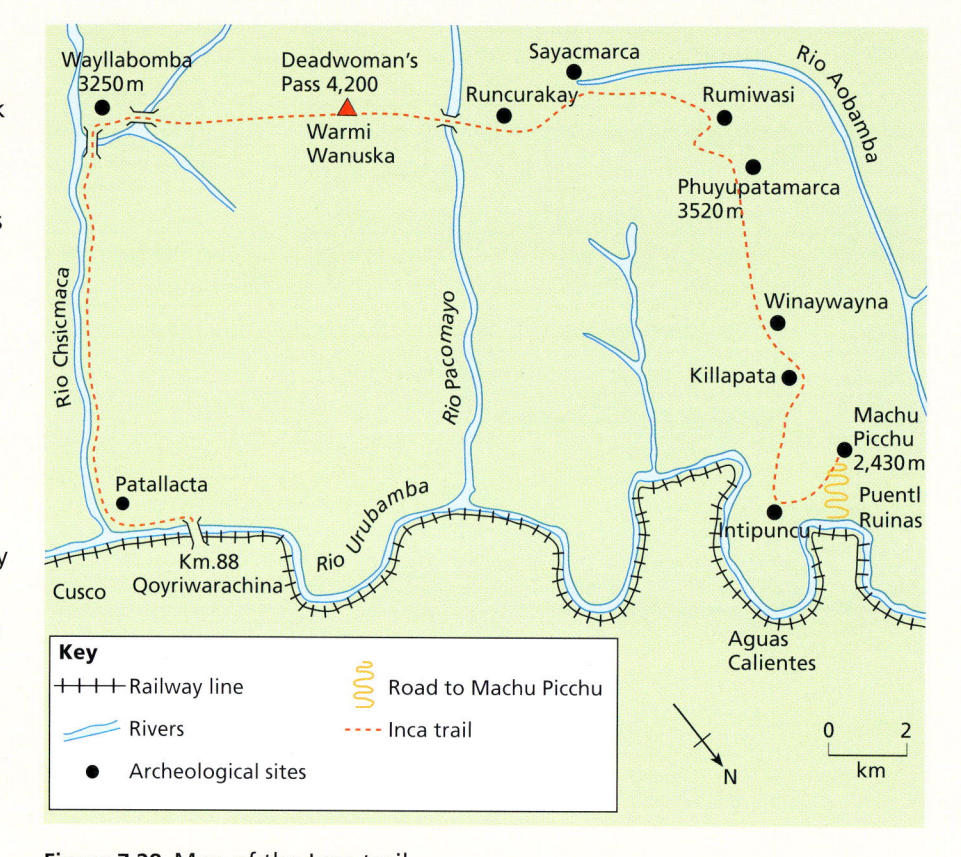

Figure 7.28 Map of the Inca trail

Figure 7.29 Guide on the Inca trail

Managing tourism

Figure 7.30 Machu Picchu

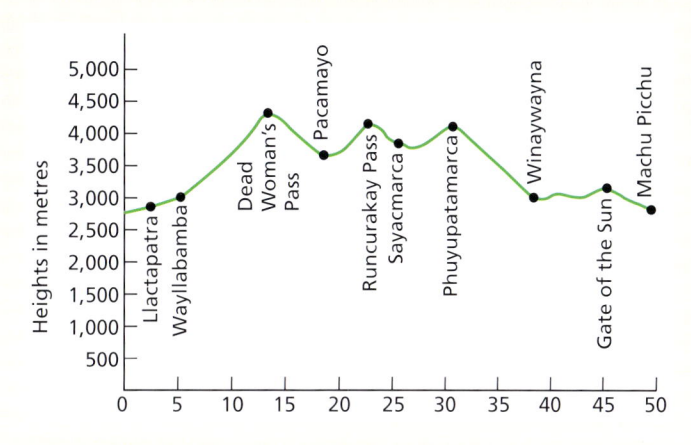

Figure 7.31 Cross-section of the Inca Trail

Figure 7.32 Porters on the Inca Trail

Figure 7.34 The market at Pisac

Figure 7.33 Numbers of people on the Inca Trail

Year	Trekkers on the Inca Trail
1992	5 000
1994	14 500
1996	30 500
1998	53 500
2000	82 000

What are the impacts of tourism on the area?

The impacts of tourism on the area are both positive and negative. In recent years there has been a great increase in the popularity of the area (see Figure 7.33).

The general reasons for this have been dealt with earlier in this chapter (see page 137). This increase in popularity has brought with it many problems as well as opportunities. The impacts of tourism can be social (affecting the people's culture and the way that they live), economic (affecting their wealth) and environmental (affecting the area that they live in).

Social

The local villagers who are employed as porters are not treated well by some of the tour companies or some of the tourists. This causes them to gain a false impression of all visitors. The local villagers are affected by the clothes of the western visitors and wish to dress like them rather than in native garments.

Economic

The economic impact of tourism is, for the most part, positive. Tourists spend money in the area which has a positive impact on the incomes of local residents. At the local market in Pisac on a Sunday morning, for example, a handicraft market has developed just for tourists.

Shops selling locally produced handicrafts for visitors have opened in Cuzco. These provide jobs both in the shops and in related industries (see page 138).

Every tour party of 18 visitors has 27 porters, 2 guides and 3 cooks. The porters are paid US$10 each day for the 4-day trip. The more reputable tour companies also request that their clients tip the porters. A tip of US$12 dollars is given by each member of the tour party and shared between the porters. This amounts to considerably more than hotel workers are paid. The tourists also pay US$17 dollars each to travel the Inca Trail, which contributes to the upkeep of the area.

THE IMPACT OF TOURISM ON THE INCA TRAIL TO MACHU PICCHU – continued

Environmental

The large increase of tourism in the area is causing concern not only to the local people but also to environmentalists around the world. The area is a World Cultural Heritage Site due to of the Inca ruins and the Inca Trail. It is also a World Natural Heritage Site due to the flora, fauna and aesthetic value of the environment. The tourists cause direct and indirect problems. The following have been identified as major concerns in the area:

Direct concerns	Indirect concerns
Erosion is beginning to occur on the Inca Trail due to the pressure of 500 tourists a day. In 1998, 53 500 tourists walked the trail.	The hotel at Aguas Calientes received permission in 1998 to build an extension. This was shelved due to the intervention of UNESCO World Heritage committee.
All tour groups cook on open fires because it is cheaper. This can cause forest fires. It is also causing destruction to vegetation close to the official camp sites.	The Peru Hotel group who owns the hotel have permission from the government to build a cable car from the hotel at Aguas Calientes to Machu Picchu. This has also been shelved for the present.
The rubbish bins along the trail are picked up by park wardens and simply dumped, usually in an open pit about 50 metres from the trail.	The toilet blocks at Machu Picchu have red roofs and stand out distinctly against the ancient ruins.
Tourists pick orchids growing among the ruins and along the trail.	Kiosks selling water, Coke and chocolate are located about every 2 hours along the trail.
Garbage is thrown into rivers, such as the Urubamba, or left close to the trail. This includes human excreta.	Rise in crime, especially on tourist trains. Many people have been robbed whilst sleeping and pickpockets operate in all the major towns.
The number of tourists at the ruins means that soon there will be no quiet places for reflection which, for many, is the whole point of the visit.	In November 2000 (due to its increasing popularity) Machu Picchu was used for a Peruvian lager advert. The crane used collapsed and broke off part of the Temple stone, one of most important features of the ruins.

These points highlight a number of issues which are causing concern to environmentalists around the world. The building of the extension to the hotel and the proposed cable car are two of their main concerns. The comments in Figure 7.36 were made by interested parties.

Due to the increase in tourist numbers, a number of management initiatives were implemented on 9 August 2000 (see Figure 7.37).

Figure 7.35 The train track at Aguas Calientes

Managing tourism 155

'The increase in visitor numbers due to the increased accessibility of the site will improve my profits.'

Local shopkeeper in Aguas Calientes

'Visual pollution of cable cars will be great. The buses are self-regulating because only a few can use the road at one time.'

Concerned resident of Aguas Calientes

'At present people arrive by train or on foot. The train travellers are then bussed to the site. This restricts the numbers. The developers see more trains and cable cars carrying 45 people per car. This would mean 400 tourists per hour reaching the ruins. It will take 2 hours for a trainload of tourists to get on the cable cars. So there will be lines of queues ruining the scenery.'

UNESCO's representative in Peru

'All rubbish from the trail is put in a truck and dumped near the Urubamba river. It gradually slides into the river.'

Peter Frost, resident of Cuzco

'It will deprive tourists of the feeling of awe at the magnitude of the mountains and the remoteness of the site.'

Catholic priest of the church in Aguas Calientes

'Usually when I trek it is customary to greet others you meet. The numbers of people on the Inca Trail already makes this impossible. What will it be like in the future?'

Kate Findlay, British trekker

'I will lose my job driving the tourist bus, where else will I find work?'

Machu Picchu bus driver

'There will be more opportunities for jobs in hotels, there are already too many mouths to feed in my village.'

Local young villager

Figure 7.36 People's opinions on the tourist development of Machu Picchu

THE IMPACT OF TOURISM ON THE INCA TRAIL TO MACHU PICCHU – continued

1. All tour operators must be licensed.
2. Groups of up to 10 independent travellers will be allowed to hike the trail if they contact an independent and licensed guide to accompany them as long as they do not hire, porters or cooks.
3. Porters should be limited to a carrying load of 20 kilograms.
4. Maximum of 500 people on the trail per day.
5. No plastic water bottles on the trail, only canteens. No littering.
6. Entrance fees will be from US$50.

They eventually came into effect on 31 December 2000. Countries such as Finland have offered to cancel several million dollars of Peru's national debt; in return, Peru must show an active commitment towards protecting Machu Picchu for future generations.

Figure 7.37 Management initiatives for Machu Picchu

ACTIVITIES

Higher

1a Where is Machu Picchu located?
b How long is the Inca Trail?
c When was the site rediscovered?

2 Describe the physical and human attractions that draw people to the area.

3 Explain the impact of visitors on the area using the headings: social, economic and environmental.

4 Figure 7.37 lists the management initiatives that are to be implemented at Machu Picchu. Working in a group, discuss the initiatives, then devise a group management plan for Machu Picchu to present to the class.

5 Write a letter to the Peruvian government stating the case for the protection of this ancient site. You may include quotes from Figure 7.36

Foundation

1a Where is Machu Picchu located?
b How long is the Inca trail?
c When was the site rediscovered?

2 Describe the physical and human attractions that draw people to the area.

3 Visitors have a major impact on the area. Complete the table below to explain this impact.

4 Figure 7.37 lists the management initiatives that are to be implemented at Machu Picchu. Working in pairs, discuss the initiatives and write your own set of initiatives. You may use the ones listed, but try to think of others.

5 You are on holiday in Peru and have visited to Machu Picchu. Write a postcard home describing your impressions of the ancient site.

Type of impact	Positive	Negative
Environment		
Economic		
Social		

Managing tourism

Case Study: THE IMPACTS OF TOURISM HAVE LED TO THE NEED FOR MANAGEMENT OF THE MALDIVES

Key

Tourist Resorts
1 Aribeach resort
2 Reethi Rah. resort
3 Kanifinolhu island resort
4 Kurumba island resort
5 Filitheyo island resort
6 Fonimangoodhoo island resort

Uninhabited islands
7 Ifuru
8 Ungoofaaru

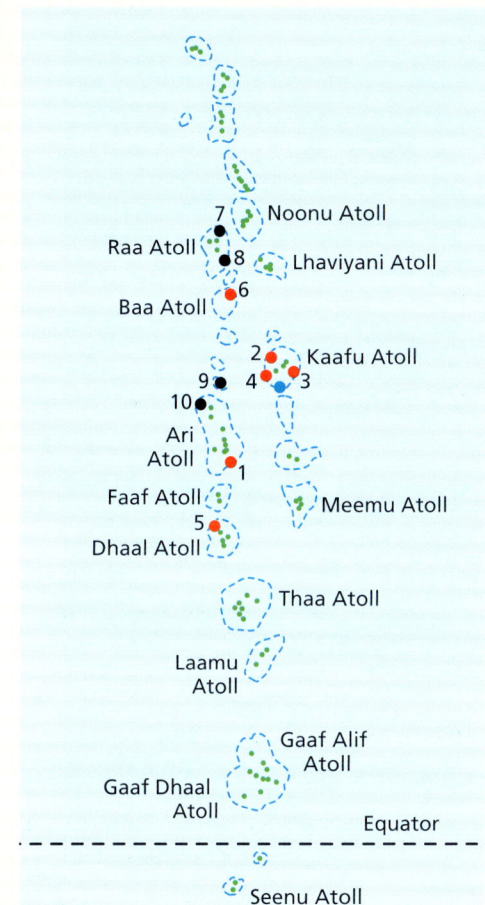

Home islands–(fishing villages which tourists are allowed to visit)
9 Rasdoo
10 Ukulash

● Male and Hulule airport

Figure 7.38 Map of the Maldives

The Maldives is an island republic in the Indian Ocean, located to the south-west of India. It stretches for 800 km north and south of the equator and is made up of 1,190 coral islands in 26 atolls (see Figure 7.38) which are only 2.4 metres above sea level at their highest point. Only 280 of the islands are inhabited, 80 as tourist resorts. All of the islands are owned by the government. The climate is tropical with temperatures ranging between 26 and 30 °C, with an annual rainfall of 1,900 mm. Tourist development of the Maldives has been rapid since the first resort was built in 1972 (see Figure 7.39).

Figure 7.39 Tourist numbers

Year	Tourist numbers
1992	235 900
1993	241 000
1994	280 000
1995	314 900
1996	338 700
1997	365 600
1998	395 700
1999	429 700

However, from the start, the development of tourist resorts has been carefully monitored to reduce negative impact on the social life of the Maldivians and their unique environment.

How has tourist development on the Maldives been managed?

In 1970 President Gayoom investigated policies and strategies to develop tourism as a sustainable and viable industry. All local people were consulted about these strategies, and because of this, the impact of tourism in the Maldives has not had the effect that it has had in other LEDCs. Guidelines were laid down which had to be fulfilled before any resort could be built:

- Resorts are to be built on uninhabited islands only.
- No resorts could be built without first carrying out an environmental impact analysis.
- All resort buildings are to be set back 5 m from the vegetation line.
- No buildings are allowed to be taller than the tree tops.
- No more than 20 per cent of an island can be built on. If water bungalows are built, then these cannot be in excess of the 20 per cent.

Over the years, new initiatives have been introduced:

- Resorts must build incinerators to deal with non-biodegradable waste.
- Many resorts are now recycling water for use in gardens.
- Solar hot water systems are being built because resources for producing electricity are scarce. Each island has to have its own generator.
- Resorts have to build septic tanks to deal with sewage waste.
- Desalination plants are being built at newer resorts to help stop the depletion of ground water supplies.

THE MALDIVES – continued

Figure 7.40a Maldivian island

Figure 7.40b Maldivian island

What help has the Maldives received?

In 1990, after 20 years of tourist development, the UN categorised the Maldives as one of the world's 29 least developed countries. There has been much aid given to the islands to help them achieve sustainable development. Aid has been given by the UN Development Programme and the World Bank. The islands have also received aid from the EU and individual countries such as Japan and Norway.

Since 1981 the EU has given US$3.75 million in aid. Projects that have been supported have not only been for the development of tourism but also for improvements in other industries such as fishing. Tourist projects have involved help with training, technical assistance and drawing up the Tourist Master Plan for 1996–2005.

The Japanese government has funded a project costing US$14m to build breakwaters along Male's shores to help with the problem of rising sea levels. The Norwegian Agency for Development Assistance (NORAD) financed a scheme to build incinerators for tourist resorts. In 1994, 49 incinerators were installed with resorts paying 15 per cent directly to the supplier, with 42.5 per cent of the cost given as a grant and 42.5 per cent given as a loan to be paid back in instalments over 10 years. In 1998 the government was in negotiations for further grant aid from NORAD.

UNDP and WTO aid came in the form of a resort management and tourism training project. In 1992 on-the-job training was provided in resorts and short-term overseas fellowships were awarded. A *Manual of Resort Management Practices* was produced. In addition, a school for hotel management and catering has been set up and is affiliated to the Birmingham College of Food, Tourism and Creative Studies. Here students can take a BTEC course in Hotel, Catering and Institutional Operations.

The future: what must the Maldivians do to ensure sustainable development of their tourist industry?

The Maldivian government has applied to the UNDP and WTO for further funding to support the Maldives in their unique tourist initiatives and to establish a sustainable framework for managing their tourist resources in the short and long term'.

A number of areas have been highlighted as a cause for concern.

The coral blasting that has occurred to provide access for the new resorts has resulted in the erosion of the island's beaches. This also allows tides to erode the beaches. Many of the resorts have built breakwaters to try to combat this. Thousands of dollars have been spent on beach nourishment programmes on remote islands

Coral reef habitats have as yet not been affected by tourism. However, the effects of nutrient run-off, especially from sewage, has caused some damage.

Development will continue to be guided with more occurring in the northern atolls of Baa, Lhaviyana and in the southern atolls of Meemu and Dhaalu. There will continue to be strict, if not stricter, guidelines on development.

At present tourists are allowed to visit designated home islands which are specially equipped with tourist souvenir shops and model schools. This will continue to occur so that the local inhabitants do not come into contact with the tourists. Groups of 15–30 tourists arrive at a time by boat, on excursions that are carefully monitored.

More local inhabitants will be encouraged to work in the tourist industry. At present only 5,961 of the 10 610 tourist jobs are filled by Maldivians and the majority of these are menial tasks. The problem is that the Maldivians do not like to live on the tourist islands away from their families and prefer to work in the informal sector where there are no strict rules of employment.

More local products need to be produced. At present cheap goods are imported from Sri Lanka and India. Tourists spend very little (around US$10–15 each) on souvenirs so this is an area of the tourist industry that needs to be developed.

If the Maldives is to maintain its unique character, the government, with the help of outside agencies must continue to improve its Tourist Development policies. This was recognised in 1994 with the commissioning of the 1996–2005 Tourist Development Master Plan which was paid for with EU aid. There also needs to be stricter and frequent monitoring of existing resorts to ensure that they remain within the guidelines for waste disposal and other environmentally sensitive issues.

Figure 7.41 The home islands

ACTIVITIES

1. Where are the Maldives?
2. Draw a suitable graph to show the increase in tourist numbers to the Maldives as shown in Figure 7.39.
3. Design a poster which shows what the Maldives has to offer tourists.
4. The development of the Maldives has been carefully managed. Describe 5 of the management initiatives and explain why each one was implemented.
5. Study the photographs of the Maldives. Does the tourist development conform to the guidelines given for resort development by the government?
6. Describe two of the schemes that have been paid for by aid from other countries.
7. Do you think that the Maldives have been sustainably managed? Give reasons for your answer.

Figure 7.42 The physical attractions of the Maldives

Case Study: YOSEMITE NATIONAL PARK, USA

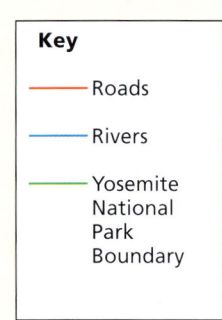

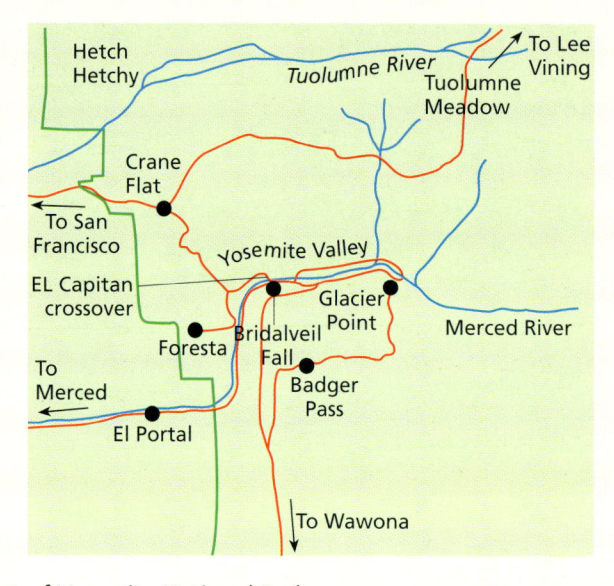

Figure 7.43 Map of part of Yosemite National Park

Figure 7.46 Yosemite Falls

Yosemite Valley is in the heart of Yosemite National Park in the state of California. The valley is approximately 2 km wide and 11 km long; it is the Park's most popular attraction and is under considerable pressure from visitors (see Figure 7.44).

Figure 7.44 Visitor numbers to Yosemite for selected years

Year	Visitors (m)
1954	1
1967	2
1987	3
1994	4
1995	4.2

The visitors come to see the sheer rock faces, such as El Capitan and the magnificent entrance known as El Portal, and Tuolumne Meadows, a large area of sub-alpine plants and the spectacular Glacier Point where people get magnificent views of the whole valley. It is the most famous glacially carved landscape in the world. However, all of this beauty is being destroyed by the people who queue to see it. As the National Parks Service (NPS) say, 'Yosemite is being loved to death by the American public.'

It is the National Park Service's mission to 'conserve the scenery and the natural and historic objects and wildlife therein and to provide for the enjoyment of them in such a manner as will leave them unimpaired for the enjoyment of future generations'. The popularity of the park and especially Yosemite Valley (which received 8,000 visitors a day in August), meant that the NPS was finding it impossible to uphold its mission statement.

Figure 7.45 El Capitan

What were the first identified problems and solutions in Yosemite Valley?

There are a number of problems which have been identified in the valley. At first, the increasing numbers of visitors were catered for by providing more car parks and widening the roads. A visitor centre was also opened in the valley and more and larger campsites were developed. By 1980 it became clear that continued development of this kind would encroach on the scenery of the area and a more sustainable policy needed to be developed. A number of proposals were made, such as reducing traffic congestion by implementing a one-way system in the valley, which allowed for a two-lane road either side. This is still in operation today. Visitor numbers have continued to increase, to the extent that the valley has to be closed on some weekends in the summer. The National Park Service intends to introduce a more radical policy which should ensure that the park is protected for future generations.

Yosemite's problems in the late 1990s

The following problems have been identified in the park:
- traffic congestion, especially in July and August,
- pollution from car exhausts as well as the normal visitor pollution,
- lack of car parking places.

The problems came to a head in January 1997 when the valley experienced flooding which damaged a lot of the infrastructure, including a number of camping sites and parking areas. This gave the NPS the initiative and funds (US$197m) to start the discussion process for the major restructuring in Yosemite Valley.

Yosemite: the plan for the future

The final Yosemite Valley plan was developed with these specific purposes in mind:
- to restore, protect and enhance the natural and cultural resources of Yosemite Valley,
- to provide opportunities for high quality, resource-based visitor experiences,
- to reduce traffic congestion,
- to provide effective park operations, including employee housing, to meet the mission of the National Park Service.

The public were involved and 14 meetings were held locally in California and nationally in some of the major cities of the USA. Over 10,000 public comments were received during this period. The National Park Service took the public's comments into account before coming up with its final plan. It will take more than a decade to implement the plan and it will cost approximately US$343 000 000.

Figure 7.47 The Yosemite Valley before and after removal of the north-side of the Valley road

Yosemite: the detailed plan

The plan can be split into a number of headings, but the main difference to most visitors will be the fact that cars will no longer be allowed in the park. This has caused the most controversy. A proposal has also been made to remove the north-side valley road and a number of the bridges and junctions, leaving in their place a bridle and cycling path.

The specific details of the plan can be seen on the map in Figure 7.48. By implementing these proposals, the NPS will both safeguard Yosemite for future generations and allow visitors to enjoy the magnificent scenery without the problems they encounter at present. The Yosemite Valley plan was signed on 29 December 2000.

Category	Action
Visitor experience	- Park at an out-of-valley car park and ride a shuttle bus (which could be a tractor and trailer) through the valley. - New visitor centre located near the day parking area. - More information on the park available. - More pedestrian and bike trails.
Parking	- Overnight visitors would still be able to drive into the valley and park at their lodge or campsite. - Day visitors park at the 550-space day visitor parking area in Yosemite village or at other out-of-valley parking areas and use the shuttle buses.
Lodging	- Some lodging removed from highly valued natural resources such as riverbanks. - Housekeeping camping is to be allowed set back from the river
Camping	- A greater range of facilities will be provided at camp sites, such as shower units.

Case Study: YOSEMITE NATIONAL PARK, USA – continued

Yosemite Falls
- Enlarge viewing area
- Improve trail for disabled

Yosemite Creek → To Yosemite Falls

North-side Drive
closed to motor vehicles from El Capitan Crossover to Yosemite Lodge, converted to multi-purpose (bicycle and pedestrian) paved trail

Sunnyside

River Merced

Yosemite Lodge
- Remove 5 motel buildings
- Build more lodges instead

To El Capitan

Southside Drive
Converted to two-way from El Capitan crossover to Curry Village

To El Capitan Crossover

Yosemite Village – Present park headquarters
- Present and future visitor centre
- 550 day-visitor vehicles parking spaces
- 3 other out-of-valley car parks for peak season at El Portal, Badger Pass, Hazel Green
- Shuttle busses to locations in valley and out-of-valley car parks
- Employee housing
- Firestation

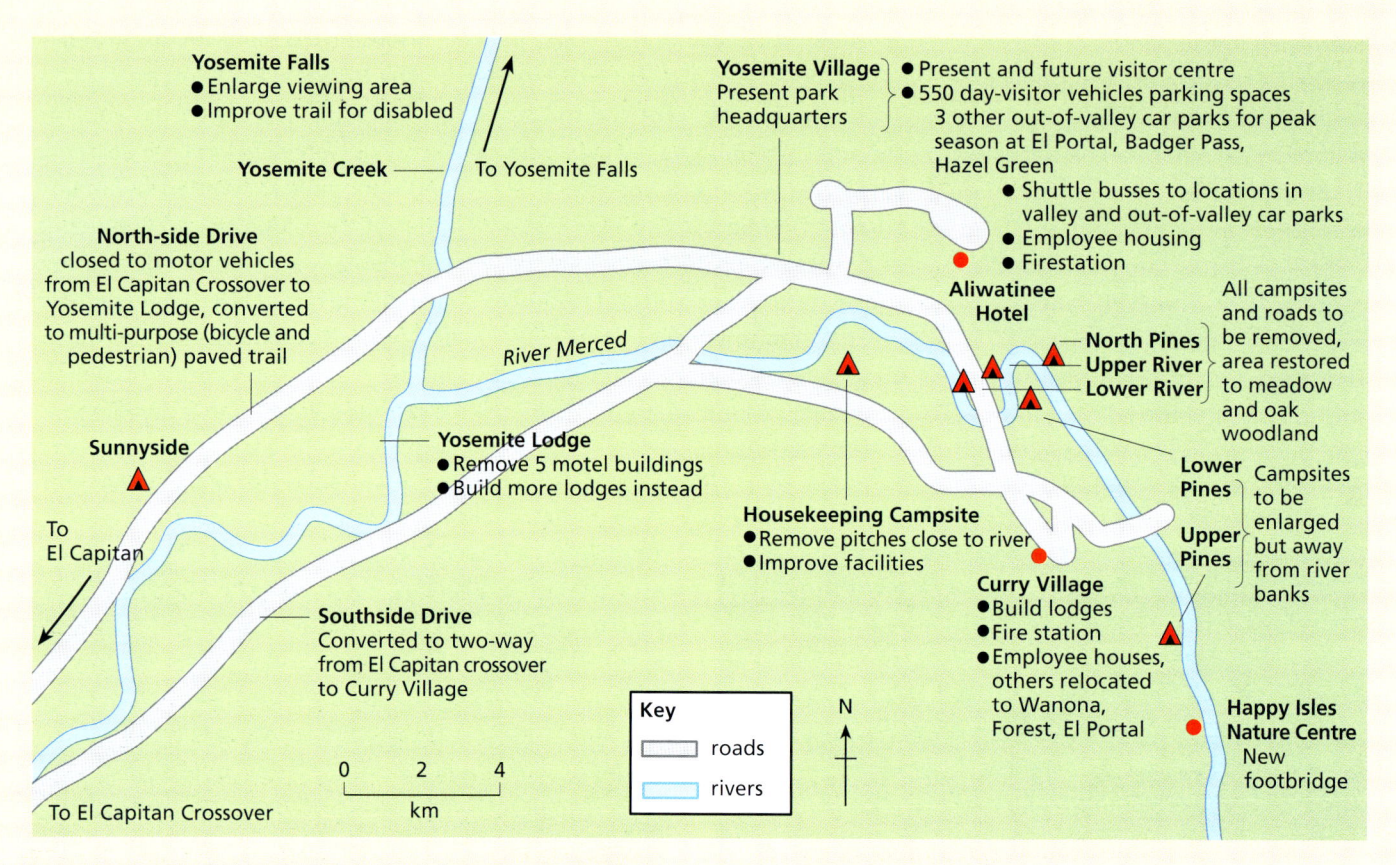

Aliwatinee Hotel

North Pines / Upper River / Lower River – All campsites and roads to be removed, area restored to meadow and oak woodland

Housekeeping Campsite
- Remove pitches close to river
- Improve facilities

Lower Pines / Upper Pines – Campsites to be enlarged but away from river banks

Curry Village
- Build lodges
- Fire station
- Employee houses, others relocated to Wanona, Forest, El Portal

Happy Isles Nature Centre – New footbridge

Key: roads, rivers
0 — 2 — 4 km

Figure 7.48 Map showing detail of the Yosemite Valley

ACTIVITIES

1. Where is Yosemite National Park?
2. Draw a suitable graph to show the increase in tourist numbers to Yosemite as shown in Figure 7.44.
3. Design a poster which shows what Yosemite has to offer tourists.
4. Read the details of the Yosemite Valley plan. Copy out the table below and complete it. The first one has been done for you. You may wish to add to the advantages and disadvantages of this initiative.

Management initiative	Advantage	Disadvantage
1. Refuse access to visitor's private cars in Yosemite Valley.	Cuts down on pollution.	People prefer to drive in the privacy of their own cars than to share a tourist bus.
2.		
3.		
4.		
5.		

5. The plan has been introduced to conserve the Yosemite Valley for future generations. What are your views on the plan? (Hint: take the initiatives one by one and state if you agree or disagree with them and why. You may wish to work in a group to complete this task.)

Sample Examination Questions

Higher tier

1 Refer back to the case study on Zanzibar, in particular the tourist numbers in Figure 7.18 on page 145.
   a Describe the changes shown in the numbers of tourists visiting Zanzibar. Use data in your answer. (4 marks)
   b Suggest reasons for these changes in tourist numbers. (4 marks)

2 Refer back to the case study on Machu Picchu, in particular Figures 7.28 and 7.31 showing the Inca Trail.
   a What is the highest point on the Inca Trail? (1 mark)
   b Name two archaeological sites on the Inca Trail. (2 marks)
   c In the first 13 km of the Inca Trail how high would you climb? (1 mark)
   d The Peruvian government have identified a number of indirect concerns which are caused by tourist usage of the Inca Trail. Explain these indirect concerns. (4 marks)

3 Some people are for the development of tourism in mountainous areas and others are against it. Give reasons for these differing opinions. Use actual examples in your answer. (6 marks)

4 Choose an LEDC which has developed its tourist industry.
   a Describe the management initiatives which have been implemented in the LEDC.
   b In what ways have other countries helped with the management of the development? (8 marks)

Total 30 marks

Foundation tier

1 Refer to the case study on Zanzibar and look in particular at Figure 7.18 which shows tourist numbers for Zanzibar. Then circle the correct answer in the sentences below.
   - Tourist numbers for Zanzibar increased by more/less than 50 per cent between 1980 and 1988.
   - The largest increase was between 1988 and 1992/1984 and 1988.
   - Many tourists go to Zanzibar for the scuba diving and snorkelling. These are known as active/passive tourists.
   - UK visitors are most likely to go to Zanzibar for a weekend break/summer holiday. (4 marks)

2 Refer to the beginning of this chapter on the growth of the tourist industry. Tourism has grown rapidly since the Second World War. Two of the reasons for this are greater wealth and developments in transport. How might these two reasons have influenced the growth of tourism to Zanzibar? (4 marks)

3 Refer back to the case study on Machu Picchu, in particular Figures 7.28 and 7.31 showing the Inca Trail.
   a What is the highest point on the Inca Trail? (1 mark)
   b Name two archaeological sites on the Inca Trail. (2 marks)
   c In the first 13 km of the Inca Trail how high would you climb. (1 mark)
   d Explain two problems caused by tourists on the Inca trail. (4 marks)

4 Some people are for the development of mountainous areas for tourism others are against it. Using actual examples explain why.
   Arguments in favour
   Arguments against (6 marks)

5 Choose an LEDC which has developed its tourist industry.
   a Describe three management initiatives which have been implemented (3 marks)
   b In what ways have other countries helped with the management of the development (5 marks)

Total 30 marks

8 Managing urban areas

Urban areas in LEDCs are subject to very rapid growth

What were the causes of urbanisation in MEDCs?

Urbanisation is the process by which increasing numbers of people within a country live in cities and towns. In the UK, urbanisation has been going on for the past 200 years and approximately 90 per cent of the population live in urban areas. Cities in the UK started to increase in size during the nineteenth century when the Industrial Revolution led to a huge demand for labour in the new factories. At the same time, more machinery was being used on farms and so fewer farm labourers were needed. These labourers migrated to towns and cities and found jobs in the factories or in mining villages, for example, in South Wales. The growth rate at this time was approximately 10 per cent and most of the migrants managed to find housing. Some factory owners even provided housing for their workers, for example, Bourneville and Port Sunlight.

The move to towns continued into the twentieth century, especially from remote rural areas (known as rural depopulation), even though the growth rate was declining. Rural depopulation in the twentieth century is mainly due to the pull of the 'bright lights' (better entertainment facilities) that towns and cities offer. Some people, however, still migrate for better employment opportunities. There is also movement in the UK from large urban areas to more rural areas in search of a better quality of life. This is known as counter-urbanisation.

What were the causes of urbanisation in LEDCs?

Since the 1950s LEDCs have been experiencing rapid urbanisation. The reasons for this are twofold:
- There is migration from rural to urban areas because of the lack of jobs and the low salaries in rural areas.
- There is a high natural increase being experienced in the cities because of the youth of the migrants and improvements in medical care.

What is the global pattern of urbanisation?

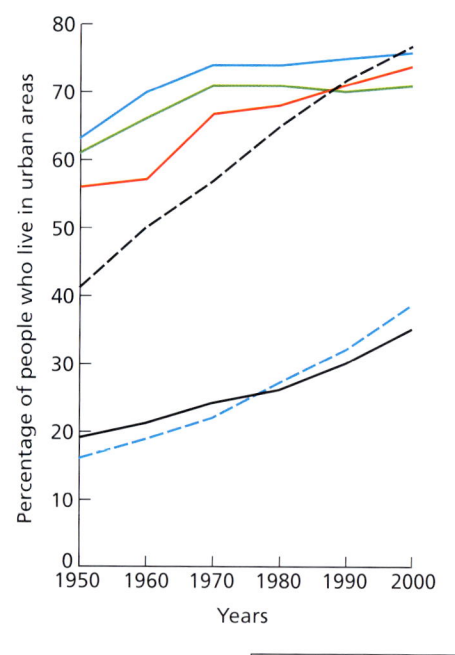

Figure 8.1 % urban population

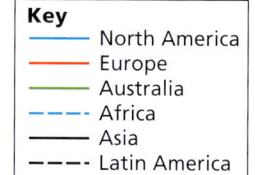

Key
- North America
- Europe
- Australia
- Africa
- Asia
- Latin America

Managing urban areas

During the twentieth century the rate of urbanisation in LEDCs has been very rapid. The world's population doubled between 1950 and 1990, but the world's urban population trebled. There are two features of urbanisation in the twentieth century:

1 The main growth in urban areas has been in LEDCs. São Paulo in Brazil, for example, has grown as follows: 1920 – 579 000; 1960 – 6m; 1985 – 12m; 1991 – 15m; 2000 – 20m.
2 This increase in the numbers of urban dwellers has meant that there has been a redistribution of the largest cities in the world. In 1900 London and Paris were the only millionaire cities in the world (cities with a population of over 1 million). Now the ten largest cities in the world all have populations of over 10 million. The use of the term 'mega city' is now being used to describe these very large urban areas.

In MEDCs the majority of people live in urban areas; in the USA, 76 per cent of the population live in urban areas, in Australia, 85 per cent of the population do and in France the figure is 73 per cent. However, in LEDCs the population is concentrated into a few very large cities within the country. If one city is much larger than all the cities in that country, then it is known as a primate city; examples include Lima in Peru and Manila in the Philippines.

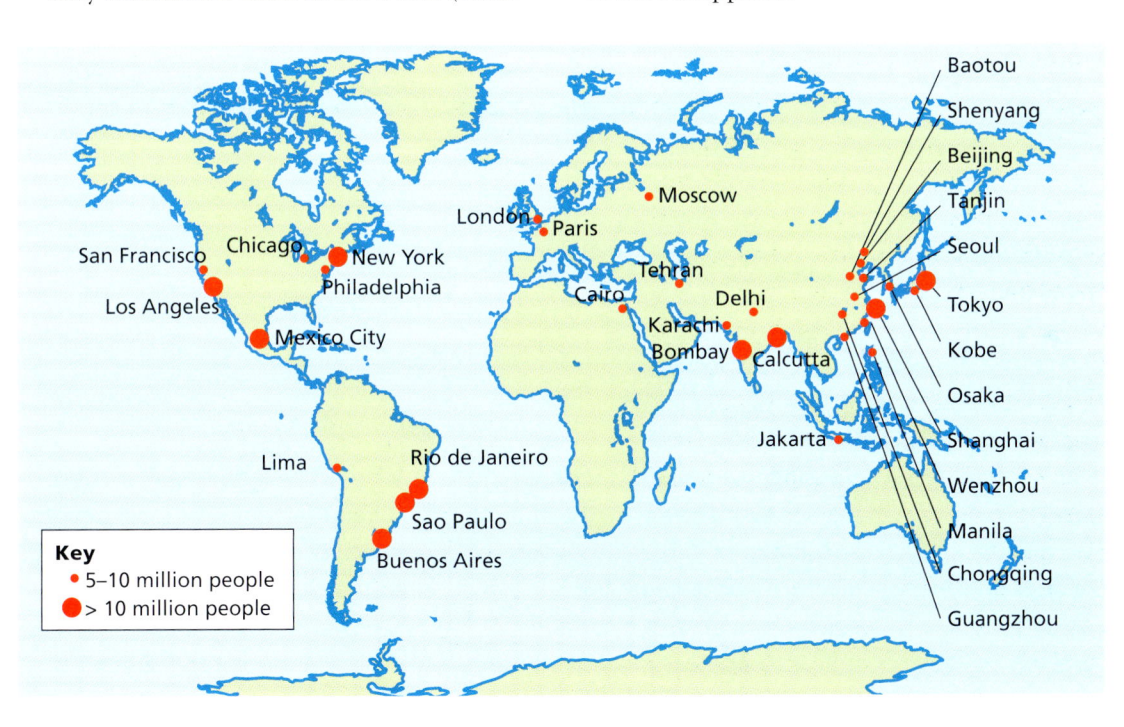

Figure 8.2 Map showing large cities in the world

ACTIVITIES

1 When and for what reasons did rapid urbanisation occur in:
a the MEDCs,
b the LEDCs.
2 Describe what happened to the percentage of people living in urban areas in LEDCs between 1950 and 2000.
3 Look at Figure 8.2. Which continent has the most cities with a population of over 5 million?
4 Describe the distribution of the cities with populations of over 10 million people.

Case Study: São PAULO, BRAZIL

São Paulo is the largest city in Brazil and the fifth largest city in the world. It is situated in south-east Brazil, 800 metres above sea level. It has a large concentration of industry, including the Ford, Toyota and General Motors car manufacturing companies. It has become the foremost centre in Brazil for computing and e-commerce. Its GDP is the same as New South Wales in Australia. In 1960, 75 per cent of Brazilians lived in rural areas and only 25 per cent lived in the city. In 2000, 75 per cent live in the cities and 25 per cent live in rural areas.

Why has São Paulo grown so quickly?

There are two reasons for the rapid growth of São Paulo: migration and high natural increases in population. Migration can be further split into:

- push factors, which are all the reasons why people want to leave rural areas,
- pull factors, which are all the reasons why they are attracted to São Paulo.

Push factors:

1 In Brazil, 31 per cent of rural households have no land. They have to rent land or find work as labourers and as farms become more mechanised, there is the risk of losing their jobs. There is very little to keep people in the rural areas, so they move to the cities in search of work.

2 Infant mortality is higher in the rural areas – 175 per 1,000 – than in the *favellas* of São Paulo where it is 82 per 1,000.

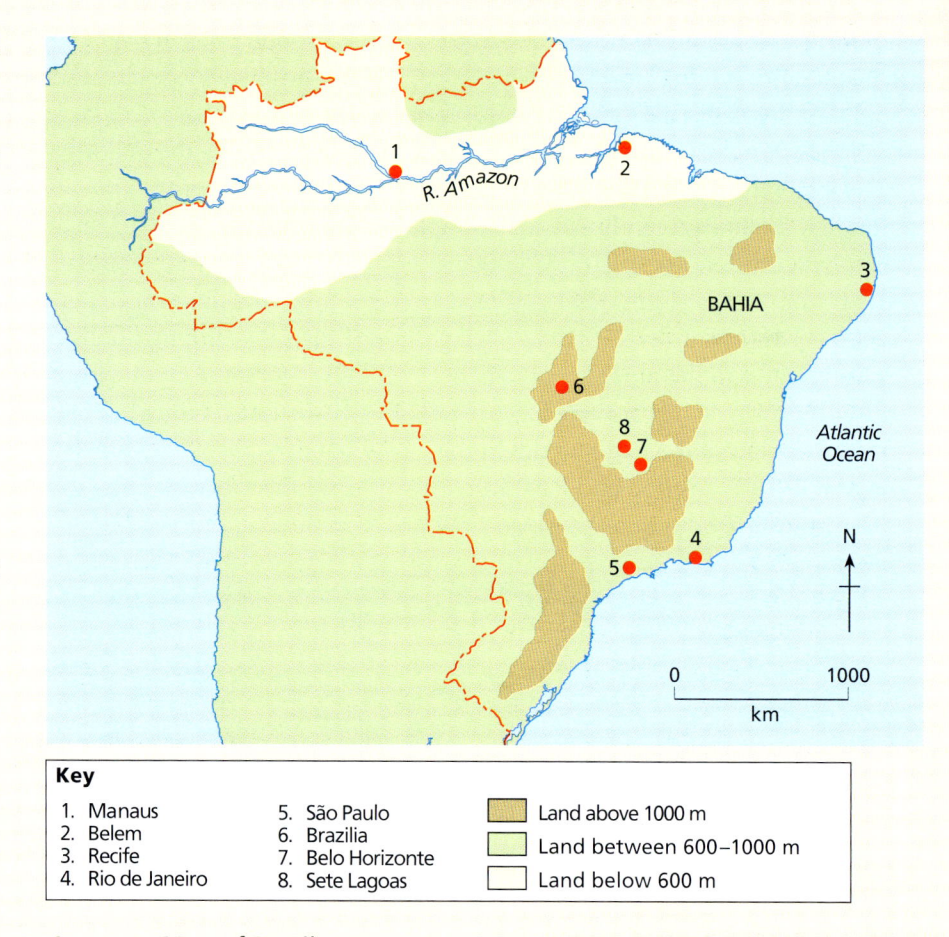

Key
1. Manaus
2. Belem
3. Recife
4. Rio de Janeiro
5. São Paulo
6. Brazilia
7. Belo Horizonte
8. Sete Lagoas

- Land above 1000 m
- Land between 600–1000 m
- Land below 600 m

Figure 8.3 Map of Brazil

3 Housing in rural areas is even worse than it is in the city. If a housing area in the city has no electricity or sewage, these services are at least close by, unlike rural areas in which there is no electricity or sewage treatment works.

4 Bahia in northern Brazil is very poor and suffers periodically from drought. It has been estimated that in this region of Brazil 32 million people suffer from chronic malnutrition. Farmers often have to stand by as their animals starve to death. Aid has been given by internationally funded projects to grow sustenance rice by rivers, but there is little money left after local officials and bankers have taken their cut. The local people have little option but to migrate to the cities.

5 Overpopulation has led to a shortage of jobs and shelter in the rural areas.

6 Land in rural areas has been taken from the subsistence farmers who have been renting it for years from large landowners who use the land to grow cash crops. Only 18 landowners control an area 6 times the size of Belgium. Brazil leads the world in the production of coffee and orange juice and as this earns foreign exchange, the landowners' actions are tolerated by the government.

Managing urban areas

Pull factors:
1. In the 1950s and 1960s there was a shortage of labour in São Paulo due to rapid industrialisation of 226 per cent. Advertising campaigns were run in the rural areas to attract workers to the city.
2. The rural dwellers have high expectations of a better quality of life in the city. There are more schools and doctors as the government puts more money into services for urban areas.
3. Word sent back to the villages by successful migrants makes life in the cities seem much better than it actually is.
4. Migration from rural areas has slowed down in Brazil, although there is still migration between urban areas. The growth in urban areas can now be attributed to the high birth rate and low death rate. The growth rate has, however, started to slow down: it declined from 1.2 per cent between 1980 and 1991 to 0.3 per cent between 1991 and 1996.

What are the results of this rapid growth?
The results of the rapid growth of urban areas are generally seen as being detrimental. There are, however, certain advantages.

Advantages of growth:
1. Farmers around São Paulo can increase their profits by producing more food for the urban market.
2. The informal sector of São Paulo still pays better than the farmers in the countryside.
Wages from workers in São Paulo are sometimes sent back to the countryside and so help the economy there.
3. Even a job in the informal sector of São Paulo is seen as better than the life of a landless peasant farmer in north-east Brazil.

4. The growth of the urban areas eases the population pressure in north-east Brazil so that there are more jobs available and fewer mouths to feed.

Disadvantages of growth:
1. The shanty towns (*favellas*) around the city consist of makeshift houses which are made from anything that the owners can find, such as wood, corrugated iron and cardboard. There are usually only one or two rooms shared by the whole family. São Paulo's *favellas* have no electricity supply and bottled gas is expensive. This situation is unlikely to change as the electricity supply company has just been sold by the government to a US–French consortium, who have increased prices and laid off 1,000 workers.

Figure 8.5 Self-help housing in São Paulo

Figure 8.6 A self-help home

Figure 8.4 The centre of São Paulo

São PAULO, BRAZIL – continued

2. Clean water is only available from standpipes, which have to supply hundreds of people.
3. Sewerage and pit latrines are inadequate to cope with the population numbers. The rivers that run through the city are very polluted as much sewage runs down the streets of the *favellas* into the rivers.
4. São Paulo has the same problems as most large cities with 9 million cars, trucks and buses and 250 km of gridlocked roads in peak periods, which also increases air pollution.
5. Agricultural production in rural areas might decrease because so many of the young adults have migrated.
6. There is a shortage of housing. It is estimated that 650,000 people are living in 600 *favellas*, a further 3 million live in *corticos*, which is very poor rented accommodation usually in tenements.
7. Unemployment in São Paulo is high at 19 per cent (1998 figure) which is surprising as it is the wealthiest city in Brazil.

How have planners in São Paulo coped with this rapid growth?

For many years the city of São Paulo was allowed to expand haphazardly without much planning. *Favellas* sprang up on land on the outskirts of the city or on sites that were not prime property, such as steep hillsides or marshy areas. This meant that the *favellas* were very susceptible to natural hazards such as landslides or flooding. In the 1970s the government decided that the way to deal with the *favellas* was to bulldoze them. However, with the return of the civilian government in 1985, this was stopped.

Since then a number of schemes have been instigated. Perhaps the best known of these have been the self-help schemes of the *periferia* in the late 1980s and early 1990s. The necessary building materials were provided by the city council to build

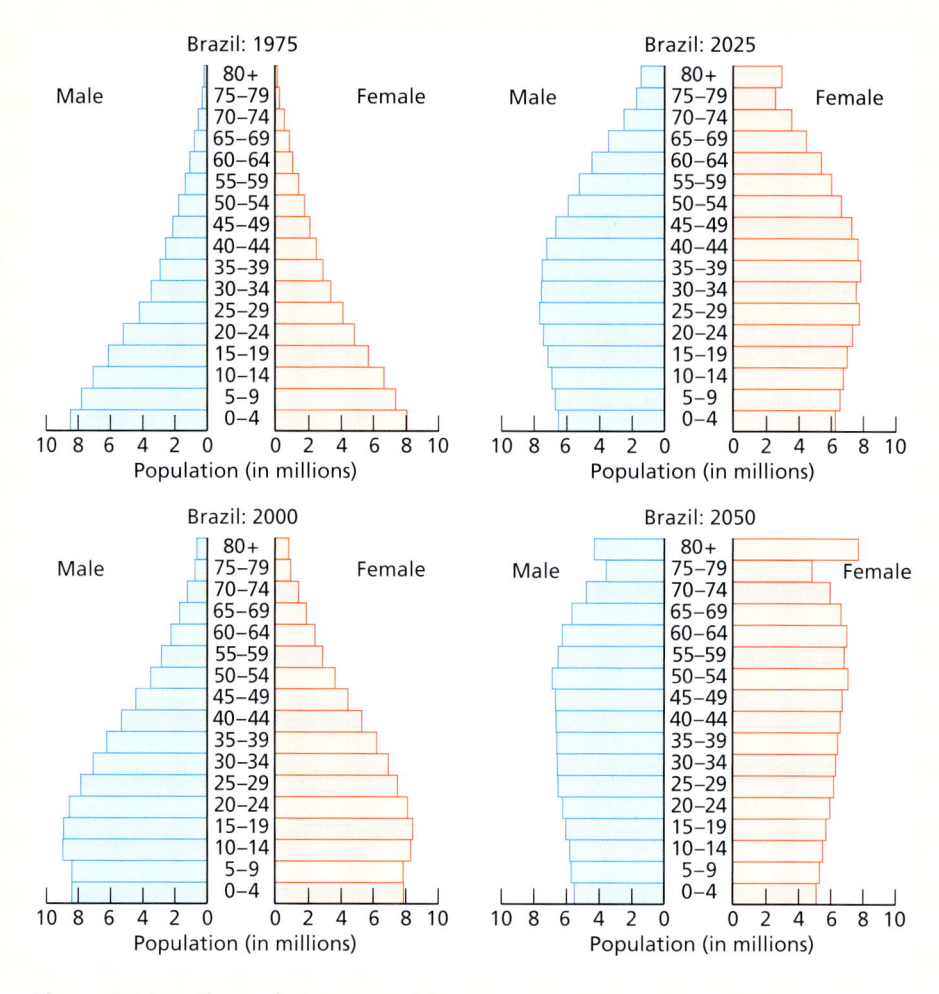

Figure 8.7 Brazil population pyramids

Figure 8.8 Cingapura scheme homes

a secure dwelling. Money has also been made available to provide running water and sewage disposal.

Perhaps the biggest scheme to be implemented by the municipality of São Paulo was the Cingapura Housing Project. Between 1994 and 1995 US$227 million were invested by the municipality and another US$84 million was invested by the government bank, international loans and the World Bank. It is estimated that this project will assist 42 000 people, which is approximately 2.2 per cent of the population of the *favellas* of São Paulo.

The project will replace *favellas*' dwellings with buildings 5 to 11 storeys high, with four apartments per storey. Most apartments will have an area of 42 square metres, with two bedrooms, a sitting room, kitchen, laundry and bathroom. Those that have already been built have nothing inside – no flooring or tiles and only the front door and bathroom have doors. Part of the *favella* is cleared to build the apartments and displaced families are housed in temporary barrack-like accommodation.

When the apartments have been built, families who can afford to, move in. No studies have been done to determine whether the *favellas*' residents want this type of housing or what happens to the people who cannot meet the economic requirements. This project does not provide for the informal sector which normally flourishes in *favellas*. Householders will have to pay an initial US$60 and then between US$18 and US$26 a month on a 20-year mortgage. This is a big commitment to *favellas*' dwellers who usually pay no rent.

The new apartments have been built close to the better areas of the city and on major routeways. In order to finance these developments, other housing projects have been scaled down. *Multiroes* (self-help schemes), for example, have lost 32 per cent of their funding, the provision of electricity to *favellas* has lost 54 per cent of its money and money for improving *corticos* (tenement housing) has been cut by 90 per cent.

In the 1990s the inhabitants of some of the *favellas* started their own self-help schemes:

Favella Monte Azul

This site lies alongside a polluted stream. It is home to 3,800 people living in 400 huts and slum tenement housing which stretches up the hillside from the stream. It is situated in the southern suburbs of São Paulo, one mile from the capital trading centre.

Seventeen years ago, Ute Craemer, a German teacher, established the Associacao Comunitaria Monte Azul in a log house near the shanty town. Since then this organisation has organised day nurseries, schools, workshops, clinics, a bakery and even a cultural centre with a library and art and theatre workshops. It now involves 120 volunteers. One of the first projects was to clean up the stream to provide fresh water through pipelines and to provide sanitation. In 1985, a wooden clinic was built; it was soon rebuilt as a three-storey brick house. The medical centre is run by 12 doctors and 4 dentists.

The association then began to focus on the residents' quality of life and as a result the cultural centre was built and is run by volunteers. Ute Craemer started a woodshop which has become so successful that it now sells products outside the shanty town. The weaving department, started by Sonia Camargo in 1995, sells its products in markets in São Paulo. The bakery, started in 1981, now employs 3 people and 3 students who are learning about the business,

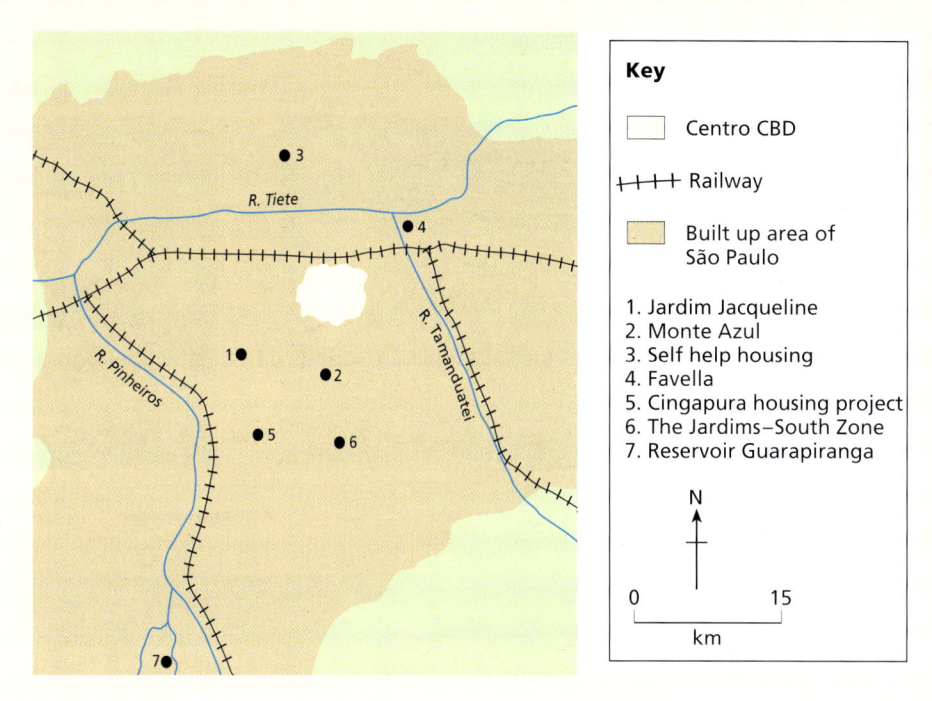

Figure 8.9 Map of São Paulo showing location of places mentioned in the case study

Key:
- Centro CBD
- Railway
- Built up area of São Paulo

1. Jardim Jacqueline
2. Monte Azul
3. Self help housing
4. Favella
5. Cingapura housing project
6. The Jardims–South Zone
7. Reservoir Guarapiranga

Managing urban areas

São PAULO, BRAZIL – continued

Figure 8.10 Polluted river in São Paulo

Figure 8.12 Industrial estate in São Paulo

Figure 8.11 (Jardims) gardens in São Paulo

including production and sale costs. Another business which is proving very successful is furniture restoring – many people who live in the *favellas* bring their furniture there to be repaired. All garbage and selected paper is recycled.

The money for these developments comes from a number of different sources, such as the São Paulo municipality and a number of charitable organisations such as the Tobias Charitable Association as well as from private donations.

Favella Jardim Jacqueline
Favella Jardim Jacqueline is situated next to São Paulo's wealthiest suburb, Caxingui. Its proximity to this suburb means that it does have some services, such as electricity. However, its residents still experience severe cases of malnutrition. In 1994, 190 families a month were receiving baskets of food, organised by a committee of 9 who begged for food and money to get the project started. The committee then turned to building a day-care centre for the *favellas* children who otherwise roam the streets. It is hoped that it will eventually employ 18 staff and look after 240 children. There are many other projects on the go; the most ambitious is a job creation project within the *favellas*.

The Focolare Movement
The church is also involved in the *favellas*. One project involves local businessmen who, after they've paid their production costs and salaries, split their profits 3 ways; to the poor, to reinvestment and to spiritual centres, where these ideas can be spread. Rudi and Henrique Leibholz run their steel foundry on these lines. They employ 75 people who have a pension fund and a medical insurance plan. They have also introduced profit sharing, which is unheard of in Brazil.

Industrial estates
Industrial estates have been set up, one on a 37-hectare site which has developed due to a multitude of small share holders. Water, sewerage, electricity and roads have been completed and 3 factories are in operation, a printing works, an industrial solvents company and a clothing factory. The industrial estates provide jobs for the people who live in the *favellas*. This is one of the ways that São Paulo has coped with employment problems.

Sustainable policies
Caritas, an Australian charity, has helped residents in some *favellas* to set up their own bank accounts, with each resident making a small contribution. The intention is to use the fund to buy the land on which the *favella* is situated, for example.

The *favellas* of São Paulo seem to be turning into slums of hope, through their own efforts and those of charitable organisations, the church and the municipality of São Paulo. However, perhaps the best way to manage the growth of the *favellas* is to stop it from occurring. One way of doing this is to encourage young people to stay in their villages.

In the poor village of Pedra Bela, 100 km from São Paulo, young people used to think that the only route to fortune was to go to the city, but times have changed. In 1989 a group of 15 villagers, including doctors, farmers and teachers, decided to set up the Pedra Bela Association. Led by Kirsten Herlow Balonyi, it started out with a grant of US$45 000 from the Danish government. It has taught local woman and young people to grow crops other than potatoes and to sew and weave. Villagers are taught many skills, including making rugs and cheese. The lessons now take place in a carpentry workshop, built and equipped with donations from a number of European countries, including Britain. Three hundred young people (20 at a time) have received this training. Their crafts are sold in São Paulo once a month and several shops in the city now sell the produce without charging any commission.

The association has now been asked by the Brazilian Rural Syndicate to give weaving lessons at Braganza, a village 50 km away, for a fee. This village is one example of how to keep people in the village of their birth. If there were more initiatives of this kind, it might be possible to stem the tide of people moving to the cities.

Housing is not the only problem that results from the rapid growth of cities; its environment is also badly affected. Congestion is another problem that results from rapid growth. In the 1960s, São Paulo built an underground train system. When it was opened in 1974, it not only cut down on congestion but also on air pollution. The system provides a cheap and reliable way for shanty town dwellers to get into the city. The subway now carries 2.5m passengers a day. It is 49 km in length and has 46 stations. However, it is very crowded and extensions are planned.

The city has also instigated busways (similar to our bus lanes). The buses have sole use of the busways, although there are still parts of the city where the buses have to mingle with the other traffic. The government is working to alleviate this problem.

Figure 8.13 The metro in São Paulo

ACTIVITIES

Higher

1 Describe the reasons for the growth of São Paulo's population.

2 Explain the disadvantages of São Paulo's rapid growth.

3 Choose one of the *favellas* written about in the text. How are people who live in the *favellas* and charities trying to improve their conditions?

4 Look at the photographs in Figures 8.5 and 8.8. Imagine that you live in a *favella* in São Paulo. The government has offered you either one of the flats shown in Fig 8.8 or the materials to build your own basic home as shown in Figure 8.5. Which would you choose and why?

5 Can you think of any reasons why the government changed its policy from self-help schemes to the Cingapura Housing Project?

Foundation

1 List three pull factors responsible for the growth of São Paulo.

2 Explain the problems caused by the rapid growth of São Paulo's population.

3 Choose one of the *favellas* written about in the text. How are people who live in the *favellas* and charities trying to improve their conditions?

4 Describe two of the governments schemes for improving the city.

5 Look at the photographs in Figures 8.5 and 8.8. Imagine that you live in a *favella* in São Paulo. The government has offered you either one of the flats shown in Fig 8.8 or the materials to build your own basic home as shown in Figure 8.5. Which would you choose and why?

Managing urban areas

Case Study

URBAN AREAS IN MEDCs ARE SUBJECT TO CONSTANT CHANGE IN THEIR LAND USE
READING, BERKSHIRE, UK

Reading is one of the largest urban areas in Berkshire. In 1901 the population was 73 000 (see Figure 8.15); today it has a population of approximately 160 000.

This growth has caused many changes to the town as it has expanded to cope with its growing population. Recently there has been a major redevelopment and renewal programme (see page 173). This has not only included change on the edge of the city but also in the CBD.

Changes in the CBD of Reading started in 1969 with the opening of the Inner Distribution Road (the IDR). This involved the demolition of some of the inner city area, mainly terraced housing and some derelict factories.

Figure 8.14 Employment structure of Slough, Reading and UK

Sector	UK	Reading	Slough
Primary	3	2	4
Secondary	25	22	28
Tertiary	72	76	68

The road was intended to be an inner ring road which would take traffic away from the centre of Reading. All major routes were to feed into it and then car parks were to lead off it. However, the road has never been completed and the traffic in Reading continues to be congested, especially in the peak hours.

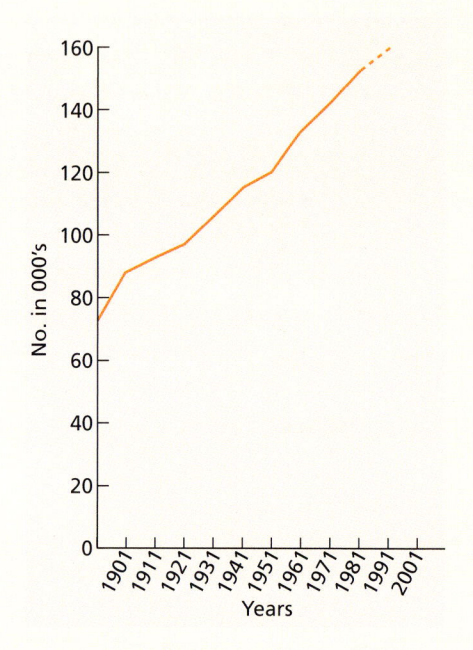

Figure 8.15 Population figures for Reading

Figure 8.16 Aerial photograph of Reading

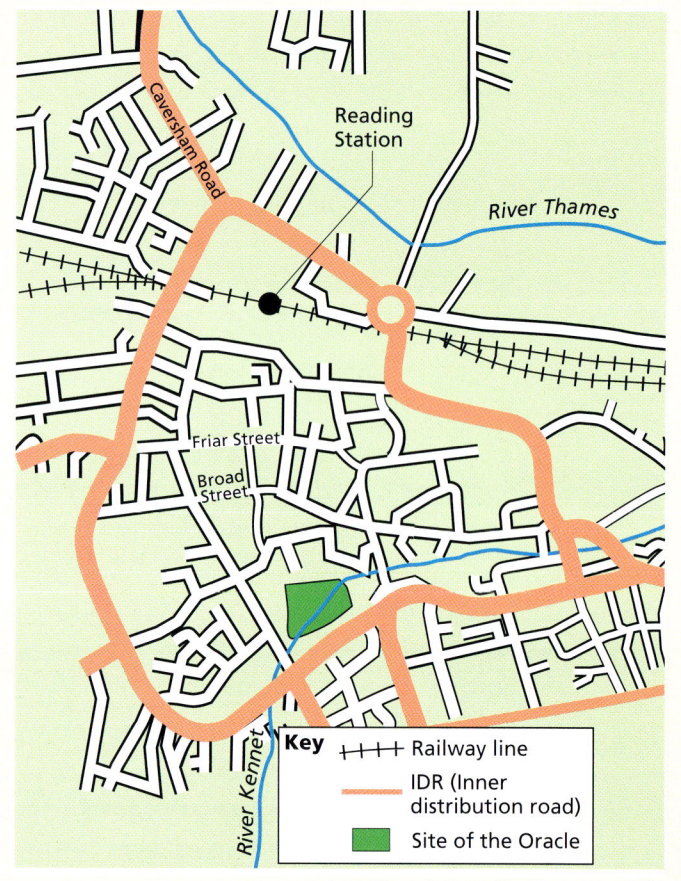

Figure 8.17 Map of Reading CBD

In 1970, Broad Street was closed to all but essential traffic. In the 1990s Friar Street was pedestrianised. The council wanted to improve the environment of the CBD by decreasing vehicle pollution with pedestrianised streets. The area became much safer for young families who no longer had to worry about the traffic. Disabled parking was provided at both ends of the main street.

At this stage Reading still did not have a large indoor shopping centre which was unusual for a town of its size. In 1998 Reading came fourth in the UK Shopping Index, which compares the catchment affluence of a number of UK towns, cities and shopping centres. It uses a 15-minute drive-time to define the catchment area. This confirmed to the council that they needed to update the CBD and provide more retail space. They had already started on a major project of redevelopment and renewal with the 1997 Oracle project. The project was to be completed by 2000. A large area of the CBD, including the old bus garage, was demolished and a new shopping centre, car park and Warner Village cinema were built.

Figure 8.18 Oracle Shopping Centre

The development spans the River Kennet. The area beside the river has been improved and is set out in the summer with pavement cafes making good use of the river banks, which originally were a polluted wasteland. Many of the shops in the Oracle, such as the Discovery store, Disney and Warner Brothers, are new to Reading. Other, such as Boots, Top Shop and Debenhams, have relocated from the main shopping streets. It is estimated that 40 per cent of the shops that were in the two main streets have relocated into the Oracle. Heelas has renewed the front of its shop on the high street, but also has access through to the Oracle.

Due to the movement of the main stores out of Broad and Friar Street, the council decided that it needed to act otherwise they would decline. Other businesses, for example, banks have been encouraged to relocate from Friar Street to Broad Street. Friar Street has now become the main entertainment area with many new trendy pubs (see Figure 8.19a and b).

Other brownfield sites within Reading have also been redeveloped. These include the Rose Kiln Lane flats and the Rex cinema site on Oxford Road. The Rose Kiln Lane flats were built on the site of derelict factories. The site of the Rex cinema, which closed because of the new cinema next to the Oracle, is at present being redeveloped into flats called Lexington Court.

There is a shortage of housing in the area: Berkshire needs another 67 000 houses by 2016. The council is hoping to build a large proportion of these on brownfield sites. In many ways, it has no alternative, as much of Berkshire is either greenbelt land or an area of outstanding natural beauty. The government has also set a 60 per cent target for new development on brownfield sites.

Figure 8.19a, b Renewal in Reading

174 | Managing urban areas

URBAN AREAS IN MEDCs ARE SUBJECT TO CONSTANT CHANGE IN THEIR LAND USE
READING, BERKSHIRE, UK – continued

Figure 8.20 Aerial photograph of Junction 11 area, new road and developments

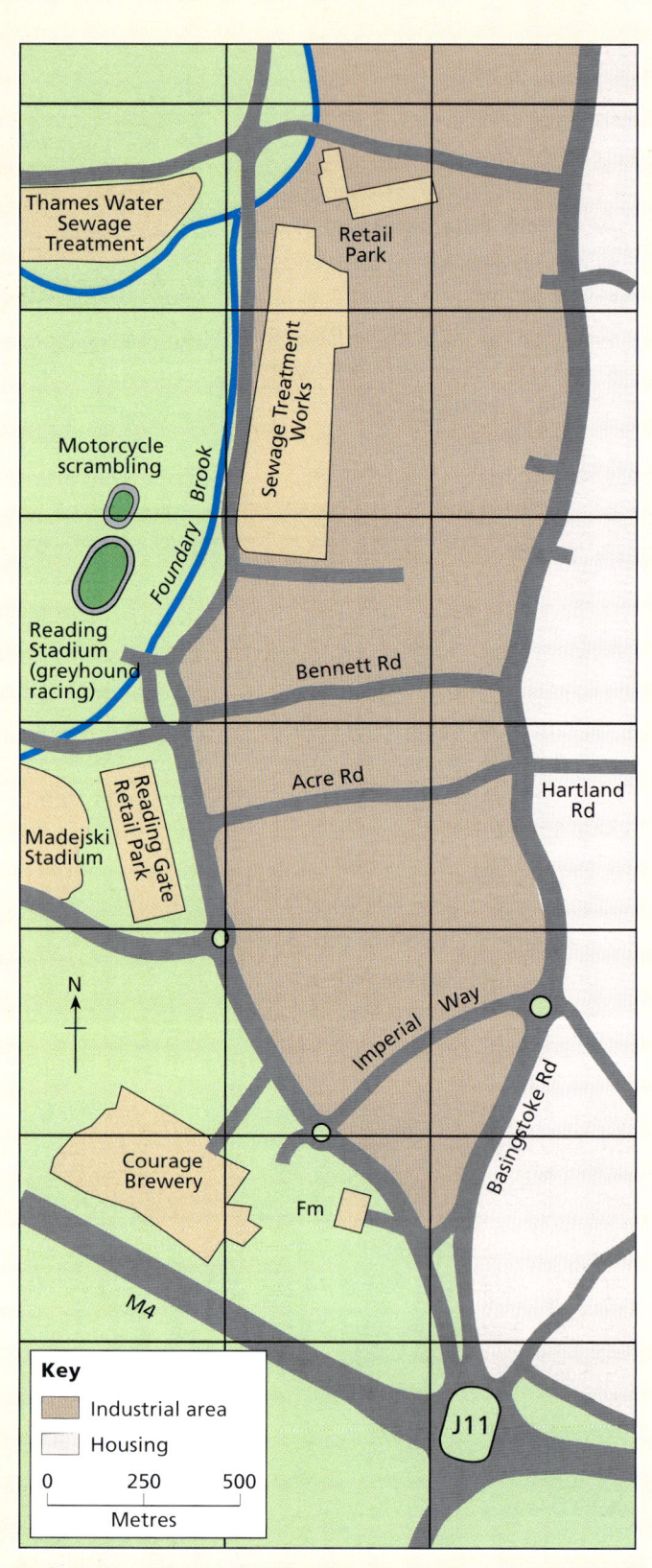

Figure 8.21 Map of Junction 11 area, new road and developments

Managing urban areas 175

The edge of Reading has also changed dramatically over the past five years, especially in the area to the south of the town between the original outskirts of the town and the M4 motorway. This area used to be landfill sites and old gravel pits; the only building was the Courage Brewery (see Figure 8.21).

The area was earmarked for major development. The first development on this greenfield site was the building of a new road to join the IDR with the M4. This was also to relieve the pressure off the A33 road to Basingstoke which was continually congested. The new road is a dual carriageway and therefore has the capacity for many more vehicles. The next development was the relocation of Reading football club from Elm Park, which was in the inner city area, to a new stadium known as the Madejski Stadium. The old Elm Park site has been redeveloped for housing. Next to the new stadium is an out-of-town shopping centre (Reading Gate) which includes B&Q and Comet (see Figure 8.22). The building continues in this area with many new office buildings in the new Reading International Business Park being developed to cope with the demand for business space (see Figure 8.23).

A new business/science park called Green Park is being built right next to the motorway. It is a typical science park with modern buildings, plenty of car parking and a landscaped environment, including a lake.

Other changes at the edge of Reading have been the building of a new housing estate, called the Beansheaf estate, and the retail and entertainment development close to Junction 12 of the M4 which was built in the late 1980s. In the early 1990s a large modern housing estate with mainly 3- and 4-bedroomed houses with gardens front and back and garages was built. A Sainsbury's Savacentre, Allied Carpets and Superbowl entertainment centre, containing a night club and bowling alley, are provided on this site. The other side of the motorway junction where the village of Theale is located has also been redeveloped as a science park.

These developments are on the edge of Reading. Although they have occurred on greenfield sites they have utilised land which was previously urban landfill on old gravel pits. It could, therefore, be argued that the land is now being put to good use, although it could have reverted to farmland.

Figure 8.22 Out of town shopping area – Reading Gate

Figure 8.23 Reading International Business Park

URBAN AREAS IN MEDCs ARE SUBJECT TO CONSTANT CHANGE IN THEIR LAND USE
READING, BERKSHIRE, UK – continued

Figure 8.24 Green Park, Reading

Redevelopment: this is when buildings in a city which are no longer of use are demolished and replaced with buildings that are in current demand.
Renewal: this is when old buildings are renovated and brought up-to-date, combining the best of the old with the new.
Brownfield site: this is an area within a city which is no longer used. It may contain old factories and housing, or it may have been cleared ready for redevelopment.
Brownfield potential: the number of brownfield sites which are available for redevelopment within a city.
Greenbelt: this is an area around the city which is composed of farmland and recreational land. There are strict controls on the development of this land. Its purpose is to control the growth of cities.
Greenfield site: an area on the edge of the city which has never been developed in any way.

ACTIVITIES

Higher

1 What is a brownfield site?
2 What is the difference between renewal and redevelopment?
3 Study the map and aerial photograph of Reading CBD (Figures 8.16 and 8.17). Draw a plan of the photograph. Mark on your plan:
   - the CBD and the IDR,
   - the site of the new Oracle shopping centre,
   - the railway line and station,
   - Broad Street and Friar Street,
   - the River Kennet.

Foundation

1 What is a greenfield site?
2 What does the word redevelopment mean?
3 Look at the map and aerial photograph of Reading CBD (Figures 8.16 and 8.17). Draw a plan of the photograph. Mark on your plan:
   - the CBD and the IDR,
   - the site of the new Oracle shopping centre,
   - the railway line and station,
   - Broad Street and Friar Street,
   - the River Kennet.

Managing urban areas   177

ACTIVITIES – continued

Higher

4   What is a census and why is the information collected?

5   Study Figure 8.14 which is a graph of population numbers for Reading.
    - A census was not taken in 1941. Why?
    - There was a boundary change in 1911. What effect did it have on population numbers?
    - Compare the population growth before 1931 with that after 1951.

6   Figure 8.15 shows the employment structure of Reading, Slough (a large town in Berkshire) and the UK.
    - Draw three separate pie charts of the information
    - Compare the information.

7   Study the section on Reading. Then put the following places in Reading into the correct place in the Table 1: the Oracle shopping centre, Yates bar, Beansheaf estate, the Pitcher and Piano bar, Heelas, Superbowl, Rose Kiln Lane flats, Rex cinema, Green park.

Foundation

4   What is a census?

5   Look at Figure 8.14. It is a graph of population numbers for Reading.
    - Describe the pattern of population growth since 1951.
    - What was the population of Reading at the beginning of the twentieth century and the end of the twentieth century.

6   Figure 8.15 shows the employment structure of Reading, Slough (a large town in Berkshire) and the UK.
    - Draw three separate pie charts of the information.
    - Compare the information.

7   Look at the section on Reading. Then put the following places in Reading into the correct place in Table 1: the Oracle shopping centre, Yates bar, Beansheaf estate, the Pitcher and Piano bar, Heelas, Superbowl, Rose Kiln Lane flats, Rex cinema, Green park.

Table 1

Redevelopment	Renewal	Greenfield site

8   Study the aerial photograph and map of Reading (Figures 8.20 and 8.21).
    - Copy the map.
    - On your copy of the map, mark the new A33 road, the out-of-town shopping centre (Reading Gate), the Madejski stadium, Green park, the M4 motorway, junction 11, Courage brewery, Foudry Brook and the sewage treatment works.

8   Look at the aerial photograph and map of Reading (Figures 8.20 and 8.21)
    - Copy the map.
    - On your copy of the map, mark the new A33 road, the out-of-town shopping centre (Reading Gate), the Madejski stadium, Green park, the M4 motorway, junction 11, Courage brewery, Foudry Brook and the sewage treatment works.

Managing urban areas

Case Study

THERE ARE MANY CHALLENGES FACING MANAGERS OF ALL LARGE URBAN AREAS, ENVIRONMENTAL PROBLEMS IN CAIRO, EGYPT

Cairo is situated on the River Nile about 200 km south of the Mediterranean Sea. Greater Cairo extends along the sides of the Nile for 30 km. It is the largest city in Egypt as well as its capital and is home to approximately 1/4 of the country's population. Cairo is now one of the 20 most populated metropolitan areas in the world and the largest city in Africa. Cairo's population has grown very rapidly (see Figure 8.25).

Cairo's growth has been greatest in the areas west of the Nile and to the north in Shoubra El Kheima. The population growth in Cairo is a direct result of people migrating there from the rural areas and from increased life expectancy, which went up from 41 years in 1960 to 64 years in 2000.

The average population density in Cairo is 30 000 people per square kilometre. Despite the fact that the most crowded areas in Cairo only have buildings three or four stories high, this is higher than Manhattan in New York. Housing is overcrowded and in short supply. Other elements of the urban infrastructure including transport, health, education, water and sewerage also face severe pressure from the ever-expanding population. City planning and attempts to control development through building permits or other means have been largely ineffective.

Cairo grapples with pollution woes

The following is extracted from a front page feature taken from the *Wall Street Journal*, 19 January 1999.

'A lingering black fog of vehicle exhaust fumes, including lead and other suspended particles, have made Cairo one of the world's most polluted cities. The US Agency for International Development says the city's air pollution kills between 10,000 and 25,000 people a year. The lead content of the air probably reduces the average child's IQ by four points. Other environmental problems include unregistered lead smelters and backyard dumps and primitive solid waste recycling methods.

The government is aware of the problems, but environmental protection isn't Egypt's strong suit. There were no environmental laws until 1995, and enforcement has been sporadic. The country phased out leaded gasoline in 1997, but it has not yet set up an emissions inspection system for Cairo's 2 million ageing vehicles – 60 per cent of all cars in Cairo are more than 10 years old.'

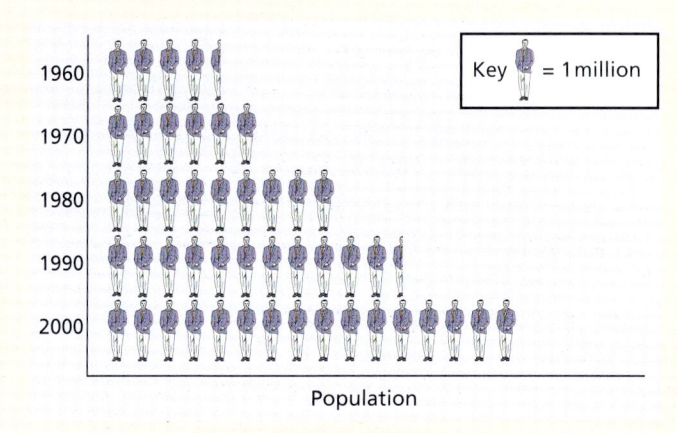

Figure 8.25 Cairo's population 1960–2000

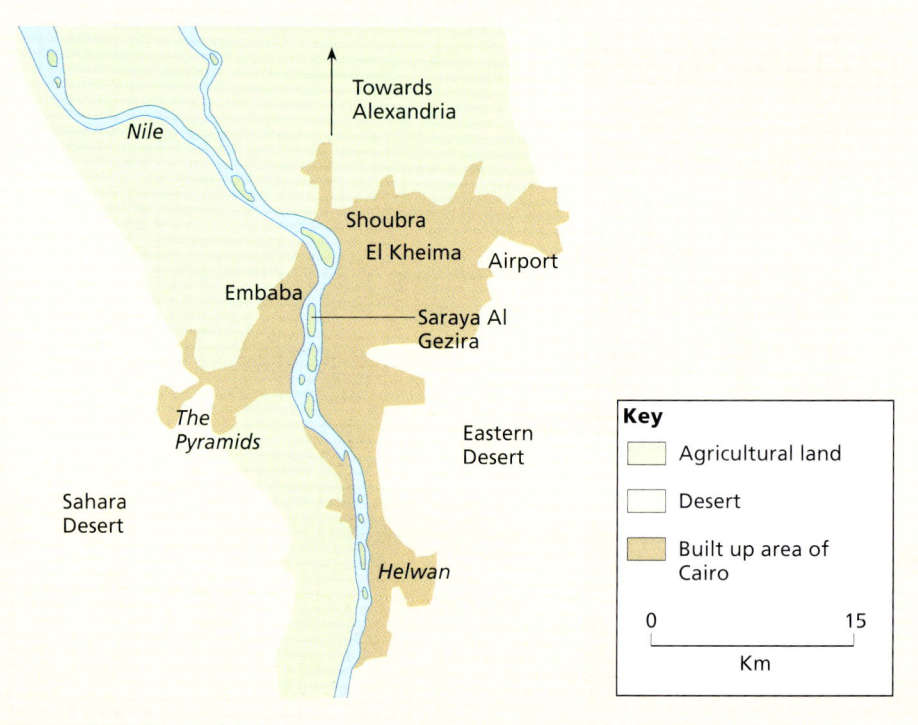

Figure 8.26 Map of Cairo

Air pollution

In the final months of 1999, Egypt was forced to take a serious look at the quality of its air when mysterious clouds of choking smog began to descend regularly on Cairo and northern Egypt.

Fumes from Cairo's 2 million vehicles combined with suspended particulate matter, plus sand blown into urban areas from the neighbouring Sahara desert, to create an almost permanent haze over the city. The concentration of suspended particulate matter in Cairo is 5 to 10 times higher than World Health Organisation guidelines. On average, sulphur dioxide is four times higher, smoke and lead three times higher and nitrogen oxides twice as high.

This situation is worst in industrial areas and busy traffic spots, where air pollution is between three and four times the accepted level of 70 micrograms per cubic metre. Levels of suspended particulate matter and lead pollution in Cairo are perhaps the highest in the world. Lead pollution is a serious threat to human health because high lead concentrations can lead to high blood pressure, kidney problems, infertility, decreased IQ levels in children and disorders of the nervous system. Particulate matter is a significant health hazard because fine particles enter the respiratory system during inhalation and are taken deep into the lungs. Air pollution in Cairo is estimated to cause between 10 000 and 25 000 deaths per year.

In the Helwan district of Cairo 100 000 workers are employed in the production of cement, iron and steel, fertilisers, textiles, bricks and chemicals. In Shoubra El Kheima, the northern industrial area, 87 000 workers are employed in over 450 industrial units like lead smelters, ceramic and glass factories and other pollution-making heavy industries. Many of these factories were built to Russian or Czech design with little or no pollution controls. Large populations have grown up around the factories: about 1 million people living in these two polluted areas.

Land pollution

The huge population of Cairo produces 10 000 tons of solid waste each day. Only about 60 per cent of this is collected and managed. The remainder is discarded into streets, canals, drains and neighbourhood dump sites where it is left to rot. The 60 per cent that is collected is done so by the Zaballeen and the Cairo Cleaning and Beautification Agency. The Zaballeen collects waste from residents for a monthly fee and transports it by donkey cart or truck where it is carefully picked over for recycling. Most of the remainder is deposited in open dumps (see Figure 8.28). Rubbish incinerators are broken and have not been repaired.

Hazardous wastes from chemical plants are also not disposed of safely. Large toxic stockpiles, as much as 50 000 tonnes, have accumulated in Helwan, Shoubra and Embaba.

Medical and hospital waste present special problems. They are generally disposed of with other solid wastes and can lead to the spread of infectious diseases. Rats and other vermin live in plague proportions on the waste dumps.

Noise pollution

The vast number of vehicles in Cairo leads to noise levels well above those considered acceptable by the WHO. The roads are gridlocked throughout the day and night leading to an almost permanent rush hour.

Figure 8.27 Industry in Cairo

THERE ARE MANY CHALLENGES FACING MANAGERS OF ALL LARGE URBAN AREAS, ENVIRONMENTAL PROBLEMS IN CAIRO, EGYPT – continued

The Nile itself has a constant flow of old boats carrying cargo in and out of the city. It is not only cargo boats, however, which cause problems.

The residents of Saraya Al Gezira have been subjected since 1994 to constant nightly noise from the floating nightclubs moored on the banks of the Nile. The residents of the 240 apartments in the area want the boats closed down. Residents complain that even if they wanted to give up the use of their Nileside rooms, retreat to the back of their apartments only exposes them to the same problem coming from the Gezira club. 'Noise from the clubs isn't the only problem,' said one resident, 'there are literally hundreds of cars looking to park at the nightclubs. By 9 pm residents can't get back in to park their cars.'

How can the urban environment in Cairo be more sustainably managed?

In 1999 an air quality monitoring system, an undertaking of the Cairo Air Improvement Project (CAIP), was set up to track particulate matter and lead in the atmosphere. The system has 36 monitoring stations in operation around Cairo. CAIP is funded by USAID, which is providing $60 million over an expected five-year period. The network will enable the government to measure the success of its pollution control initiatives. The aim of the projects is to install a monitoring system so the Egyptian Environmental Affairs Agency (EEAA) can continue to demonstrate a reduction in pollution. The air quality manager said that they were monitoring to get a baseline and hoped, in two or three years, to be able to report a significant reduction in the worst polluted areas such as Shoubra El Kheima.

The air monitoring project is just one aspect of CAIP's strategy, which also involves programmes to reduce pollution from the lead smelters that account for so much toxic smog. They are doing this by installing new equipment, designing new smelters and assisting in relocating the factories.

CAIP's Vehicle Emission Testing, Tune-Up and Certification (VET) component aims to reduce harmful vehicle emissions from the 120 000 vehicles on Cairo's roads. Traffic officers have been stopping cars on main roads so that EEAA-trained inspectors can conduct emissions tests.

Another aspect of the project is a programme to promote the use of compressed natural gas fuel in motor vehicles. CAIP is working with the Cairo Transit Authority and the Greater Cairo Bus Company to switch their fleet of buses to gas. Apart from being cleaner than other fossil fuels, it is a good economic move for Egypt, which is rich in gas reserves. The first phase introduced 50 buses operating on gas but, with 20 000 buses in the city, there is a long way to go.

Cairo has developed an underground metro which it is hoped will help stem the ever-increasing number of vehicles on the roads.

Figure 8.28 Waste dump in Cairo

Figure 8.29 Cairo rush hour

ACTIVITIES

1. What was the population of Cairo in: **a** 1960, **b** 2000.
2. Why did the population of Cairo increase so rapidly between 1960 and 2000?
3. Figure 8.29 illustrates one of the causes of pollution in Cairo.
   a State how vehicles have led to air pollution in Cairo.
   b What other factors have contributed to pollution in Cairo?
4. What is being done by the Egyptian government to improve the urban environment?
5. Imagine you are a resident in Saraya Al Gezira. What could you do to improve the urban environment in Cairo?

Sample Examination Questions

Higher tier

1. Study Figure 8.1 on page 164 which shows the growth of urban population in the world.
   a Which continent experienced the greatest growth in population between 1950 and 2000? **(1 mark)**
   b Which continent has experienced the least growth in urban population? **(1 mark)**
   c Why are the numbers of people in urban areas in LEDCs increasing rapidly? **(4 marks)**
2. Study the photographs in Figures 8.16 and 8.17.
   a What does the term 'renewal' mean? **(1 mark)**
   b What evidence can you see in the photographs that the council are trying to improve the environment? **(3 marks)**
   c Why do you think that these buildings in Reading were renewed while others have been redeveloped? **(3 marks)**
3. Study the population pyramids for Brazil (Figure 8.4).
   a How many people were aged 0–15 in 1975? **(1 mark)**
   b Compare the population pyramids for 1975 and the year 2025. Use data in your answer. **(5 marks)**
   c Explain the shape of the pyramid in the year 2050. **(3 marks)**
4. Policy makers in both MEDCs and LEDCs are trying to develop sustainable strategies. Look at one city that has developed sustainable policies to deal with the problems of rapid growth. Evaluate the decisions the policy makers have made to solve the city's problems. **(8 marks)**

Total 30 marks

Foundation tier

1. Look at Figure 8.1 which shows the growth of the urban population in the world.
   a Which continent had the highest percentage of urban population in 1950 and in 2000? **(2 marks)**
   b Why are the numbers of people in urban areas in LEDCs increasing rapidly? **(3 marks)**
2. Look at the photographs in Figures 8.16 and 8.17.
   a What does the term 'renewal' mean? **(1 mark)**
   b What evidence can you see in the photographs that the council are trying to improve the environment? **(3 marks)**
   c List 3 redevelopment schemes that have occurred in Reading. **(3 marks)**
3. Study the population pyramids for Brazil (Figure 8.4).
   a How many people were aged 0–15 in 1975? **(1 mark)**
   b How many people were over the age of 65 in 1975? **(1 mark)**
   c Compare the population pyramids for 1975 and the year 2025. Use data in your answer. **(5 marks)**
   d Describe some of the problems that this increase in population will cause for cities in Brazil. **(3 marks)**
4. Policy makers in both MEDCs and LEDC are trying to develop strategies which are sustainable. Look at one city that has developed sustainable policies to deal with the problems of rapid growth.
   a Describe the policies. **(3 marks)**
   b What are the views of the local citizens about these policies? **(5 marks)**

Total 30 marks

Appendix A: Sample Examination Answers

Chapter One: The Physical World

Higher tier – mark scheme

1 a *Point mark* (4 marks)
   Information for examiners
   - Expect to be able to recognise the drawing of the feature.
   - One mark per correct feature.

   b Low. (1 mark)
   c *Point mark* (2 marks)
   Information for examiners
   - Low tide because the stump is visible (1). Stumps can only be seen when the tide is out (1).

   d *Point mark* (3 marks)
   Information for examiners
   - One mark for first answer, rock or chalk.
   - Terminology: slumping (1).
   - Two marks for description of slumping.
   - It fell from the cliff (1).

2 *Point mark* (2 marks)
   Information for examiners
   - Little usage in the upper stage – farming (1).
   - Much usage in middle stage – tourism (1).

3 a *Point mark* (2 marks)
      Haweswater is a long thin lake whereas Blea Tarn is a circular lake (2).
   b North, north east. (1 mark)
   c U-shaped valley (1), mention of glaciation processes receives extra mark. (2 marks)
   d Follows river valleys (1). Above level of lakes or rivers it is close to (1).
      Reserve one mark for map evidence. (3 marks)

Foundation tier – mark scheme

1 a *Point mark* (4 marks)
   Information for examiners
   - True, false, true, true.

   b Low. (1 mark)
   c *Point mark* (2 marks)
   Information for examiners
   - Low tide because the stump is visible (1). Stumps can only be seen when the tide is out (1).

   d *Point mark* (3 marks)
   Information for examiners
   - One mark for first answer. Rock or chalk.
   - Terminology: slumping (1).
   - Two marks for description of slumping.
   - It fell from the cliff (1).

2 *Point mark* (2 marks)
   Information for examiners
   - Tourism (1), farming (1), power station (1).

3 a *Point mark* (2 marks)
      Haweswater is a long thin lake whereas Blea Tarn is a circular lake (2).
   b North, north east. (1 mark)
   c U-shaped valley (1), mention of glaciation processes receives extra mark. (2 marks)
   d Follows river valleys (1). Above level of lakes or rivers it is close to (1).
      Reserve one mark for map evidence. (3 marks)

Chapter Two: The Human World

Higher tier – mark scheme

1 a Northfield. (1 mark)
   b Camp/caravan site. (1 mark)
   c Coquet. (1 mark)
   d A1068. (1 mark)
   e North or north east. (1 mark)

2 *Point mark* (4 marks)
   Information for examiners
   Four differences at one mark each, e.g. area C the houses are larger, have gardens, not packed so close together/spread out along the road, different colour roofs. There will be other acceptable answers.

3 *Point mark* (3 marks)
   There needs to be three areas pointed out with a simple reason for each at one mark each.
   - Not close to the river because of flooding (1).
   - The central area is used for allotments (1).
   - The area in the foreground is used for recreation/cricket/ farming/cows (1). (3 marks)

4 *Levels mark* (5 marks)
   Level 3
5 The answer must be explanatory in style with, probably, two developed points. One of the points above could be further developed – perhaps the idea of a route centre with its advantages for trade.
   Level 2
   3-4 One point has some clear explanation. It is sited inside a meander, so is protected from attack on three sides by the wide river. It has developed at a bridging point of the River Coquet, therefore routes converge here to cross the river. These statements would be worth two marks each.
   Level 1
   1-2 Undeveloped points that are correct but do not explain. It is in a meander, it has a flat site, it is a bridging point.

5 *Point mark* (3 marks)
   Allow maximum of one mark if there is no evidence.
   Points from the map
   - Large number of farms shown
   - Little built up areas
   - Some large areas of gently sloping land.
   Points from the photograph
   - Large areas of flat land
   - Different coloured fields showing crops
   - Field of cows in the foreground.

Foundation tier – mark scheme

1 a Northfield. (1 mark)
   b Camp/caravan site. (1 mark)
   c Coquet. (1 mark)
   d A1068. (1 mark)
   e North or north east. (1 mark)

2 *Point mark* (4 marks)
   Simple comparative statements will be worth one mark each.

Sample Examination Answers

- The houses at C are larger than those at D (1).
- C has large gardens; D has small/no gardens (1).
- C is along the road/on the edge of the village/backing on to the river, whereas D is in the village/packed together (1).
- One other difference not to do with size, gardens or location, e.g. roof colour (1).

3 *Point mark* (2 marks)
- E: allotments, accept gardens or farming (1).
- F: anything to do with flooding (1).

4 a Two simple points or one developed point. (2 marks)
  b *Point mark* (4 marks)
  Could be given 2 marks for each reason or if one point is well developed, three and one. The meander gives protection on three sides from possible attack (2). The river could be crossed by a bridge which allowed routes to continue north and south of the river (2). If the concept of route centre and trade is mentioned, likely to reach 3 marks.

5 *Point mark* (3 marks)
Maximum of 1 mark if there is no picture evidence.
Points from the photograph
- Farm buildings are shown
- Not any large built up areas
- Large areas of flat land
- Different coloured fields showing crops
- Field of cows in the foreground.

Chapter Three: The Economic World

Higher tier – mark scheme

1 a Stack. (1 mark)
  b Wave-cut platform. (1 mark)
  c Beach. (1 mark)
2 a Quarry. (1 mark)
  b Oil drilling 972 854, farming – a number of farms mentioned 987 808, forestry 00 84. (3 marks)
3 *Point mark* (4 marks)
Many examples; only credit one of each. Must quote map evidence to achieve more than 2 marks.
Information for examiners
- Gives tourist facilities: caravan/camping sites.
- Beaches: Swanage and Studland.
- Railway line.
- Information centres/parking 032 773, 031 773.
- Country park 02 77.
- Hotels.
- Corfe Castle.

4 *Point mark* (2 marks)
Information for examiners
- Straight boundaries.
- Roadways within it.
- Possibility of local knowledge – screens oil wells.

5 Pastoral, sheep. Not hill. The relief of the land. An answer that refers to the contours. Lack of rivers in the area – poor dry soils because of rock types. Chalk and limestone. (2 marks)

6 *Levels mark* (5 marks)
Information for examiners
- Roads on either side of chalk escarpment.
- A351 in the river valley.
- No roads in the south by the coast, steep cliffs.

Level 3
5 Makes three good points concerning the pattern of the roads and railway. May refer to the lack of roads in certain areas.

Level 2
3-4 Makes two good points about the roads for top of level. Makes one good point to enter the level. There must be evidence of explanation to enter this level.

Level 1
1-2 Makes general descriptive points with no explanation

Foundation tier – mark scheme

1 a Stack. (1 mark)
  b Wave-cut platform. (1 mark)
  c Beach. (1 mark)

2 *Point mark* (4 marks)

Grid reference	Primary activity
00 84	Forestry
972 854	Oil drilling
968 784	Quarry
987 808	Farming

3 *Point mark* (4 marks)
Many examples only credit one of each. Must quote map evidence to achieve more than 3 marks.
Information for examiners
- Gives tourist facilities: caravan/camping sites.
- Beaches: Swanage and Studland.
- Railway line.
- Information centres/parking 032 773, 031 773.
- Country park 02 77.
- Hotels.
- Corfe Castle.

4 *Point mark* (2 marks)
Information for examiners
- Straight boundaries.
- Roadways within it.
- Possibility of local knowledge – screens oil wells.
- Pastoral. The relief of the land. An answer that refers to the contours. Lack of rivers in the area – poor dry soils because of rock types. Chalk and limestone.

5 *Levels mark* (5 marks)
Information for examiners
- Roads on either side of chalk escarpment.
- A351 in the river valley.
- No roads in the south by the coast, steep cliffs.

Level 2
4-5 Makes two good points about the roads for top of level. Makes one good point to enter the level. There must be evidence of explanation to enter this level.

Level 1
1–3 Makes general descriptive points with no explanation.

Chapter Four: The Natural World

Higher tier – mark scheme

1 a Anticyclone or high. (1 mark)

b A line that joins places of equal pressure. (1 mark)

c South east and 13–17 knots. Both required for mark. (1 mark)

d *Levels mark* (4 marks)

Level 2

3-4 Pressure and wind have to be mentioned to reach this level. Understanding of a pattern and variations should be shown. Winds are generally light with the highest 13–17 knots on the west coast of Ireland. The winds blow clockwise away from the centre of the anticyclone. There is a gentle pressure gradient especially in the east.

Level 1

1-2 One or two points made at 1 mark each. Might only mention the pressure or the winds. The pressure increases towards the centre of the anticyclone. The pressure ranges between 1016 and 1024 millibars. The winds are light/gentle. Highest winds are 13–17 knots.

2 a *Point mark* (3 marks)

Information for examiners
Each statement plus data is worth 1 mark.
- Small temperature range of 11 °C.
- Summer high of 17 °C.
- Winter low of 6 °C.
- Small monthly change of temperature maximum of 3 °C.

b *Point mark* (4 marks)

Information for examiners
Expect comments on rainfall and temperature. Question asks for reasons. Mark on degree of reasoning.
- Small temperature range due to the effect of the sea which keeps the land warm in the winter and stops it getting too hot in the summer (2).
- Similar monthly rainfall totals caused by Atlantic depressions tracking eastwards throughout the year (2).

3 *Levels mark* (6 marks)

Level 3

5-6 Could be three points described and explained or two points with further depth of explanation, e.g. they could take the second point above and then explain that this is necessary because the trees grow in an area of low annual precipitation.

Level 2

3-4 Description and explanation of two points for maximum at this level.
Conifers have sloping branches so that snow does not accumulate and snap off the branches.
Because the leaves (needles) have a small surface area and are waxy, transpiration is reduced.

Level 1

1-2 Short descriptive points, e.g. conical shape, shallow roots, sloping branches, etc.

Foundation tier – mark scheme

1 *Point mark* (5 marks)

a Anticyclone or high. (1 mark)

b Pressure and millibars both correct for 1 mark. (1 mark)

c One mark for each correct answer. Units must be stated.
  i Temperature: 14 °C.
  ii Wind speed: 13–17 knots.
  iii Wind direction: south east.
  iv Cloud cover: 8 oktas/eighths.
  v Precipitation: rain shower.

2 a 17 °C. (1 mark)
b 6 °C. (1 mark)
c 11 °C. (1 mark)
d *Point mark* (4 marks)

Information for examiners
Maximum of two marks if there is no data.
- Winter maximum (1).
- Lowest rainfall in April (1).
- Lowest rainfall of 52 mm in April (2).
- Total rainfall 939 mm (1).

3 *Levels mark* (6 marks)

Level 2

5-6 One explanation required to reach the top of this level. For examples see higher tier.

Level 1

1-4 Short descriptive points, conical shape, fir trees, sloping branches etc.

Chapter Five: Managing the Environment

Higher tier – mark scheme

1 a i *Point mark* (3 marks)

Information for examiners
- Geology, rock type.
- Rock structure.
- Coastal processes: cliff face – weathering and mass movement; cliff foot: erosion by the sea.

ii *Point mark* (4 marks)

Information for examiners
- Build up of beach material on one side.
- Dissipates wave energy due to build up of material.
- Material no longer moves along the coast.
- Waves break before they reach the cliff.

iii *Levels mark* (5 marks)

Information for examiners
Expect the following management techniques but there may be others:
- Managed retreat.
- Beach nourishment.
- Cliff regrading.

Level 3

5 Sound explanation of engineering techniques, 2 to be covered in detail for this level.

Level 2

3-4 To reach Level 2, 1 technique should be explained in detail.

Level 1

1-2 May be lists of different techniques. Description rather than explanation.

b i *Point mark* (4 marks)
Information for examiners

Hard engineering techniques
Afforestation
Distance Embankments
Washlands
Flood warning system

Soft engineering techniques
Dams
Channelisation
Embankments
Flood relief channels

ii *Levels mark* (6 marks)
Information for examiners
Expect answers from b i.

Level 3
5-6 Sound description and explanation of engineering techniques. Both types to be covered, in detail for the top of this level.

Level 2
3-4 To reach Level 2, both types of technique should be dealt with.

Level 1
1-2 May be lists of different techniques. Description rather than explanation.

c *Levels mark* (8 marks)
Information for examiners
- Specific case study information on any type of damage by agriculture.
- Soil erosion.
- Desertification.
- Modern farming techniques.

Level 3
7-8 For top of level, the effects of the damage and the opinions of actual groups of people for both sides of the argument need to be covered in detail.

Level 2
4-6 For the top of Level 2, the effects of the damage should be covered. The opinions of groups of people will be covered although only one actual group will be mentioned. To enter this level the effects of the damage should be covered and different opinions mentioned.

Level 1
1-3 General points about farming and the environment, no clear case study. Groups of people may be mentioned.

Foundation tier – mark scheme

2 a i *Point mark* (2 marks)
Information for examiners
- Weathering
- Corrasion

ii *Point mark* (4 marks)
Information for examiners
- Groynes
  Advantages: prevents longshore drift, cheap, provides beach for tourists, easy to repair.
  Disadvantages: unattractive, easily damaged.
- Gabions
  Advantages: cheap, easy to construct, adsorb wave energy.
  Disadvantages: ugly, easily damaged, restrict beach access.

iii *Point mark* (3 marks)
Information for examiners

Soft engineering technique	Description
Beach nourishment	The coastline is built up with sand and pebble from elsewhere.
Managed retreat	The land by the sea is made into a gentle slope instead of a steep one.
Cliff regrading	The sea is allowed to flood areas which were once defended.

iv *Levels mark* (5 marks)
Information for examiners
Expect soft engineering techniques such as:
- Beach nourishment
- Cliff regrading.
- Managed retreat.

Level 3
5 Both advantages and disadvantages are described in detail.

Level 2
3-4 Top of level, either advantages or disadvantages described in detail. The other is mentioned. To reach Level 2 both should be mentioned.

Level 1
1-2 General comments about beach defences.

b i *Point mark* (2 marks)
Information for examiners
- Planting of trees (1), to limit surface run-off (1).

ii *Point mark* (6 marks)
Information for examiners

Hard engineering techniques
Afforestation
Distance Embankments
Washlands
Flood warning system

Soft engineering techniques
Dams
Channelisation
Embankments
Flood relief channels

c i *Point mark* (3 marks)
Information for examiners
- Answer is dependent upon case study.
- Expect 3 distinct effects, 1 mark each.
- Or fewer effects covered in more detail. The rain washes chemicals into rivers (1), this causes algae to bloom (1), fish die due to lack of oxygen (1).

ii *Levels mark* (5 marks)
Information for examiners
- Detail expected on any type of damage by agriculture.
- Soil erosion.
- Desertification.
- Modern farming techniques.

Level 2
4-5 For top of level must be an actual case study that discussed and actual groups of people.

Level 1
1-3 General points about farming and the environment. No actual groups, although there may be opinions.

Chapter Six: Managing Hazards

Higher tier – mark scheme

1 a Africa or Antarctica, do not allow Australia. **(1 mark)**

b *Point mark* **(3 marks)**
With one mark for each relevant point.
- Most are on the edge of the continents.
- They are on land and in the sea.

Negative points as in 1 a.

c *Information for examiners*
This requires an answer that focuses on a destructive plate boundary and the processes that take place there.
Mark according to how well developed the answer is. A diagram is likely to be helpful; indeed, full marks could be achieved with a good annotated diagram. Don't double credit writing and diagram. **(4 marks)**

d *Levels mark* **(5 marks)**

Level 3

5 One of the above statements in greater detail or a specific example, e.g. full explanation of the gap theory including precise located example of Loma Prieta could reach four marks. The question asks for attempts so two or more attempts are needed.

Level 2

3-4 Some understanding is shown. Seismographs which register earthquakes often show minor tremors or foreshocks which come before a larger earthquake. Previous earthquakes can be plotted which help to pinpoint areas at risk, those areas where there have not been earthquakes are most at risk. A radon gas counter shows different measurements before some earthquakes. Two statements similar to above required for top of this level.

Level 1

1-2 Simple ideas with no amplification such as: they use monitoring equipment or animals behave differently

2 a Simple statements from the passage at one mark each. Allow reasons not in the passage that might be appropriate for Etna. **(3 marks)**

b *Levels mark* **(6 marks)**

Level 3

5-6 The answer contains detailed statements and has at least one example to illustrate level two themes.

Level 2

3-4 Understanding shown, e.g. in the past there were no emergency services and buildings would be poorly built. In an MEDC there are emergency services and warning systems. Two points required for top of this level, although only one need be well explained.

Level 1

1-2 Simple statements, e.g. some are more violent, close to large cities.

c *Levels mark* **(8 marks)**

Level 3

7-8 The impact needs to be evaluated at this level. The difference between short- and long-term effects will be clearly understood.

Level 2

4-6 At this level the cyclone must be specific. It is case study driven. Factual detail and understanding of the impacts will be shown. At the top of this level, impact on the people and the environment must be mentioned.

Level 1

1-3 Simple statements about the damage done by the cyclone. May well be generalised and not located. Could be about people or the environment.

Foundation tier – mark scheme

1 a 1999 **(1 mark)**

b Africa **(1 mark)**

c *Point mark* **(3 marks)**
With one mark for each relevant point.
- Most are on the edge of the continents.
- They are found on land and sea.
- There are not any in Africa/Antarctica.
- Several are found around the rim of the Pacific Ocean.

Information for examiners

d No specific boundary type is mentioned in the question therefore the candidate can focus on one boundary or more general on several boundary types. At this level expect most answers to be generalised. Credit all good geographic points.
- At conservative margins plates rub against each other (1).
- Pressure builds up and the plates jerk causing an earthquake (1).

Full marks could be achieved by explaining friction more clearly and giving a located example. **(3 marks)**

e No explanation is required just two examples at 1 mark each e.g. monitoring seismographs, radon gas counters, watching animals, earthquake plotting.

f Some understanding of the methods is required for the candidate to say whether the scientists are or are not successful. **(5 marks)**

2 a Simple statements from the passage at one mark each. Allow reasons not in the passage that might be appropriate for Etna. **(3 marks)**

b *Levels mark* **(6 marks)**

Level 2

4-5 Understanding shown e.g. in the past there were no emergency services and buildings would be poorly built. In an MEDC there are emergency services and warning systems. Two points required for top of this level although only one need be explained.

Level 1
1–3 Simple statements e.g. some are more violent, close to large cities.

3 a *Point mark* (4 marks)
Allow one mark for each statement that shows how local people were affected e.g. relief, aid deaths disease.
b *Point mark* (4 marks)
Allow one mark for each statement that shows how the environment was affected, e.g. floods, storm surge, crops ruined, land devastated. Allow marks to cross over between **a** and **b**.

Chapter Seven: Managing Tourism

Higher tier – mark scheme
1 a *Point mark* (4 marks)
Reserve one mark for data.
Information for examiners
- Largest increase between 1988 and 1992 (2).
- Numbers increased by more than 50% between 1980 and 1988 (2).
- Increase slowed down to 5,250 between 1992 and 1996 (2).

b *Point mark* (4 marks)
Information for examiners
Refer to reasons for growth of tourism at beginning of Chapter 7.
- People have more money (1), therefore they can afford holidays that are further away (1).
- Transport has been developed, for example planes (1). This means that people can travel further more easily (1).

2 a 4,200 m. (1 mark)
b Patallacta, Wayllabamba, Runcurakay, Sayacmarca, Rumiwasi, Phuyupatamarca, Winaywayna, Killapata, Intipuncu, Machu Picchu. (2 marks)
c 1,450 m. (1 mark)
d *Point mark* (4 marks)

Information for examiners
- Rise in crime rate (1).
- Tourists being robbed when they are asleep on trains (1).
- Toilet blocks have red roofs (1).
- This stands out in the beautiful landscape, not pleasing (1).

3 *Levels mark* (6 marks)
Information for examiners
- Information on environmental problems such as traffic congestion in Malham.
- Economic advantages, jobs created although they are seasonal in many cases.
- Social: price of houses in Malham.
- Litter on the Inca Trail.

Level 3
5–6 Both sides of the argument are covered in detail for the top of the level. Good use of examples for both sides of the argument; actual groups of people are mentioned.

Level 2
3–4 Top of level has both sides of argument mentioned with specific information, one side developed better than the other. To reach this level there must be mention of both sides of the argument and a specific group for one side.

Level 1
1–2 General information about people's views on tourism in mountainous areas.

4 *Levels mark* (8 marks)
Information for examiners
- Maldives: only 20 per cent of the island should be built on.
- Maldives: islands to have own incinerators.
- EU gave money for training schemes.

Level 3
7–8 Specific detail of case study should be evident both for management initiatives and aid from other countries.

Level 2
4–6 Top of level: both areas mentioned briefly with specific information. To enter the level there must be specific information on one of the points.

Level 1
1–3 General information about management initiatives and/or aid.

Foundation tier – mark scheme
1 *Point mark* (4 marks)
Information for examiners
More, 1988–1992, active, summer holiday.
2 *Point mark* (4 marks)
Information for examiners
- Greater wealth so people have more money (1), they can therefore afford holidays that are further away (1).
- Developments in transport, for example planes (1). This means that people can travel further more easily (1).

3 a 4,200 m. (1 mark)
b Patallacta, Wayllabamba, Runcurakay, Sayacmarca, Rumiwasi, Phuyupatamarca, Winaywayna, Killapata, Intipuncu, Machu Picchu. (2 marks)
c 1,450 m. (1 mark)
d *Point mark* (4 marks)
Information for examiners
- Tourists pick flowers (1).
- Tourists pick orchids (2).
- Garbage is thrown into rivers (1).
- Rubbish is thrown into the Urubamba River (2).

4 *Levels mark*
Information for examiners
- Information on environmental problems such as traffic congestion in Malham.
- Economic advantages: jobs created although they are seasonal in many cases.
- Social: price of houses in Malham.
- Litter on the Inca Trail.

Level 2
4–6 Top of level has both sides of argument mentioned with specific information on one side of the argument. To reach this level there must be mention of both sides of the argument.

Level 1
3-1 General information about people's views on tourism in mountainous areas.

5 *Point mark* (3 marks)
Information for examiners
- Maldives: only 20 per cent of the island should be built on.
- Maldives: islands to have own incinerators.

Levels mark (5 marks)
Information for examiners
- EU gave money for training schemes.
- Loans from Norway.

Level 2
4-5 Top of this level: specific information about a case study. To enter level: points are more logical but still cannot be linked to a specific example.

Level 1
1-3 General information about aid given to countries for tourist development.

Chapter Eight: Managing Urban Areas

Higher tier – mark scheme
1 a South America. (1 mark)
  b Australasia. (1 mark)
  c *Point mark* (4 marks)
  - Maximum of 3 marks without both points mentioned below.
  - Migration from rural areas into cities.
  - Rapid natural increase due to youth of migrants and improving medical care.

2 a Renewal: this is when old buildings are renovated and brought up-to-date, combining the best of the old with the new. (1 mark)
  b *Point mark* (3 marks)
  - Traffic calming.
  - Smart paved streets and pavements.
  - Stylish litter bins.
  - Cycle racks.
  - Neat bus shelters that have no graffiti.
  c *Point mark* (3 marks)

- Old buildings with character.
- Terraced, so demolition more expensive.
- Cheaper.
- Only doing part of the street not whole area so more difficult.

3 a 45 million people.
  b *Levels mark* (5 marks)
  - Traditional LEDC in 1975; 2025 slight lowering of birth rate (fewer in 0–4 age range).
  - Definite lowering of death rate.

Level 3
5 Both areas covered birth rates and death rates. In detail with data for this level.

Level 2
3-4 Top of level has both areas mentioned with specific data. One might be better than the other at this level.

Level 1
1-2 General information about the pyramids. No data.

  c *Point mark* (3 marks)
  - Shanty towns with all their problems.
  - Pollution.
  - Traffic congestion.

4 *Levels mark* (8 marks)
Level 3
7-8 Specific detail of case study should be evident. A number of policies (dependent on depth) should be discussed and evaluated.

Level 2
4-6 Top of level must have specific detail of two policies and good evaluation of one. To enter the level there must be specific information on a policy with some evaluation of it.

Level 1
1-3 General information about policies.

Foundation tier – mark scheme
1 a North America and South America. (2 marks)
  b *Point mark* (3 marks)

- Migration from rural areas into cities.
- Rapid natural increase due to youthfulness of migrants and improving medical care.

2 a Renewal: this is when old buildings are renovated and brought up-to-date, combining the best of the old with the new. (1 mark)
  b *Point mark* (3 marks)
  - Traffic calming.
  - Smart paved streets and pavements.
  - Stylish litter bins.
  - Cycle racks.
  - Neat bus shelters that have no graffiti.
  c *Point mark* (3 marks)
  - Rose Kiln Lane flats.
  - The Oracle.
  - Rex cinema site.

3 a 45 million people. (1 mark)
  b 4 million. (1 mark)
  c *Levels mark* (5 marks)
  - Traditional LEDC in 1975, 2025 slight lowering of birth rate (fewer in 0–4 age range).
  - Definite lowering of death rate.

Level 2
4-5 Both areas covered birth rates and death rates. One in detail for this level. Some data must be included.

Level 1
1-3 General comments about the pyramids. There may be some vague data.

4 a *Point mark* (3 marks)
  - Description of policies from case study, e.g. self-help schemes.

Levels mark (5 marks)
Level 2
4-5 Top of level must have specific detail of policies and people's views given. Or specific groups of people and less on the specifics of the policies.

Level 1
1-3 General views which are unspecified. No groups mentioned.

Index

Africa, Sahel desertification case study 104–105
agriculture *see also* farming systems
agriculture 100–101, 102
air masses 68–69, 71, 72
Amazonian rainforest (South America), oil extraction case study 108–109
anticyclones 73
arches 7
Arctic Maritime (Am) air masses 69
arêtes 17
aspect and shelter for settlements 35
attrition 3
Ayia Napa (Cyprus), tourism case study 141–143

Bangalore (India), land use case study 44–45
Bangladesh, Cyclone One Bravo case study 117–119
bars 9
bays 6
beaches 8
biological weathering 4
birth rates 24–25, 26–27
Bracknell (UK), computer development case study 62–63
Brazil
    car manufacture case study 65–66
    São Paulo urbanisation case study 166–171
British anticyclone weather 73–74
brownfield potential 176
brownfield site 176

Cairo (Egypt), urbanisation case study 178–180
car manufacture case study 65–66
car ownership 139
caves 7
census data 29, 40
chemical weathering 3
cirques (corries) 17
cliffs 6
cliffs, recession 89
climate
    east European continental 75–76
    factors 77–78
    west European maritime 75
cloud types 69, 71, 113
coastal defences 89–90
coastal deposition, characteristic landforms 8–9
coastal erosion 3, 89
    characteristic landforms 5–7
    management 89–93
Common Agricultural Policy (CAP) of the EU 59–60
communications 36
concentric ring model 38
conservation 83
conservative (transform) margins 123
constructive (divergent) margins 122
consumer demands 139
continental crust 120
continental drift 120
convection rain 70

convergent (destructive) margins 121–122
corries (cirques) 17
corrosion 3
crevasses 17
cumulonimbus clouds 113
Cyclone One Bravo (Bangladesh), case study 117–119
cyclones (tropical storms) 111–119
Cyprus, tourism case study 141–143

dams 95
death rates 24–25, 26–27
defence of settlements 35
deforestation 108
deltas 15
demographic transition model 26–27
dependency ratio 32
depressions 71–72
desertification, case study 104–105
destructive (convergent) margins 121–122
divergent (constructive) margins 122
Doñana National Park (Spain), fragile environment case study 106–107
droughts 104

earthquakes 120
    case studies 128–131
    characteristics 126–128
    global distribution 123–125
East Africa, Zanzibar tourism case study 144–147
Ecuador, oil extraction case study 108–109
Egypt, Cairo urbanisation case study 178–180
employment patterns
    changes over time 50–51
    national differences 49
epicentre 126
eutrophication 101
exploitation 83, 101

farming systems *see also* agriculture
    characteristics 52
    diversification 57–58
    EU policies case study 56–60
    factors 52–53
    intensive rice farming case study 54–55
favellas (Brazilian shanty towns) 166, 167, 168–169, 170–171
flood plains 15
flooding 94–96
    management 95, 96–99
    warning codes 97
fold mountains 120, 122
forests
    coniferous 81
    distribution 79
    tropical rainforests 80
fragile environments 100–109
    management 103
frontal rain 69
fronts 69, 71

Germany
    employment patterns 49
    population pyramid 30
glaciers 16
    characteristic landforms 16–20
greenbelt 176
greenfield site 176

hanging valleys 19
headlands 6
Himalayas, formation 122
Home Farm, West Midlands (UK), farming case study 56–58
Hurricane Floyd case study 113–116
hurricanes (tropical storms) 111–119
hydraulic action 3

Inca Trail (Peru), tourism case study 152–156
India, Bangalore land use case study 44–45
India, birth rates 25
Indian Ocean, Maldives tourism case study 157–159
industry
    employment patterns 49–51
    formal and informal sectors 64
    hi–tech 62–63
    secondary location 61
    sectors 48
interlocking spurs 11

Japan, Tottori earthquake case study 131

Kenya, population pyramid 29

latitude 77
leisure facilities 63
levees 15

magma 121, 122
Maldives (Indian Ocean), tourism case study 157–159
Malham (UK), tourism case study 148–151
Mali, employment patterns 49
mass movement 4
meanders 12–13
Mid-Atlantic Ridge 122, 123
Midlands (UK), flooding 94
Mississippi River (USA), flooding case study 98–99
moraines 20
Mount Pinatubo (Philippines), volcano case study 132–135
multiple nuclei model 38
multiplier effect 138

Negros Occidental (Philippines), rice farming case study 54–55
nitrates, used in agriculture 100, 101, 102, 103
Norfolk Broads (UK), fragile environment case study 102–103

ocean currents 77
ocean trenches 121

Index

oceanic crust 120
oil extraction, case study 108–109
ox-bow lakes 14

Papua New Guinea, forestry case study 82–86
Pennine Way (UK), tourism case study 148–151
Peru, Inca Trail tourism case study 152–156
Philippines
    Mount Pinatubo, volcano case study 132–135
    Negros Occidental, rice farming case study 54–55
physical weathering 3
plate tectonics 120–123
Polar Continental (Pc) air masses 69
Polar Maritime (Pm) air masses 69
pollution 106–107, 178–179
population
    dynamics 24–27
    growth 22–23, 29–30
    pyramids 29–30
    rural and urban 32
    structure 28–29
    youthful and ageing 32–33
prevailing winds 78
pyramidal peaks 17
pyroclastic flows 133

rain 69–70
Reading (UK), land use case study 40–43
Reading (Berkshire, UK), urbanisation case study 172–176
redevelopment 176
relief rain 70
renewal 176
resources 37
resources, exploitation 101
ribbon lakes 19
rice farming, case study 54–55
Richter scale 126
river valleys, characteristic landforms 11–15
rivers
    characteristics 10–11
    flooding 94–99

São Paulo (Brazil), urbanisation case study 166–171
Sahel (Africa), desertification case study 104–105

San Andreas Fault 123
sector model 38
settlements
    economic factors 36–37
    patterns 37
    physical factors 34–36
shanty towns and *favellas* 45, 166, 167, 168–169, 170–171
socioeconomic circumstances 138
Somalia, floods 95
South America, Amazonian rainforest oil extraction case study 108–109
Spain
    birth rates 25
    Doñana National Park 106–107
spits 8–9
spurs, interlocking 11
stacks 7
stumps 7
subduction 121
suburbs 42
sustainable development 83, 84

Taiwan, employment patterns 49
tectonics 120–123
Tottori (Japan), earthquake case study 131
tourism 137–138
    case studies 141–162
    classification 140
    growth 138–139
toxic waste 106–107
transform (conservative) margins 123
transportation of materials 7
Tropical Continental (Tc) air masses 68
Tropical Maritime (Tm) air masses 68
tropical rainforests 80
tropical storms (hurricanes, cyclones, typhoons, willy-willies) 111–119
Turkey, earthquake case study 128–130
typhoons (tropical storms) 111–119

U-shaped valleys 19
UK
    air masses 68–69
    Bracknell, computer development case study 62–63
    Midlands flooding 94

Norfolk Broads, fragile environment case study 102–103
Pennine Way, tourism case study 148–151
Reading, land use case study 40–43
Reading (Berkshire), urbanisation case study 172–176
Walton-on-the-Naze, coastal erosion case study 92–93
weather variability 69–74
urban land use 41, 44–45
urban structure models 38–39
urbanisation 164–165
    case studies 166–171, 172–176, 178–180
USA
    Mississippi River, flooding case study 98–99
    population distribution 28
    population pyramid 30
    Yosemite National Park, tourism case study 160–162

V-shaped valleys 11
volcanoes 120, 121, 122
    global distribution 123–124
    Mount Pinatubo case study 132–135

Walton-on-the-Naze (UK), coastal erosion case study 92–93
water supplies 34
waterfalls 12
wave action 5
wave-cut platforms 6
weather charts and symbols 72, 73, 88
weathering 3–4
winds
    prevailing 78
    tropical storms 111–119
world population 22–23

Yosemite National Park (USA), tourism case study 160–162

Zanzibar (East Africa), tourism case study 144–147